A HISTORY OF THE WORLD

The Modern World

A History of the World

Volume III
THE MODERN WORLD

EDITORS:

JOHN A. GARRATY

PETER GAY

 HARPER & ROW, PUBLISHERS

NEW YORK, EVANSTON, SAN FRANCISCO, LONDON

The quotation on page 231 is from "the first president to be loved by his" by E. E. Cummings in *Poems, 1923–1954,* published by Harcourt Brace Jovanovich, Inc. Used with permission.

Maps by Harry Scott

A HISTORY OF THE WORLD: THE MODERN WORLD. Copyright © 1972 by Harper & Row, Publishers, Inc. All rights reserved. Printed in the United States of America. No part of this book may be used or reproduced in any manner whatsoever without written permission except in the case of brief quotations embodied in critical articles and reviews. This book first appeared as a portion of THE COLUMBIA HISTORY OF THE WORLD, copyright © 1972 by Harper & Row, Publishers, Inc., published simultaneously in Canada by Fitzhenry & Whiteside Limited, Toronto. For information address Harper & Row, Publishers, Inc., 49 East 33rd Street, New York, N.Y. 10016.

FIRST EDITION

STANDARD BOOK NUMBER: 06-042256-4

LIBRARY OF CONGRESS CATALOG CARD NUMBER: 72-75674

Contents

Maps

Introduction

We live in the Age of World History, and as ages go, ours is relatively young. Until the fifteenth century, the many cultures of this earth developed in comparative isolation, their boundaries breached only by occasional traders, by border warfare, and by spectacular mass migrations, such as the "barbarian" invasion of the Roman Empire in the early centuries of the Christian Era. But after Columbus and Cortez had awakened the people of Western Europe to the possibilities, their appetite for converts, profits, and fame was thoroughly aroused and Western civilization was introduced, mainly by force, over nearly all the globe. Equipped with an unappeasable urge to expand and with superior weapons, conquerors made the rest of the world into an unwilling appendage of the great European powers; Africa, Asia, and the Americas became sources of raw materials, markets, objects of scientific curiosity, and places for the permanent settlement of Europeans. The peoples of these continents were, in short, the victims of a ruthless, unrelenting exploitation.

But then came the scientific and technological revolutions of modern times, which, in transforming the Western world, also transformed its non-Western dependencies. We are now witnessing two simultaneous, only apparently contradictory developments. World civilization is becoming more uniform, as the West imposes its techniques and its ideas. And the dependent nations are breaking away from the domination of the West, using these very Western techniques and ideas to establish their separate identities, and find their places in the councils of power. Isolation has become impossible; ancient empires like China and the newly self-conscious nations of Africa alike involve the whole world in their activities. Thus both the traditional division between Western and non-Western history and the patronizing assumption that non-Western is a kind of footnote to Western history have become obsolete. This, as we have said, is the Age of World History. It is therefore supremely the age *for* world history.

The difficulty with most currently available world history textbooks is that they look at this enormous, multifaceted subject from the present backward and from the perspective of Western society. Recognizing that the world is no longer a congeries of unrelated nations and civilizations, the authors of such books pay lip service to a global conception of history, but more often than not they actually write about the development of Western civilization and discuss other civilizations only as and when they influenced or were influenced by "the West." Typically they trace history from its "roots" in Mesopotamia and Egypt through Greece and Rome and medieval Europe and on to the present, and only begin to pay serious attention to Asia, Africa, and other regions when Western civilization came "in contact" with the cultures of these areas. When they do treat non-Western civilizations as separate entities, they usually attach the material to the main narrative without either relating it to the rest or concerning themselves with the continuity of the histories of these "exotic" societies.

Our approach has been quite different. We have tried to examine human development as it might be studied by a visitor from outer space and also to write our history in a truly chronological way—looking at the whole globe and all its civilizations at each stage of development. Of course we devote far more space to human history than to the remote eons during which the universe and our planet evolved, and more to recent centuries than to ancient times. Generally speaking, the closer our account approaches the present, the more detailed and extensive it becomes. Similarly we devote more space to the history of the West than to other civilizations. We do so partly because more is known about recent times and about the West, and partly because we (and our readers) are modern Westerners. To take an obvious example, we use throughout the Western calendar, dating events backward and forward from the birth of Christ. No other system would be intelligible. Nevertheless, we are writing world history, not merely a history of how the rest of the world has affected us, or we it. Our book is meant to be equally relevant to anyone who can read English, without regard for "race, creed, or national origin." And while it is also designed to be read as a whole, the separate histories of all major civilizations can be followed from their origins on without loss of continuity. Volume I commences with the still-unsolved mystery of the origin of the universe and proceeds through the evolution of the earth and of life and of the human animal to the earliest civilizations. It carries the story down to about 1500 A.D. Volume II treats the emergence of the modern world in the 16th, 17th, and 18th centuries. Volume III attempts (the task becomes increasingly difficult!) to describe the development and interactions of the societies of the world in the last 200-odd years.

World history conceived of in this manner is difficult to write under any circumstances. Surely no individual possesses the factual knowledge or has the "feel" that comes only from deep and prolonged study of a period or culture that are necessary if one is to describe and evaluate all history and all cultures authoritatively. We have dealt with this problem by assembling a group of experts (forty in number), thus bringing together their special knowledge and insights in a collaborative enterprise. Naturally a history of the world written by forty specialists presents other problems that would not arise in a work by a single author; it runs the risk of becoming a mere collection of encyclopedia articles, held together only by the covers in which the parts are bound. Aware from the beginning of this danger, we sought to surmount it in several ways. First our historians and other experts all know one another personally. Throughout the writing, we were in frequent contact and could repeatedly consult, debate, compare, and criticize in order to fuse our several efforts into a unified intellectual construct. This process went on at each stage of the book's development, over a period of more than five years.

Consider our first and most crucial tasks: the preparation of an outline and the allocation of space to various regions and periods of time. How should the history of the early civilization of India be related to that of Egypt and China or, for that matter, of Mexico and Peru? How many chapters should the history of Africa occupy as compared with that of South America or Eastern Europe? As editors—one a historian of the United States, the other of Western Europe—we knew that any answer we could devise for such questions would be inadequate and surely distorted. We therefore asked our specialists to tell us how they proposed to organize their material and how much space they needed, bearing in mind the ultimate limitation imposed by our decision to produce a work of roughly half a million words. Using draft outlines prepared by the contributors, and consulting with them at every stage, we eventually worked out the structure of our history.

The collaborative effort did not, however, end at this point. Whenever appropriate our authors consulted with one another in order to avoid repetition and omission, and they read and criticized their colleagues' manuscripts in all cases where they had special knowledge, and in many—out of friendship or curiosity—where they did not. Many of the following chapters bring together the writing of two and even three authorities, yet it is our belief that the parts of such chapters fit together as smoothly and as logically as those produced by a single mind.

Finally, our contributors have generously allowed us a remarkable latitude in organizing and editing their manuscripts. Given our common commitment to the production of an integrated synthesis of world history, all conceded that a more-than-ordinary editorial license was essential. Our object as editors has been to try to impose a basic uniformity of approach, to supply connecting passages and cross-references, and to alter the individual prose styles of the authors (without too great artistic loss, we hope) in the interest of creating the illusion not that we two have written what follows, but that all of us have written it all. It goes without saying, however, that each author has remained the ultimate arbiter of the facts and opinions in his own sections. Each has carefully read and corrected our "final" version.

Our original thought in planning and writing this book was that it was to be aimed at the so-called general reader. Only when the project was well under way did we realize that it might also serve as a text in world history courses. In retrospect, we believe that our original "oversight" was a fortunate one. If we had planned to write a conventional textbook we might have crowded our pages with too many dates, with the names of too many kings and battles and the like, and thus have lost the forest in the trees. Our assumption that our "general reader" would be impatient with enormous masses of detail led us to focus instead on the meaning of events and their broad influences, upon whole civilizations and their patterns of development, upon the shape of world history rather than the billions of discrete facts from which that shape emerges. And of course this is exactly what a world history textbook should also do. Perhaps students can be compelled to learn the names and dates of all the kings of England, and the terms of every major treaty that the many nations of the world have negotiated with one another over the centuries—although we doubt it. More important, they should not be asked to do so. Such matters are part of the history of the world it is true, but they do not help much in making *world history* meaningful. Our book is crowded with facts, but our facts have been chosen to explicate the whole, not simply as ends in themselves.

Consider the matter this way. To answer the question "What is man?" one does not put a slice of human tissue under a microscope, however necessary microscopic study may be in seeking the answer to many questions about man. Similarly, to answer our question, which essentially is "How has mankind fared on this earth?" one must view the history of mankind in its widest outlines. On the other hand, the reader's understanding of world history can and should be greatly increased by the study of selected parts of the whole in greater detail. We assume that instructors will want their students to delve more deeply at many points as they proceed with the subject. Thus, at the end of each chapter we have listed the best available special works on the topics covered. In addition, the instructors' manual designed to accompany this text contains extensive annotated bibliographies, again organized by chapters.

Much of whatever merit this volume possesses it owes to Cass Canfield of Harper & Row. His faith in our idea encouraged us to work out the details, and his generosity enabled us to enlist the services of the many busy scholars whose brains and energies produced this book. He has guided and supported our efforts through countless drafts and around a hundred unforeseen difficulties. Beulah Hagen of Harper & Row has laboriously, patiently, and with a fine intelligence supervised the design of the book and seen our complicated manuscript through the press. Cass Canfield, John Ryden, Mary Lou Mosher, Mel Arnold, and John Gordon, also of Harper & Row, have made important contributions to our project. We are deeply grateful. To thank individually all those who have helped our authors would be impractical in the space at our disposal; we leave that happy task to our colleagues. But we, as editors, wish to extend our loving thanks and appreciation to our wives, Gail Garraty and Ruth Gay, whose critical reading of the manuscript has been of great help and whose support at every stage has been truly invaluable.

JOHN A. GARRATY
PETER GAY

Contributors

René Albrecht-Carrié Professor Emeritus of History, Barnard College and the School of International Affairs, Columbia University

Herman Ausubel Professor of History at Columbia University

A. Doak Barnett Senior Fellow in the Foreign Policy Studies Division of Brookings Institution

Jacques Barzun University Professor at Columbia University

Elias J. Bickerman Professor Emeritus of History at Columbia University and Professor of Jewish History at the Jewish Theological Seminary

Hans H. A. Bielenstein Professor of Chinese History at Columbia University

Shepard B. Clough Professor Emeritus of European History at Columbia University

Gerson D. Cohen Jacob H. Schiff Professor of Jewish History at The Jewish Theological Seminary of America

Robert D. Cross President of Swarthmore College and Professor of American Social History

Ainslie T. Embree Professor of History at Duke University

Rhodes W. Fairbridge Professor of Geology at Columbia University

John A. Garraty Professor of History at Columbia University

Nina G. Garsoïan Professor of Armenian Studies and Professor of History at Columbia University

Peter Gay Professor of History at Yale University

J. Mason Gentzler Professor of History at Sarah Lawrence College

Henry F. Graff Professor of History at Columbia University

Lewis Hanke Clarence and Helen Haring Professor of History at the University of Massachusetts, Amherst

Richard Hofstadter De Witt Clinton Professor of American History at Columbia University (d. 1970)

Graham W. Irwin   Professor of African History at Columbia University

Charles Issawi   Ragnar Nurske Professor of Economics at Columbia University

Edward P. Lanning   Professor of Anthropology at Columbia University

William E. Leuchtenburg   De Witt Clinton Professor of History at Columbia University

Maan Z. Madina   Associate Professor of Arabic at Columbia University

John A. Moore   Professor of Biology at the University of California

Richard B. Morris   Gouverneur Morris Professor of History at Columbia University

John H. Mundy   Professor of European History at Columbia University

Ernest Nagel   University Professor Emeritus at Columbia University

Peter A. Pardue   Associate Professor of Religion at Indiana University (Bloomington)

Orest Ranum   Professor of History at the Johns Hopkins University

Eugene F. Rice, Jr.   Professor of History at Columbia University

Henry L. Roberts   Professor of History at Dartmouth College

James P. Shenton   Professor of History at Columbia University

Jacob W. Smit   Queen Wilhelmina Professor of History at Columbia University

Morton Smith   Professor of History at Columbia University

Fritz Stern   Seth Low Professor of History at Columbia University Visiting Professor at the University of Konstanz in Germany

Alden T. Vaughan   Professor of History at Columbia University

Immanuel Wallerstein   Professor of Sociology at McGill University

Hershel Webb   Associate Professor of Japanese History at Columbia University

Robert K. Webb   Managing Editor of the American Historical Review

Lodewyk Woltjer   Rutherford Professor of Astronomy at Columbia University and Editor of the Astronomical Journal

A HISTORY OF THE WORLD

The Modern World

Reaction and Rebellion

1 The Napoleonic Era

For two generations at least, in every European country, the memory of the French Revolution—still in some ways central to the French themselves—was a profound psychological fact. For most respectable, established, and propertied men and women, the main ingredient in that memory was fear, though they differed greatly over the means of exorcising the specter of revolution—whether by resistance, repression, or reform. But in their common anatomy of revolution, a cardinal assumption, preached in and out of season to those less fortunate souls who might imagine it a way out of their troubles, was that revolution inevitably ended in military despotism and the loss of the very liberties the revolutionaries had sought to gain. The historical text they had chiefly in mind was Napoleon Bonaparte, the man they had fought for so long at so much cost in blood and treasure. Despite their efforts, he was remembered by the dispossessed and ambitious as a deliverer, a guarantor not a destroyer of the Revolution. In time it became clear that he had also, unwittingly, stimulated still another profoundly creative force—the nation, as the nineteenth and twentieth centuries have understood it. If one had to choose a single man to stand at the turning point when we can begin to see the world as we know it—a man who summed up what was creative in eighteenth-century Europe and who prefigured (by design, accident, or reaction) the main impulses of the past 150 years, no one could qualify so well as Napoleon. It was surely Napoleon, more than Caesar, more than Luther, whom the German philosopher G. W. F. Hegel had in mind when he spoke of that rare but powerful phenomenon, the "world-historical individual." Hegel and Napoleon were after all, almost exact contemporaries.

Napoleon Bonaparte was born in Corsica in 1769 to a family of decayed but proud petty gentry. A year earlier, France had acquired Genoa's claims to that embattled and clan-ridden island. Born French by accident,

A.D.	1768	French take Corsica
	1769	Napoleon Bonaparte born at Ajaccio, Corsica
	1784	Napoleon enters the École Militaire
	1789	Meeting of the Estates General; beginning of the French Revolution
	1790	Edmund Burke's *Reflections on the Revolution in France* published
	1791–1792	Legislative Assembly
	1792–1795	Convention
	1793	Execution of Louis XVI; English evacuation of Toulon; Napoleon becomes brigadier general
	1794	Fall of Robespierre
	1795–1799	Directory
	1796	Napoleon assumes command of the army of Italy
	1797	Treaty of Campo Formio
	1798	Napoleon sails from Toulon to begin Egyptian campaign; Battle of the Nile
	1799	Napoleon returns to France; 18th Brumaire; Napoleon overthrows the Directory
	1799–1804	Consulate
	1800	Battle of Marengo; Battle of Hohenlinden
	1801	Treaty of Lunéville; Alexander I becomes czar of Russia; French concordat with papacy
	1802	Treaty of Amiens; Napoleon becomes life consul
	1803	Bank of France founded
	1804	Napoleon proclaimed emperor; Napoleonic Code promulgated
	1805	Battle of Trafalgar; Battle of Austerlitz; Treaty of Pressburg
	1806	Death of William Pitt; Battle of Jena; Berlin Decree, establishing the "Continental System"
	1807	Great Britain abolishes the slave trade; Napoleon forces Ferdinand VII of Spain to abdicate and installs his brother Joseph as king of Spain; Battle of Friedland; Treaty of Tilsit; Milan Decree
	1807–1808	J. G. Fichte delivers his *Addresses to the German Nation*
	1809	Battle of Wagram; Treaty of Schönbrunn

Napoleon was revolutionary by inheritance: his father was a close associate of General Pasquale di Paoli, the veteran Corsican patriot who had
fought against Genoa and then against France until his defeat three months
before Napoleon's birth. Napoleon's father chose to submit to the French
rather than flee with Paoli to England; his noble status, however insub-
stantially based in wealth, was accordingly confirmed. Napoleon, the
second of eight surviving children, benefited much from this decision. With
the help of a benevolent patron, he got the best education that France
could offer, first in one of the twelve recently founded royal schools for
sons of nobles, at Brienne, then, after 1784, at the distinguished École
Militaire in Paris, a training school for officers (like Sandhurst or West
Point) founded in mid-century as one of the military reforms of the reign
of Louis XV. Napoleon's small size and Corsican accent subjected him to
taunts from the boys at Brienne, and his unimpressive lineage brought him
up against the snobbish contempt of the cadets in Paris. But he was an
ambitious, hard-working, and brilliantly successful student. Completing his
course, astonishingly, in the space of a year, he was posted at an advanced
rank to one of the best regiments in the army.

The Revolution found Napoleon in full sympathy, hardly surprising in
view of his experience, his inheritance, or, perhaps more to the point, his
thorough allegiance to the ideals of the Enlightenment and above all to
Rousseau. With his brothers, he took the lead in implementing the Revolution in Corsica, but the influence this decision won for his family soon
dissolved in defeat and exile: Corsica rebelled against France, and General

Paoli returned to deliver the island to the English. Forced to be wholly French, Napoleon managed to survive the kaleidoscopic changes of the early years of the Revolution. He was helped, of course, by the emigration of royalist officers, and he was able in one way or another to avoid postings that might have slowed his progress; but he also gave convenient and genuine support to successive Republican factions as they seized power.

In 1793, with Spanish assistance, the English had occupied the Mediterranean naval base at Toulon, situated in a region honeycombed with disaffection and torn by civil war. Sent to command the artillery in the place of a wounded officer, Napoleon so distinguished himself in the action that forced the English evacuation that he became a brigadier general at the age of twenty-four. Six months later occurred the Thermidorian reaction. Napoleon was then in service with the army of Italy, and though he was briefly imprisoned, the distance from Paris and some helpful connections protected him from the logical consequences of his close association with the Robespierrists. The next year, no doubt serving ambition and conviction as much as his professional obligations, he accepted command of the artillery that the Convention summoned to protect itself from popular protest against the new constitution of the Year III. Napoleon's famous "whiff of grapeshot" on 13 Vendémiaire (October 5) dispersed the insurgents, secured the Directory in power, and assured him of their gratitude. Reinforced by the patronage of Paul François Barras, one of the directors, and by his marriage to Josephine de Beauharnais, an able, flamboyant woman, somewhat older than himself (she had once been Barras' mistress), that gratitude brought the young general a further promotion and, at the age of twenty-six, command of the army of Italy. He now began to sign himself Bonaparte, rather than Buonaparte. It is a fitting sequel to this final commitment to France that his victories in Italy made his native Corsica, from which he had been driven three years before, untenable for its English conquerors.

Spain had quickly withdrawn from the First Coalition of 1793, leaving Austria standing alone with England against a revolutionary France victorious almost by default. To attack England—busy though she was picking up French overseas possessions—was not then practicable; but Austria could be fought on land most effectively in her valuable possessions in northern Italy; by 1797 Napoleon had brought a defeated Austria to the Treaty of Campo Formio and had made northern Italy a French possession.

Napoleon's military success did not lie in a revolutionary technology; even massed fire, his later contribution to the art of artillery warfare, depended on tactical insight, not technical innovation. Like his equipment, most of his tactical devices—the combination of line and column, for example—were well known earlier in the century to royalist officers who had had to plan almost continual wars against England. Revolutionary leaders had already evoked the nation in arms (less novel in theory than in practice), with its irresistible resource of numerous, enthusiastic citizens. What Napoleon brought to bear on this heritage was his skill at disposing and manipulating forces—which in the course of his wars grew to triple the size of mid-eighteenth-century armies—hurling them at the most decisive spot with startling speed and effect. The success of this maneuvering arose partly from his insistence on mobility: he preferred light to heavy cavalry, and his armies, independent of base stores, lived off the country—successfully in Italy, disastrously fifteen years later in Russia. But there was another explanation of his ability to move vast numbers of troops farther and faster than earlier generals: it lay in the steady appeal he made to the self-interest and loyalty of both officers and men. No one better exploited that potent corollary of the nation in arms—the career open to talents: fighting ability brought promotion, and privates could literally become field marshals. No one was better at the equally important task of maintaining or restoring morale by a timely appearance among tired troops to urge them on to the last ounce of effort. To the end Napoleon was a soldier's soldier, and (one is reminded of Erwin Rommel in the Second World War) he cast his spell over his opponents too.

Having beaten Austria in Italy, Napoleon turned to strike at the remaining enemy—not by direct assault but by invading Egypt, a romantic choice that was also rational, for Egypt was the key to control of the East and the route to India, where Britain was finally victorious over the French. But the only French victories in Egypt were those of the scholars and scientists whom Napoleon took along with him; they attained a new level of geographical knowledge, made striking reforms in public health, started the science of Egyptology, and indirectly inspired a new fashion in architecture and interior design. At the beginning of August, 1798, a British fleet, commanded by Horatio Nelson (soon to be Lord Nelson), sailed into the harbor at Aboukir Bay, east of Alexandria, and destroyed the French fleet in the Battle of the Nile, cutting off Napoleon's forces and leaving them to be mopped up slowly by a British army. Napoleon himself escaped to France, arriving on October 13, 1799; he was of course still celebrated for his performance in Italy.

He returned not merely to garner laurels, though they were his in plenty as he journeyed north to Paris. He went to Paris to secure himself in a political situation once more in rapid flux. The Directory was in trouble. Faced with a Second Coalition of Austria, Russia, and England, the French government was overextended in Italy and in financial difficulties, and its members were in disagreement among themselves. Emmanuel Joseph Sieyes, the former priest who had trumpeted the cause of the third estate in 1789 and had survived to become a director, intended to overthrow the system to his own advantage. For his coadjutor, he chose Napoleon, protected as he was by public acclaim from the suspicion rightly felt by the other directors of the young general's ambition. Napoleon's stated price was a central place in the new constitution. To get the constitution, the legislative councils were to be moved from Paris to St. Cloud, where, under Bonaparte's inevitable protection, they could deliberate with only the right pressures applied. But the Councils did not willingly take direction, and their openly expressed distrust of the "dictator" led Napoleon on November 9 (18th Brumaire), 1799, in the riskiest gamble of his career, to drive out the protestors, leaving a rump to agree to the new constitution.

In drafting the Constitution of the Year VIII, which followed the successful coup d'état, Sieyès ingeniously limited the ostensible grant of universal suffrage to the right of local electors to nominate "notabilities," who in turn would nominate a higher level of notabilities, and so on until from a final list the emasculated legislative bodies of the nation would be drawn. The executive power was conferred, as Napoleon wished, on three consuls; but, in the choosing, Napoleon outmaneuvered Sieyès, to emerge himself as first consul assisted by two henchmen. In 1802 he became consul for life, with power to nominate the other consuls and his successor. In some ways it was little more than a change in title when in 1804 Bonaparte became the Emperor Napoleon I. What was new, however, was reversion to the hereditary principle, necessary to the stability of the regime, faced as it was with a renewed war and internal dissension. A pretext was found in an abortive assassination plot early in 1804. The principal conspirators were quickly rounded up—one veteran antirevolutionary wryly remarked that they had set out to give France a king and had given her an emperor—but a grander victim was needed. The leader of the émigrés, the Comte d'Artois, eluded Napoleon's net; the Duc d'Enghien did not. Enghien, certainly not implicated in the plot, was reportedly about to lead an invasion; he was arrested illegally in the German state of Baden, kidnapped, brought to France, tried in secret, and executed. Napoleon thus put his opponents on notice and drove Ludwig van Beethoven, in a rage, to tear out from his *Eroica* symphony the dedication to Napoleon, who had shown himself, after all, a mortal who could turn tyrant. Most of Europe did not need reminding that the Napoleonic regime, still illegitimate, depended on force. To fulfill the hereditary principle, Napoleon needed an heir, and Josephine had been unable to bear him a child. Their marriage, damaged by Josephine's infidelity, had become an arrangement of mutual convenience, softened by a measure of respect and even affection. In 1809, the Emperor finally and reluctantly brought himself to divorce her; early the next year

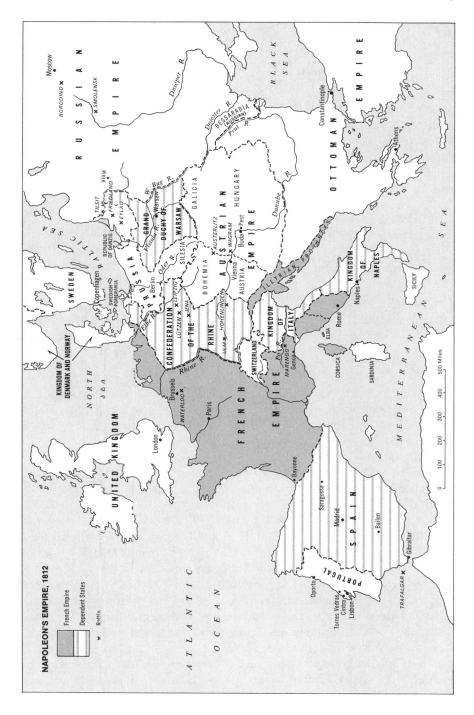

NAPOLEON'S EMPIRE, 1812

French Empire
Dependent States
✕ Battle

he married Marie Louise, a daughter of the Emperor of Austria. A son, known as the King of Rome, was born in 1811.

Meanwhile, Napoleon had carried French arms and influence to un-imagined heights. At the end of 1799, while talking peace, he was preparing for a lightning descent, through the Alps, on Italy; there in June, 1800, he defeated the Austrians decisively in the hazardous Battle of Marengo. A further victory over the Austrians (won by General Jean Moreau, later to be exiled for his part in a plot against Napoleon) at Hohenlinden in Germany led Austria to sign a separate peace at Lunéville. Czar Paul I at once turned about face to form an "armed neutrality" of the Baltic powers against England, and it was only a matter of time until the Peace of Amiens was arranged with Great Britain in March, 1802.

Conflicting interests and the clash of Napoleonic ambition with British strategic imperatives brought the uneasy peace to an end a little more than a year after it was made. But the Third Coalition proved as unstable as the others. Austria, defeated at Austerlitz, signed the Treaty of Pressburg in 1805. Prussia, which had held aloof in the hope of getting the German state of Hanover, belonging to the English crown but occupied by Napoleon, came in only to be beaten at Jena in 1806. The Russians, also caught in the debacle at Austerlitz, were decisively defeated at Friedland in 1807. The result was the Treaty of Tilsit in that year, the high-water mark of Napoleonic success. Having defeated Prussia and Russia, Napoleon made them his allies. France held Italy completely, far surpassing the grasp of Charles VIII four hundred years before. On the Rhine, France had got not only the natural frontiers so dear to Louis XIV but a series of client states in southern Germany; even Holland, so long an unattainable goal of Bourbon ambition, had been reduced to a dependent kingdom.

Only Great Britain had eluded the Emperor, thanks to her navy. Nelson had followed his victory at the Nile by wrecking the Czar's Armed Neutrality in a raid on Copenhagen in 1801. Then, in 1805, as plans for an invasion of Britain were mounted and after a trans-Atlantic race resulting from a French attempt to lure the English fleet from the Channel to the West Indies, Nelson lay in wait off the Spanish coast until the French fleet decided to dash from their refuge in Cádiz for the safety of the Mediterranean. They were caught and decisively beaten in the Battle of Trafalgar on October 2, 1805; Nelson fell a victim, but only after the outcome was clear. The invasion plans were canceled; indeed many troops from Boulogne had already been dispatched to the east to face the Allies at Ulm and Austerlitz. For another ten years France and Britain confronted each other, the one supreme on land, the other at sea.

The Napoleonic era meant more, however, than the triumphant achievement of Valois and Bourbon dreams. Were the consuls right in declaring as

they did in 1799 that the Revolution was complete? To say that would be
to deny much of Napoleon's persistent appeal. It was in fact his greatest
accomplishment that he consolidated and secured the creative impulses of
the 1790's in viable form and, in actuality or by challenge, extended them
to nearly the whole of the Continent. One could argue that Napoleon
violated the basic Revolutionary principle of equality when he restored an
aristocracy, or even when he instituted the Legion of Honor in 1802. But
the Napoleonic aristocracy—in contrast to the aristocrats of the *ancien
régime* for whom the Emperor retained a healthy contempt—was an *open*
aristocracy of service, even though tarnished by the corruption of some
Napoleonic nobles by power or honor or money; while the Legion of
Honor was the canonization of merit and the institutional warrant of the
career open to talents. Napoleon's religious policy could also be used as an
argument against a revolutionary interpretation of his career. The Concordat with the papacy in 1802 retreated from the advanced secularism of
Revolutionary France and from Napoleon's own unreligious outlook; it
created a host of problems for future statesmen by deeply embedding the
Church (the clergy were paid directly by the state) in the fabric of national
life. Yet it was a clear-eyed recognition of the social utility of religion, and
it made a signal contribution to the pacification of the country. The majority of French citizens were not yet prepared for the heady laicism to
which the Jacobins had called them and which republican politicians a
century later were to echo.

Perhaps one could even condemn the Napoleonic Code, the great codi-
fication of law proclaimed in 1804, for its retreat to authoritarianism,
particularly in the realm of family life. But the main legal victories of the
Revolution—equality of men before the law, the rights of citizens, the
abolition of manorial privileges—were retained and embodied in a form
that has been France's most important cultural export. Indeed, the Code—
in striking contrast to the chaotic, creaky, and often inequitable libertarian-
ism of English law—points to the persuasiveness of the central legacy of
the eighteenth century, rationality. Rationality was forced on every front.
Administration was centralized with clear lines of responsibility running to
the Council of State from new officials called prefects, each at the head of a
department; with subprefects in the departmental subdivisions called arron-
dissements and a tight control over the selection of mayors, local government
was established in the form it retains today. Taxation and national finances
were recast, and in 1803 the Bank of France was founded to cap the
nation's financial system as the Bank of England had done across the
Channel for more than a century. Centralization was also rigorously applied, for good or ill, to the educational structure, culminating in the University of France. Here the regime built on foundations laid by the Con-

vention and the Directory, but the Napoleonic period saw the effective beginning of those institutions—the lycées and the grandes écoles, above all the École Normale and the École Polytechnique—that have shaped the intellectual life of modern France. The Empire was a despotism still. The secret police, headed by the able Joseph Fouché, was new only in its efficiency; but in its contempt for opposition, increasingly stringent control of the press, and the systematic use of propaganda, the Napoleonic system points forward more than back. Still, this negation of rationality was itself rational: to the very end, Napoleonic France remained a state—a modern state—at war.

While the Revolution was consolidated at home, it was aggressively exported. Again, at first sight, one might be led to doubt that statement. Echoing the Corsican tradition of family loyalty, Napoleon put his relatives on the thrones of client states—he was himself king of Italy, with his stepson Eugene Beauharnais as viceroy, his brother Joseph was king of Naples and later of Spain, Louis was king of Holland, and Jerome king of Westphalia; only Lucien, having made a marriage of which his masterful brother disapproved, retired to private life. The client kingdoms paid tribute and (Italy especially) yielded up their art treasures. But French institutions were used to reduce the vast conquests to order and submission; above all, the Napoleonic Code was used to bring states, hampered by feudal survivals and administrative inefficiency, with a single lurch into the modern world. The example and philosophy of the Revolution went abroad as well. Ultimately the revolutionary parties, most evident in Italy, failed: they were tied too closely to France to survive the reaction of the victorious nation-states. But the legacy remained. The Neapolitan and Spanish constitutions of 1812, extreme and impracticable though they were, enshrined French principles and survived the reaction as spurs to generations of "liberals"; liberal principles informed new parties of the left and inspired recurring revolutions in one country after another.

The countries that escaped French occupation or reduction to the level of client states responded rather to the French challenge than to French principles. Here the best example is Prussia, where reform rested on the impressive Enlightenment that had flourished in the late eighteenth century, with borrowings from the British, notably Adam Smith and Edmund Burke. Indeed certain piecemeal reforms had been accomplished in Prussia before there was a French example, including some freeing of the serfs. But Prussia remained a congeries of scattered feudal segments. Its economy was overwhelmingly given over to agriculture, which became steadily more backward as one proceeded to the east. Its hardened military and bureaucratic tradition was less a viable system than a memorial to the Great Elector and Frederick the Great. But in the years after 1804, through the imagination and drive of a group of enlightened though far from radical administrators, Prussia was remade into a modern nation-state; chief among these legislators was the Freiherr vom Stein, an enlightened Anglophile descended from a family of Rhineland knights. The serfs were freed throughout Prussia, local and provincial governments were remodeled, commerce and industry were relieved of many of the old restrictions and controls, and the army (ultimately based on conscription) was made more efficient and humane. In education above all, the ideals of the Enlightenment were evident. The new *Gymnasien* (equivalent to English grammar schools or French lycées) were henceforth to mold Prussia's elite, and German universities leaped into the vanguard of European intellect. With education, Prussian reform touches most vitally the rapidly growing sense that Germany was a nation, its unity evoked in the potent *Addresses to the German Nation* by the philosopher J. G. Fichte, delivered in 1807–1808, and symbolized by the founding of the University of Berlin in 1810. Napoleon too had contributed to German unity by refusing in 1806 to recognize any longer the existence of the Holy Roman Empire; he thus turned the Hapsburg emperor back on his Austrian and east European domains, while the French consolidation of many petty German states laid the groundwork for still larger agglomerations and ultimately for unification. But the essential spirit, the capacity to think of Germany as something other than a geographical expression, sprang above all from the vision and passion of German philosophers and men of letters.

The three remaining Great Powers were much less touched by French-exported or French-inspired reform. Exhausted from defeat for much of the period, Austria had also reacted against the wholesale reforms of the enlightened emperor Joseph II; Joseph's nephew, Francis I, was far from a reformer. A brief flurry of reform after 1806, under Count Philipp Stadion, was a pale reflection of the Prussian marvel and a gesture at reclaiming German leadership. These reforms underlay, in their military aspect, one more effort against the French that ended disastrously at Wagram in 1809; the brief alliance that followed gave Napoleon his new empress. Thereafter, Francis fell under the influence of Count Metternich, who raised negative policy to the level of principle.

Russia showed no such consistency. More than any other European state, she took her character from her ruler. The early Revolutionary period had seen Russia ruled despotically, with relative efficiency and a decorative overlay of enlightenment, by Catherine the Great; she was succeeded in 1796 by Paul I, whose bitter opposition to Revolution was the only constant in an erratic policy that reflected his madness. His assassination in 1801 brought the young Alexander I to the throne. Himself unstable, and deeply affected by the horrible circumstances of his accession,

Alexander emerged from two mild but abortive reforming movements, one early in his reign, the other after Tilsit, into a conservative mysticism that was to leave its mark on the peace settlement and the postwar world.

In Great Britain, although the period of the Revolution is always counted (rightly) as a serious setback for the movement toward mild political, economic, and religious reform that had begun in the 1770's, a number of administrative and financial reforms were made under the aegis of the country's brilliant prime minister William Pitt. He was in office from 1783 until his death in 1806, except for three years after 1801, when he was forced to resign by the refusal of King George III to contemplate the quid pro quo that Pitt had promised the Irish for the loss of their parliament in the legislative union with Great Britain in 1800—the admission of Catholics to high office and to parliament.

French ideas had certainly infected some Englishmen, most evidently in the early 1790's, when radicalism took an enormous step, both forward and down in the social scale. But a country at war, increasingly impressed by Edmund Burke's arguments in his *Reflections on the Revolution in France*, could not tolerate that kind of dissent, and by 1800 a savage repression had brought open radical activity to an end. Though political and trade-union organizations were proscribed, admiration for French principles and even for Napoleon survived among workingmen and some of the more radical Dissenters from the Church of England, who had not entirely forgotten Cromwell. But throughout the period the invocation of French principles was rather a rhetorical addition to native radical ambitions, running back at least to the seventeenth century. These impulses barely touched a wide public opinion until the last years of the war, when signs of revolutionary ideas and organization reappear among the working classes in the Luddite risings—so called from their mythical leader King Ludd—of 1811–1813. But even among middle-class circles with grievances, the wars against Napoleon brought an upsurge of patriotic sentiment. Unlike Continental peoples, the English did not have to learn the lesson of nationalism; they had learned it at least as early as the sixteenth century and had so far assimilated it as to find newer manifestations of it incomprehensible. But whatever its discontents, the English nation benefited from the essential freedom of its institutions—the lesson that Bonaparte could never learn—and from a sudden, vast expansion of wealth resulting from economic revolution and war.

Robbed of his invasion, Napoleon determined to attack the "nation of shopkeepers" economically. Having got control of the Continent, he proclaimed "the Continental system" in the Berlin and Milan Decrees in 1806–1807, an attempt to exclude British goods to which the British replied with a blockade. The British navy enforced the blockade so efficiently that it became embroiled with neutral nations whose ships it insisted upon searching. This resulted in war with the United States in 1812. But even with his system of client rulers and subject peoples, Napoleon found it hard to enforce his ban on British trade. At times he frankly needed what the British could produce and had to license violation; there was a continual drain through smuggling. But in the two periods when enforcement was really tried, the impact on Britain was extremely harsh—in 1807–1808 and again in 1810–1812; the second of these crises underlay the Luddite risings.

The collapse of Napoleon's dominion began in its extremities, first in Spain. Determined to include Spain effectively in the Continental system, and appalled by the squalor and corruption of the Spanish king and queen and their favorite Godoy, Napoleon forced their abdication in favor of his brother Joseph. The Spanish people never agreed. They rose against the French, in regular and guerrilla military activity. Meanwhile, the flight of the Portuguese royal family to Brazil and the rejection of Joseph by Spanish colonies overseas gave the British two valuable footholds, the one strategic in Portugal, the other economic, on which a century of Latin American economic penetration was based. Although the British began the Peninsular War in 1808, as they were to begin their Continental campaigns in 1914 and 1939, with a brilliant retreat and evacuation, the forces sent to Portugal under Arthur Wellesley, later Duke of Wellington, paid careful attention to fortification, were willing to fall back on their bastions to wait, and finally wrecked the superbly mobile French forces by making them sit still. In 1811 the turning point came, and Wellington and his Spanish allies pushed slowly through Spain to enter southern France in 1814.

Meanwhile, to block the drain at the other end of the Continental system, Napoleon launched an invasion of Russia in 1812. At heavy cost, the Russians retreated to Moscow and beyond, drawing the French a thousand miles from home, where in time they were dealt with cruelly by cold and hunger. The long, tragic retreat from Moscow triggered revolts in other European nations. A Fourth Coalition was formed of Britain, Austria, Prussia, and Russia, and while Britain pushed up from the Peninsula (and provided, as always, endless subsidies) the other three allies massed their armies in Germany. At the Battle of Leipzig in October, 1813, they won a crushing victory, leaving France open before them. After futile negotiations, the allied march resumed, slowed but not stopped by Napoleon, for the numbers he could formerly command were shrinking away and the old spirit was gone. Behind the lines, one after another dignitary sought accommodation or peace, including Joseph Bonaparte and that inveterate schemer Talleyrand, who had already come to terms with Louis XVIII, commenting that treason was a matter of dates. Betrayed and deserted, Napoleon abdicated early in April, 1814. Louis XVIII was proclaimed as the allies entered Paris, and the victors sent the defeated emperor to his new kingdom, the island of Elba in the Mediterranean.

By the Treaty of Chaumont in March, 1814, the coalition was converted into an alliance, and in fairly short order the first Treaty of Paris was signed, providing generous terms for France, which, while losing her natural frontiers and her far-flung acquisitions, still kept more territory than she had had when Napoleon began his conquests; she was not to be occupied or forced to pay an indemnity. To deal with the vastly larger problem of remaking Europe, the powers adjourned to a congress that opened at Vienna in September, graced or overawed by the presence of the Czar, the Emperor of Austria, and the King of Prussia, by a number of lesser monarchs, and by a remarkable set of negotiators—Castlereagh and Wellington from England, Hardenberg from Prussia, Metternich from Austria, and the resilient Talleyrand.

Certain "principles" have been discerned in the settlement: the containment of France; the legitimacy of displaced dynasties; the compensation of states either for their sufferings or for lands they gave up in the general settlement; and, above all, the balance of power. Into the mill went those territories refashioned by Napoleon in southern Germany and the Low Countries; those kingdoms, like Saxony, that had collaborated with the French; and those regions so long subject to manipulation by the great powers, such as Italy or Poland, the latter three times partitioned already and temporarily rescued by Napoleon as the Grand Duchy of Warsaw. France was encircled by an enlarged kingdom of Holland, including the former Austrian Netherlands, by a strong frontier on the Rhine where Prussia was more firmly entrenched, by a revived and neutralized Switzerland, and by Austrian dominance in northern Italy, reinforced by the addition of Venetia (the republic had fallen to Napoleon in 1797) by way of compensation for the loss of her Belgian territories. Poland survived not at all, and Saxony only in truncated form. Denmark ceded Norway to Sweden, the Spanish and Portuguese royal houses were returned to their thrones to face two generations of intrafamily squabbling and civil war, and the Bourbons were restored to misgovern in Naples. Except perhaps for the declaration against the slave trade, inserted at the insistence of Great Britain, where that humanitarian reform had been accomplished in 1807–1810, the settlement was thoroughly obedient to the canons of eighteenth-century diplomacy; only the scale was different. Though in retrospect we can see nationalism as the most powerful solvent of Napoleon's conquests, it was something neither named nor appreciated. The statesmen at Vienna did not recognize it, and it counted only in the future by way of challenging or modifying the settlement.

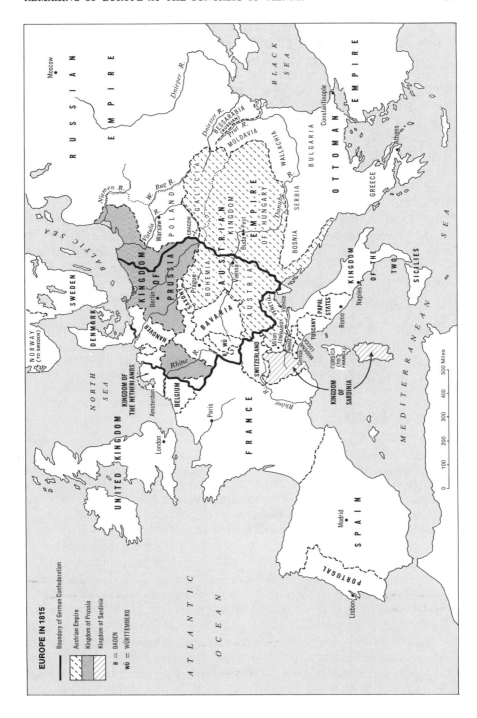

The splendor, gaiety, and sense of accomplishment in Vienna were crudely shattered in March, 1815, when Napoleon escaped from Elba. As he moved swiftly to Paris, joined by his old soldiers and heartened by an amazing outpouring of loyalty, the coalition was at once renewed, and Wellington and the Prussian general Blücher took up a stand in Germany. The end of the "Hundred Days" came on June 15–18 at Waterloo in Belgium, a battle that Napoleon came close to winning. Louis XVIII returned once more, and this time Napoleon was sent far away to the island of St. Helena in the South Atlantic, to spend the remaining six years of his life spinning reflections, self-justification, and a legend. The Allies had signed the final settlement at Vienna a few days before Waterloo; they went back to the conference table to fashion a second Treaty of Paris, reducing France's territory to the limits of 1790 and subjecting her to occupation and the payment of an indemnity; France was isolated but not ostracized. Other than the Treaty of Paris, the one new element in the settlement was the Czar's harebrained, mystical scheme for a Holy Alliance, by which the monarchs pledged themselves to a policy based on Christian precepts. The monarchs agreed to it as a gesture, except for the King of England, who kept aloof. It was the renewed Quadruple (and later, thanks to Talleyrand's skill, the Quintuple) Alliance on which the Concert of Europe rested in succeeding years. But the Holy Alliance, signed by three despots, became a new bogey to unite heated liberal imaginations that were only temporarily in eclipse.

For Further Reading

Connelly, Owen, *Napoleon's Satellite Kingdoms.*
Lefebvre, Georges, *Napoleon from 18 Brumaire to Tilsit, 1799–1807.*
Simon, Walter M., *The Failure of the Prussian Reform Movement, 1807–1819.*
Thompson, E. P., *The Making of the English Working Class.*
Thompson, J. M., *Napoleon Bonaparte.*
Webster, Sir Charles, *The Congress of Vienna, 1814–1815.*

2   The United States: 1789–1823

The men who made the American Revolution had hardly won independence when they turned to the task of making a nation. Most shared in some measure the mixed expectation of Alexander Hamilton when he wrote, "Happy America, if those to whom thou hast intrusted the guardianship of thy infancy know how to provide for thy future repose, but miserable and undone, if their negligence or ignorance permits the spirit of discord to erect her banner on the ruins of thy tranquillity." Few thought the task would be easy. Their newly independent domain encompassed a territory of imperial dimensions, and history seemed to militate against the success of republics, especially when expanded beyond the confines of a single city. Equally dangerous was the narrow parochialism that permeated the thinking of so many Americans. Only the smaller states, fearful of absorption by their larger neighbors, seemed committed to real cooperation.

But the severe economic and social dislocations that beset the country in the immediate post-Revolutionary years provoked a deepening uneasiness about the future and a growing readiness to consider closer ties. Efforts to resolve commercial difficulties at a meeting in Annapolis, Maryland, during the late summer of 1786 had attracted delegates from only five states, but this assemblage had called for an expanded convention of states to meet the following spring at Philadelphia. This call resulted in the drawing up between May and September of 1787 of the Federal Constitution, a document that defined the basic governmental structure of the new nation.

The liberal philosophy that informed the Constitution evolved from the Puritan and Glorious Revolutions. It expressed a profound concern for protecting the rights of the individual against the pretensions of authority. To assure a balance, it divided power through a system of checks and balances, a process which the Constitution's principal author, James Madison, explained as "giving to those who administer each department the necessary constitutional means and personal motives to resist encroachments of the others." Lest anyone misunderstand his intent, Madison added: "Ambition must be made to counteract ambition."

The founding fathers defined the dimensions of central authority broadly, but they retained also the already existing structure of state and local authority as a check on this central authority. Unlike the French, who

A.D. 1786 Annapolis Convention
1787 Philadelphia Convention
1789 George Washington inaugurated
1791 First Bank of the United States established
1795 Jay Treaty ratified
1796 Washington's Farewell Address
1797 John Adams inaugurated
1798 Alien and Sedition Acts; first Kentucky and Virginia Resolutions
1799 Second Kentucky Resolutions; undeclared naval war with France
1801 Thomas Jefferson inaugurated
1803 Louisiana Purchase
1804 Alexander Hamilton killed
1807 Embargo
1808 African slave trade ends
1809 Nonintercourse Act; James Madison inaugurated
1811 First Bank of the United States expires
1812 War of 1812
1814 Hartford Convention; Treaty of Ghent ends War of 1812
1816 Second Bank of the United States established
1817 James Monroe inaugurated
1820 Missouri Compromise
1823 Monroe Doctrine

produced a Napoleon as an aftermath of their Revolution, Americans accepted a strong central government reluctantly, and only after most stringent efforts to restrict its activities. Ratification of the Constitution was assured only when it was agreed that it be amended to include a Bill of Rights, not the least of which was the right of the separate states to reserve to themselves all powers not "expressly delegated" by the Constitution to federal authority.

Once the great states of Virginia and New York ratified the Constitution in late June, 1788, the new government was launched, but it possessed only the barest administrative apparatus: a foreign office consisting of a secretary, two diplomats, and three clerks; a military establishment made up of one secretary and an 840-man army; and a bureaucracy of twelve (unpaid) clerks. The new government was burdened with a formidable if uncounted debt, and only the barest revenue and no credit with which to resolve its financial problems. Despite this somber inheritance, within less than a decade the new republic was a going concern.

Success in establishing the new government resulted from the unstinting efforts of men such as George Washington, Thomas Jefferson, Alexander Hamilton, James Madison, and John Adams. Washington's enormous prestige gave the Republic a legitimacy no one else could have bestowed, and when in 1797 he voluntarily surrendered the presidency, he set a precedent for the peaceful transfer of power that went far toward guaranteeing its stability. More immediately, as Alexander Hamilton acknowledged, Washington provided the "aegis" under which the Secretary of the Treasury could secure the national credit. He accepted without protest the large role assigned to him, aware that each of his acts converted the broad constitutional principles into the procedures which would guide his successors.

No less formidable, although more controversial, Hamilton persuaded the Congress to fund its inherited indebtedness. Overriding stubborn opposition, he also persuaded Congress to assume the outstanding state debts. The price he paid for this was minuscule: he surrendered the placing of the future federal capital to Jefferson, who located it in the present District of Columbia.

Hamilton was dubious about the prospects of the Constitution, a document which he feared conceded too much authority to the states, but he felt that an effective federal government must nonetheless be established. A weak central government would attach "to itself the disrespect incident to weakness and [be] unable to promote the public happiness." Subtly he set to work extending federal power at every opportunity. To secure the national finances, he maneuvered the First Bank of the United States through Congress. This agency assured the new government of a central bank through which its fiscal needs would be effectively managed. Over the opposition of Jefferson and Madison, he persuaded Washington that the "necessary and proper" clause of the Constitution allowed for the establishment of the Bank.

Hamilton's labors "to establish in this country principles more and more national" triggered deep-rooted fears of central authority and its concomitant threat to state sovereignty. Under the leadership of Madison and Jefferson, opposition arose that by the end of the first decade had become a political party. Unable to prevail within the Washington administration, Jefferson withdrew as Secretary of State to allow him free scope in speaking out for those interests he felt were slighted by the administration.

Central to the Jeffersonian appeal was his confidence in the people, and especially "those who labor in the earth," a group he designated "the chosen people of God." On more than one occasion, Jefferson challenged the idea that government should be "trusted to the rulers . . . alone." Instead he took the position that "the people themselves are its only safe depositories." Possessed of a supreme confidence "in the common sense of mankind in general," Jefferson expressed his "earnest wish . . . to see the republican element of popular control pushed to the maximum of its practical exercise." A government so controlled was bound to be "pure and perpetual." This attitude differed from that of Hamilton, who proclaimed: "Take mankind in general, they are vicious—their passions may be operated upon." Hamilton claimed to be "affectionately attached to the republican theory," but felt obliged to add that he was "far from being without doubts."

But it would be a mistake to identify Jefferson with modern equalitarian doctrine. "There is a natural aristocracy among men," he wrote John Adams. "The grounds of this are virtue and talents." Shaped in his youth by the deferential politics of Virginia, he anticipated that a knowledgeable public would choose to be ruled by the "natural aristoi." And he had no doubt that he was an "aristo" of the blood, a conviction confirmed by his frequent election to office. He also shared the attitudes that characterized the Virginia gentry. Although a staunch supporter of vigorous state government, at least while not himself in control of the federal apparatus, he firmly opposed development of a large federal establishment. "Let the general government be reduced to foreign concerns only," he wrote on the eve of his election to the presidency, "and our general government may be reduced to a very simple organization and a very unexpensive one: a few plain duties to be performed by a few servants."

The divergences between Hamilton and Jefferson were real, but as the first Treasury chief shrewdly observed, "while we were in the administration together, [Jefferson] was generally for a large construction of the

Executive authority and not backward to act upon it in cases which co-incided with his views. . . . To my mind a true estimate of Mr. Jefferson's character warrants the expectation of a temporizing rather than a violent system."

Hamilton was close to the mark. Both men started from political premises derived from seventeenth-century British revolutionary tradition; both made ready reference to Locke, Harrington, and other revolutionary apologists. Each at a different point in his career posed the great Leveller question, "Men begin to ask, everywhere: Who is this tyrant that dares to build his greatness on our misery and degradation?" Where they parted was in the tone of their expectations. Jefferson in the twilight of life asserted, "It is a good world on the whole. . . . I steer my bark with Hope in the head, leaving Fear astern." Hamilton shortly before his own tragic death said: "Every day proves to me more and more, that this American world was not made for me."

Hamilton's last remark had its ironic touch, for even as he made it, Jefferson, now President, confirmed the permanence of the administrative apparatus Hamilton had erected. Nonetheless, by 1804, Hamilton was an anachronism. In the late 1790's, unable to dominate the Federalist party, he had broken with his nominal chief, John Adams. As that stuffy but sturdy New Englander struggled to contain the undeclared naval warfare raging with France, Hamilton pressed for an open declaration of war. Made uneasy by the savagery of the Terror in France, Hamilton concluded: "None can deny that the cause of France has been stained by excesses and extravagances for which it is not easy, if possible, to find a parallel in the history of human affairs, and from which reason and humanity recoil." Adams did not dissent from that judgment, but he did not believe that the cause of France's enemy Great Britain was that of America. Instead, he insisted that the interests of America were best served by remaining neutral.

Such differences of opinion were significant only as they reflected more deeply rooted national sentiments. The future relations between the new nation and the outside world were at issue. The controversial nature of these differing views speeded the development of the new national parties, a situation many found alarming. "The situation of the public good, in the hands of two parties nearly poised as to numbers, must be extremely perilous," mused John Taylor of Caroline. "Truth is a thing, not of indivisibility into conflicting parts, but of unity. Hence both sides cannot be right." Despite such sentiments, the excitement generated by the signing of the Jay Treaty with Great Britain reached a climax with the emergence of two distinct political parties, the Federalists and the Democratic Republicans.

The Federalists had intended that the Jay Treaty would avoid the outbreak of war, but by failing to settle such issues as the impressment of seamen, ship seizures, and Indian depredations on the northwest frontier, it precipitated bitter protests from among Republicans. It also blighted relations with the French, who claimed that it violated the Franco-American treaty of 1778 and controverted current American sentiment. On the latter point at least, the French were correct. Washington hesitated to act on the treaty, well aware that his decision was bound to aggravate party divisions. "The peace of our Country stands almost committed in either event," the Federalist Noah Webster noted. "A rejection sacrifices Mr. Jay & perhaps many of his friends, a ratification threatens the popularity of the President, whose personal influence is now more essential than ever to our Union." After Washington approved it and obtained Senate ratification, the opposition tried to prevent the House of Representatives from appropriating the funds necessary to implement the treaty. This hurdle was overcome, but Washington sadly observed that public agitation was "higher . . . than it has been at any period since the Revolution."

Contemporary reactions to the Jay Treaty dispute ran the gamut of American fears. The prospect of foreign war, the threat of political dissolution, sectional antipathies, and hidden conspiracies conjured up a witches' brew that unnerved the victorious Federalists, even as it deepened the hostility of the defeated Republicans. Passion threatened to supersede reason. "What has been the conduct of government?" demanded one group of Virginians. "Under the corrupt influence of the [Hamiltonian] paper system, it has uniformly crouched to Britain." Within Congress, elemental decencies faded. Washington's Farewell Address was actually an effort to turn the tables upon those political opponents who were making his final presidential days miserable. With the collaboration of Hamilton, he set to work undermining what vestiges remained of the French Alliance. His famous "great rule of conduct" warned against a *"political* connection" with any foreign power. Alliances should be transitory, and only "for extraordinary emergencies." Washington recommended both neutrality and unilateralism, a combination he expected to be easily obtained, and he predicted that if the people remained united, national weakness would be succeeded by a strength which would make foreigners hesitant to challenge the country. The United States could then "choose peace or war, as our interest . . . shall counsel." The attainment of this objective became the central theme of American foreign policy.

Between the goal and its fulfillment stood the great European powers, battling for world supremacy. In their conflicts, the rights of neutrals fell by the wayside. Domestic tranquillity suffered further disruption as partisan politics intensified. Crusty and stubborn John Adams, ostensibly the head of the Federalist party, was undercut by Hamilton, even within his own cabinet. Yet he refused to engage in open warfare with France, settling instead for what has been called a quasi-war, while he worked to reconcile misunderstandings. (Adams, however, was no appeaser, while he worked to reconcile misunderstandings. "If infidelity, dishonor, or too much humiliation is demanded, France shall do as she pleases, and take her course," he said. "America is not SCARED.")

A further complication arose when, in response to Republican attacks, Adams reacted with a monumental blunder, the Alien and Sedition Acts. These laws were intended to silence "alien" agitation against the government and prosecute domestic "pests" and disturbers of order and tranquillity 'who write, print, utter, or publish false, scandalous, and malicious writings against the government of the United States.' " Jefferson denounced the Sedition Act as a "gag law," which prompted one Federalist editor to retort: "Nothing can so completely gag a Jeffersonian Democrat as to restrain him from lying. If you forbid his lying, you forbid his speaking."

Portentous with danger for the future was the response of Jefferson and Madison, who put their pens to resolutions, passed by the legislatures of Kentucky and Virginia, which defined federal authority in the narrowest of terms. If the federal government exceeded its constitutional powers, Madison contended, the states had the duty to interpose their authority against "the usurpations of Congress." Jefferson even advocated nullification, a demand that was included in the second set of Kentucky Resolutions of 1799. Although other state legislatures did not follow the lead of Kentucky and Virginia, the resolutions effectively rallied Republican opposition, thus contributing to Jefferson's triumph in the election of 1800.

But once in office, Jefferson, albeit reluctantly, left the Federalist administrative apparatus intact. The threatening tone of his language of the previous decade faded; he appealed for reconciliation and emulated his predecessors in seeking to detach the United States from European involvements. "We have a perfect horror," he declared at the inception of his administration, "at everything like connecting ourselves with the politics of Europe." The world struggle shaking Europe he interpreted as an opportunity to gain advantages in the New World. When Napoleon's plans for an American Empire went awry, Jefferson, uninhibited by his previous strict-constructionist arguments, purchased the vast Louisiana Territory.

But when confronted with renewed British and French attacks on American shipping, he could find no better response than an embargo on all foreign commerce. This boycott, designed to force the belligerents to relax their hostile orders and edicts, boomeranged. Federalist New England resorted to civil disobedience and, with fine irony, contemplated nullification. As Jefferson's second term drew to a close, Albert Gallatin, then Secretary of the Treasury, gloomily confessed: "A majority will not adhere

to the embargo much longer. . . ." Congress shortly confirmed his predic-
tion by repealing the act and replacing it with the less onerous Nonintercourse Act.

The Madison administration continued the search for a way to compel
respect for American maritime rights. It was a task made doubly difficult
by the unimpressive performance of Madison, who revealed a remarkable
inability to control Congress or shape public opinion. Within Congress,
discontent grew, allowing the more energetic members of the august body,
dubbed "war hawks," to shape a policy committed to redeem national
honor. Madison succumbed, calling for the expansion of federal arms. By
the spring of 1812, Congress had taken so belligerent a stance that few
members questioned the correctness of one Pennsylvanian who declared,
"If we now recede we shall be a reproach to all nations." With the renewal
of an embargo in early April, the drift toward war accelerated. On June 18,
1812, the United States went to war with Great Britain.

In short order, the ill-prepared American forces invaded Canada and
were repulsed. Within a year, despite a few early naval successes, the
American navy had been swept from the seas. The final indignity came in
late August of 1814 when British forces seized and burned Washington.
The obvious weakness of the federal government, more specifically its
inability to protect the American coastline, excited renewed clamor in New
England for an end either to the war or to the Union; a protest meeting at
Hartford issued a vigorous defense of states' rights and contemplated
secession. But the movement collapsed when peace was negotiated at
Ghent in December, 1814. American spirits received an unexpected boost
when news spread that Andrew Jackson had won a great battle over the
Redcoats at New Orleans.

The war had ended with both belligerents about where they had
started. Nonetheless, changes had occurred. Republicans could claim to
have won "an honorable peace with a powerful and arrogant enemy."
Federalists found it impossible to shake loose from the reputation of
treason; the party disintegrated. With the accession of James Monroe to
the presidency in 1817, the old divisions faded; seemingly a political
consensus had been achieved.

In fact, a massive restructuring of political alignments moved along
under a deceptive calm. The long preoccupation with European affairs
ended as Americans turned their attention to domestic affairs. "The people
have now more general objects of attachment with which their pride and
political opinions are connected," Gallatin observed. "They are more
American; they feel and act more like a nation; and I hope that the
permanency of the Union is thereby better secured."

Events further conspired to ensure the United States greater security from foreign intervention. Napoleon's effort to establish French hegemony over Europe hastened the collapse of Spain's Latin American empire. The long rift between Britain and America was healed by the expectation of security and mutual profit at Spain's expense. When the other major European powers utilized the Holy Alliance to restore governments overthrown by revolutions, Americans moved to recognize the newly independent republics to the south. Any doubt about American views was stilled by the straightforward statements of the Monroe administration. "It may be observed," Secretary of State John Quincy Adams wrote, "that for the repose of Europe, as well as of America, the European and American political systems should be kept as separate and distinct from each other as possible." The government was, therefore, in a highly receptive mood when the British foreign secretary, George Canning, proposed a joint Anglo-American statement supporting Latin American independence. London acknowledged the United States as the dominant American power, a situation that made an understanding of the "great political and commercial interests which hung upon the destinies of the new continent" imperative.

When Britain backed away from implementing the proposal, Monroe and Adams decided to go it alone. The result appeared in Monroe's 1823 Annual Address. The United States unilaterally declared its decision "that the American Continents, by the free and independent condition which they have assumed and maintain, are henceforth not to be considered as subjects for future colonization by any European Power." No less emphatically, American policy renounced any intention of interfering in the internal concerns of Europe.

The long tutelage had ended. Whereas only a decade earlier, Americans had struggled to gain respect for their rights, Adams justified the new doctrine with a simple statement. "It would be more candid, as well as more dignified, to avow our principles explicitly to Russia and France than to come in as a cockboat in the wake of the British man-of-war." The experiment in independence had been completed triumphantly, at least as far as the outside world was concerned.

At home, one haunting doubt remained: the existence of slavery. Through 1819 and 1820, a legislative battle over the extension of slavery into Missouri had raged. It was settled by compromise, but as Jefferson anxiously exclaimed, a geographical line, coinciding with a marked principle, moral and political, had been exposed to angry passions, never to be stilled in the lifetime of man. More ominously, another observer wrote: "The impression produced upon my mind by the progress of this discussion is, that the bargain between freedom and slavery contained in the Constitution of the United States is morally and politically vicious, inconsistent with the principles upon which alone our Revolution can be justified." John

Quincy Adams would one day publicly air his views, and when he did the nation would be well on its way toward civil strife. The United States had avoided destruction from without. Could it avoid disruption from within?

For Further Reading

Dangerfield, George, *The Era of Good Feelings.*
Miller, John C., *The Federalist Era.*
Smelser, Marshall, *The Democratic Republic.*

3   Liberation Movements in Europe

In 1790 the citizens of Avignon declared theii wish to be united with the rest of the French nation. They were French, but Avignon was papal territory. Their action nicely illustrated an issue that would become one of the most important sources of conflict and change during the nineteenth century: the principle of self-determination, the right of a people to choose its own allegiance, which ran counter to the generally accepted principle of the day, that a ruler's sovereignty ultimately rested on divine sanction.

The right of self-determination, like the democratic principle, was a vital part of the French Revolution. There was nothing peculiarly French about the idea; what had been done in France had equal validity anywhere. But it began in France: the course of events which resulted in war between revolutionary France and the rest of Europe saved the revolution in France, and the success of French arms spread the revolutionary principle abroad. Napoleon, for all that his regime was an empire and a dictatorship, worked to the same effect. Moreover, the Napoleonic conquests, being French, induced a strong anti-French reaction in which national feeling was crucial. This was particularly marked in Spain and in the Germanies. Modern nationalism, which contains the claim to the right of self-determination as an integral part, had its origin in the French Revolution and its Napoleonic sequel.

Napoleon and France were, of course, eventually defeated, and as we have seen, the Congress of Vienna attempted to restore the old order. But Europe could never be the same again; force can master force but is impotent in coercing ideas. Despite the "settlement" of 1815, the principles of the French Revolution remained the core of nineteenth-century liberalism. In post-Napoleonic Europe many people found themselves under alien

A.D. 1814–1815 Congress of Vienna
      1820–1821 Revolution in Naples; rising in Piedmont
      1821–1830 Greek War of Independence
           1823 The Monroe Doctrine proclaimed
           1830 Greece recognized by the Powers; Otto of Bavaria king; revolution in Paris; Louis Philippe "king of the French"; rising in Brussels; proclamation of Belgian independence
      1830–1831 Belgium recognized by the Powers; Leopold of Saxe-Coburg king
           1831 Revolution in Warsaw; risings in central Italy
      1819–1844 German Zollverein
           1836 Palacký's *History of Bohemia*
           1837 Rebellion in Upper and Lower Canada
           1839 Durham Report on the organization of Canada
           1840 Union of Canada
      1847–1848 Irish famine; *Young Ireland*
           1848 *Communist Manifesto;* revolution in Paris; Second French Republic; revolutions in central Europe; Austro-Sardinian War; Piedmontese Statuto; Frankfurt Parliament; counterrevolution in France and in central Europe; Louis Napoleon elected President of the Republic
           1849 Roman Republic; Austro-Sardinian War; Frankfurt constitution; Russian intervention in Hungary; the French in Rome
           1867 British North America Act creates Dominion of Canada

rule, and the course of the century saw their increasingly successful struggle to escape this domination. Save for the Scandinavian peninsula, the
Atlantic states had long achieved national identity, but the area between
the Rhine and the Alps and the Russian border was dominated by multinational empires. The struggle for national identity in mid-Europe took on
two different aspects: in Germany and in Italy it sought to bring together
separate political entities that "belonged" to a variety of "legitimate"
rulers; elsewhere it attempted to disrupt existing political units.

This generalization calls for some qualification, both in the West and in
the East. The Kingdom of the Netherlands, a creation of the Vienna settlement, compensated William of Holland for some Dutch colonial losses by
giving him the Austrian Netherlands. Austria in turn was compensated with
Lombardo-Venetia. The Netherlands had not been united since the days of
Spanish rule in the sixteenth century; hence its northern and southern parts
had developed quite differently. They were diverse in religion no less than
in their economic life. While the Dutch Republic had become an imperial
and maritime trading nation, manufacturing flourished in Belgium, the
region which, after England, first felt the impact of the Industrial Revolution. In addition to these sources of tensions, the constitution of the new
kingdom and the character of King William's rule created grievances
among the Belgians who felt themselves treated as conquered subjects
rather than equals.

These troubles might have come to a head even sooner than they did
had it not been for conflicts within Belgium: Flemish-speaking Catholics
stood against French-speaking Walloons, who were strongly influenced by
the anticlerical French Enlightenment. The two groups eventually reconciled their differences, however, and the revolution of July, 1830, in Paris
was the signal for a rising in Brussels in August. The intransigent attitude
of King William led to a complete break and to the proclamation of
Belgian independence in October.

Here was clearly a breach of the existing order of Europe which had
been guaranteed by the powers at Vienna. William's appeal for support
against the Belgians fell upon receptive ears in the conservative courts, the
Russian most of all, but the powers had to reckon with the possibility that
France might come to the rebels' assistance. But the new "king of the
French," Louis Philippe, was a moderate, inclined to peace: he agreed not
to intervene in Belgium provided others did not. The British attitude was
crucial; when London became convinced that the French entertained no
aggressive designs, the possibility of British intervention evaporated. Thus
the Belgians were able to make good their independence. The powers,
meeting in London, officially recognized it in December. The frontiers of

Belgium were drawn, its neutrality guaranteed, and Leopold of Saxe-Coburg was recognized as king. The Belgians went on to draft a liberal constitution later used as a model for many others. The Dutch king bowed to the inevitable, although he did not formally recognize the new nation for another nine years. The birth of an independent Belgium was a major achievement of liberalism and nationalism acting in unison.

It has been said that the independence of Belgium was won in Warsaw. Czar Nicholas I had assembled an army ready to march to the assistance of King William, but the Poles disliked Russian rule as much as the Belgians the Dutch. The proclamation of Polish independence in Warsaw in January, 1831, provided full employment for Czar Nicholas' army. Surrounded by unfriendly powers, and without the possibility of assistance from sympathetic western states, the Polish rebellion was doomed, though the Russians did not reenter Warsaw until September. The repression was harsh; Poland was virtually reduced to a Russian satrapy. But Polish nationalism did not die.

The events in Poland illustrate a much larger problem: outside of Russia proper the Slavic peoples of Europe were all under alien rule—Prussian, Austrian, or Ottoman. Most of them had lost their independence long before the Poles, but nationalism was everywhere on the rise. German philology and romanticism, searching for the identity of the *Volk,* stimulated it by reviving interest in languages—Czech, for example, which had no current literary status. A number of Czech scholars set about restoring their language to a more dignified position. František Palacký's *History of Bohemia,* written in German in 1836, became in 1848 the *History of the Czech People,* written in Czech. This work of erudition was duplicated elsewhere, among the South Slavs for example, and cultural revival became a characteristic preliminary to the assertion of political claims.

The progression from cultural to political nationalism had manifested itself in Greece as early as the eighteenth century. The Greeks could appeal to ancient glories that all Europe acknowledged. Together with the impact of French revolutionary ideas and Turkish maladministration, cultural nationalism produced revolution, and the proclamation of Greek independence in 1822. During the rest of the decade a struggle, often brutal, went on with alternating fortunes until British, Russian, and French intervention finally procured Greek independence.

The Greek problem was part of the larger "Eastern Question," the fate of the whole Ottoman domain. In Turkey's European possessions the Balkan peoples, Christians for the most part, all wanted independence. The continued decay of the empire, the possibility of the demise of "the Sick Man of Europe," and the question of how his corpse should be disposed of

muslim, orthodox, Catholic

were the constant concern of the powers, ever jealous of each other yet reluctant to break the peace.

Russia, Britain, France, and to a lesser extent Austria had interests in the Mediterranean. The Czar was torn between sympathy for his coreligionists and respect for the legitimacy of the Sultan's rule over Greece; but he was ever alert to the possibility of Russian expansion southward toward the Straits. Britain and France were opposed to Russian expansion, and the result was a compromise of concerted action, the Treaty of London of 1827. The intervention of the three powers led, in 1830, to their recognition of the independence of a small part of the Greek-inhabited world; in 1832 Otto, the second son of the king of Bavaria, was named king of Greece. The Greeks' struggle for independence was far from over; it was to continue throughout the century.

The decades of the thirties and forties were generally quiet in Europe, but agitation went on. The flames of nationalism could not be extinguished by repression or partial concessions. Then, in 1848, revolutions broke out across Europe, some nationalist, some liberal, in inspiration. The first sign of general trouble came in February, 1848, in France.

King Louis Philippe abandoned all thought of resistance and took the road of exile. The triumphant rebels proclaimed the Second Republic. The regime at first reflected the more radical tendencies of the Parisian proletariat and proceeded to hold country-wide elections under universal manhood suffrage. But the country as a whole was less radical than Paris, and the new National Assembly balked at the ambitious program of social reforms proposed by the men of February. By June there was a counter-revolution, in which the workers were ruthlessly put down by the armed forces. By the time elections were held for the presidency, in December, an overwhelming majority endorsed Louis Napoleon, a nephew of the first Napoleon, who had presented himself as the candidate of "order" and had also skillfully capitalized on the magic of his name.

Though change took somewhat longer to effect and the course of events was more tortuous, a broadly similar pattern emerged in mid-Europe, where political liberalism was reinforced by demands for self-determination. This whole area had been under Metternichian direction since 1815, and to Metternich nationalistic aspirations were anathema. In March, 1848, a revolution in Vienna caused his downfall, and Metternich, like Louis Philippe, sought refuge in England. For the better part of two years turmoil prevailed. Taking advantage of the Austrian predicament, the Italians enthusiastically rose in rebellion. But the Austrian army remained loyal, and Marshal Radetzky, following some initial setbacks, retrieved the situation. Simultaneously, Prince Windishgrätz reestablished "order" in

Prague where the nationalistic Czechs had also revolted. The uprising in Vienna, led by liberal students and workers, was crushed as well. As in France, so in Austria, the months from June to December undid what the months of February and March had done.

In 1849 the Italians renewed the war with Austria, but the outcome was a repetition of the preceding year. In Italy as in the Austrian empire, the old order successfully regained the upper hand. All that remained was a constitution in the Kingdom of Sardinia, plus the ironic fact that the pope was restored in Rome through the intervention of French force. It took a little longer to subdue the Hungarians, who were not finally put down until a Russian army intervened.

In Germany, too, the tide of revolution rose and fell, and with the same rhythm. In May a parliament was convened in Frankfurt to frame a constitution and to answer the question: What is Germany?—the old Holy Roman Empire, with its variegated populations, or only German-speaking territories? The high intellectual caliber of the Frankfurt assembly proved on the whole an impediment to the making of decisions, and the national question was a fatal stumbling block. The German Confederation was tied to the Hapsburg domain proper, and by the time the delegates decided to exclude Austria itself and Bohemia from Germany it was too late. Frederick William IV, the Prussian king, had recovered from his initial fright and withdrawn the concessions he had originally granted. In 1849, though tempted, he turned down the offer of a crown made by the Frankfurt Parliament; in 1850, he proposed a scheme of his own for German unity. But confronted with an Austrian ultimatum he yielded. The Frankfurt Parliament exhausted itself in high-sounding but irrelevant talk and expired.

The revolutions of 1848 and 1849 did not affect Britain or Russia. The Irish famine of the mid-forties, terrible as it was, produced no clear movement for independence, and the Poles remained subdued. Britain was not unsympathetic to the liberal agitation across Europe but feared above all the extension of the revolutions into an international conflagration. What interventions there were—the Russian in Hungary, the French in Rome, and a brief German one in the Danish Duchies—thus remained localized. Most important, France, to which central European liberals looked for leadership and assistance, early proclaimed a policy of nonintervention. She saved the peace at the cost of killing the revolution.

The revolutions of 1848 failed; their promoters were too inexperienced and lacked a sufficiently broad base of popular support. The opposite ends of the social scale (the peasantry and the large landowners) resisted the penetration of liberal ideas, while the new industrial working class was still too small to have much influence. Thus the characterization "revolution of the intellectuals" is, especially in central Europe, largely justified. The *democratic self-determination , despotic search't*

residue of the upheavals was very small. There were constitutional changes in some small states, but fundamentally control remained everywhere in the same hands, even in France, now again a republic. One notable legacy of the revolutions, especially in the Austrian empire, was the setting of the forces of liberalism and of nationalism against each other.

The disturbances took on, nevertheless, considerable significance as a warning to the defenders of the old order. The forces of change, of liberalism, democracy, and nationalism, though momentarily defeated, were making progress. One relevant development was the altered tone of the social thinking of the revolutionaries. In France the socialism of Louis Blanc was no longer of the utopian kind. And Karl Marx's *Communist Manifesto* was published in 1848. Even though it had no effect on the course of contemporary events, it was a landmark in the evolving social and economic outlook.

Inevitably the passion for self-determination that redrew the map of Europe in the nineteenth century spilled over into European settlements overseas. England's largest collection of overseas settlers in America had of course won independence late in the eighteenth century, but there were settlements to the north of the young United States that remained within the British Empire. They too clamored for some sort of autonomy. The situation was complicated by the ethnic composition of the Canadian settlements. The French had come to the St. Lawrence valley in the sixteenth century, and through times of prosperity and defeat, they had resisted all attempts at assimilation into the dominant English culture. They were French and remained French.

From the beginning, the British recognized the delicacy of the situation, though not, in French eyes, sensitively enough. The Peace Treaty of 1763 had put all of Canada into British hands; in 1774, with the Quebec Act, the British government guaranteed the French settlers the free exercise of their religion (which was Catholic), their language (which was, of course, French), and their law (which was the old French civil law). But after the American colonies had won their independence, thousands of American Loyalists—Protestant, English-speaking, English-oriented—streamed into Canada, obtained land, and agitated to make Canada more clearly British than the Quebec Act had made it. The usual consequences of a moderate policy emerged in Canada, as they often emerged elsewhere: neither nationality was satisfied with the concessions made to the other.

Considering the difficulties, the British government acted wisely. In June, 1791, Parliament passed the Canada Act which divided the region into Upper Canada and Lower Canada, thus dividing (though not with perfect neatness) the British, who dominated the first, from the French, who dominated the second. The government of the two provinces was precisely alike: each had its governor, its appointed legislative council, and its elective assembly. And both were part of the British Empire: London was empowered to disallow colonial legislation. Moreover, the Canada Act undertook to respect the religious sensibilities of both sides: it set aside land for the maintenance of the Protestant clergy and guaranteed the traditional rights of the Catholic Church.

For a quarter-century there was peace in Canada; this was the time of westward expansion and exploration. The Canadian Pacific coast had been sailed as early as the 1780's; in 1792 Captain George Vancouver, an intrepid sailor, carefully explored and surveyed the region that bears his name. In the following year, Alexander Mackenzie reached the Pacific coast overland. The inland remained mostly barren, but by 1800 trappers and traders had crisscrossed the continent many times. Canada was becoming an economic reality, one the mind could grasp. The British-American War of 1812, in which Canadians fought loyally and well, even produced a temporary coalescence of sentiments between English and French Canadians—a convergence of feeling and action that did not long survive the settlement of the war in 1814.

In fact, however, discontent with the Canada Act of 1791 sprang less from national rivalries than from the desire for self-government. Both in Upper and in Lower Canada, new immigrants—mainly Scotch and Irish —complained of the old self-serving plutocracies which monopolized the governments of both provinces. In 1837 and 1838 rebellions broke out; they articulated the demands for a democratization of the government that had been voiced, with increasing irritability, since 1815. The British, heady with reforming fervor after the great Reform Act of 1832, responded with moderation and constructive statesmanship. In May, 1838, the Earl of Durham reached Quebec as the new governor-in-chief of both provinces. "Radical Jack" proved tactless and even more conciliatory to the rebels than the British government had instructed him to be. He resigned under pressure in October, but early the following year, in February, 1839, he issued a celebrated document, the *Report on the Affairs of British North America,* which outlined the policy an enlightened Britain should follow in Canada. The Durham Report, as it came to be known after its author, looked to the creation of Canadian self-awareness through political and economic means. It called for the gradual extinction of French separatism through the creation of a sense of Canadian citizenship, for intensive economic development supervised by the Crown, the reunification of the two provinces, and responsible self-government that would leave mainly the conduct of foreign affairs in British hands.

Much of what Durham asked for was granted with uncommon speed:

in 1840, Parliament enacted the Durham Report into law, although the Canadians did not enjoy fully responsible government until the governorship of Lord Elgin (1847–1854). This was vast progress in a short time. Nor was it all: in these years, Canada regulated its relations with its powerful neighbor to the south. In 1842, with the Webster-Ashburton Treaty, and in 1846, with the Oregon Boundary Treaty, Canada and the United States drew their frontiers to mutual satisfaction. Progress in self-government continued: in 1856, the legislative council was turned from an appointed into an elected body.

But progress in one area created discord in another. Durham's United Canada could not in the long run satisfy the French Canadians, especially since immigration from France was negligible and from Britain sizable. In this atmosphere, replete with tension but still open to reason, a solution emerged: a confederation. That solution was embodied in law in March, 1867, with the British North America Act. It was a piece of legislation of vital importance, for Canada to be sure, but for the rest of the British Empire as well; it was a model for other British colonies. The act provided for a Dominion of Canada, which included the provinces of Nova Scotia, New Brunswick, Quebec, and Ontario. The Dominion had a federal parliament with representatives from each of the provinces, and each of these, in turn, had its provincial government. What Britain had failed to do with its thirteen rebellious colonies, it did in Canada, illustrating that rarest of lessons: that men can learn from experience.

For Further Reading

Marriott, J. A. R., *The Eastern Question.*
Namier, L. B., *The Revolution of the Intellectuals.*
Rath, J. R., *The Viennese Revolution of 1848.*
Robertson, P., *Revolutions of 1848: A Social History.*

4   Liberation Movements in Latin America

The dissolution of the great European empires created by Portugal and Spain in the sixteenth century has long been considered the central event of the first half of nineteenth-century Latin American history. Historians have minutely examined the origins of the revolutions of 1808–1826 that resulted in political independence for thirteen nations. Among the explana-

A.D. 1804 Haiti declares its independence
      1808 Portuguese Court flees to Brazil
      1810 Autonomous governments set up in Argentina, Chile, Colombia, and Venezuela
      1815 Brazil declared a kingdom
      1816 Bolívar issues a decree against slavery
      1817 José de San Martín crosses the Andes to defeat Spaniards at Battle of Chacabuco
      1821 Victory of Bolívar at Carabobo, last major engagement of war in Venezuela; Mexico wins its independence, followed by short-lived (1822–1823) rule of Emperor Agustín Iturbide
      1822 Brazilian Empire declared independent under Pedro I
      1824 Battle of Ayacucho, last major engagement in South America
      1826 Congress of Panama, convoked by Bolívar
      1830 Death of Bolívar

---

tions they have found for these fundamental changes are the administrative ineptitude of Spain and Portugal, the influence of Britain, France, and the United States, the growing economic and political maturity of the colonies, and the impact of the European Enlightenment upon traditional values in the New World. But it was Napoleon's invasion of the Iberian peninsula which precipitated the events that led to the violent disruption of the Spanish empire in America and the peaceful entrance of Brazil into the society of independent nations.

The martial exploits of such figures as the Mexican priest-patriot Miguel Hidalgo, the dashing liberator Simón Bolívar, and the respected José de San Martín have until recently dominated the story of the revolts against Spain. Diplomatic maneuverings in European chancelleries and Washington have also been emphasized. Little attention has been paid to cultural, economic, and social developments. We have it on the authority of Bolívar himself that the revolutionary years brought no basic changes to the structure of Latin American societies. On his deathbed the Liberator declared that he had "plowed the sea," so far as changing the character of South American life was concerned.

More recently Marxist-oriented Latin American historians and others have made detailed studies and sophisticated analyses of the nonmilitary aspects of these turbulent decades. In certain respects independence marked no sharp break with the past, for despite the clash of arms and the multitude of pronunciamentos, many economic and political institutions persisted throughout the revolutionary era. But there were some decisive changes. Foreign trade increased when the old mercantilistic monopolies collapsed. Already strong movements for the suppression of the slave traffic and the abolition of Negro slavery grew still more powerful. During the revolutionary wars, although Negroes and Indians served chiefly as cannon fodder on both sides of the struggle, persons of mixed blood rose more easily in the social scale and mestizo army officers became more numerous. On the other hand, the colonial protective laws generally vanished with independence, and the missions which had protected many Indians were ruined. In the new competitive society the ill-prepared Indians suffered greatly.

The most marked social change, however, was the rift that developed between the urban elite who dominated the seaports and the capitals and the rural, provincial societies of the interior. Historian Charles C. Griffin explains it this way:

At the seats of government and in the ports upper and middle classes began to be affected by the streams of foreigners (diplomats, visiting scholars, pedagogues, merchants, soldiers and sailors). . . . Fashions began to ape the styles of London and Paris; new sports and pastimes replaced colonial recreations; even habits of food and drink changed. Provincial cities were but little affected by these newfangled notions and the countryside was largely unconscious of them. Thus, the wider, European outlook of the elite in almost every country began to show itself in minor ways long before it was enshrined in law, educational institutions, and in the arts.

Brazil's independence was accomplished far differently. The Prince Regent Dom João fled from Napoleon's army across the Atlantic, protected by the British fleet, and landed with some 15,000 courtiers in Rio de Janeiro in 1808. Thus, Rio became the temporary capital of an empire which included, besides Brazil, the islands of Cape Verde, Madeira, and the Azores, the vast unexplored territories of Angola and Mozambique in Africa, and scattered establishments in China, India, and Oceania. This momentous event both enhanced the pride of Brazilians and brought solid economic advantages. The old Portuguese mercantile monopolies were abolished and Brazilian ports opened to the trade of all friendly nations. The manufacture of iron and textiles was undertaken; a bank, a naval college, a medical faculty, a botanical garden, a public library, and a printing press were established. Agriculture improved as coffee production expanded under royal protection, and the Botanical Garden introduced the cultivation of Oriental tea.

To the capital came many distinguished foreigners, often under royal patronage. A mission of French artists in 1816—architects, musicians, painters, sculptors—became the nucleus later for an Academy of Fine Arts. European scientists arrived and prepared learned reports which greatly increased the world's knowledge about Brazil. But the presence of the Portuguese court brought some problems. Taxation increased, and arrogant courtiers, officials, generals, and hangers-on monopolized the offices of government, much to the chagrin of the Brazilians whom they displaced.

Even after Dom João granted the colony equality with the mother country in 1815, serious economic and political differences divided Brazilians and Portuguese. Dom João returned to Portugal in 1821, accompanied by some 3,000 courtiers and most of the cash in the Bank of Brazil. He left his son Crown Prince Pedro to govern Brazil. Aware of the growing Brazilian desire for independence and strengthened by the advice of the most distinguished Brazilian of the age, José Bonifácio de Andrada, Pedro led Brazil into independence with his famous "Cry of Ipiranga" (September 7, 1822): "Independence or death! We have separated from Portugal." Pedro was proclaimed emperor. But in 1831 he too departed, having proved almost as autocratic as the Portuguese parliament. He left behind his infant son, Pedro II, who was crowned emperor in 1841 at the age of fifteen, the only monarch in the Americas. Thereafter for almost forty years Pedro gave Brazil a degree of peace and stability unique in Latin American history. (Another unique phenomenon was that Negro slavery lingered on until 1888; Brazil was the last country in the Americas to abolish the peculiar institution.)

A deep cleavage between port and hinterland society also developed in Brazil, evidenced by the generational gap between the younger landed gentry who became urban leaders trained largely in the law and their patriarchal families who remained in the provinces: "In their material environment and, to a certain extent, in their social life," Gilberto Freyre has written, "the majority of the Brazilians of the fifties were in the Middle Ages: the elite only was living in the eighteenth century. Only a few men, such as the emperor himself, and a few women . . . were conscious of the Europe of John Stuart Mill, hoop-skirts . . . four-wheeled English carriages, and Pius IX."

Elsewhere in Latin America confusion and dictatorship often reigned. Mexico during these decades was bitterly divided between Federalists and Centralists, the latter group led by the colorful demagogue Antonio López de Santa Anna. This sorry period in Mexican history reached its nadir in

LATIN AMERICA AFTER
THE WARS FOR INDEPENDENCE

European possessions

● Capitals of independent countries

0   500   1,000 Miles

the war with the United States, 1845–1847, when internal politics as much
as the American army resulted in the fall of Mexico City. In Central
America the second quarter of the nineteenth century was so chaotic that
one American diplomat traveled over the length and breadth of the Central
American federation in vain search for a government to present his cre-
dentials to. Elsewhere confusion, sometimes chaos, prevailed. The Argentine revolutionary movement of 1810 gave the liberals an opportunity to
organize the country politically and to reform it socially and economically.
Despite the efforts of such able men as Mariano Belgrano, Manuel

Moreno, and Bernardino de Rivadavia, they failed, and Argentina fell under the dictatorship of the bloody tyrant Juan Manuel de Rosas (1835–1852). Defenders of Rosas (and they still flourish in Argentina) point to his maintenance of independence against attacks by France and Britain, which was indeed no mean achievement. But he also began the distribution of land to army veterans, which led to the growth of the enormous ranches which have so notably influenced Argentine economic and political life. In nearby Paraguay José Gaspar Rodríguez de Francia, an even more despotic dictator, kept his nation sealed off from effective contact with the outside world for most of the period 1814–1840.

Chile's revolutionary experience illustrates the difficulties confronting the friends of real reform. Bernardo O'Higgins possessed great power during his rule (1818–1823), but he could neither change the popular addiction to religious processions, cockfighting, and gambling nor take away from the aristocracy their privileged positions and great entailed estates. The principal result of the Chilean revolution was the transfer of economic and social control from a Spanish-led society to one dominated by conservative Creoles.

The monopoly of the Latin American Catholic Church was only slightly shaken in the post-revolutionary years. The British insisted in their 1810 treaty with Brazil on permission to hold Anglican services, but even this modest toleration found no favor in Spanish America. Despite the beginning of anticlerical movements, priests had an important voice in fashioning the basic policies of the new nations. In Peru, surprisingly, some religious leaders proposed to make the Church more relevant to the life of the people. They proposed to celebrate Mass in the vernacular, make church services less ornate, reduce the influence of Rome, do away with the Inquisition, and even relax the rule of celibacy for at least some of the clergy. But the priests who advocated these remarkable reforms were ahead of the times; the hierarchy condemned them and they were silenced.

The dreams of Bolívar for one Great Colombia were also dashed: Ecuador, Colombia, and Venezuela went their separate ways. Thus, nearly everywhere the immediate aftermath of the revolutionary wars was often frustration. Even in Brazil, regional rivalries and discontent led to disturbances that were not quelled before the middle of the century.

But did Bolívar and the other liberators really "plow the sea"? In large measure the answer to this question, unfortunately, is yes. The new nations were not stable enough or advanced enough to confront their fundamental problems—education, land reform, transportation, agricultural and industrial development—with any marked success. Yet the economic devastation and social changes that the wars caused permitted some new developments as traditional ways weakened. The political liberation of the Iberian

empires in America made possible choices that would not have been open
had Latin America remained in colonial bondage. The liberated nations,
now open to world influences, aroused keen interest among European investors. Visions of El Dorado danced before the eyes of merchants, manufacturers, entrepreneurs.

British enterprises were particularly imaginative: Cornish miners were
to bring new techniques, the Pacific and the Atlantic were to be joined by a
canal, milkmaids were to be sent to Buenos Aires to improve butter production. Capital was available to launch a joint stock company for almost
any project: to navigate the rivers of South America by steamboats, to fish
for pearls in Colombia, to establish the unemployed poor of Great Britain
and Ireland as agricultural colonists in the United Provinces of the Río de
la Plata. Many of these schemes resulted in severe losses to European
investors, but others helped to bring Latin America into the modern age.
Ideas as well as techniques, capital, and manufactured goods flowed across
the ocean. Although for many years her role remained passive, Latin
America was becoming a part of the larger world.

For Further Reading

Bushnell, David (ed.), *The Liberator, Simón Bolívar: Man and Image.*
Humphreys, R. A., and Lynch, John (eds.), *The Origins of the Latin Ameri-
can Revolutions, 1808–1826.*
Masur, Gerhard, *Simón Bolívar.*
Robertson, William S., *The Rise of the Spanish American Republics as Told
in the Lives of Their Liberators.*

5   The Near East

The eighteenth century marks one of the lowest points in the long history of
the Middle East. Various causes, from the twelfth century onward, had
contributed to the decline: the Crusades, the Mongol invasions, the breakdown of some of the major irrigation systems and the salination of the soil,
the infiltration of nomadic tribes and the diversion of trade routes. In the
fifteenth to sixteenth centuries the Ottoman Empire, and in the sixteenth to
seventeenth Iran under the Safavids, had enjoyed a temporary revival,
marked by strong government, economic recovery, and a high level of
artistic creation—without, however, any accompanying technological or

A.D.

1774	Russo-Ottoman Treaty of Kuchuk Kainarji
1792–1793	Nizam-i Jedid; New Regulations reorganizing Ottoman military and civilian institutions
1794	Founding of Qajar dynasty in Iran
1804	Serbian revolt against Ottoman rule
1804–1812	Russo-Persian war, ended by Treaty of Gulistan in 1813
1805	Muhammad Ali becomes governor of Egypt and founds dynasty
1807–1808	Revolt of Janissaries, murder of Selim III, succeeded by Mahmud II as Ottoman Sultan
1811	Muhammad Ali massacres Mamelukes and consolidates his rule
1820–1822	Muhammad Ali conquers Sudan
1821–1830	Greek war of independence
1825–1828	Russo-Persian war, ended by Treaty of Turkmanchai, 1828
1826	Mahmud II massacres Janissaries and reorganizes Ottoman army
1832–1833, 1839–1840	Ottoman-Egyptian wars
1837–1838	Persian-Afghan war
1839	Hatt-i Sherif of Gulhane: reforms guaranteeing liberties of Ottoman subjects; British occupy Aden
1854–1856	Crimean War
1856	Hatt-i Humayun: extending of rights granted by Hatt-i Sherif; Anglo-Persian War
1860–1861	Communal conflicts in Lebanon and Syria
1868–1876	Ottoman Civil Code
1869	Opening of Suez Canal
1875–1878	Balkan and Russo-Turkish wars
1876	Proclamation of Ottoman Constitution, accession of Abdul Hamid II

1881–1882	Arab revolt in Egypt, followed by British occupation
1883–1885	Mahdist revolt in Sudan ending Egyptian rule
1896	Assassination of Nasiruddin Shah of Iran
1896–1898	Anglo-Egyptian reconquest of Sudan
1901	Oil concession granted to W. K. D'Arcy in Iran
1905–1909	Constitutional Revolution in Iran
1908–1909	Young Turk revolt restores constitution in Turkey; deposition of Abdul Hamid in 1909
1912–1913	Balkan wars
1914	Turkey enters war on side of Central Powers; Egypt becomes British protectorate
1916	Arab revolt against Turkey
1917	Balfour Declaration, promising Jewish national home in Palestine
1919–1922	Turkish war of liberation against Greek and Allied forces
1923	Treaty of Lausanne between Turkey and Allied Powers; deposition of sultan; Turkey proclaimed republic
1920	League of Nations assigns mandates to France over Lebanon and Syria and to Britain over Iraq, Palestine, and Transjordan
1921–1925	Riza Khan establishes control over Iran, deposes Ahmed Shah and founds Pahlavi dynasty
1922	Britain declares Egypt independent
1924	Ibn Saud conquers Hijaz and establishes rule over most of Arabian Peninsula
1932	Iraq granted independence

intellectual progress. But from 1514 until the middle of the eighteenth century these two empires were engaged in almost uninterrupted and inconclusive wars, which exhausted their strength and devastated the borderlands, especially Iraq and Azerbaijan. From the end of the seventeenth century, in both states, the central government's hold on the provinces gradually weakened. Revolts and tribal raids proliferated, order broke down, communications crumbled, and economic activity declined. In the course of the eighteenth century European commerce with Iran, Syria, and Egypt dwindled and cultural contacts diminished, increasing still further the already great isolation of the region. However, in Constantinople and the Balkans, both trade and cultural exchanges increased rapidly, setting in motion economic, social, and political forces that were to transform that region.

The Middle East was pulled out of its isolation by international political and economic rivalries. At first the main clash was between Britain and France, then between Britain and Russia, and finally, toward the end of the nineteenth century, between Britain and Germany.

From the time of Peter the Great, Russia had been encroaching on both the Ottoman Empire and Iran, while Britain's expanding empire in India made it increasingly anxious to secure the land and sea routes leading to the subcontinent. But it was Napoleon's conquest of Egypt in 1798, and his dispatch of a military mission to Iran in 1807, that drew attention to the strategic importance of the Middle East and made it a center of Great Power struggle.

Between 1804 and 1827 Russia defeated Iran in three wars, annexing Georgia and Azerbaijan. But no significant Russian conquests were achieved at the expense of Turkey because the British, and sometimes the French, resisted Russian expansion. Their opposition expressed itself most dramatically in the Crimean War. Russia's efforts did help to liberate the Balkan peoples, but did not lead to the domination of the area that the czars desired.

After the expulsion of Napoleon's troops from Egypt—owing to Nelson's victories—France lost all direct power in the Middle East; every French attempt to regain control of the area was frustrated by the other Great Powers. But France retained much influence in the region, thanks to its investments in the Suez Canal and various railways, its trade, its numerous cultural and religious contacts, and its acknowledged position as protector of Catholics in the Ottoman Empire. Britain became the dominant power in the Middle East after 1815. By its steady support of the Ottoman government it exerted much influence until the end of the century. Its naval supremacy was unchallenged, and its economic strength far exceeded that of its rivals. Except for the brief war with Turkey in 1807 and the expedition of 1840 against Muhammad Ali—undertaken at the request of the Porte—the short Persian War of 1856 was Britain's only direct clash with a major Middle Eastern state. In 1820–1853 treaties suppressing piracy and the slave trade ensured its predominance in the Persian Gulf. In 1839 it annexed Aden—for use as a coaling station and to guard the entrance to the Red Sea—and in 1878 Cyprus; in 1882 it occupied Egypt; and in 1896–1898 an Anglo-Egyptian force conquered the Sudan.

The rise of German power, and the increasing economic and military cooperation between Turkey and Germany, which culminated in the alliance of 1914, forced a realignment of the rival forces. Britain settled claims with France in Africa in 1904—relinquishing Morocco in return for Egypt—and in 1907 came to an understanding with Russia about Iran, dividing the country into spheres of influence. Starting in 1915, Britain, France, Russia, Italy, and Greece began partitioning the Ottoman Empire. The Bolshevik Revolution and Turkey's victorious struggle against the Allied forces in 1918–1922 rendered many of the provisions of these treaties inoperative, but France emerged with control over Syria and Lebanon, thus fulfilling an ancient dream, and Britain was granted mandates over Iraq, Palestine, and Transjordan. Thereafter, with France as a junior partner, Britain dominated the Middle East until after the Second World War.

Repeated defeats by Austria and Russia and the successful Balkan national uprisings persuaded the Ottoman rulers to take radical steps in hopes of saving their empire. Selim III (1789–1807) and Mahmud II (1808–1839) broke the power of the Janissary army—once the finest and most disciplined infantry in the world, but by now an unruly, destructive mob—and cleared the way for the Tanzimat reforms. The army and the bureaucracy were reorganized; control of the central government over the provinces was greatly strengthened. In 1908 the Young Turk movement destroyed the absolutism of Abdul-Hamid II, ushering in a brief constitutional period that lasted until Turkey's entry into World War I. Underlying these political changes was steady, if very slow, modernization of the legal and judicial systems and some progress in economic, social, and intellectual activity.

Until shortly before the First World War, the official ideology continued to be "Ottomanism." All subjects of the Sultan were encouraged to think of themselves as equal. In 1839 even Christians and Jews were granted formal equality with Muslims. But the successful encroachments of the Balkan states, which by 1912 had absorbed practically the whole of European Turkey, along with Armenian national aspirations—which were ruthlessly repressed—and the rising tide of Arab nationalism, brought

THE MIDDLE EAST, 1880-1914

Maximum extent of the Ottoman Empire, 1880-1914

0   100   200   300   400   500 Miles

about a sharp change in policy. Recognizing that the strength of the empire lay in its Turkish component, the government tried to "Turkify" the other peoples. This only exacerbated national feelings still further and led to the Arab Revolt of 1916. In 1918 the empire was shorn of many of its Asian provinces and occupied by Greek, British, French, and other troops. The ensuing war of liberation revivified Turkish nationalism. It was led by Mustafa Kemal Atatürk, a general who had won fame and popularity by his brilliant defense of Gallipoli in 1915 and his dogged resistance to the British advance in Syria in 1918. The ramshackle, multinational, archaic Turkish empire emerged as a compact, homogeneous republic which, in the course of the 1920's and 1930's, rapidly modernized its economic, social, and cultural institutions. The power of the Muslim clerical establishment was broken, the Arabic script was replaced by one based on Latin, the veil and polygamy were abolished, and education was expanded.

In the Arab provinces four separate forces eroded Ottoman rule. In Egypt Muhammad Ali, a tobacco merchant of Turkish origin, born in Albania in 1769, with no education but endowed with ability amounting to genius, landed as a soldier of fortune in the Ottoman army. By 1805 he had become pasha, or governor, and soon secured virtual independence and founded a dynasty that ruled the country until 1952. With the help of French and other foreign advisers, he established a modern army and navy and the most efficient government in the region and started a process of rapid economic and social development. In Arabia a puritanical religious revival, Wahhabism, enabled the house of Saud, after many vicissitudes, to extend its rule over the greater part of the peninsula under the leadership of Adul-Aziz ibn-Saud (1880–1953), the founder of modern Saudi Arabia. National movements in Lebanon, Syria, and Iraq took the form of secret societies which inspired the Arab Revolt during the First World War, under the leadership of the Sherif of Mecca. Lastly, Britain, France, and Italy occupied various countries in the Middle East and North Africa.

The postwar settlement caused great disappointments. Egypt, after much agitation, secured a limited measure of independence in 1922, which broadened in 1936 but still fell short of nationalist demands. The Fertile Crescent was placed under British and French mandates, and Palestine was declared a national Jewish home, to which more than 300,000 Jewish immigrants came by 1939. The interwar years witnessed continual agitation and revolts against the British and French but except in Iraq, which became independent in 1932, the results achieved were slight. And the nationalist struggle led to the frequent disruption of the constitutional processes introduced in these countries in the 1920's.

In Iran, which was less exposed to Western influences than the Ottoman Empire, the absolute rule of the Qajar dynasty (1794–1925) was not seriously challenged until the Constitutionalist Revolution of 1905–1909. After an initial success constitutionalism was, however, crushed with the help of Russian troops and the Russian-led Cossack Brigade. During the First World War Iran, notwithstanding its official neutrality, became a battle ground for Turkish, Russian, and British troops. The collapse of the Ottoman Empire and Russia left Britain as the predominant power, but a nationalist uprising and diplomatic pressures forced British withdrawal. One of the leaders of the uprising, Riza Pahlavi, an army officer of humble birth and little education but great ability, proclaimed himself shah in 1925, and started rapidly to modernize the country.

Western interest in both raw materials and swift connections with India led to the establishment, as early as the 1830's, of regular steamship services between Europe and the eastern Mediterranean and between India and Suez. Then the opening of the Suez Canal, in 1869, channeled a huge amount of traffic through the Middle East. Ports and internal transport were developed: the first Egyptian railway was opened in 1854, and others soon followed in Anatolia, Lebanon, Syria, the Sudan, and Iraq. Steamboats cruised the Nile, the Tigris-Euphrates, and the Karun. After the First World War road building was greatly accelerated.

All this, together with the inflow of European capital (nearly $2 billion by 1914) and the development of banking and other financial services, made it possible to integrate the Middle East in the international economy. Cash crops grown for export, such as cotton and tobacco, began to dominate the economy. The area under cultivation was greatly extended and large irrigation works were built, notably in Egypt.

The value of the foreign trade of the Middle Eastern countries multiplied manyfold in 1815–1914. And although population was growing everywhere, thanks mainly to improved hygiene, total output seems to have increased faster, with a consequent rise in the level of living. However, transport also opened the way for European factory products, which soon overpowered the Middle Eastern handmade goods, causing great hardships to the ancient handicraft centers—and to certain segments of the population.

In the 1920's, and still more in the 1930's, exports suffered greatly, because of the sharp decline in world agricultural prices. This brought home the need for industrial development, and by 1939 a start had been made in Turkey, Egypt, Iran, and Palestine. Foreign oil companies began drilling in the region before World War I, in Iran and Egypt, and by the beginning of World War II the Middle East accounted for some 6 per cent of world output.

Increased trade and the reorientation of trade and communications through the Middle East helped to spark an intellectual renaissance. Missionary schools were established in Lebanon in the eighteenth century and in the other countries in the nineteenth. All the main Christian sects participated in this movement, but the most active countries were France and the United States. In addition to elementary and secondary schools, foreign missions provided the Middle East with its first liberal arts colleges, notably the American University in Beirut (1866) and Robert College in Istanbul, and military schools, with technical branches, were founded in Istanbul, Cairo, and Tehran. But full-fledged national universities did not come into being until the decade of World War I. The Egyptian, Ottoman, and Iranian governments began sending students, mainly prospective technicians, to European centers early in the nineteenth century, and the number has expanded steadily down to the present time.* Soon Western books were being translated into Turkish, Arabic, and Persian, and were brought out, in large numbers, by the newly established printing presses. For although a printing press had been set up in Istanbul in the eighteenth century—and there had been even earlier ones among the Christian sects of Lebanon and Syria—it was not until the nineteenth century that printing attained significance. Almost simultaneously, newspapers began to appear in Egypt, Lebanon, Turkey, and Iran, spreading new ideas among a broad circle of readers. This was accompanied by a literary revival, marked by greater simplicity and clarity of style, enrichment of vocabulary to cope with modern needs, and the introduction of hitherto unknown forms such as novels and plays. And although by 1939 the Middle East had made no significant technical, scientific, intellectual, or artistic contribution, it had carried out a far-reaching and irreversible internal transformation. Writers of distinction, some of whose works were translated into various foreign languages, had appeared: for example, Peyami Safa and Zia Gök Alp in Turkey, Taha Husain and Tawfiq al-Hakim in Egypt, Muhammad Ali Jamal-Zadeh and Sadiq Hedayat in Iran. For the first time in centuries, women began participating in intellectual activity, notably the Turkish novelist Halide Edip and the Lebanese Mayy Ziadeh. Some sculptors and painters began to attract international attention. Scientists were grappling with local problems. Altogether, the intellectual and artistic horizons of the Middle East were being immeasurably broadened.

For Further Reading

Avery, Peter, *Modern Iran.*
The Cambridge History of Islam. (2 vols.)
Fisher, Sydney N., *The Middle East: A History.*
Hourani, A. H., *Arabic Thought in the Liberal Age.*
Hurewitz, J. C., *Diplomacy in the Near and Middle East.*
Issawi, Charles, *The Economic History of the Middle East.*
Lewis, Bernard, *The Emergence of Modern Turkey.*
Vatikiotis, P. J., *The Modern History of Egypt.*

---

* The only previous mission had been the sending of Iranian painters to study in Rome, in the 1640's. A few members of minority groups—Greeks, Armenians, Jews, and Catholic Lebanese—did, however, pursue theological or medical studies in Italy and other European countries.

The Industrial Revolution

6   The Industrial Revolution in England

The Industrial Revolution was essentially a rapid change in methods of producing goods other than crops, a change that involved a transition from making things by hand with the aid of simple tools to their production by increasingly complicated machines and chemical processes. In this great transformation, which quickened dramatically in the second half of the eighteenth century and continues to this day, mechanical contrivances performed more and more human tasks; machines were moved by energy derived from inanimate rather than animal, including human, sources; and goods increasingly came to be made out of inanimate materials. Not only did the Revolution put millions of mechanical slaves at the disposition of man, but it also permitted him greatly to increase the supply of raw materials at his disposal. It allowed him to tap the riches in the earth's crust that had been stored up over eons. Man was no longer restricted for the satisfaction of his needs and wants mainly to the current output of plants and animals—he could turn to his own purposes a wealth that would have made Midas seem like a pauper.

The advances which gave this great economic change the name Industrial Revolution occurred in Great Britain, yet it would be contrary to the facts to regard the mechanization of industrial processes as strictly an English experience. More in accordance with the evidence would be the view that this great transformation of industry and subsequently of society itself was a product of Western civilization, which in turn had borrowed widely from many civilizations. Indeed, one should remember that spinning and weaving, the making of pottery on the potter's wheel, the grinding of grain by composite mechanisms, the moving of machines by windmills and water wheels, the transmission of power by shafts and gears, the operation of atmospheric pumps like the water pump, and the fundamental processes of metallurgy were transmitted from the ancient past to modern man and

A.D.   1694   Founding of the Bank of England
              1733   James Kay invents the flying shuttle
              1769   Josiah Wedgwood opens pottery factory at Etruria,
                     near Stoke-upon-Trent; James Watt patents the
                     steam engine after years of experimentation;
                     Richard Arkwright invents the water-powered
                     spinning frame
              1770   James Hargreaves patents the spinning jenny
              1776   Adam Smith publishes *The Wealth of Nations,* the
                     classic of classical political economy
              1784   James Watt patents a locomotive, two years after
                     Oliver Evans patents a similar device
              1785   Edmund Cartwright patents the power loom
              1793   Eli Whitney invents the cotton gin
              1798   Eli Whitney builds a factory for the mass produc-
                     tion of firearms near New Haven
              1811   Pittsburgh's first rolling mill opens
              1821   Great Britain adopts the gold standard
              1822   First textile mills in Lowell, Massachusetts
      1824–1825   Repeal of the Combination Acts in Britain, permit-
                     ting trade unions to burgeon
              1829   George Stephenson perfects the steam locomotive
              1830   Railroad is put to its first serious uses in the United
                     States
              1846   Great Britain repeals the Corn Laws
              1849   Great Britain repeals the Navigation Acts
              1858   Henry Bessemer (later Sir Henry) builds Bessemer
                     Steel Works at Sheffield, using a new process that
                     makes large-scale production possible
              1869   Transcontinental railway across the United States is
                     completed

were developed and refined by Continental Europe. England, more than any other state between 1750 and 1850, had a number of advantages which joined in felicitous proportions and with proper timing to effect rapid industrial change. In this case, as in so many great movements in the past, the doctrine of *necessary concomitants* provides a framework for the most rational and most complete analysis of what took place.

England achieved its breakthroughs primarily, as we shall see, in the manufacture of textiles, especially cottons, in iron metallurgy, and in the development of the steam engine as a prime mover. Yet changes in spinning and weaving and in smelting were accompanied by a host of improvements in production—the invention of the circular saw and the rotary plane in the lumber industry, the slide rest on the lathe, the boring mill which allowed the making of more accurate guns and cylinders for engines, better glazes in making chinaware, breechloading and percussion guns, the cylindrical press for printing cloth, and new methods of making the basic industrial chemicals, sulfuric acid and soda. It seemed that "Necessity" had mothered a great brood of inventions in one mammoth birth.

England was the leading innovator of methods for rendering raw materials more useful to man, but it by no means had a monopoly of inventions. A Frenchman, Antoine Lavoisier, discovered the chemical nature of combustion; another Frenchman, Claude Louis Berthollet, developed prussic acid (hydrocyanic acid) and used chlorine for bleaching; still another, Nicholas Leblanc, discovered a way of making soda from sea water; and a fourth, Louis Robert, invented the process of making paper in continuous strips. An American, Eli Whitney, invented the cotton gin. And a German, Justus von Liebig, determined the chief chemical components of plants and thus laid the basis for a chemical fertilizer industry.

England had, however, a clear head start in the mechanization of industrial production, which gave her enormous economic advantages down to at least World War I. In the cotton textile industry England long held an overpowering position. In 1821, it took over 70 per cent of American exports of raw cotton. In 1840, Great Britain mined 31 million tons of coal, as against 4 million tons produced by Belgium, and 3 million by Prussia. Ten years later, Great Britain owned more net tons of commercial shipping than France, the United States, and the German states together, and in 1870 it produced more steel than France and Germany combined. In that year the United Kingdom produced 31.8 per cent of all the world's manufactured goods, and accounted for as much of the world's trade as France, Germany, and the United States put together.

The extraordinary jump that Great Britain got on other powers of Western civilization in the hundred years from 1750 to 1850 also gave that country important noneconomic advantages. It attained a position of military, especially naval, dominance that in turn gave it great "diplomatic" power. This meant that Britain's role in the affairs of Europe was greater than it had been in the seventeenth century and enabled it to capture the lion's share of the colonial areas that were being divided, especially in Africa, in the New Imperialism. Furthermore, industrialization and trade so elevated Britain's per capita national income that by the middle of the nineteenth century it was about twice that of France or Germany. Thus it became apparent to all other nations that if they were to play an important role in international affairs and if they were to enjoy a higher standard of living they must industrialize. Indeed, the history of the last century and a half has been characterized by a struggle to industrialize—and no end to that effort is in sight.

However, awareness of an "industrial revolution" as a great divide between an old world and our world was hardly paralleled by a similar awareness on the part of the people who lived through it. In the eighteenth century many well-informed Englishmen were barely conscious of factories, so often tucked away in inaccessible parts of the country, knew little of the men who ran or worked in them, and had little time or understanding to spare for the economic and social problems that are so likely to engage our attention. Nor did entrepreneurs or the hard-pressed if narrow-sighted local government officials who had to cope directly with those problems think in terms of a revolution; most of the problems—child labor, for example—and the remedies found by the state or by philanthropic individuals were commonplaces in preindustrial England, and the changes seemed only of degree, not kind. The new processes that appear to us so revolutionary were seen by their initiators rather as pragmatic solutions to immediate practical problems, and devoid of wide social significance. There were, moreover, many earlier innovations in both technology and organization, while in parts of the economy old methods persisted until the present century. Still, at some point in time, probably in the late eighteenth century, a crucial corner was turned, or, to borrow W. W. Rostow's phrase, there occurred a "take-off into sustained growth." To understand how it happened, we must reckon with economic developments that—like the optimism that suffused men's minds or the demand for political change that swelled toward the century's end—were deeply rooted in preindustrial circumstances.

In agriculture, the predominant industry in which the wealth and interests of England's social and political leadership lay, the eighteenth century saw the maturing of a series of important changes. From about the time of the Restoration, the owners of large landed estates began to consolidate and to add to them, frequently at the expense of small owner-occupiers (often called yeomen) handicapped by lack of capital, heavy taxation, and inefficiency. The most capable of small owners might in fact better their lot by becoming tenant farmers, and some managed to survive on their own lands into the nineteenth century. Others sold out and went into trade; many more no doubt declined into the ranks of laborers. Thus emerged the typical Victorian rural pattern of landlord—living primarily on his rents—farmer, and landless laborer.

The need to administer large estates profitably gave rise to changed methods. The most important and famous was enclosure, replacing the old system of open fields containing the scattered strips of individual holdings by the walled or hedged fields of compact, separately held farms. Parts of the country had been enclosed for hundreds of years, and in many places enclosure had gone on regularly by agreement among owners. But elsewhere the old system survived until the eighteenth century; then, helped in part by lower rates of interest, the process went on rapidly to create more or less the modern look of the English countryside by the early nineteenth century. Enclosure made possible new crop rotations and improved stock-breeding, and many proposals were made for the application of machines to agriculture. But machinery could not come into general use until there was industry to produce it, and much bad farming continued alongside the improved farming that attracted so much attention from contemporaries. Crop yields seem not to have increased markedly during the eighteenth century, and the growing population had to be fed more and more from imported grain.

Rooted in England's natural and political advantages, a striking prosperity came to English towns, reflected in improved standards of living, a flourishing provincial culture, and a growing pride and confidence. Early in the century what passed for public opinion found expression largely in a jingoistic hatred of the French or in sporadic outbreaks of hostility against town oligarchies or the central government; by the end of the century it had grown into a demand for political participation and reforms. But the forms of trade and industry that underlay these developments were not fixed, and, as in agriculture, the century saw important changes. In some industries—shipbuilding, for example, or brewing—the size of firms steadily increased. In others traditional organization was beginning to approach the limits of practicability; such was the "domestic system" of the textile industry in which outworkers in small villages or the countryside round about a large town were employed by a clothier who supplied them with raw materials and marketed the goods. In foreign trade, where the largest profits and the greatest risks had lain, England's markets were shifting. England's principal trade had always been with the Continent, but because she wanted more Continental wines, steel, naval stores, raw wool, and luxury goods than the Continental demand for English woolen cloth could pay for, the difference had had to be made up by reexporting tropical products from Africa, the Americas, and the Indies. The gradual shrinkage of the European market in the eighteenth century was, however, more than compensated for by a rising demand for English goods in the tropical areas and, above all, in the flourishing North American colonies. The growth of England's foreign trade provided a surplus of capital for investment and strengthened her commercial machinery.

The most fundamental change was probably the rapid growth in population that began in the 1740's. There was no census before 1801, but Malthus' essay on the principle of population, published three years earlier, gave powerful form to an awareness pressing in on all sides. The causes of this increase are obscure. In recent years historians have shifted their attention from a declining death rate to social and environmental factors raising the birth rate—the decline in apprenticeship, say, or lowered age of marriage. Whatever the causes, between about 1750 and 1820 the English population doubled. The growing population had to be fed, clothed, and housed. Towns, growing much more by natural increase than by immigration from the countryside, spawned problems far beyond the capacities of old medieval urban institutions.

The upward surge in population forced English industry to find ways of meeting the demand. But the hard-headed men who took the decisions did not all follow one particular course or turn at once to the use of machines and bringing together large numbers of workers in factories. Indeed, the more natural and profitable way in many industries lay in the increasing subdivision and specialization made possible by an expanding market. At one level the process led to a growing differentiation among those individuals or firms vaguely called merchants. In the early eighteenth century, a large merchant might buy and sell a wide variety of goods, own or hire ships, and function as an insurer or banker; by the latter part of the century these functions had generally split apart, and even those who bought and sold specialized increasingly in particular commodities. A similar course was followed in some of the metal trades—hardware among them—and thus some cities, like Birmingham, remained towns of small workshops until the late nineteenth century.

In other industries more obviously revolutionary means were employed. One such industry was iron. Steel was used only for fine work like cutlery; its widespread use had to wait until after the middle of the nineteenth century when ways were found to produce high-quality steel in quantity. So the first century of the Industrial Revolution was an age of iron, though the demand for it tended rather to follow the spread of industrialization than to anticipate it. The ancient English iron industry, based on small, migratory, charcoal-fired furnaces and forges, could not meet the challenge even after the discovery of the coking process early in the eighteenth century enabled manufacturers to substitute coal for vanishing supplies of English charcoal. It was not until the steam engine in the 1770's made possible the hot blast, and the Cort process the production of high-quality wrought iron, that the industry could move forward. Its rapid progress thereafter and the large, permanent installations of the new technology required larger units and huge investments. The iron industry also helped to revolutionize the mining industry; although the nature of the coal seams precluded much mechanization until fairly recent times, mines went deeper and required more expensive and sophisticated equipment for hauling, lifting, and pumping.

The textile industry did not require such high-cost and impressive equipment, but a seemingly insatiable world demand called for vastly greater productivity of both labor and capital. Wool, long England's major industry, was no longer in the vanguard: technical difficulties delayed the invention of machinery, and the complex structure of the industry, shot through with vested interests and stubborn traditions, was another powerful brake on progress, at least in the traditional textile centers in the west of England and East Anglia, which lost the initiative and ultimately succumbed to the more progressive ways of the new, less tradition-bound woolen manufacturers of the West Riding of Yorkshire. What the world wanted was cotton cloth. A new commodity in world trade, first introduced from India in the seventeenth century, cotton progressed slowly in early eighteenth-century England. But, unhampered by inherited organization and able to draw on a rapidly growing supply of raw material, English cotton manufacturers took advantage of a series of important inventions that first speeded up handwork (e.g., the flying shuttle) and that then, through the application of mechanical power, superseded handwork in one after another operation, improving quality at the same time. Mechanization came first to the spinning side of the industry; the expanded supply of yarn was made into cloth by handloom weavers who flocked into that easily learned and highly respectable trade to face a terrible future when it in turn was mechanized early in the nineteenth century. Prices fell dramatically, and it was soon possible for English calicoes, spun, woven, and printed by machine, to undersell handmade calicoes in India itself. Until well into the nineteenth century, the prosperity of England's export trade rested above all on cotton cloth.

The cotton industry was the first to turn to full-scale factory production. The reliance of cotton mills on water power imposed limitations on the industry as to location and, in dry seasons, even operation. In 1769, James Watt, a Scottish instrument maker, had found a way to bring new speed and efficiency to the cumbersome steam engines used since the late seventeenth century to pump out mines. Watt's steam engine was quickly applied to the iron industry to provide the hot blast and to power steam hammers. Then, in the eighties, Watt found a way to convert his engine's lateral stroke to circular motion; this made it possible to bring factories into towns, close to the supply of labor.

But what probably made most men aware for the first time of the extent of the industrial change that had come over the country was the use of the steam engine for still another purpose. The railway, fully launched with the opening of a line between Liverpool and Manchester in 1830, had grown out of the earlier use of railed ways over which stationary engines hauled heavy loads, coal particularly. The locomotive steam engine effected a major revolution. Intended at first as supplementary to the net- work of turnpikes and canals that had spread throughout England in the late eighteenth century, this new triumph of industrial organization ended by sweeping the field of transportation. Supported by local interests and by a remarkable outpouring of the nation's capital, but built without a na- tional plan, English railways lurched through a succession of speculative booms, some spectacular failures, much trial and error, and far too many horrible accidents into approximately the modern system by the 1870's. Nearly all of English life was affected: the movement of passengers, mail, and goods was speeded up; bulky raw materials and manufactured goods were made available throughout the country; the look of the country was dramatically altered by viaducts, cuts, and tunnels; and men's imaginations were deeply stirred.

The Industrial Revolution was the work of thousands of men with an eye to profit, as much efficiency as they could afford, and survival, of men willing to work hard and to take sometimes disastrous risks. These en- trepreneurs were drawn from a wide spectrum: merchants, yeomen, landed gentlemen (who were not prevented by social custom, as on the Continent, from open participation in trade), even dissenting clergymen. Their social and political attitudes varied as much as their origins. Some were narrow, bigoted, self-serving, and harsh; perhaps not far removed themselves from being workmen, they had to pinch every penny and exploit their workers as ruthlessly as they dared. Others were educated, enlightened men who did their best to provide as good working and living conditions for their workers as could be managed, took the lead in the religious and cultural life of their communities, held local office, and aspired to a role in national politics. More, in between the two extremes, moved toward the latter pole in the second or third generation or even escaped into the ranks of the landed gentry.

By law and inherited prejudice, they were denied the advantages of the modern joint-stock company: not until 1844 did it become easy and relatively inexpensive to incorporate, and not until 1855, and then against strong resistance, was limited liability allowed. But the family firms or partnership provided sufficient resources for all except the most extensive, capital-devouring enterprises like the railways. The railways performed an important service, however, in accustoming wealthy men and women to invest in industry rather than in land or government securities. By the 1870's and 1880's more and more firms were outgrowing limited resources, even when fed by plowing back profits, and the limited liability corporation began to come into its own.

England was fortunate in having a well-developed banking system that could make loans to investors or to firms and that moved funds from areas where money was plentiful to those where it was in short supply. At the head of the system was the Bank of England, founded in 1694, a privately owned joint-stock bank dealing primarily in government business. Beyond the well-established and generally solid London private bankers were the rapidly growing numbers of country bankers. But the system was remarkably freewheeling and betrayed a degree of ignorance of sound banking practice that seems appalling to modern eyes. The Bank of England did its best to avoid becoming a true central bank, a role it did not exercise fully until toward the end of the nineteenth century. With often the dimmest notions of liquidity, and with little experience to guide them in such important questions as the proper proportion of loans to deposits or the extent of reserves needed to support the issue of paper money, English bankers helped to feed the inflation of the period of the Napoleonic wars and often to worsen the cyclical fluctuations of the economy that came with such terrifying regularity in the early nineteenth century. Usually triggered by a crop failure or by some adverse development in international trade, these periodic crises were heightened by the lack of knowledge as to how to deal with them and by panic. Even the best firms could suffer, and those with the fewest resources or the most incompetent managements simply disappeared, and with them the livelihoods of their workers and the capital, and often the reputations, of the owners.

The men, women, and children who supplied the sinew and skill for English industry present a similarly complicated picture. In the eighteenth century English labor consisted of a mass of skilled and unskilled workers who fell into a complex hierarchy of income and social position. Industrialism increased this complexity by opening a new range of skills and responsibilities to the most able and ambitious and, at the other end of the social scale, by isolating workers in old, decaying industries from which the only escape was likely to be death or the workhouse. Moreover, industrialism gave new opportunities for the employment of women and children, often indeed in greater demand in some industries than men. Not only the economic but also the social and psychological effects of this development were enormous. Workingmen were well aware of the distinctions conferred by training, skill, and education; at the same time, they came increasingly to think of themselves as forming a class, with common interests to be defended against their masters.

It would be dangerous to take this essentially political self-evaluation at its face value, but English labor did have a few common characteristics. Workingmen were far better disciplined in the middle of the nineteenth century than they were at the beginning. To a considerable degree, this was the result of their having been broken to or having grown into an industrial discipline unlike the life of an agricultural or domestic-industrial community. The organization of a factory, the incessant demands of a single, tireless source of power, meant living by the clock, keeping the pace, and obeying orders, a hard set of lessons enforced by fines, discharge, the blacklist, and (on children) by beatings. The foreman, or overlooker, represented immediate authority, and a gulf opened between the owner and his workers that could not exist in a workshop. The most generous and foresighted provision by an employer for education or the improvement of his workers could seem condescending or self-serving at a distance. So too employers, fearful of any compromise of their authority, sometimes sought out the most docile labor—women and children where possible—and set themselves resolutely against trade unions. Trade unions had been outlawed in 1799 and 1800, but were again permitted, for dealing with wages and hours of labor, in 1824; after a succession of false starts, trade unionism took deep root among the skilled trades in the 1840's and 1850's, and within a generation they were strong and confident enough to seek for new economic and political conquests.

It is impossible to speak categorically about the effect of the Industrial Revolution on standards of living. Probably most workingmen who thought about such things would have said that their condition had deteriorated: the myth of a golden age in a rural past was strong. It was also largely untrue, if one considers the quality of the life of the poor in the eighteenth century. Certainly for most nineteenth-century workingmen and their families the expectation of life was increasing (save for the stubbornly high rate of infant mortality), and the disappearance of traditional, often brutal pastimes was matched by the appearance of others, among them by mid-century the music hall and organized sport. But to try to argue the case for either improvement or deterioration from statistics is a nearly hopeless task. Not until the middle of the century can one speak confidently about the pattern of wages and purchasing power: from then until nearly the end of the century, there was fairly steady improvement in standards of life throughout the working class, except in the worst of the so-called sweated trades, the remnants in tailoring, dressmaking, cigar making, and some other examples of a domestic system that had all but disappeared from the industrialized trades. Earlier in the century, however, such survivals created widespread social problems and provided the main mass support for radical movements like Chartism. Still, whatever improvement can be pointed to, nothing can gainsay the awful threat that lurked throughout the century in sickness, being orphaned or widowed, or being thrown out of work in a depression. Despite the enthusiastic and sometimes misguided work of private charities, such calamities more likely than not meant resort to the Poor Law, and that for many of its "beneficiaries" meant the hated workhouse. Leaving aside the small numbers of highly skilled "aristocrats of labor" who could limit entry into their trades and for whom trade unions or friendly societies provided insurance against illness or unemployment, the most constant and appalling characteristic of working-class life was a terrible sense of insecurity.

The most impressive and to some attractive guide to understanding the working of this complex and changing economy was the system of economic thought that has come to be known as classical political economy. To a large degree its categories were preindustrial. Adam Smith's seminal *Inquiry into the Causes of the Wealth of Nations* was published in 1776, and even David Ricardo's systematization of economic thought forty years later was obsessively concerned with problems drawn from agricultural experience, such as the interrelations of landlord, capitalist, and laborer, and the nature of rent. Still, classical economics could lead to highly relevant analyses of industrial society, and in time even to socialism, by way of the labor theory of value, as central to Ricardian as to Marxian economics. The essentially optimistic outlook of Adam Smith was given a gloomy turn by the engrafting of the Malthusian principle of population, and much Victorian economic and social thought was dominated by the notion of a wages fund, a fixed and not easily alterable supply of capital that had to be parceled out among available workers: the greater their numbers, the smaller the share of each. Despite the enlightened attitude toward labor of many of the leading economists, the popular version of the system often supported a fatalistic view of the possibilities of improvement and an ideological justification of the arbitrary power of the capitalist.

Many other currents of the age, however, led to a softening of this harshness and a blurring of the lines of the class struggle that men in all segments of opinion were not slow to discern. The stream of voluntary charitable activity had broadened to a flood by the end of the eighteenth century; much of it was foolish, but some was magnificent, finding expression in the founding of hospitals, schools, and other institutions to better the quality of human life. To its most devoted practitioners, such voluntary work seemed a far more certain and rewarding means of alleviating suffering than appealing to a state that had, in everyone's experience, proved to be lamentably inefficient and corrupt. It was even possible to imagine the creation or evolution of a perfect society through the generalization of education, discipline, and humanity. The notion of a creative individualism —so idealistic in its own time, so harsh in both appearance and reality in retrospect—was made more tolerable by the persistence and strengthening of certain social arrangements that men then took for granted—a newly humane but still stern administration of law, made the more efficient by the new police forces of which London's, founded in 1829, was the prototype; the social discipline of the family; the tradition of a hierarchical order in which, while men could rise and fall, they generally knew their place and kept to it. Above all, perhaps, a moral revolution spread rapidly beginning in the late eighteenth century. It rose partly from the demands of a more populous and interdependent society that could not tolerate the old laxity, partly in response to the imperatives of a revived and Evangelical religion. Attitudes toward work, sex, and private and public behavior were human- ized, and the goal of "respectability," though peculiarly prized by a rapidly growing middle class, exerted an appeal throughout society. As with fac- tory discipline, much was lost through the imposition of this new moral discipline—color, freedom, amusement, and possibly some important psy- chological outlets. Yet surely more was gained, for it helped to create a society that, for all its faults, was increasingly safe, comfortable, and peaceful.

The most enthusiastic advocates of laissez-faire could not, however, refrain from demanding that the state clear away mercantilist obstacles to free enterprise, revise the tax system in the interest of free trade, and ease the movement of labor and capital. Increasingly the state was called upon to deal with the consequences of urban and industrial civilization, conse- quences beyond the capabilities of the best-motivated and best-supported voluntary charity. Thus in 1802 factory legislation had begun with a pious injunction to cotton manufacturers to look to the welfare of children in their employ; by the sixties there was a broad regulatory code, enforced by government inspectors. Education long remained the province of private religious societies, but the state intervened in 1833 to provide building grants, to which inspection was soon attached, followed by ever more detailed regulation of curriculums and by state encouragement of a new profession of primary school teachers. Finally after 1870, public primary schools were founded to supplement the voluntary system, and secondary education followed in 1902. Railways, the formation of companies, bank- ing, and communications all came to greater or lesser degree under state regulation, and in the case of railways the notion of state ownership was openly discussed as early as the 1840's, though it was not to come for another century.

Above all, the state had to cope with poverty. It did so harshly, if with a certain crude efficiency, through the hated New Poor Law of 1834. It also attacked problems of housing and public health in the rapidly growing towns. By mid-century the towns themselves, their governments reformed in 1835, were playing a larger and larger role of self-improvement, extending in some cases even to "municipal socialism," the ownership of gas and water works. Nearly inconceivable as an instrument of reform at the end of the eighteenth century, by the middle decades of the nineteenth century the state had become the major engine for controlling and guiding the lives of Englishmen. It made that transition because it had itself been reformed and had provided, in a new professional civil service, a means for analyzing its problems and working out solutions.

By the 1860's industrialization had stretched its original assumptions to the limit. The railway network was substantially completed, traditional English farming had reached its peak with the costly drainage and heavily capitalized methods of "high farming," and classical political economy had not yet attracted the critics who were soon to undermine it from within. Free trade had been firmly established as British policy (following a steady liberalization from the 1820's) with the repeal of the Corn Laws in 1846 and of the Navigation Laws in 1849; in 1860, the Cobden Treaty with France had brought a major competitor to look at trade in much the same way. In trade as in foreign policy, Britain was the unchallenged leader of the world, free trade, of course, being most likely to benefit the nation with a long industrial and commercial lead over other nations.

But, profitable though it is to be first, the lead can be lost to competitors who are keener, less set in their ways, and determined to beat the nation to which they have so long been tributary. From the 1870's, England had to face a new, more complex, less fortunate revolution—agricultural disaster overwhelmed the growers of wheat and meat, the mainstays of high farming, and more intense industrial competition appeared from new industrial countries. Britain did not lose her ability to innovate or adapt: in the late Victorian age, large-scale industry became the rule; new industries and technologies like steel, chemicals, and electricity were absorbed; the distributive trades were revolutionized by the coming of department stores and chain stores; and even in depression many parts of the economy prospered. But the industries on which the Agricultural and Industrial Revolutions had been built were in decline as other nations, often doing their jobs better, needed them less. England gradually lost her supremacy, to face a new century with a host of nearly insoluble problems and the cold comfort that she had once been an example to the world.

Further reading suggestions follow chapter 7.

7   The Spread of Industrialization

To a large extent the story of the industrialization of Western Europe, of America, and then of various other parts of the world is a study of diffusion. In general, whether they be inventors of spinning jennies, of flying shuttles, of steam engines, or creators of new styles in dress or painting, or new forms of business organizations, compared to the imitators or borrowers of what is new, originators are few in number. In the spread of the Industrial Revolution, the process of diffusion began with the realization by other nations that the British had certain industrial processes which gave them price and style advantages. In fact, so valuable did the new industrial secrets appear to be that the English enacted many laws, consolidated in 1795, intended to prevent the new machines, or their designs, or even workmen who could reproduce them, from leaving England. These laws were not abolished until 1843. The French, aware of the advantages which the new processes gave the English, sent industrial spies to England and offered large payments to English workers who could bring their techniques to France. As one result of this effort, William Wilkinson, an ironmonger and metalworker, went to France and aided in setting up the metallurgical center at Le Creusot. In a similar way William Cockerill and his son, John, brought plans for textile machines to what is now Belgium. The textile machine and metallurgy industry which they founded at Seraing, near Liège, still exists today. And Samuel Slater, a maker of textile machines, left his native Derbyshire for Rhode Island and in company with Moses Brown created a successful spinning business there.

In the first diffusion of industry, the new techniques went to areas which were in close communication with England, where economic conditions were very similar to those in which the breakthroughs of new methods of production had been made. Also, the industries which moved first and got the best foundations were those which were very close to processes in handicraft production and thus were relatively familiar to workers. Furthermore, except for blast furnaces, the industries which spread early in the nineteenth century did not require great initial investments. Capital could be built up gradually out of profits. And lastly, the new industries went to areas where markets already existed or where some local advantage like water power, iron ore, fuel, or an abundant labor supply seemed to assure low-cost production. In this way the cotton textile industry spread to such places as Mülhausen in Alsace, where water power

A.D.   1793   Alexander Hamilton, "Report on Manufactures"
       1859   Value added by manufacturing exceeds value of agri-
              cultural products sold
       1901   U.S. Steel Corporation, first business capitalized at more
              than a billion dollars, formed

----

from the streams coming out of the Vosges mountains was available, to
New England, where there was also water power, and to Alpine regions.
Soon it went to places like Ghent in Belgium and Chemnitz in Germany,
where fuel to generate steam power was cheap.

By the middle of the nineteenth century the first period of the diffusion
of mechanization had come to an end and the spread of industry entered a
new phase that was to continue until World War I. Government efforts to
retain the secrets of technological advance had broken down and were used
thereafter only in rare instances, like that of nuclear fission, in which
problems of national defense were involved. To be sure, individual firms
continued to guard jealously their techniques and methods of production in
order that their rivals could not compete with them so readily. Inventors
won the legal right to a monopoly of their findings for a specified number
of years. But in spite of such restrictions, indeed in part because of them,
technical information became available to nearly everyone capable of
understanding it almost as soon as it was discovered. Patents made known
general conceptions of what was new and thus allowed experts to figure out
what had been achieved. Firms that established branches abroad to tap
new markets unavoidably exported their capital and their knowledge of
production to other areas, and trained foreign workers in necessary new
skills. Technical books had to be written, and these were sold everywhere.
And trade associations published journals that revealed both what was
being developed in their industries and what productive equipment was
available in the market. Indeed, the second wave of diffusion was aided
throughout by the older industrialized areas. As had happened so many
times in the past, economically advanced regions were exporting the very
things which had made them the most advanced and had given them positions of military and political superiority.

In this second period, industry moved first to peripheries of the earlier
industrialized sections and then to places where raw materials could be

assembled cheaply for processing. Inasmuch as coal had become "king" of all these materials because it provided power and heat energy for smelting iron, heavy industry tended to locate where coal could be had at low cost. Therefore regions like the Ruhr Valley and Silesia in Germany, the north of France, the Walloon part of Belgium, and cities or towns on the sea, on canals, and on rivers became favorable sites for industrial plants. To be sure, water power remained important for textiles and light industries generally; and some industries, like the needle trades, sought cheap labor. Still others, like baking, had to be near their markets and thus contributed to the self-industrialization of urban centers.

In this way the period from 1850 to 1914 saw the extension of mechanized industry to most of France, to more of Belgium, to all of Germany west of the Elbe, especially along the Rhine, in Hanover, and in Saxony, to Bohemia, the central part of Austria, and to the northern part of Italy, particularly Piedmont and Lombardy. Accordingly it was possible by 1914 to regard Europe as divided into two main regions, one industrial or "black" and the other agricultural or "green." The frontier between them ran roughly from the Elbe River to Budapest and thence to Rome. Indeed, in 1870 the United Kingdom, France, Belgium, Germany, Italy, and Sweden accounted for 83 per cent of all European manufacturing and even in 1913 for 74 per cent of it.

France progressed rapidly in its efforts to catch up with England until the Franco-Prussian War of 1870, but thereafter Germany made the most phenomenal economic strides forward. The reasons for the decline in the rapid rate of growth of both the United Kingdom and then of France are multitudinous, but some are particularly striking. Perhaps the most important was the fact that Germany acquired from England and France both capital and technology for its own industrialization. In addition, however, Germany seemed more determinedly bent on industrialization than did France, which put much of its resources into colonialism, invested its capital abroad, and refused to give up its style of gracious living. Then, too, Germany, with its coal and chemical resources, had advantages in raw material which France could not match. And lastly, Germany developed its scientific educational system and its research facilities far beyond those of its competitors. By its industrialization, it upset the previously existing balance of military power and became the center of a political alliance which was in a position to challenge the former leaders. And challenge them it did in two world wars.

Still another aspect of the second period of industrialization in Europe was the sizable contributions to the technology of mechanization made on the Continent. In the development of methods for making cheap steel, a product which was essential to large-scale and high-speed industrial production, important inventions were made by William Siemens, an Englishman of German birth, and by two French brothers, Émile and Pierre Martin, who patented their findings in 1866. Portland cement was invented by an Englishman, but methods of producing it were improved by both French and Germans. Aluminum was discovered by a German; the internal combustion engine was developed to the point of practicality by a German, Gottlieb Daimler; the electrolytic process for producing soda from common salt was developed by a Belgian, Ernest Solvay; Alfred Nobel, of Sweden, invented a cheap explosive in the form of dynamite; and an Italian, Guglielmo Marconi, invented radio.

Transportation developed along with the growth of industrial production in western Europe. Europe was crisscrossed with railways which tapped new markets and made available for processing raw materials located in remote places. Concurrently, ocean shipping grew rapidly, with steamships finally taking over from sail in the last quarter of the nineteenth century, and with interocean or sea canals like the Suez, the Panama, and the Kiel greatly shortening the distance between important shipping centers. In 1914 the world tonnage of ocean shipping was about 20.5 million tons, and 96 per cent of this tonnage was accounted for by Europe and the United States.

The great improvement of transportation permitted the exchange of goods over long distances and allowed areas with competitive advantages to specialize in producing particular goods. In a very general way, Europe may be said to have become the "workshop" of the world, selling to the rest its industrial surpluses and importing in exchange raw materials and foodstuffs. A system of multilateral commerce came into being which maintained a general and intricate balance of trade and payments. In the exchange of goods, the industrial states had a distinct edge, for at the going prices manufacturers required fewer "inputs" of capital and labor than did agricultural products.

In spite of the enormous increase in industrial output, the advance was not uninterrupted; the ascent was marked by declines as well as rises. Fluctuations in the progress of mechanized industry came to be known as business cycles or, to avoid the impression of extreme regularity, as business fluctuations. These waves went from crest to trough between two to four years and seemed to be generated by the operation of the economic system itself. The upward swing was characterized by optimism on the part of businessmen, by plant expansion, fuller employment, and rising prices. When a point was reached at which entrepreneurs believed that they could not sell more goods at existing prices, they stopped expanding plants, laid off workers, and began to cut prices to move inventories. The deepest of all the depressions was that of the 1930's, but before that catastrophe the

prob. dehumanizing labor us quality 2 machine
unequal distribution of profit
exploitation
of labor, extorted labor underenting negotiation

Western world had experienced a "long depression in prices" (which is to be distinguished from the business cycle phenomenon) that lasted from 1873 to 1896. Between these years prices fell so low and so far that many economists thought that the possibility of further economic expansion was dependent upon Europe's geographical expansion of its sphere of operation —an opinion that contributed much to the new wave of European imperialism which characterized the period from 1870 to World War I.

Another aspect of industrialization causing concern pertained to the labor force. Workers no longer owned the means of production and were dependent on their wages, which in turn were dependent upon the employer and his success. Many philosophers in accordance with their interests or sentiments endeavored to rationalize the situation of workers under capitalism. Capitalist economists usually took a laissez-faire attitude and thought that everything would work out under a scheme of "survival of the fittest." Economists who sided with the workers criticized the capitalist system and wanted either to supplant it with some utopian scheme or to overthrow it entirely. The solutions most widely adopted were, first, a great improvement in the condition of labor effected by employers on their own initiative or under pressure from trade unions; second, the gradual devolution to workers of many of the products of their labor; and, third, the growth of the "welfare state" idea—the notion that the state is responsible for the welfare of all and must, either by providing jobs or by social insurance schemes, protect the individual all the way from "the womb" (maternity insurance) to "the tomb" (death insurance).

The same industrializing forces that were transforming Great Britain and the Continent were also affecting the United States. The pattern of American development was somewhat different from that of the Old World; indeed an economic historian looking at the United States in the early twentieth century might well contend that the country had experienced no "industrial revolution" comparable to that which shook England and western Europe in the eighteenth and nineteenth centuries. Compared to conditions in 1815, American economic life in 1907 was incredibly more diverse, more productive, more highly capitalized, more technological, but the process of becoming a "developed" economy did not involve America in a dramatic revolution from an old economic order. Instead, there was simply a steadily accelerating evolution from a colonial economy which was production-oriented in spirit, capitalistic in character, and technological insofar as possible. Because there never was an *ancien régime,* there could be no real revolution. And because there was no real economic revolution, nineteenth-century America was largely spared the traumatic political, social, and intellectual repercussions produced by the

Industrial Revolution in other lands. The change, in other words, was gradual.

In a similar vein, John Adams once argued that the military conflict between the American colonies and Great Britain lasting from 1775 to 1783 was an anticlimax. The real revolution, he thought, had taken place much earlier, when the colonials began to think of themselves not as Englishmen living in the provinces, but as Americans. Later historians have extended Adams' argument to suggest that the revolution had begun with the act of emigration, which, consciously or not, constituted a declaration of independence from Old World politics, society, and culture.

At no time in the seventeenth or eighteenth century did the United States have a stable, settled agricultural economy. Despite the myth of the self-sufficient frontiersman entirely dependent on his own resources, as soon as a new area was opened for settlement, the pioneer, subsistence farmer quickly succumbed to commercial agriculture. He regarded land as a commodity to be exploited, not a place on which one "settled." Rural Americans never envisioned themselves as part of a timeless scheme of things, in which the climate, the seasons, and the configuration of the landscape established norms and disciplines for men. If the land "wore out," or if there was a prospect of better land over the next ridge, they simply "moved on." The symbols of the American countryside have not been the hearth, the barn, and the old oaken bucket, but the ax that felled the forest, the plow that broke the plains, the Conestoga wagon that carried the farmer to his next opportunity, and, eventually, the Model T Ford that took him to the main chance in the big city.

America never sustained a genuine "country interest," comparable to the squirarchy of England, the peasant proprietor parties in France, or the Junkers in Prussia. Not that there have not been, on occasion, wistful voices. Thomas Jefferson, for example, hoped that with the acquisition of the huge Louisiana Territory in 1803, America might remain (what in fact it had never been) a country of contented yeomen. But Jefferson lived long enough to see that the farmer in the Mississippi Valley, like his progenitors in the East, was neither yeoman nor contented. Take the Lincoln family. Thomas Lincoln moved frequently in the early nineteenth century, from Kentucky to Indiana to Illinois, always in search of better land; he never established an "old homestead" to blur young Abraham's recognition of the desirability of escaping from the country to such urban careers as storekeeping and the practice of the law.

Meanwhile, in the South, the development of large-scale plantations producing tobacco, rice, sugar, and cotton, along with the existence there of several million Negro slaves, led politicians, priests, and poets to proclaim that at least in this region a stable country interest had evolved. They were right in the limited sense that for a long period of time the region competed successfully in world markets with these staple crops. But there was nothing traditional or precapitalistic about these plantations. Analogies drawn between plantation owners and landed European nobility, and between Negro slaves and serfs or peasants, were spurious. Plantation owners, like other American farmers, ruthlessly exhausted the fertility of their lands and then sought out new ones. The "old mansions" which then and later seemed to symbolize the stability of Southern rural life flourished no longer than the farmhouses of other regions. Harriet Beecher Stowe's *Uncle Tom's Cabin* catches the precarious nature of plantation life far better than any song Stephen Foster ever wrote. When profits declined, slaves were "sold down the river," in the same matter-of-fact way a capitalist would get rid of any unproductive asset. In every important respect, southern agriculture was far closer to modern capitalistic enterprise than to the traditional rural order with which romanticists compared it.

Toward the end of the nineteenth century, a congeries of rural-based organizations appeared—Granges, Farmers' Alliances, Agricultural Wheels —to articulate the conviction of many farmers that national political life was increasingly oblivious to the aspirations and needs of rural America. Though on occasion almost all borrowed from the rhetoric of a pastoral, preindustrial society, the only desire held in common by a southern white sharecropper, a bonanza wheat farmer from the Red River Valley of North Dakota, and a Missouri corn-and-hog producer was for political-economic changes that would bring each greater profit. So William Jennings Bryan of Nebraska may be taken as representative of late-nineteenth-century agrarianism when, speaking to the Democratic national convention in 1896, he moved easily from an assertion of the moral primacy of tillers of the soil to the claim that farmers were, after all, just as much businessmen as the speculators who inhabited the Chicago Board of Trade.

In short, America did not experience, and did not need to experience, the kind of agricultural revolution that everywhere in Europe was the precondition to the development of modern industrialism. It was not necessary to shake people loose from the soil, destroy hereditary tenures, subvert a politically potent country interest, or replace a pastoral ethos with a capitalist one. The marked changes in American agriculture that took place in the nineteenth century—the disappearance of subsistence agriculture from all but scattered areas of America, the growth in the size of farms, mechanization, the sharp upturn in the amount of capital required for land and equipment, and the development of national and international markets —all these simply continued trends that had been apparent since the first settlements.

But if industrial development in America was not retarded by stubbornly entrenched agrarians, it was to some extent hampered—and to some extent aided—by a shortage of labor. No other country except Russia began industrialization with a surplus both of land and of economic opportunity, available to the man in search of work. Of course, it was romantic, even in America, to imagine that a young man from a worn-out Vermont or North Carolina farm could easily strike out for the rich virgin lands of Dakota Territory or Oregon. Yet publicists and historians who have described "the frontier" as a safety valve have been right in principle, if not always in their description of the precise mechanism by which men bettered themselves. Wages in the East, if usually lower than in the West, remained throughout the nineteenth century consistently higher than wages for comparable work in Europe.

At about the time the Englishman Thomas Malthus was making his dire predictions about the effect of the rapid growth of population on human well-being, in America Alexander Hamilton was explaining to Congress how the new nation might go about developing the manufacturing sector of the economy. One of the great benefits of industrialization, he argued, was that factories made women and children, often of only marginal benefit in farming, important productive assets. Given the labor shortage, this was an especially potent consideration.

Though Congress refused to take any of the steps Hamilton recommended to promote manufactures, his words were prophetic of the exigencies confronting industrialists. One of the wonders of the Western world in the 1830's was the textile mills of Lowell, Massachusetts, where girls from respectable farm families labored in a kind of paternalist Arcadia with their company-sponsored literary societies and their prim, chaperoned boardinghouses. A later generation would dismiss such enterprises as "company towns" designed to exploit the workers as efficiently as possible; but this was a misconception. The Lowell girls were not wage-slaves; most returned to the farm after a few years of work had earned them a competence, or at least a trousseau.

The Lowell experiment did not provide a long-range solution to the shortage of labor. More fundamental assistance came from the massive influx into America between 1830 and 1924 of some 35 million immigrants, the large majority of them men and women in their twenties and thirties, attracted by the greater opportunities and higher wages America offered. A few of these immigrants brought with them skills and technological knowledge acquired in the mines and manufacturing enterprises in western Europe; they played a very important role in speeding the development in America of efficient coal mines, canals and railroads, and of the textile and iron-and-steel industries. Dramatic as their contribution was, however, these skilled workers probably contributed less to American economic growth than the mass of newcomers who arrived with no industrial skills at all. Constituting a large mass of virtually unconditioned labor, they were available for any kind of task in any part of the country. The needs of the New England textile manufacturers were effectively met by the middle of the nineteenth century by Irish and German immigrant families (and later in the century by newcomers from French Canada and Italy). The canals and railroads of the Mississippi Valley and the Great West were constructed by Irish and Chinese, the timber of the north exploited by Scandinavians, the subways of New York dug by Italians, the steel mills and meat-packing plants of the Middle West manned by immigrants from eastern Europe, the clothing industry of New York by Jews. Because most of these immigrants brought no ingrained craft tradition with them, entrepreneurs encountered little resistance in introducing technological change. When, for example, it became technically possible to mechanize much of the production of boots and shoes, the old artisans were easily replaced (actually most of them became supervisors) by willing hands, as new to the trade as to the country. Conversely, immigrants—especially of the first generation—were by and large uninterested in unionization. For one thing, most of them could find more valued fraternity in associations of fellow immigrants in their neighborhood or church than with fellow workers, often of different ethnic origin, in the mines or factories. Even more important, they usually received wages that were recognizably better than those paid in the home country. And even those who were warned by American workers or alerted by socialist theory to the inclination of employers to reduce wages to subsistence levels had to cope with the fact that real wages in the United States rose every decade in the nineteenth century.

Like all industrializing countries, America needed large amounts of capital, for economic growth and for the "social overhead" of an urban, technological society. Immigration played some part in meeting this need. Willy-nilly, European countries had to pay the costs of nurturing immigrants who, when ready to become productive members of society, left for America. In the nineteenth century, the subsidy this practice bestowed on the American economy amounted to at least $1,000 for each new settler.

At the same time, European—and especially English—investors were attracted by the growth potential of the country. Much of the capital invested in canals and cattle ranches, in banks and commercial ventures, in textile factories and steel mills, and even in state and municipal bonds came from Europe. Until early in the twentieth century there continued to be a net flow of capital into the United States; the country benefited enormously from undergoing industrialization in that period in history when the flow of private capital was least hindered by governmental controls.

It would be a mistake, of course, to conclude that most investment capital was generated abroad, just as it would be a mistake to argue that the absence of an entrenched agrarian interest, or the influx of immigrants, was primarily responsible for the pace and relatively painless character of American economic development. The key factor, almost certainly, was the American ethos which gave unreserved sanction to all behavior conducive to rapid growth. Opinion in the United States stigmatized sloth and self-indulgence, and saw little virtue in humility or contemplation. It also firmly insisted that work was good in itself, and, besides, would lead to success. And success, it was agreed, was best measured by the capacity it bestowed to perform more work. Preoccupied with the duties and opportunities of the individual, it took pretty much for granted that the well-being of society would result automatically from the achieved well-being of individuals. Though each detail of this ethos had its origin or parallel in European attitudes, it enjoyed a singular power in America. Informing the expectations of most of those leaving Europe for America, it was reinforced by the spectacular "progress" and "success" it helped engender in this favored land.

Certainly it encountered no sustained, substantial criticism from religious leaders, those to whom Americans characteristically looked for intellectual guidance. The majority of churchgoing Americans adhered to evangelical Protestant denominations, which not only acknowledged one another's legitimacy but also agreed on the essential harmony of the "gospel of work" and the Sermon on the Mount. When Andrew Carnegie in 1889 combined the traditional doctrines of Christian stewardship with strictures against the least public interference with individualism, private property, competition, and the process of accumulation, most Protestants agreed that he had articulated a "gospel of wealth" that was both true and also characteristically American. A few Protestant ministers were beginning to call for a more "social Christianity," but they did not seriously threaten the commitment of Protestantism to a rugged individualism.

The same bourgeois ethic characterized the outlook of most Catholic, Lutheran, and Jewish leaders. Though obligations to orthodoxy made them somewhat tentative in endorsing a "Protestant ethic," they were powerfully attracted by its emphasis on work in the world. John Ireland, Roman Catholic Archbishop of St. Paul, was a prime exponent of this ethic. Affected no doubt by his own spectacular rise from humble immigrant antecedents, and by the success of many laymen in his diocese, he was able to declare to a stock-market group in the 1890's that "it is energy and enterprise that win everywhere; they win in the Church, they win in the State, and they win in business." Few orthodox churchmen were quite so confident. Yet it is hard to imagine a culture so formally committed to religions of otherworldliness so wholeheartedly endorsing a gospel of individual worldly enterprise.

Americans generally agreed that one of the most fundamental respon-sibilities of the political order was to foster economic growth; the best government was that which least inhibited the enterprise of the private individual, and—by so doing—created conditions favorable to progress. Education, it was believed, ought to be available to every young American, and by the middle of the nineteenth century most states had some kind of law requiring cities and villages to offer a free elementary education to all. By the end of the century, most states had taken the considerably more radical step of compelling each child to attend some school. Though the education was the responsibility primarily of the states, the federal gov-ernment in the 1860's provided land grants to support state universities, and in the early twentieth century began to provide funds for specially deserving groups, like farm children.

So striking was the American commitment to public education that it is tempting to describe American political philosophy as faith in anarchy plus a schoolmaster. But most Americans wanted government to provide more than teachers. Towns and villages vied with one another in offering tax benefits to builders of canals, railroads, and factories. State legislatures offered bonuses to nascent enterprises, and state courts redefined ancient common law principles to permit railroads to use eminent domain powers which had not been allowed simpler kinds of transportation companies. The courts also strictly limited the railroads' liability to either passengers or employees, acknowledging that a new enterprise needed elbow room to thrive. By the middle of the nineteenth century, most states had passed "general" incorporation laws which extended to whole classes of would-be entrepreneurs the benefits of corporate organization.

The federal government was neither indifferent nor inactive to the needs of enterprisers. In defining the "American system," Henry Clay, like Hamilton before him, thought it essential to impose a tariff that would protect American industry from foreign competition, and to maintain a federally chartered bank that would perform for American businessmen services analogous to those provided by the Bank of England. He also favored federal transportation and communication projects. Between 1830 and 1860 the Congress was too riven by sectional conflicts to sustain coherent programs in any of these areas, but the Supreme Court proved able, then and throughout the rest of the century, to guarantee that capital-istic enterprise would not be *inhibited* by capricious state action. First by interpreting the prohibition in the federal Constitution against impairing the obligation of contracts, and—after the Civil War—by a strained con-struction of the Fourteenth Amendment denying to the states the right to deprive citizens of life, liberty, or property without due process of law, the Court zealously protected "the enterprise of a free people." It also jealously guarded the rights of corporations chartered in one state to do business in other states. American federalism, with its overlapping and at times competing jurisdictions, instead of retarding the development of a national economy, in practice maximized the possibility of innovation by the individual.

It goes without saying that rapid industrialization was not the only spectacular development in nineteenth-century America. Expansion across the continent was largely independent of the Industrial Revolution; efforts of Marxist scholars to see American expansion as the last stage of industrial capitalism are unpersuasive. The slow but steady growth of democratic political institutions, which, superimposed upon America's republicanism, made the country unique among nations, was not immediately dependent upon the Industrial Revolution, though it certainly gained strength from the prosperity industrialism fostered.

Furthermore, even if industrialization was the central theme of nineteenth-century American history, it is clear that the course of that development was not linear or uniform; three periods of markedly different character can readily be discerned. By 1859, the progress of industrialization was such that the value added by manufacturing surpassed the value of agricultural products sold, but the great majority of Americans still lived on farms, or in small towns in rural communities, and very little of the manufactured product was exported. In other words, in 1859 American manufacturing was still directed almost exclusively at a domestic market, expanding rapidly because of the construction of canals and railroads, and the widespread use of the steamboat.

During the second stage, which lasted until the turn of the century, industrialization broadened its base and extended its range enormously. By the late nineties steel manufactured in Pittsburgh undersold English steel in Liverpool, and American capital exports exceeded the infusions of capital from abroad. Even the agricultural sector became more broadly international: American wheat was being sold in ports as distant as Stockholm, Stettin, and Odessa.

In these last years of the nineteenth century, both factories and corporations grew dramatically in size; when the United States Steel Corporation was founded in 1901, it was capitalized at more than a billion dollars. Such corporations, enjoying broad legal privileges, engendered hostility among smaller businesses directly threatened by their economic power, fear among laborers whose unions proved quite incapable of coping with management, and unease among middle-class Americans startled by this emanation of "private enterprise." But hostility, fear, and unease did not produce in the nineteenth century any pronounced reaction against the prevailing government policies.

Then early in the twentieth century, the pace of economic development quickened still more. Consumer goods that were to be the hallmark, and the cherished vindication, of the twentieth-century American capitalism— the automobile, the household appliances, the suburban home itself— assumed a steadily increasing importance. New industrial and commercial processes accompanied this revolution. The larger corporations established research and development divisions charged with discovering new products. The factory assembly line appeared, producing identical items in profusion at high speed. Massive advertising campaigns stimulated demand. National distributing systems—chain stores and licensed dealerships, for example—satisfied customers wanting products with nationally known names.

These years also saw the welling up of the idea that the state had a moral obligation to act positively and firmly to promote the general welfare. The idea took a somewhat different form than it did in Europe. Its advocates called themselves "progressives." Convinced that government had largely failed in its task because of "corruption," these progressives saw a remedy in making public officials more responsive to "the people." If city bosses could be eliminated, senators elected directly rather than by state legislators, the legislators themselves made subject to recall by the citizenry, even judges deprived of their immunity from public control, the progressives believed that government would become pure in character, democratic in procedure, and scientific in the regulation of business. Most reform energies were invested in crusades for these essentially political goals; as a result, there was in America no such extensive regulation of business enterprise as occurred in industrialized countries of western Europe in these years. Nevertheless, American progressives played an indispensable role; by insisting that the government had the right and duty to shape the course of economic development, they readied their countrymen to accept the drastic regulation of industry which took place first during World War I, and later during the Great Depression.

For Further Reading

Cipolla, Carlo M., *The Economic History of World Population.*
Clough, Shepard B., *European Economic History: The Economic Development of Western Civilization.*
Cochran, Thomas, and William Miller, *The Age of Enterprise.*
Deane, Phyllis, *The First Industrial Revolution.*
Henderson, H. O., *Britain and Industrial Europe, 1750–1850.*
League of Nations, *Industrialization and World Trade.*
Svennilson, Ingvar, *Growth and Stagnation in the European Economy.*

8   A World Economy

Although industrialization was, in the nineteenth century, chiefly centered in western Europe and the United States, its *effects* were world-wide. Indeed, as early as the late eighteenth century, the outlines of a world economy were clearly discernible. Centered in western Europe, it included Russia, India, the East Indies, the Middle East, northern and western Africa, and the Americas. Trade had increased manyfold in the course of the century, shipping had grown in volume and speed, and strong financial links had been forged. The result was to connect the markets of the world more closely than ever before. Within three weeks after the signing of the treaty in 1814 ending the war between Great Britain and the United States, coffee prices in Jidda, on the Red Sea, had dropped 30 per cent. The expansion of Europe was also well advanced. In the Americas, an area equal to that of western Europe had been settled by a European population of somewhat less than 10 million, and more than half a million Russians lived in Siberia. Trade, migration, and settlement led to the diffusion not only of ideas, techniques, and products but also of basic crops—thus Old World plants like sugar, coffee, and cotton were grown on a large scale in the Americas while such New World crops as corn, potatoes, and tobacco were becoming the mainstay of many farmers in Europe, Asia, and Africa.

The world market, however, was confined to the coasts; except along rivers, its effects were rarely felt a hundred miles inland. The outline of a world economy remained sketchy and had not yet been filled in. The expansion of the rimland economy into the hinterlands, and its spread throughout China, Japan, Oceania, and Africa, was the task of the nineteenth century. It was accomplished through the transport revolution; the migration of huge numbers and the settlement of vast areas; the development of European industry, which required hitherto unknown quantities of raw materials; the investment of immense amounts of European capital overseas; and the manifold expansion of trade.

From the fifteenth century on, the sailing ship had been the main instrument of European economic and political expansion. Constantly growing in carrying capacity and speed because of improvements in design, built of cheap and easily available materials and needing no fueling stations, sailing ships continued to carry the greater part of international trade until the 1870's. American clipper ships represented the supreme achievement of the age of sail. Capable of speeds of up to 15 knots, a clipper could carry 5,000 tons across the Atlantic in less than two weeks.

A.D.   1807   Robert Fulton sails from New York to Albany in steamboat
              Clermont
       1816   Regular transatlantic service, in sailing ships, between
              Liverpool and New York
       1819   *Savannah* crosses Atlantic, mostly under steam
       1821   Adoption of gold standard in England
       1825   Opening of Stockton and Darlington railroad, in England
       1844   Electric telegraph opens between Washington and Balti-
              more
       1846   Repeal of Corn Laws
       1866   Laying of first transatlantic cable
       1869   Opening of the Union and Central Pacific's transconti-
              nental railway; opening of Suez Canal
       1876   Invention of telephone
       1884   Invention of compound turbine in steam navigation
       1887   Daimler's internal combustion engine automobile
       1901   Marconi's first transatlantic radiotelegraphy message
       1902   First transpacific cable
       1903   Completion of trans-Siberian railway; airplane flight by
              Wright brothers
       1909   First cross-Channel flight, by Louis Blériot
       1914   Opening of Panama Canal
       1919   First transatlantic flight by John Alcock and Arthur Brown
       1924   First flight around the world by United States Army planes
       1936   First television broadcast

No corresponding progress had been made in land transport; the bulk of internal trade continued to be carried by water. In western Europe attempts had been made for several centuries to supplement the excellent river network with canals, but it was the exigencies of the Industrial Revolution, and more particularly the need to move huge quantities of coal, that led to large-scale canal building in the years 1760–1850, first in Britain and then in western Europe and the United States. The introduction of steamboats gave a further impetus to river navigation and canal construction. In spite of some improvements, however, road transport continued to be slow, uncertain, and expensive. When, during the Cabinet crisis of 1834, Sir Robert Peel rushed back from Italy to London, his journey took as long as it would have in Roman times.

The obstacle to economic development presented by inadequate land transportation was overcome by the railroads. Following George Stephenson's success with the *Rocket* in 1829, railways began to spread rapidly; by the 1840's they had superseded roads in the more advanced countries, and canals could hardly stand their competition. By 1850, the United States had 9,000 miles of track, Britain almost 7,000, Germany nearly 4,000, France nearly 2,000, and small stretches were to be found in most other European countries, including Russia. In the 1850's railways began to be built in India, Egypt, Turkey, Algeria, South Africa, Argentina, and elsewhere—but not in Japan and China until the 1870's. By that decade the era of the transcontinental railways had begun: the United States in 1869, India (Bombay–Calcutta) in 1870, Canada in 1885, Europe (Calais–Constantinople) in 1888, Russia (Trans-Siberian) in 1903, South America (Argentina–Chile) in 1910. By 1913 the world's railway mileage was close to 700,000, of which 257,000 were in the United States, 49,000 in Russia, 40,000 in Germany, and 35,000 in India. Freight rates were sharply reduced, falling by a half or more in the last quarter of the nineteenth century. After World War I, however, railway building slowed down greatly, owing to the competition first of the automobile and then of the airplane; indeed, in several advanced countries many lines were abandoned. Today there is considerably less track in the world than in 1914.

Railway construction, which required enormous amounts of capital, was financed in very diverse ways. In England and America private companies built hundreds of uncoordinated projects, but on the Continent the state provided not only overall control but a large, and often predominant, share of capital. British capital also financed the greater part of the railways built in India, Canada, and Latin America, generally with financial guarantees by the national or state government concerned. French capital was active in building southern and southeastern European lines.

Steamboats proved their worth on American rivers in the 1810's, spread to Europe and Russia soon thereafter, and by the 1850's were navigating the Ganges, Nile, Amazon and La Plata, and other rivers. By the 1830's regular services were also operating in the Mediterranean, connecting with other steamship lines to India and England. Over the next few decades several innovations—the use of iron instead of wood, the replacement of paddlewheels by screw propellers, and the introduction of the compound engine—enabled steamships to compete with sailing ships on the oceans. Further boons to steam navigation were the opening of the Panama railway in 1855 and the Suez Canal in 1869. By the late 1880's maximum tonnage had risen to 11,000 and speed to 21 knots, and the Atlantic run had been reduced to six days. All this greatly raised the cost of ships, and led to the formation of large shipping companies. Competition, however, continued to be intense, and the economies achieved were such that freight rates, which had shown a downward trend since the end of the Napoleonic wars, dropped by a half to two-thirds between the 1870's and about 1900, when they began to be stabilized by the formation of "rings" and "pools" between the leading lines.

The shift from sail to steam was also one from American to British predominance, which lasted until World War II. Around 1890, Britain owned three-quarters of the world's tonnage and was launching two-thirds of all new ships, but thereafter both figures were steadily reduced by competition from Germany, the United States, Norway, Japan, and other countries. In 1914, total gross registered tonnage was 49 million, of which 21 million was under British flag, 5.4 under German, and 5.4 under American.

By World War I, the oil-burning internal combustion engine was widely used on ships, but the automobile was still an expensive luxury and the airplane in the experimental stage. The subsequent development of the car and plane not only greatly reduced travel time but also opened up large areas of the world hitherto unreached by modern transport. The concurrent rise of petroleum as the leading fuel necessitated new forms of transportation, notably tankers, which now account for one-third of all world shipping, and pipelines, many of which cross international frontiers.

Modern transport both facilitated and required the development of better communications. The fact that the declaration of war by Spain on England in 1779 was not known in Madras for nearly twelve months shows how slowly news then traveled, and even in the 1840's the swiftest steamship mails between London and Bombay took a month. However, the telegraph, first used in 1844, spread rapidly; in the United States it reached the Pacific coast by 1861. By the 1850's, European telegraph wires and underwater cables stretched as far south as Sicily and Malta, and long lines were in operation in India, the Middle East, and other parts of the world. The growing needs of commerce and finance spurred the laying of deep sea cables, and in the 1860's India was linked with Europe, and Britain with the United States. By 1902 the Pacific had been spanned and a network of more than 300,000 miles of submarine cables, mostly owned by Great Britain, crossed the oceans and seas. The previous year the first radio message had been sent across the Atlantic, inaugurating a new era in communications.

It has been estimated that, in the course of the nineteenth century, some 8 or 9 million square miles of land were settled in North and South America and Oceania, an eightfold or ninefold increase over the area occupied in those regions in 1800. To this should be added a vast stretch of land in Siberia. This was made possible by the decline in transport costs, which greatly extended the area from which bulky crops, notably grains, and minerals could be marketed. Especially noteworthy was the introduction of refrigeration on railways and steamers in the 1870's, which opened huge markets for meat, dairy products, and fruit in the eastern United States and Europe. Other important factors were the rapid growth in capital accumulation, which financed much settlement, the free land and various facilities offered to immigrants, and the lowering or removal of duties on imports of agricultural products into western Europe. Spurred by such incentives, population, both immigrant and native-born, spread westward in the United States and Canada and northwestward in Australia, at an accelerating pace, so that by 1914 the process of settlement had been substantially accomplished in these countries. A similar movement in Argentina and Brazil started later and made relatively less headway, while in Africa—except for its Mediterranean and southern coasts—even the beginning of settlement had to await the establishment of European rule in the last quarter of the nineteenth century and the control of tropical diseases.

The migrations that accompanied this settlement were on a far larger scale than any previously known, and have since been matched only by the displacement of populations during and after World War II. Five main streams of intercontinental migration may be distinguished: from Europe, and elsewhere, to the Americas, Oceania, and South and East Africa, a total of about 60 million between 1815 and 1914; from Russia to Siberia and Central Asia; from southern Europe to North Africa; from China and Japan to eastern and southern Asia; and from India to southeastern Asia and South and East Africa. All five drew mainly from the lower strata of society, all were primarily motivated by the prospect of economic betterment, and all were greatly facilitated by the new cheap and swift means of transportation. Their effects on the countries from which the migrants came were diverse. Only in Europe, for example, did emigration significantly reduce population pressure. And their impact on the receiving countries also differed greatly.

Immigrants and their descendants accounted for more than half the population growth of Argentina and Siberia, two-fifths of that of the United States and Brazil, and less than one-fifth of that of Canada, from which emigration to the United States was always heavy.

Since the vast majority of immigrants were unskilled workers their main contributions were the raw labor they supplied, the external economies they created by raising the density of settlement, and the added inducement they provided for foreign investors.

The other streams of migration were very different in their character and effects. Starting around 1830, hundreds of thousands of southern Europeans (French, Spanish, Italian, and Greek) settled in North Africa, from Egypt to Morocco. At their peak, in the 1930's, they numbered more than 2 million. They controlled practically all industry, trade, and finance, and a large segment of agriculture. They formed the bulk of the entrepreneurial and professional classes and in some countries even provided most of the skilled workers. But since, for religious and cultural reasons, there was practically no intermarriage or social fusion between them and the local population, they remained a sharply distinct group whose privileges aroused increasing animosity in a region where national self-consciousness was rapidly growing. Hence, with the decline of European power during and after the Second World War, nationalist pressures forced a mass exodus which practically eliminated European settlement in North Africa.

The same has been generally true of Asian migration. The Japanese sent settlers to their overseas empire, providing it with capital, skills, organization, and enterprise. But following the loss of the empire in 1945, 6 million returned to the homeland—2 million from China alone. Similarly, Indians and Chinese spread along the shores of the Indian Ocean, in the wake of the colonial powers; at their peak Indian settlers in these areas numbered more than 3 million, Chinese some 12 million. Occupying an intermediate position between the Europeans who controlled the large enterprises and the local population, they worked as petty traders, moneylenders, clerks, and, where local labor supply was inadequate, as coolies. But they too did not fuse with the local population, and the financial success of many of their members made them an object of suspicion and resentment. With the achievement of independence they have come under heavy pressure in several countries. Thus, for example, large numbers of Indians in Burma and of Chinese in Indonesia have been forced to return to their original homelands.

"In the fifty or so years before 1914," the distinguished British economist R. C. O. Mathews writes, "the different parts of the world were linked together by trade and lending in a relationship closer, perhaps, than any that has existed before or since." The links were provided by convertible currencies based on gold; by a rapidly spreading network of international banking; by massive capital flows; and by the liberalization of trade, which led to a large increase in its value. The relative stability of prices prevailing in this period greatly helped this linkage and integration. In all these processes, the leading role was played by Great Britain, which continued to dominate the commercial and financial scene until the outbreak of the First World War, but France, Germany, and the United States were increasingly important.

As regards currency, until 1870 bimetallism was common, but after that the gold standard spread swiftly. Gold had begun replacing silver in England and France in the eighteenth century. The world trend was accelerated by the adoption of the gold standard in England in 1821 and by the liberal policy pursued throughout the century by the Bank of England. The successive increases in gold supplies from Siberia, California, Australia, and South Africa made it possible to expand the reserves of the central banks and to meet the rapidly growing needs of world production and trade. A further important source of finance was provided by the banking system, which was consolidated in the leading countries in the first half of the century and thereafter began to branch abroad. British, French, German, and other banks greatly facilitated the overseas trade of their homelands, and some of them served as channels for foreign investment.

Viewed as a whole, the period of the British gold standard, 1821–1914, was one of relative price stability. However, prices fluctuated quite sharply during the business cycles that succeeded each other in swift succession. The close relation between the levels of prices and business activity in all the highly developed countries shows the increasing interconnection of the world's leading trading and financial centers.

Still another link was provided by capital flows. Immediately after Waterloo, Britain began lending abroad on an unprecedented scale and, helped by a consistent surplus in its current accounts, rapidly raised its foreign holdings. By 1866 these had passed the £500 million mark, by 1874 £1,000 million, and by 1891 £2,000 million. At the outbreak of the war they stood at £4,000 million; by then nearly half the annual flow of British savings was being channeled abroad. French foreign investment became significant in the 1850's, accelerated in the 1880's, and soon absorbed about one-third of domestic savings. Germany gained importance in the 1890's but rarely invested more than a tenth of its savings abroad. A United Nations estimate put total long-term foreign investment in 1914 at $44 billion, of which Britain accounted for 18, France for 9, Germany for 5.8, and Belgium, the Netherlands, and Switzerland for 5.5. The United

States was still, on balance, a debtor, owing $6.8 billion and holding foreign investments worth $3.5 billion.

The bulk of this capital had flowed to areas of new settlement: the United States, Canada, Argentina, Brazil, Australia, New Zealand, South Africa, and Russia. Much of it was invested in railways and other "social overhead capital," either directly by the investor or by the local government. Hence it is not surprising that capital investment tended to proceed in spurts, being attracted by a wave of railway building associated with higher prices of primary products, and by accelerated migration and intensified settlement in new areas. Similarly much of the investment in India and Egypt was connected with cotton booms, particularly the sharp one provoked by the diminution of American exports during the Civil War. Most of this capital investment contributed significantly to the economy of the borrowing countries, but a substantial amount was put to unproductive use and left a heavy burden of debt, particularly in the Middle East and some Latin American countries. As for the lenders, experience varied, the generally good record of British overseas investment contrasting with the heavy losses sustained by France and Germany as a result of the First World War.

By developing transport and increasing the output of primary commodities, foreign investment helped to expand international trade. The value of all imports and exports skyrocketed from about £340 million in 1820 to £8,360 million in 1913, and in real terms the increase was even greater. Such a rate of growth was unprecedented, and has since been matched only in the years following the Second World War.

Here again Britain set the pace, by removing restrictions on foreign shipping and on commerce with the colonies, by abolishing prohibitions on the export of gold and machinery, and, above all, by reducing tariff barriers. The latter process, begun in 1824, was substantially completed by 1860, when almost all goods were admitted free of duty. Britain's example was followed by Germany, France, and other states, and the 1850's to 1870's were a period of virtually free trade between the major countries. The Great Depression of the 1870's, and other factors such as intensified national and imperial rivalries, set in motion a new wave of protectionism in most countries, but nevertheless trade in 1914 was far less restricted than it had been a hundred years earlier or than it was to be for nearly fifty years after that date. What made Britain's liberal policy still more important was the fact that it constituted by far the largest market in international trade, accounting for one-third of the total in the 1840's, a quarter in the 1870's and a sixth in 1913. Furthermore, both its total imports and its import surplus rose steadily, thus providing its suppliers with rapidly growing export proceeds. The buying power of these proceeds was further increased by the fall in the cost of textiles and other manufactured goods caused by the improvement in production methods.

In other words, British industrial development, capital exports, and commercial policy greatly stimulated the development of primary production overseas, a process from which Britain and western Europe benefited, both as importers of raw materials and as exporters of finished goods and equipment. When, after 1860, the terms of trade turned against primary products, importers of these goods derived a further benefit while exporters, such as the United States, Canada, Italy, Sweden, Russia, and Japan, gained an added incentive for industrialization. The wide diffusion of industry created new streams of trade. Alongside the exchange of manufactured products for raw materials, which had dominated the nineteenth century, there developed a swiftly expanding trade in manufactured products between industrial countries—a trade that has continued to grow in both absolute and relative importance and now exceeds the traditional exchange between advanced and backward countries.

By the turn of the century a clear pattern of world trade and payments between the main regions of the world had emerged, which can be schematically presented:

A. *Tropics* (agricultural and mineral producing tropical countries of Asia, Africa, and Latin America)—large export surplus, particularly in trade with the United States and western Europe.
B. *United States*—large export surplus except with Tropics.
C. *Regions of Recent Settlement* (Canada, Oceania, South Africa, Russia, and temperate zone of South America)—large export surplus with western Europe and Britain, partly offset by import surplus with United States and Tropics.
D. *Western Europe*—large import surplus except with Britain.
E. *Britain*—large import surplus except with Tropics.

Thus the two capital exporting areas, Britain and western Europe, had a huge import surplus in their merchandise trade with the rest of the world. This was, however, more than covered by their earnings from shipping, insurance, and various financial services, as well as by interest payments on their investments; hence their overall current account showed a surplus, enabling them to continue making foreign investments overseas. Conversely the debtor regions had a large overall export surplus, which enabled them to service their debt and, in the case of the United States, to redeem it. Within this broad division there were complex multilateral patterns, such as the triangular trade between the Tropics, the United States, and Britain.

The firmness of the ties that bound together the economies of the various parts of the world was dramatically demonstrated by the dislocations caused by the First World War. The advanced countries had become deeply dependent on the rest of the world for their food, raw materials, and certain essential producer goods like fertilizers. The backward countries were no less dependent for manufactured goods and equipment.

The war, however, shattered the international financial system and disrupted the flow of capital. It also created powerful pressures to reduce dependence on foreign trade and to develop domestic production through autarchy and national planning. The result was to accelerate the growth of nationalism all over the world; each "people," the theory dictated, must be both politically independent and industrialized in order to be strong.

The diffusion of industry, therefore, went on apace and along previous lines, but now the areas chiefly affected were eastern and southeastern Europe, the United States and Canada, and Asia. The proportionate share of western Europe in world manufacturing declined and with it the place in the sun of that part of the world. However, western Europe recovered its industrial capacities in some five or six years after the catastrophe, an eloquent testimony to the recuperative powers of the system. Indeed, even World War II did not destroy it. Germany, France, and Italy experienced economic recovery and expansion after 1949 which was universally recognized as "miraculous."

This most recent phase of industrialization has witnessed the development of machines that revolutionized transportation and communications. The motor truck gave a flexibility to carrying that allowed light industry, particularly, to leave urban centers; high-tension electrical lines gave greater mobility to power and to light; and radio and television changed very drastically the entertainment industry and the spreading of information. The automobile made it possible for man to live at a considerable distance from his work, to explore new regions, and to have a new form of recreation. Furthermore, automatic, computer-controlled machinery made technological unemployment a more pressing problem than it had been in the past and instilled a new sense of urgency in the need for men to determine the wisest and richest uses of their expanding leisure.

In these changes the sciences played a strikingly important role. The next "revolution" seemed destined to come from chemistry and physics, for from these disciplines must come new materials and sources of power to replace the natural resources that industrial societies were so rapidly exhausting. Chemistry had already performed wonders, and it continued to do so with the development of such things as artificial fibers and plastics, which brought important changes to the textile and packaging industries. Undoubtedly the most dramatic achievement of the sciences was the creation of a new source of power from nuclear fission. Here was an advance that showed promise of changing the power pattern of the world and of allowing the industrialization of areas devoid of conventional sources of power.

By the middle of the twentieth century, the most developed nations began to realize that it would be to their benefit to have the economically backward areas of the world industrialized; that they themselves would profit from a greater division of labor, an increase in international trade, and a general improvement in the world's standard of living. The United States undertook the greatest "foreign aid" program in history, and many of the other industrial states adopted similar programs, although of lesser magnitude. This turn of events, a far cry from the restrictive policies of England at the beginning of the Industrial Revolution, was strengthened by the fact that political colonialism was coming to an end and that the new form of "imperialism" was economic in nature.

As one comes to the conclusion of the study of any great change like that of industrialization, one cannot escape the question: Did the change redound to the benefit of mankind? To answer such a question is very difficult. But at least the analyst may point out that the new system did extend man's control over his physical environment—it allowed him to live better and with less fear of want. Indeed, the expectation of life at birth in western Europe rose from some thirty years in 1750 to some seventy years in 1965. Industrialization allowed the population of Europe to increase by nearly four times within this same span of years, despite the fact that more than 50 million emigrants left its shores between 1846 and 1930. Beneficial as such results appear to have been, industrialization has pushed people off the land into cities (only some 10 per cent of the occupied population in the more advanced economies are engaged in agriculture), where conditions of life leave much to be desired. In short, industrialization has helped to solve many of man's physical problems but has contributed to social problems of enormous gravity and complexity.

For Further Reading

The Cambridge Economic History of Europe, Vol. VI.
Feis, Herbert, *Europe, The World's Banker.*
Ferenczi, Imre, *International Migrations,* Vol. I, *Statistics.*
Hawtrey, R. G., *The Gold Standard in Theory and Practice.*
Imlah, Albert M., *Economic Elements in the Pax Britannica.*
Jenks, Leland H., *The Migration of British Capital to 1875.*
League of Nations, Economic Intelligence Service, *The Network of World Trade.*
Rostow, W. W., *The Economics of Take-Off into Sustained Growth.*
Thomas, Brinley (ed.), *Economics of International Migrations.*
Willcox, Walter F., *International Migrations,* Vol. II, *Interpretations.*

New Forces, New Ideas

9   Romanticism and After

If it is appropriate to speak of the machine as the symbol of Rationalist thought during the Enlightenment, then the proper symbol for Romanticist thought is the living organism. The favorite mode of the Age of Reason was analysis and simplification: the system of Newton and the model of the good society alike consisted of a few intelligible parts that worked smoothly together and could be readily understood by any unprejudiced observer. But analysis led to abstraction, which led to skepticism. In the end it seemed as if the love of simplicity and generality had simplified nearly everything out of existence. In Hume, as we know, the real world and its objects are reduced to a set of habitual impressions; the universe is no longer ruled by cause and effect; hence there is no science and certainly no God.

Besides these losses, which the mind of the post-Enlightened generation could grasp, the deeper self suffered a starvation of the feelings. The dwelling among abstractions, the business and duty of being Enlightened, is dry work. Any experience of life suggests that advising the soul to be lofty and the heart to keep calm while the intellect works out all the geometries needed by man and society is *too* simple. Rousseau had been the first to point this out. He had reminded Europe of the existence of emotion, not in order to have it substituted for reason, but in order to warn against an exclusive attachment to either. Speaking of religion and philosophy, he said categorically: "General and abstract ideas are the source of the greatest human errors; never has the jargon of metaphysics led to a single discovery, and it has filled philosophy with absurdities that make one ashamed as soon as one has stripped off the big words."

The Romantic generations, which span the half-century from one European crisis to the next—1789 to 1848—knew better than to confuse life with abstraction, or human salvation with comfortable reasoning. They

A.D.   1761–1762   Rousseau's *Émile* and *Nouvelle Héloïse*
       1767–1769   Lessing's *Hamburgische Dramaturgie*
            1774   Goethe's *Sorrows of Young Werther*
            1790   Goethe's *Faust: A fragment*
            1796   Erasmus Darwin's *Zoonomia* (evolutionary theory)
            1798   Wordsworth's and Coleridge's *Lyrical Ballads*
            1803   Death of Herder; birth of Berlioz
            1804   Beethoven's *Eroica* Symphony
            1807   Hegel's *Phenomenology of Mind*
            1814   George Stephenson's first locomotive
       1820–1830   Rediscovery of Diderot's *Rameau's Nephew, The
                   Memoirs of Benvenuto Cellini,* the poems of Fran-
                   çois Villon, and the philosophy of Spinoza
            1822   Stendhal's *Racine et Shakespeare*
            1824   Death of Byron in Greece; Delacroix's first modern
                   painting
            1827   Victor Hugo's Preface to his play *Cromwell;* death
                   of Beethoven
            1830   Berlioz's *Symphonie Fantastique;* Revolution in
                   Paris, Belgium, Italy, and the German Rhineland
       1830–1842   Comte's Positivist philosophy
       1833–1839   Invention of photography
            1835   David Strauss's *Life of Jesus;* Tocqueville's *Democ-
                   racy in America*
            1837   Pugin's *Contrasts;* deaths of Leopardi and Pushkin
            1839   Turner's painting *The Fighting Téméraire*
            1845   Alexander von Humboldt's *Cosmos*
            1848   Revolutions on the Continent; Chartism threatening
                   in England
            1850   Death of Wordsworth

violent enthusiasm   *ambitious*   *romanticized in memory / bystander*

had been marked by the tremendous experience of the revolution followed
by Napoleon—twenty-five years of wars and overturns, of heroism and
passion, of destinies made and unmade with dramatic suddenness—and
they could tell at sight that the ironic anecdotes of Voltaire, the prose of
Gibbon, or the bland indifference of Hume did not correspond with reality *the future*
as the later comers knew it. Romanticism, before it was a movement or
even a name, was a radically changed sensibility.

The first truth about Romanticism, then, is that its so-called reaction
against the previous age was not born of mere impatience with outworn
forms of art and inadequate social philosophies; rather, it sprang from the
immediate awareness of a new world. That this awareness expressed itself
in forms and concerns that sometimes seem remote from that new world is
an appearance readily explained when we consider how the Romanticists
undertook to revise rationalism, that is, to include reason in a larger view
of experience; or putting it still another way, to transform the machine into
an organism.

At the outset, almost any cultural change occurs by simply taking in
neglected opposites. To find a new basis for reason one goes back to
experience. When weary of established forms and admired models, one
hunts out older forms and remote models. Instead of tired abstractions, one
looks for the concrete instance. Whereas Sir Joshua Reynolds, say, had
taught his academy students to paint the most general forms they could
imagine, Blake says that all art consists of particulars. The particular is
individual, unique, vivid. Fresh and original, it arouses strong feelings—
possibly feelings of repulsion in some, but it banishes indifference. Accordingly, the Romantic thinkers and artists stop dealing with Man, a
capital-letter abstraction. They seek out men—as Rousseau already had
done when he passed from the theory of the social contract to the needs of
the Polish nation and Corsican society.

Trusting experience and the individual, the particular, the Romanticist
looks within himself and reports on his findings; that is why he is often an
egotist, or seems so. Introspection of course makes him liable to error,
fantasy, silliness. His dreams or illusions are part of reality, to be sure, but
they need verification. Hence the Romantic passion for history, the store-
house of innumerable particulars, of countless individuals. Walter Scott, as
a modern scholar has said, "taught Europe history," by showing in his
novels how varied Man actually was, and (a subtler point) how irrelevant
to men's lives were the rationalist statements that could be made about
them. For example, the eighteenth-century conviction that "at bottom" all
universe
religions and moralities are one is quite useless for describing the Middle
Ages or understanding a particular saint. To a genuinely religious age or
being, all religions are *not* one. The saint and the crusader testify to the
truth of *their* religion, not to the syllogisms of a Deist.

reason

Other discoveries followed for the Romantics from an imaginative reading of history. They learned that the past is not a contemptible confusion best forgotten; it is a moving spectacle, a still-potent fragment of humanity. To dismiss the centuries since Rome as barbarian, to scorn Gothic architecture, to believe that human reason began with Newton, as the Enlightenment had done, was to ignore the depths of one's own life and to deny the spirit of one's own people. The people, who had made history in the revolutionary and Napoleonic wars, were now after a long neglect to be recognized as the reservoir of all genius, the agent of social continuity, the great democratic basis of western civilization.

As with the past, so with the remote or exotic parts of experience. Rousseau had shown the philosophes and the orthodox that they had no conception of the size of the world, a provincial outlook persuading them that the Christian God was *the* God, unknown though he was to three-quarters of the human race. The Romantics had the same intuition about the scenery, customs, and art of peoples lying beyond the comfortable cosmopolis of Europe. Chateaubriand drew wild word-pictures of the wild New World, Delacroix went to Morocco to paint, dozens of poets sought the Near East for its intimations of Asia. The realms of the exotic, like the Middle Ages or the hidden inner self, were not places into which to escape from contemporary reality; they were places with which to enlarge one's understanding of it.

Such feelings as these did not burst forth, in common life or in art, without the usual preparation and transition. To mention Rousseau is of course to name the great link between the earlier age and its successor. Rousseau stands out because his writings set Kant on the track of the "practical reason," which gave encouragement to resurgent piety; because he influenced Goethe's feeling for nature and shaped some of his attitudes toward science, love, and prose literature; and because his sway over the Western mind was lasting: sixty years after Rousseau wrote *The New Héloïse*, Shelley could still study it with a sense of revelation. And in his famous *Confessions* Rousseau furnished a guidebook to self-searching for all the lyricists and psychologists of the next century. If Wordsworth and the "nature philosophers" did not have to consult the credo of the priest from Savoy, it was only because the worship of nature had become a widespread cult. It aided in the rediscovery of Spinoza (freshly interpreted as a pantheist), and it gave body to the religious revivals, both Catholic and Protestant, whose common quality was now the aesthetic emotion— the *beauty* of the Christian ethic and architecture, of God's handiwork, of belief itself.

But Rousseau was not the only forerunner. The eighteenth century had felt and recorded many "Romantic" sentiments even while subduing them to physics and mathematics. The taste for Gothic architecture and wild

[handwritten annotations in top margin: optomirm [abinid] injustic / deni[] of evil]

[handwritten annotations in left margin: ego / ambition / throw off / law]

gardens came in the 1760's, first as a fad, then as genuine feeling. Repressed emotion found a vent in sentiment and pathos (the "tearful comedy" as well as the folk ballads) or in manufactured fears and mysteries (the Gothic tale of ghosts and horrors, so unlike Reason and so close to superstition).

In Germany, moreover, a revolt had begun against the domination of French taste and the writings of M. de Voltaire. The scholar, critic, and playwright Lessing was the leader of this cultural uprising, in which Shakespeare played the role of a hidden god, whose natural virtues would help the insurgents conquer the French. And as Herder, another critic, pointed out, those virtues—naturalness, depth of knowledge, and emotion—were also to be found in the ancient German literature hitherto neglected, the sagas and ballads and fairy tales that spoke of a world at once less artificial than the present and nearer the permanent human verities.

Deeper still ran the stream of old pietism which burst out in the late eighteenth century in Methodism and kindred movements marked by evangelical fervor, poetry, and humility. Finally, the French Revolution itself, though it cast patriotism in the classical roles of ancient Rome, was a school of modern heroism and a drama of contemporary life. All these elements merged in the Romanticist philosophy, which may be summed up as: the prevalence of drama in a world of animated beings. *dreams*

Drama means conflict, which presupposes differences, individuality, unexpectedness, mystery. The human mind can grasp and mold reality, especially the passionate mind, but it can never exhaust reality or reproduce its richness. Recalling Pascal, whom the philosophes had derided, the Romantics saw man as simultaneously great and wretched, hero and slave. Goethe's Faust, exhibiting these "two souls in one breast," served as exemplar to the age and established its new morality by asserting that true living is striving rather than achieving. *the life one is given.*

Romantic art naturally matched the Romantic sensibility. Its preferred forms were "open," dramatic, dynamic rather than static or seeking perfection. Blake's love of concrete particulars was shared by poets, painters, and musicians alike, and "local color" became a leading virtue. The particular—minute, significant, true—consorted well with Scott's historical novels or with Balzac's studies of society in the *Comédie Humaine,* or with Stendhal's soundings of the psychological depths. Wordsworth's *Lyrical Ballads* were imitations of the street ballads retelling strange incidents of low life. Byron's early stories in verse mixed introspection with travel in the strange Near East. Goethe and Victor Hugo, Pushkin and Mickiewicz, Heinrich Heine, Alfred de Vigny, and Leopardi, Keats and Shelley, fed the vast desire to hear an individual voice, vibrant with passion and bringing to consciousness emotions and sensations that were new.

The element of drama was so diffused throughout these artistic revelations that little or none was left for drama itself: the stage was barren. But the canvases of Turner, Bonington, Géricault, and Delacroix made up for the lack, and so did the music of Beethoven, Weber, and Berlioz, of Mendelssohn, Glinka, and Schubert, of Donizetti, Bellini, and Chopin. It was, all over Europe, an explosion of genius, as if the very idea of genius defined what Romanticism as a whole had to contribute. For genius is individuality, the dredging of the depths, the mystery of mind and of its wayward power oscillating between grandeur and misery. To those observers of the time who could not understand the necessity of all the striving and who would not read *Faust,* Stendhal would cite the nearer prototype: Napoleon. And lest the point be missed, he patiently explained that Napoleon's genius lay in vastness of plan, mastery of detail, and rapidity of execution.

The Romantics, then, were realists in the plainest sense of the word, reality-seekers. But to make a cult of experience in this way, to try to embrace so much of the given diversity, must surely lead to confusion: "mastery of detail" is a great virtue, but it ends in chaos without "vastness of plan." How to organize the teeming facts of the living universe was the Romanticists' problem. Abstractions are more manageable. They are fewer and deductive logic connects them, as the philosophes had shown.

What then was the organizing principle of all this heaving, heedless life? The Romanticists were fortunate in having at hand the pattern they needed, the "plan" which their fellow seekers, the biologists, were beginning to employ. In truth, it was no accident that biology, whose realm is Life, should have served Romanticist thought. For the desire to replace the abstract and machine-like by a richer model of experience is equivalent to replacing physics and mathematics by biology, leaving the heavens and its circlings of dead matter for the earth peopled by organic forms. This parallel motion of the artistic, scientific, and philosophic spirit led, in the Romanticist period, to the triumph of the idea of evolution.

Buffon, as we know, was an evolutionist by 1750, when his descriptive work on animals drew attention to striking analogies. His collaborator and disciple, Daubenton, extended men's knowledge of comparative anatomy; Buffon's protégé and assistant, Lamarck, made an exhaustive study of species and devised the first tenable scheme of natural evolution. The use and disuse of organs, argued Lamarck, would modify the form of individuals and by "descent with modification" would in time make species evolve. Simultaneously with him, Erasmus Darwin, botanist, physician, and poet (and subsequently the grandfather of Charles Darwin), was setting down astute speculations on the same theme as Lamarck's. With systematic insight, Darwin anticipated his grandson's subdivision of subjects as well as some of his arguments, but he posited that the need and will of the creature to achieve its ends led to the variations of form, which then descended and produced the results we call evolution.

Soon the idea was in the air. Goethe was a convinced evolutionist before 1830, and in that year of political revolution the matter was openly debated by Cuvier and Geoffroy Saint-Hilaire in the French Academy of Science. Three years later, Charles Lyell published his *Geology,* based on evolutionary theory, in which a chapter is devoted to summarizing Lamarck. At that point the biological revolution may be said to be an accepted fact in European culture, whatever remained to be proved or argued in the technical domain of biological science.

The distinction just drawn should make it clear that evolution as a *form of thought* dates from the era of Romanticism and is one of its great contributions. It is still with us, as we know from our reliance on particular "histories"—of a medical case, of corporate profits, of an art form. It is our habitual method of understanding the present and of guiding life.

None of this insistence on living and evolving means that during the half-century under review physicists and mathematicians went into hibernation. On the contrary, they pursued their work, establishing (for example) the principle of the conservation of energy and enabling chemistry to attain the status of a separate science. But the scientists of that time were still "natural philosophers," most of them still unspecialized, and therefore under the influence of the new current of vitalism: it is characteristic that in the new chemistry, the combining properties of elements were called "elective affinities," and that this technical term could serve Goethe as the title of a novel.

Outside science, evolutionary thought found its readiest application and utility in social philosophy. Readmitting so large a slice of the past as the Middle Ages called for some account of institutional change. A nobleman at Versailles was a different creature from his ancestor at the court of Charlemagne. How did the change—in manners, dress, language, beliefs, economic condition, rights and privileges, attitudes toward women and children—come about? By evolution; by gradual changes, chiefly small and invisible but relentless. Such was the pattern and principle of the new history and the new philosophy. Earlier authors had written books about the "revolutions" of states, meaning the changes of dynasty or religion— the events at the top of the social pyramid. Now the only acceptable histories were those that traced the broader evolution—of law or kingship; occasional closer studies might be called "physiologies" (of marriage, of crime)—always the organismic analogy.

This mode of understanding past and present had immediate relevance to existing fears and hopes. The fear of revolution was in part allayed by the evidence of evolution, which showed that progress was as much hindered as aided by great upheavals. Across the chasm of the violent French revolution a line of development could be traced: how much wiser, then, was the English revolution of 1688, which was such only in name and which merely took a natural evolutionary step! These were arguments that also fed reformers' hopes; for, looking back, it seemed as if mankind never did stop in its forward march. In the worst of times something was stirring, evolving, along the line of progress, which entitled each political or social advocate to expect that by aiding the natural course through a demonstration of its inevitability the evolution might be quicker and the desired Utopia nearer.

This line of reasoning is familiar to all who have ever heard its loud echo in twentieth-century Marxism. Marx inherited the faith in it from Romantic evolutionism. In his formative years it was a commonplace; and so were a number of systems designed (like his later socialism) to explain how man had reached his present state, social and intellectual. The first of these systems in point of time was that of Comte Henri de Saint-Simon, who compared the earliest times known to him (ancient Egypt) to infancy; and Greco-Roman times to youth. After a protracted adolescence, modern times expressed maturity. This "law of the three stages" prepared the mind for accepting the ultimate form of maturity, the last phase of evolution, which was to be a highly organized technocracy. Industrialists and bankers were to assure prosperity, peace, and a just distribution of technological plenty. The Saint-Simonian movement was widely influential throughout Europe in the 1820's and 1830's, both among the idealistic young and among speculative thinkers.

The magic force of three stages also inspired the great Hegel to a philosophy of history in which he sought, among other things, to explain post-Napoleonic Europe. His compass was wider than Saint-Simon's; his analysis went deeper into the confusions of the past and the impenetrability of the Eternal. An apostle of freedom, he divided the evolution of man into three steps by means of the degree to which the idea of freedom found embodiment. In the ancient or Oriental world, only one was free—the tyrant. In the medieval world, a few were free—the nobility, a class. In the modern world, all were free—the whole nation.

All men, that is, were *to be* free: there was work yet to do, and Hegel had views on the process of historical evolution. The recent past had shown unmistakably that the idea of freedom realized itself in mankind through conflict. A force or thesis (which could be an idea-bearing group as well as an embattled institution or people) claimed or held power—only to be met by an antithesis or opposition, equally determined to prevail. The outcome of the struggle was that regardless of any victory neither idea conquered; rather a synthesis resulted, which fused elements from each set purpose into a higher expression of mankind's unconscious brooding will.

Besides explaining history, Hegel's "dialectical" movement of opposites supplied, in his estimation, a new logic to replace the traditional one, which falsifies the world by showing it static: his was dynamic, able to deal with life, which is a perpetual Becoming. Hegelism in this most general sense has been one of the lasting contributions of Romanticist thought. From the New England Transcendentalists of Emerson's generation to the Chinese Marxists of today, the form (not the doctrine) of the philosophy of becoming has molded the minds of even the least philosophical.

The third evolutionary scheme contemporary with Hegel's is Auguste Comte's, in which the crowning stage is what its creator called Positivism. In the infancy of the race, says Comte, man is religious—he endows every object with indwelling gods. Later (again in those conveniently placed Middle Ages) man is metaphysical: he frames abstractions out of things and attributes the power of the thing to the abstraction. That is a great step forward, for it finally permits modern man, by dropping the abstraction, to reach the positive stage of thought: studying objects and their relationships simply as they are given by nature. To do so is to furnish positive knowledge or science. Positivism made many adherents, whose sense of historical evolution led them in various reformist directions. Proving a point while seeming only to unfold truth was the common feature of all the evolutionary histories that explained the present and forecast the future; in a word, it was the *genetic method,* fruitful, convenient, easy to misuse, but obviously the only fitting one for an age peculiarly sensitive to the energies of life.

Much has been written about the politics of Romanticism as distinguished from the speculative philosophies that spanned all of recorded time and offered a stopping place for human history where conflict was to cease and freedom without effort was to ensue. On the more mundane ground of politics, we ask: Were the less sibylline minds of the Romantic period liberal or reactionary? Did their work promote or retard the great evolution toward the parliamentary, democratic nation-state? The actual struggle of parties belongs to another chapter. At this point only beliefs concern us, and even more than beliefs, their relation to the main course of Romanticist art and opinion.

That relation, apparently, offers difficulties to some cultural historians, because they find undoubted Romanticists on both sides of the great divide. Scott was a confirmed Tory; Byron and Hazlitt were radicals. Victor Hugo and Lamennais ran the gamut from reaction through liberalism to socialism. The young revolutionists Wordsworth and Coleridge turned more and more conservative with advancing age. In Germany the confusion seems even greater. There are proponents of the self-contained nation and corporate state, like Fichte; cosmopolitan liberals like Heine; anarchists of every complexion; and converts to Catholicism who work back from liberal to reactionary positions. Obviously, statistics about thinkers mean nothing; each

individual career must be studied and understood in the light of temperament and circumstance. Is it then possible at all to speak of the politics of
Romanticism? Diffident observers are ready to deny unity to the movement
because in its leaders practical goals shifted and diverged.

The unity is there, but these observers look for it in the wrong place.
What unites a movement such as Romanticism, which virtually embraces
the whole age, is not the many solutions brought forward by individuals
and groups, but the concentration of all on a few issues. A unity of temper
has already been shown, together with the method of discovery it applied.
In politics the temper is the same, but the methods are many. The Romantics wanted for themselves and their peoples the freedom, diversity,
self-reliance, and opportunity for self-development which they praised and
used in their works of art and historiography. But they differed as to the
means of achieving them. Yet nearly all agreed that revolution must not go
on ad infinitum, for the very sake of the liberties sought.

But what was the true bulwark of those liberties? Some said monarchy
and mother church—and among them were Balzac, Bonald, Joseph de
Maistre, and John Henry Newman. Others said nothing short of universal
suffrage and a republic: Victor Hugo was one of those. The many who
turned nationalist, especially in Germany and Italy (and we may count
Fichte, Hegel, Mazzini, and Manzoni in this group) were convinced that
without a strong unified political state coextensive with the historic culture
no freedoms could survive. Past experience lent color to their view: they
had been invaded, cut up, trampled on for centuries. Some were now willing to accept tyranny rather than helpless disunity.

Finally there were the partisans of a neomedievalism (the kinship
here is with Burke's and Scott's Toryism) who saw that in large aggregates
men are rootless and unhappy. To avoid social atomism, men must work
and be ruled by traditions rather than bureaucracies, live on a familiar spot
of ground rather than in anonymous cities. Carlyle, the introducer of German Romanticism to England, became the tireless expounder of this view.

If one adds the individual variations on these large themes, the politics
of Romanticism present the usual cacophony of any political period. But it
is instructive to regard this grand debate as uncommonly consistent under
its surface confusion. For a glance ahead shows us that from the French
Revolution to the Russian, the search for freedom that inspired all Romantics led Western man to each of the solutions proposed in that earlier
time. First, the complete laissez-faire of liberalism was won and found
wanting. Then followed "Tory democracy" to protect the underdog from
the rugged and ruthless liberal. That proved insufficient, and socialisms and
communisms of every kind flooded Europe. The corporate state, totali-

tarian state, welfare state have by now tried in myriad ways to combine elements of all the hoped-for freedoms, including the utopian. The only plan that has not been gone back to is that of Church and King in close alliance. It is the only one, for by the 1960's there were signs that anarchism was once more a tempting hypothesis, especially to the young. Meanwhile it is clear that raging-blind nationalism still seems to many dissenters, even within the old unified countries, the key to all earthly blessings.

It is curious but true, therefore, that side by side with the abstract ideal of liberty which we draw from the legacy of the Enlightenment, the realized or imagined embodiments of that ideal that we still battle about or die for go back to the exuberant period that followed the French Revolution.

In one other realm likewise, the realm of art, Romanticism first brought about changes that we still take for granted as the normal order of things. There is much about Romantic art that we decry or despise and many assumptions underlying it that we wish to see discarded, but we have not yet gone beyond them. To take the most striking, it is from the time of Romanticism that art and artists have been regarded as of enormous social and spiritual importance. Gibbon would have smiled at the idea. Today art is commonly taken as the sign of true greatness in the life of a nation; art is the measure of "a healthy society"; also a precious, eternal possession of mankind; the artist (rivaled only by the great scientist) is an extraordinary being, divinely inspired and accordingly privileged. The genius, in short, is the first superman, and his deliverances have the force of revelation. The religion of art, art the twin of religion, are phrases that occur early in the Romantic century. Hegel and Walter Scott, sober men both, were not ashamed to make avowals of such feelings. Their first full-blown, widespread manifestation was Shakespeare-worship.

Nor was this Romanticist fervor what a later age would call aestheticism. The genius was worshiped for what he could create, which even in that age of renewal and exploration seemed miraculous. In technical innovations alone the Romanticists must be credited with an astonishing performance. What Goethe, Wordsworth, Hugo, and Pushkin did with language; Constable, Géricault, Bonington, and Delacroix with color and line; Beethoven, Weber, Berlioz, Chopin with rhythm and sound; Scott, Balzac, Stendhal, and Gogol with social and psychological observation— all this seems hardly believable even after 125 years.

So rich indeed was their output that they accustomed the Western world to another novelty, another aspect of the evolutionary view of the world: they created the Cult of the New and forced the public to accept pluralism in style. After the Romanticists it became a settled expectation that every succeeding wave of art should be new and that every individual artist should be original. Whatever the actuality of art in earlier ages, the professed aim was one style at a time, coupled with "perfection," which meant approaching the single ideal for the genre, not diversity but unity. Romanticism turned all these roles inside out, and in so doing helped create a rift between the bulk of polite society (the "philistines") and those who by taste or snobbery support the artistic avant-garde in its ever more startling innovations.

That split is of course reproduced in the difference between the bohemian life of the artist and those "bourgeois values" which by the end of the nineteenth century very few dared to defend openly. In the Art for Art's Sake movement, which should really be named Art for Life's Sake— art the redeemer of life—the bourgeois, ridiculed and condemned for the previous seventy-five years, could fittingly cry out, like the pagan emperor, "Thou hast conquered, O Esthetician!" So far as culture in the main is concerned, the central tendency of Romanticism in art is unbroken from its inception in 1790 to the First World War; and indeed to the present day.

What does modify it in detail about the midpoint of the last century is that all of Europe undergoes the great disillusionment and loss of hope after the failure of the revolutions of 1848. What this failure betokened is told in another chapter. Here the point is that the universal fear and despair—in both victors and vanquished—engendered in the artistic consciousness of Europe a revulsion against the enthusiasms, the energies of the period just preceding.

The need was felt for a shrinking of consciousness, a return to what was plain and possible; and as this more assured ground could only be the tangible and material, the name Realism was given to the new movement in literature and painting. It concentrated on the commonplace in order to transmute it into art, just as the new politics concentrated on things rather than principles. Realpolitik was the politics of material advantage, divorced as far as might be from loyalties and beliefs. "Look," said everyone to himself, "where faith and hope, liberalism and dreams of progress, have led us—to catastrophe. Give it up. Swallow your pride; forget your visions." That is the lesson of *Madame Bovary* and all aggressive Realism.

Yet in the works of the spirit, that mood was temporary. To it succeeded a stoical Neo-Classicism, also of short duration, and a Neo-Romanticism variously called Symbolism, Impressionism, Aestheticism. In literature, the "naturalistic" novel itself partook of the earlier exploratory zest of Romanticism, and in point of technique the later work in all genres and arts clearly owed its genesis to this or that element (sometimes a passing thought) in the earlier, inclusive, Romantic movement: evolution, descent with modification, could thereby be demonstrated again. Only now, after

still more revolutions and world wars, does its force seem to be close to
spent.

For Further Reading

Rousseau, *Confession of Faith of a Savoyard Priest.*
Scott, *Rob Roy.*
Delacroix, *Journals* (W. Pach trans.)
Goethe, *Faust* (Alice Raphael trans.)
Berlioz, *Memoirs* (David Cairns trans.)
Hegel, *Lectures on the Philosophy of History.*

10   From Liberalism to Democracy

The Congress of Vienna worked hard to make a settlement that should
bring lasting peace to Europe after a quarter-century of war. Its twin
principles of legitimacy and compensation were meant to pacify as many
peoples and rulers as possible. Yet the new era that began after Waterloo
in June, 1815, witnessed from the start a struggle among at least five
overlapping groups, not counting the divergent interests of the great
powers. Generally speaking, everybody approached the new age as the
opportunity to carry on and settle Unfinished Business.

To the extent that the aristocracy, in France and elsewhere, could feel
that it had won the long battle with the Revolution and Napoleon, they
argued: We are the victors, we must work to restore the old regime. The
liberals thought: We have had to make concessions, but the last word has
not been said; we must work to complete the design sketched by the
enlightened thinkers of the last century. The radical wing of the liberal party
was sure that only political democracy—not just the parliamentarism of
the upper bourgeoisie—would satisfy the needs of the people. And among
the people and the democrats were some who denied the validity of mere
political change. The system must be recast, by reform or revolution, so as
to abolish poverty and inaugurate *economic* freedom through socialism.

Add to these demands the nationalist passions aroused by both the new
romanticist temper and the cumulative hostility to the Napoleonic invasions, and it becomes clear why the first half of the nineteenth century in
Europe was a time of uneasy equilibrium punctuated by armed revolts and
repressions. Nationalism naturally found an enemy in the old dynastic

A.D.

1815	Waterloo; Peace by Congress of Vienna
1819	Carlsbad Decrees against liberal youth and intellectuals
1820–1830	The Carbonari revolutionists in France and Italy
1821	Death of Napoleon
1822–1823	Congress of Verona and Spanish revolution put down by the French
1823	Monroe Doctrine
1824	Death of Byron at Missolonghi
1828	Jacksonian democracy in power in the United States
1829	The Greek Revolution succeeds and is ratified by the powers
1830	Revolutions in France, Belgium, the Rhineland, Italy, and Brazil
1832	The English Reform Bill passed after a near-revolution
1831–1834	Revolutions in Poland, Spain, and Italy
1840	Napoleon's ashes brought to Paris
1840–1848	Socialism: Louis Blanc; Chartism and Parliamentary rule
1848	Revolutions in France, Germany, Austria, and Italy
1851	The Great Exhibition in London
1852	The Second French Empire: democracy, the welfare state, and dictatorship

interests, which viewed territorial concerns in other than national terms. As for the other four parties, each viewed the other three as irreconcilable. Despite the great fatigue that follows long wars, despite a general desire to "cope with revolution" and substitute other means of social change, it was apparent that a showdown would come sooner or later, because in truth the legitimacy invoked by the powers at Vienna did not exist. Its former possessors had lost it irrevocably, and the new claimants (liberals, democrats, socialists) had not yet made good their claims.

No alliances were possible among the upstarts; their creeds were too divergent. And what is worse, the warring groups were shortly to fall under the hidden sway of a material force that had nothing to do with creeds, passions, memories, or hopes—the Industrial Revolution. Out of these disparate movements a one-to-one opposition gradually emerged: the emotion of nationalism came to be pitted against the desire for political liberalism. This crystallization of feeling around one or another goal occurred at different times in different countries, but the history of regimes and revolutions between Metternich's Congress at Vienna in 1815 and his flight from the same city in 1848 can be read as the triumph of nationalist feeling over liberalism.

Even the distant Americas, North and South, went through the same collective emotion, which testified to the belief—perhaps it was nothing more than an instinct—that man could better win his freedom through nationhood than through political machinery. The sensation of being kin, of being numerous, strong, and self-determining, seemed to offer a surer hope of social bliss than the complex, laborious effort of working a parliamentary system. These generalities—or rather, clues to a broad understanding not only of the period under review but also of the travail through which the wider world is now going—must now be tested by the recital of events in the principal countries of Europe until 1848.

The practical device attached to the Vienna peace in hopes of making it permanent was the Quadruple Alliance, a banding together of Austria, Russia, Prussia, and Great Britain for maintaining stability. The powers were to meet in periodic congresses and decide on armed intervention, if it seemed appropriate to preserve the terms of the treaty. In the event, those congresses only stimulated resistance against what came to be called "Metternich's system." The system was his chiefly in the sense that it was central Europe and Italy that kept trying to shake off repression. In the Hapsburg empire, Hungarians, Croatians (Yugoslavs), Czechs, Poles, and Germans had caught the nationalist fever. It expressed itself in journalism and plays, in student societies and professional groups. Censorship and police control were imposed to uproot doctrine and prevent the exchange of ideas with other countries. By an ill-judged policy, troops from one nationality were sent to garrison another, both groups of course being strengthened in their hostility by these enforced contacts.

Outside Austria, Metternich sought to control the similar patchwork of "the Germanies" to the north and Italy to the south. On this axis, there was not a self-contained nation between the Baltic and the Mediterranean; Austrians and Spaniards governed pieces of Italy, and to the east Russia played the same role of unwanted guardian over her border states, Finland, Latvia, Lithuania, and part of Poland. Against the liberalism at work within this conglomerate, Metternich secured from a congress at Carlsbad in 1819 a set of decrees muzzling the universities and the press, providing for a spy system, and forbidding the grant of any constitution "at variance with the monarchical principle." This was a rejoinder to student demonstrations in honor of Luther and to the assassination of the playwright Kotzebue, who had been a spy in the Russian service.

Germany was held down for a time, but Italy uprose. A rebellion in Naples in 1820 forced the Spanish Bourbon King Ferdinand IV to grant a constitution. Behind this overturn was the massed force of Carbonari or pretended charcoal burners. They were in fact young liberals and nationalists, who met in the woods and plotted resistance. The Congress of Troppau declared for intervention, and the next year at Laibach, the king of Naples "invited" the Austrian army into his realm to "restore order." This was done, with the usual sequel of fierce persecution. Comparison with modern methods of conducting international affairs shows that though the means have multiplied and the time lag has shortened, the scheme remains unimproved.

Other revolts followed in northern Italy (where the enemy was Austrian Hapsburg, not Spanish Bourbon); in Russia (where the once liberal czar, taught in youth by French rationalists, had turned reactionary); in Great Britain (where industrial unrest was harnessed to liberalism); in Spain (where the army mutinied and thus set off a full-scale uprising that forced a second constitution down a Spanish Bourbon throat); and in Portuguese America (where Brazil shook off the tutelage of the mother country and made itself into an independent empire).

Within a decade of the "permanent" Peace of Vienna, revolution had become endemic. Beyond the scope of Metternich's system, the Serbs won the first skirmishes toward national liberation from the Turks and within a few years more the Greeks did likewise. This time, however, popular opinion throughout western Europe was on the side of the Greeks. Lord Byron was in the peninsula supplying money and working for unity, and three years after his death at Missolonghi the great powers not only guaranteed an independent kingdom of Greece, but also gave virtual autonomy to Serbia and the Rumanian provinces of Moldavia and Wallachia.

Freedom was obviously easier to bear at a distance and when it was freedom from another power. This exception to Metternich's system was especially clear when Great Britain broke away from the Quadruple Alliance of 1823 and supported President Monroe in his declaration supporting the independence of the South American colonies from Spain: these new nations might be easier to trade with if they were not Spanish but free. And though Britain was neither giving up colonialism nor dealing liberally with her own dissidents at home, her nineteenth-century tradition of supporting national self-determination abroad had begun.

Yet by 1829 the meaning of so much independence won and condoned was still far from clear. Was the political and emotional response of European rulers and ruled based on a growing love of *free nations,* or was it inspired by the love of *free citizens?* It took two events of wider scope to suggest a likely answer. And to come to the first of these one must ask what had been happening since 1815 to the chief culprit and warmonger, which it had been the object of the Peace of Vienna to neutralize and contain, namely France.

At the outset it was in France that the sharpest conflict occurred between the victorious, "legitimate" aristocrats and the defeated liberals. Though the restored Bourbon king, Louis XVIII, wanted to pursue a middle-of-the-road policy, he was not allowed to. The charter he had promulgated in 1814 (before the return of Napoleon for a hundred days) guaranteed representative government, religious freedom, and civil rights. But after Waterloo, the reactionary wing of the King's party, known as "ultras," demanded a return to the *ancien régime.* Without waiting for the King, they took matters into their own hands and conducted a nation-wide persecution of liberals—a "White Terror" to match the red of Robespierre's time. During this purge, elections were held under the charter and, in the absence of liberal leaders (most of them in hiding), the chamber that was returned was manned by ultras. There followed a year's worth of repressive legislation: the press was controlled, divorce disallowed, and an ad hoc judicial system set up to protract the political purge. So extreme were these measures that in order to keep his hold on the mass of the people the King had to dissolve the Chamber. The new majority proved to be moderate, which left ultras and liberals as ineffectual minorities.

Since one naturally associates liberalism with representative government, it is necessary to understand at this precise juncture what made the French Charter of 1814 ephemeral and useless as a dike against the tide of liberalism. Ultimately, of course, later and more liberal constitutions suffered the same fate under the pressures of democracy and socialism. What is true of that first charter is true of all other instruments that limit or seem to limit the sway of popular sovereignty. For popular sovereignty is the great ideal legacy of the French Revolution of 1789, confirmed in his special way by Napoleon, and productive of the series of revolutions with which Europe and the world have had to deal ever since—the democratic evolutions based on universal manhood suffrage, and the dictatorial kind, by plebiscite, by the proletariat or by any other mode of populism. The latest is the revolution by direct action for continuous, total participation, in which the sovereign people exercises its rights in the manner that these descriptive words imply.

Back in 1815, the French Charter, like those extorted by force from this or that Metternichian satellite, restricted popular sovereignty by property qualifications. Only those who paid 1,000 francs a year in direct taxes were entitled to vote. What this meant can be measured by the fact that when under the moderate royalists, the sum was reduced to 500 francs, it shifted the majority from the aristocrats to the upper bourgeoisie. Extending the franchise by lowering property qualifications was thus the first step as well as the perennial demand of liberals in France, England, and elsewhere down to the day of universal suffrage.

The second liberal requirement is a free press, for the essence of liberal politics is to drum new ideas into the popular mind. European liberalism is inherently a concern of the articulate—students, journalists, university and professional men; in short, persons who live by ideas more than by custom, to whom change, reform, progress, are vivid realities, and who invent the political machinery that progress demands. The moderate royalists in France were so far in tune with the times as to liberalize the press laws and to institute national conscription for the army, a measure tending toward recognition of the principle of social equality which Napoleon had made so potent a political force.

An integral part of the liberal and egalitarian program is the removal of disabilities once imposed on special groups. In 1815 the Congress of Vienna had been liberal to the extent of decreeing the abolition of the slave trade. The liberal constitutions of the ensuing years variously freed Dissenters, Jews, or one-time political exiles from various restrictions. The conviction grew that any citizen had both civil and political rights. The only question was whether a regime of free-for-all such as liberal theory envisaged could show any stability. Soon after the mild relaxation of controls legislated by the moderate royalists in France, the Duc de Berri, the King's nephew, was assassinated. An immediate revulsion followed the outrage, and new laws reversed the previous trend. The election procedure was complicated by a provision that gave a double vote to the thousand-franc taxpayers, and the term of the legislature was lengthened to seven years. The Church was given a stranglehold on education, and the rudiments of a police state, equipped with internal espionage, were set up. To clinch the reaction, France was assigned the task of military intervention in Spain. A year later, in 1824, Louis XVIII died, leaving the throne to his brother, Charles X, long the leader of the ultras.

These typical details of the seesaw between liberty and repression in post-revolutionary Europe suffice to show how and why Europe in the first half of the nineteenth century lived either in fear or in hopes of further revolution. The example of the United States, where the election of Andrew Jackson as President in 1828 appeared as a step toward democracy, could not serve countries in which the very principle of representative government was disputed by half the population. England, as we shall see, barely avoided a revolution like the one that was becoming inevitable in France.

The decisive overthrow of the Bourbons, symbols of legitimacy, took place in France because of several converging reasons: France had a century of liberal ideas behind her; France was the initiator of revolutions; France had not one but half a dozen doctrines of reform; France had a bourgeoisie with a powerful motive of self-interest inciting to revolution. That motive was simple: the aristocrats led by Charles X had voted themselves a large indemnity for the loss of their estates suffered in the 1790's. To pay the indemnity, the state lowered the interest rate on the national debt, that is, took the money out of the pocket of the bondholders, mostly well-to-do bourgeois. The elections of 1827 brought into the Chamber a bourgeois majority, which the King disregarded. He appointed as minister an émigré of the old days, as stubborn as the King; and when the conflict between Chamber and minister grew tense, Charles issued ordinances against the press and the chamber and called for new elections.

The ordinances did not last a day: journalists and publicists at once called for a general insurrection in the name of popular sovereignty, and in three days' fighting forced the abdication of Charles. Workingmen fought side by side with students, lawyers, and soldiers, and disposed forever of divine-right monarchy in France. The next king was not *of France* but *of the French*. Louis-Philippe, a cousin of the former reigning line, owed his position, if not to an election, at least to an invitation. The republican party was still too urban and intellectual to prevail. The "country," which is to say the peasantry, was still wedded to the old forms, and the liberal leaders from the upper bourgeoisie were content with a king provided he was constitutional, as in England. In these characteristics, the French revolution of 1830, quickly imitated throughout the Continent, is as it were the diagram of the first effective advance of liberalism to catch up with the unfinished business of 1789.

The events that paralleled in England the forward march apparent in western and central Europe betoken a different kind of arrears. To be sure, England had for forty years contended with domestic adherents of the original French Revolution; indeed among the educated there were men (such as Hazlitt and Byron) who saw even in Napoleon the principle of liberty at work. But the great popular feeling that brought England to the verge of revolution between 1830 and 1832 was due to intrinsic factors as well as to imported ideas. The chief cause was a shift in population and wealth which made the English Parliament visibly unrepresentative. While the new factory towns of Manchester, Birmingham, Leeds, and Sheffield grew in size and the factory owners in influence, the "rotten boroughs" (whose voters were for sale) and "pocket boroughs" (sometimes uninhabited) returned Tory landowners to the House of Commons.

There were, moreover, whole classes that had long been exasperated by Tory complacency: the disfranchised Catholics, the nonconformist Dissenters (disabled on religious technicalities), the intellectual classes (philosophical radicals such as William Cobbett, liberal economists such as James Mill, law reformers such as Jeremy Bentham, theoretical democrats such as Francis Place the "philosophical tailor")—none of them, under the unreformed parliament, stood any chance to exercise a fraction of power.

Finally, the new business interests, typified in such a man as Richard Cobden, the cotton manufacturer, knew that the state had long been inefficiently run by the squires, the bishops, and the lords. "Economic reform" had been called for—and defeated—as far back as the 1780's. It was time for England, on the threshold of the greatest productive expansion in history, to set its house in order, beginning with the political representation of its most energetic leaders, the new industrialists.

These were aided, on one side by the equally new working class, whose lot in the cities was dismal and precarious, and on the other by the Whig party, which having long been out of office saw in the current agitation an opportunity to reenter. As early as 1819, an influential Whig, Lord John Russell, proposed giving the vote to the manufacturing class, but it was only ten years later that Earl Grey, the party leader, made reform a stated Whig policy. The Tories in power did not respond in the approved way of stealing the opposition's thunder. Their liberalism was for export only, as in the support of President Monroe and the rebellious Latin American colonies. It was with great difficulty that a few concessions were made in the late 1820's, notably that of relieving the Dissenters and Catholics of their political disabilities. For the rest, as the Duke of Wellington, the Prime Minister, maintained in 1830, the English Constitution was perfect as it stood.

But the July Days of that year in Paris threw a new light on the situation. The country rang with noisy demonstrations, at first spontaneous, soon well led and sustained. Tories in the Commons became nervous and lost confidence in Wellington. Earl Grey formed a new ministry and introduced the first Reform Bill. It was defeated in 1831, but in fresh elections Grey was returned, bringing with him a second Reform Bill. It passed the Commons and failed in the Lords. When King William IV

refused to create enough new peers to override that opposition, Grey resigned and Wellington attempted a comeback.

It was then that the English liberal "revolution" took place. Intellectuals of the radical school joined with the manufacturers in stumping the
country and organizing protest meetings. Francis Place advocated a run on
the banks; other speakers urged the nonpayment of taxes. In the crowded
midlands, the workers were persuaded that their interest, from the price of
bread to the continuity of employment, depended on sending their bosses
to Parliament—which must be reformed before that desirable goal could be
reached.

With the sound of mass meetings in their ears the Tories gave up. Earl
Grey and his Whigs took power once more and won from the King a
grudging assent to the creation of new (Whig) peers to neutralize the
Lords' expected veto of a third Reform Bill. The threat sufficed, the Tory
Lords choosing to be reformed rather than swamped. By becoming law, the
Reform Bill of 1832, like the Paris revolution of 1830, reset in motion the
liberal transformation of Europe which the Vienna settlement had sought
to halt. Once past dead center, one reform bill begot another; each stimulated fresh demands on the part of groups deeming themselves neglected;
democracy, equality, socialism became logical necessities. No obstacles of
mind or matter could impede their forward march, though the path lay
across rivers of blood.

The provisions of the great bill of 1832 did not of course foreshadow
such consequences. The reform got rid of rotten boroughs, roughly re-
adjusting representation to population. The big new cities were given seats,
and at the same time the franchise was extended and simplified. In the
towns a voter had to pay a rent of £10 a year; in the country he had to
own land of the same rental value or be a tenant of land worth £50 a year.
It is estimated that these changes increased the electorate by 1½ per cent.
Voting continued to be by open ballot, so convenient for bribery and
coercion; but at least the polling period was reduced from two weeks to
two days, which both lessened the opportunity for traffic in votes and made
elections more sober occasions.

Besides dislodging with a minimum of violence the old English oligarchy, the chief by-products of Reform were: the liberation of the mu-
nicipalities from the control of self-perpetuating cliques; the steady reform
of the criminal law; and the emancipation of the Jews on the same terms as
the Catholics and the Dissenters.

On the Continent, the one firm result of the wave of 1830 revolutions
was the separation of Belgium from Holland, a victory of nationalism

rather than of liberalism: from the start the union imposed at Vienna had been unworkable. After some days' fighting in Brussels, in 1830, France and England joined forces to compel the Dutch king to let go his vassal state. Belgium became a liberal kingdom in its turn, but pledged to neutrality under the guarantee of all the great powers. It was the violation of that agreement in 1914 which symbolizes the breakdown of the supremacy of Europe.

Elsewhere after 1830, conservatism apparently recovered the upper hand and annulled all the concessions it had hastily made to the revolutionists. In the Germanies, particularly the Rhineland, liberals had extorted constitutions like the one France had enjoyed fifteen years earlier and had just replaced by a better one. This relationship is significant: the revolutions of Central Europe correspond in character to the advances made ten or fifteen years earlier in the westernmost countries, and down to the present this gap in time has not been closed.

In Italy, 1830 liberalism failed in the same way, thanks to the cooperation of the Hapsburgs and the pope. Russia suppressed the Poles' uprising of 1831 and seized the chance to make an end of Polish independence by annexing the kingdom, thus laying up for Europe an inexhaustible source of misery. As for the minorities ruled by Austria, their mutterings were still too indistinct to show anything more than the presence of a nationalist discontent which has in fact never yet been appeased.

One concludes that what sanguine liberals saw as political progress—the irresistible advance of enlightened mind against the forces of darkness and oppressive reaction—was in truth a double confusion and misunderstanding. On the one hand, the passion of nationalism innocently assumed the guise of love of liberty; on the other, the constitutions sought as the instrument of liberation were rarely matched by the necessary political maturity of the populations. Events proved that when national groups won freedom they did not scruple to oppress other minorities. Written constitutions did not of themselves guarantee order, justice, and civil rights. Throughout this tragicomedy the fraud was largely unconscious. Kings deceived their peoples "for their own good"; popular leaders adopted liberal slogans "as a first step" toward national selfhood; and the bourgeois who won the full franchise (as in England and France) mistook *their* coming to power as the final achievement of freedom for mankind.

On this last point the contrary demonstration was not slow in coming. Since the 1820's workmen in Paris, Manchester, Berlin, Rome, Warsaw, Naples, and Turin had fought side by side with students and journalists against the troops of the embattled monarchies. Indeed, ever since the original upheaval of 1789, the common people had been the great anonymous force behind every attempt to change the existing order. But by the

1830's the working class, whether industrialized as in England and Belgium, or still partly an artisan class, began to recognize that its lavishing of blood on the barricades did not much advance its prospects. Aristocrat or bourgeois, the men on top remained more intent on their own interests than on the workers'. In fact, the bourgeois was in several respects the less likely to favor the workers. His views (and his legislation) on economic matters were the so-called liberal ones, which regarded labor as a commodity and advocated laissez-faire as the healthiest state. This meant leaving the worker to shift for himself—out of work in bad times, starving when ill or old, dependent on the toil of his wife and small children to earn a bare subsistence. Compared with this rugged freedom of the manufacturing town, life on the land under a resident squire or lord was likely to be more bearable and secure.

These things being so, leaders and theorists of working-class liberty soon came to the fore. Their agitation followed two divergent lines. One set of reformers, divided among groups using various names, wanted to re-make society from the ground up. They planned—and carried out—utopian schemes of community life, in which everyone had a function and a reward. Prosperity and happiness were ensured by obedience to the rule *and* the ruler of the utopia. Such schemes, fathered by Saint-Simon or Fourier or Cabet or (most successfully) by Robert Owen in Scotland, might be described as benevolent despotism adapting itself to socialist ideals. The Saint-Simonian propagandists enjoyed a great vogue throughout Europe down to the 1840's. The Owenites and others inaugurated a remarkable number of communities in the United States. And their writings as well as those of purely theoretical socialists, communists, and anarchists such as Sismondi, Bell, Gray, Moses Hess, and Proudhon were the first to attack the free-for-all doctrine of liberal economics. In so doing they determined the course of the later socialist theory which leads to Russian communism and the welfare state.

These early reformers were disposed to act directly on their beliefs, but without violence: simply show the world how to reorganize itself by giving it a model. The second and much larger working-class movement had faith in representative institutions; the object of its struggle was to make them completely democratic. In England, this doctrine was known as Chartism, from the "People's Charter" of liberties which was to establish the true Parliament and open the way to all needed reforms. In substance, Chartism boiled down to six demands, all but the first of which have become commonplaces of political democracy: (1) annual elections for parliament, (2) universal manhood suffrage, (3) the secret ballot, (4) salaries for members of parliament, (5) equal electoral districts, and (6) the removal of property qualifications for members of parliament.

To achieve these goals the Chartists were ready to petition the Queen and demonstrate in public. They felt no gratitude to the men who had pushed through the reform of 1832. Lord John Russell, who thought Parliament sufficiently reformed for decades to come, was derided as "Finality Jack." By the mid-1840's mere *liberalism* was already out of date, inadequate to the swamping needs. The railroad mania proved the frivolity of parliament and capitalism combined; the Irish famine showed that political problems were grounded in economic organization. Only the rock-bottom principle of one man, one vote, could ever give to the most numerous, most indispensable class in every country the leverage necessary to bring about a decent society. That society must be democratic, and some said republican as well.

The main objection to democracy was that it would put the state at the mercy of the ignorant and the illiterate. From antiquity it was well known that the mob was the ruin of civilizations. The rejoinder was: remove the mob's ignorance, make the masses literate, "educate your masters." But the time was not ripe. Too many thought it still possible to fend off the tide. The liberal manufacturing class, having arduously made its way to the top, felt that others should do the same. When during these same "Hungry Forties," the French lower middle and working classes were grumbling about the restricted franchise, about the feeble (non-nationalist) foreign policy, about the dullness of daily life, the liberal prime minister Guizot, despite his integrity, intelligence, and willingness to extend the free educational system, could only advise the dissidents to get rich and thus qualify for a seat in the Chamber.

In England or in France, the formula did not meet the case. Nobody needed to be told to get rich and nobody believed that everybody could. What is more, the clash of interest and outlook between the old aristocracy and the industrial bourgeoisie (quite different from the great merchant families) was driving the aristocrats to side with the people against the middle layer. Protecting the factory worker through legislation became a Tory aim, at once charitable to the worker and annoying to the entrepreneur. Hence the precarious internal situation of the two countries that led the Western world. Both the ideas they broached and the tremors they felt agitated the rest of Europe. From Scandinavia to Spain and from Prussia to Italy, men, books, parties, plots, demands, outbreaks, and defeats produced a harsh orchestration whose crescendo was reached in the quasi-universal revolutions of 1848.

England, as usual, escaped the worst of the upheaval and was in fact the exiles' sanctuary as the Continental uprisings were successively crushed. English Chartism failed quietly: the great parade and petition to the Queen was doused in torrential rain. Ten thousand special constables (including Louis Napoleon, future emperor of the French) ensured order in the London streets. In France the Republic established manhood suffrage but, rent by dissension and unemployment, succumbed to the coup d'état of Louis Napoleon. In central Europe, nationalist rivalries were played off against one another to their common destruction. And the hopeful yet divided Frankfort Assembly seemed to prove that men of ideas were incapable of transacting parliamentary business, let alone run a modern nation. To the south, Mazzini's Young Italy movement had inspired multiple outbreaks with which both the new Pope Pius IX and the king of Sardinia, Charles Albert, appeared to sympathize. But soon reaction set in. The pope changed his mind and Charles Albert was defeated by an Austrian army. Count Metternich, it is true, had fled Vienna forever, and Louis Philippe abdicated, but the system of Europe appeared unshaken. Under that appearance the reality was that Western culture had come to one of its periodic turning points.

Needless to say, these revolutions, protracted through nearly four years, did not mean the same thing for all the nations affected. The common turning involved only two facts that were clear. One was that henceforth nationalism proved a more unifying and hence a more potent ideal than liberty. A second was that idealism itself suffered a permanent loss of momentum. Among men of thought there was after 1848 a failure of nerve. The appeal to "practicality," to force and numbers, to the "politics of things" (realpolitik), to cynicism and the mass mind, replaced the earlier faith in the perfectibility of man, itself premised on his essential goodness. Liberalism, democracy, universal education and welfare did become features of Western civilization after 1870, but there is a sense in which the Enlightenment and the "principles of 1789" come to an end in 1848.

For Further Reading

G. L. Dickinson, *Revolution and Reaction in Modern France.*
Tocqueville, *Democracy in America.*
Sydney Smith, *Peter Plymley Letters.*
J. S. Mill, *Autobiography.*
Louis Blanc, *History of Ten Years.*
Karl Marx, *Communist Manifesto.*

11   The Rise of Socialism

Throughout the history of the Western world, men had from time to time imagined a golden age. Usually it was placed in the past, but sometimes it was a vision of the future—a utopia in which perfection was realized and which, by indirection, was a criticism of the shortcomings or iniquities of the world in which the critics had to live. Christianity could be a powerful stimulus to this kind of thinking, through its call to love and moral perfection and, more concretely, on the basis of hints in the Bible and practice among early Christians, through the ideal of property held communally not individually; this ideal was attained in some respects by medieval monasticism and was advocated, with terrible repercussions, by some more radical reformers in the sixteenth century and by such millennarian groups as the Diggers in seventeenth-century England.

In the early nineteenth century there appeared the first advocates of a new tradition that offered both a criticism of present-day society and a blueprint for a perfect future society; by the 1830's the name socialism had been coined for it. It was, however, sharply differentiated from earlier forms of utopian thought. For one thing, although there were specifically Christian forms of it, socialism was as a rule aggressively secular; for another, it held out for the first time the possibility of realization. The sources of this new confidence can be found, no longer in Christianity, but in the thought of the eighteenth century—in its humanity and secularism, in its confidence in the possibility of human and social engineering, and, among a few Enlightenment writers, in its faith in perfectibility—and in the French Revolution. Although the French Revolution was a liberal, not a socialist, revolution, a few aspects of it provided later socialists with inspiration and heroes: the Jacobins had stringently regulated the economy in the interests of both justice and equality, and in 1795–1796 François Noel Babeuf (who, characteristically, called himself Caius Gracchus Babeuf) led a rising, the Conspiracy of Equals, that was frankly communist and that, through a lieutenant, Filippo Michele Buonarotti, transmitted a conspiratorial tradition within which nineteenth-century socialism could, indeed often had to, flourish. But these examples did not exhaust the socialist significance of the French Revolution; far more important was the fact of the Revolution itself, proof that society could be altered and altered suddenly, if not by merely applying psychological and social theory, then by violence.

A.D.   1795–1796   Babeuf leads the proto-communist "Conspiracy of
                   Equals" in France
          1813   Robert Owen publishes *A New View of Society*
          1817   Ricardo's *Principles of Political Economy and Taxa-
                   tion* published, the definitive statement of classical
                   political economy
          1818   Karl Marx born at Trier in the Rhineland
          1832   Death of G. W. F. Hegel
          1840   Proudhon publishes *What Is Property?*
          1843   Marx expelled from Germany
          1844   Marx meets Friedrich Engels
          1845   Engels publishes *The Condition of the Working Class
                   in England in 1844*
          1848   Marx and Engels publish the *Communist Manifesto;*
                   European revolutions
          1849   Marx settles in England
          1864   Ferdinand Lassalle killed in a duel; International
                   Working Men's Association (First International)
                   founded in London
          1867   Marx publishes first volume of *Capital*
          1871   Commune established in Paris following French de-
                   feat in Franco-Prussian War
       1872–1876   Torn by internal divisions, the First International
                   gradually disintegrates
          1875   Social Democratic Party founded in Germany
          1883   Fabian Society founded in London; Marx dies
          1889   Second International founded; Eduard Bernstein
                   proposes his "revisionist" departure from ortho-
                   dox Marxism
          1893   Independent Labour party founded in England
          1900   Labour Representation Committee founded in Eng-
                   land, leading to formation of the Labour party in
                   1906
          1905   Russian Revolution
          1908   Georges Sorel publishes *Reflections on Violence*
          1914   Divisions in socialist parties on the question of the
                   war result in general support of the war and col-
                   lapse of Second International

The French Revolution belongs, however, to the prehistory of socialism; its real history takes its rise in the new economic circumstances of Europe. It will not do to invoke the Industrial Revolution and to let it go at that; although Owen in England and Saint-Simon in France were prophets of a new industrial order, in neither country was industrialism far enough advanced to allow it to be put forward as a sufficient explanation of their fertile imaginations. What was more at issue was the expansion of the preindustrial economy—the growth of manufacturing, trade, and accumulated wealth; the explosion of population; and the consequent problems of greater extremes of wealth and poverty. The problems of an expanding, incipiently industrial society, problems that for the first time could seem remediable, socialists proposed to cure.

In England, socialism began with Robert Owen, himself an enlightened and progressive factory owner and manager, and his disciples; in France, it began with a remarkable cluster of unusual, even eccentric thinkers, less rooted in economic reality but quite as prophetic in some respects of the future. In both countries, these originators of socialism drew on current psychological speculation: Owen, for example, was a firm believer in the doctrine stemming from Claude Adrien Helvétius and David Hartley that man was a creature of his environment and could be changed in his very nature by changing that environment. They could draw too on another magnificent creation of the eighteenth-century mind, the developing doctrines of classical political economy; these doctrines analyzed and prescribed for the economy with remarkable perception and relevance, but in their glorification of capital, commerce, and laissez-faire they came dangerously close to rationalizing the evident maldistribution of wealth, underconsumption, and poverty. This apparent rationalization became more striking early in the nineteenth century when the gloomy conclusions of T. R. Malthus about the threat of overpopulation were grafted onto the optimism of Adam Smith and Jean Baptiste Say to produce a theory of inevitable conflict among economic classes, found in the abstract analyses of the English economist David Ricardo; curiously, some of Owen's disciples (Thomas Hodgskin being the most famous) and later Karl Marx himself were to take much of Ricardo's teaching—his insistence on the Lockean notion of the origin of value in human labor, for instance, and his view of class conflict—and turn it back on classical economics to construct a theoretical justification for socialism.

The early French socialists were at once more original than the English and more fantastical. Charles-Edmond Fourier, for example, advanced a psychology that was a remarkable mixture of humane insight and patent silliness and urged a reconstruction of society with all the realism one might expect of a man who appeared promptly at his house at a fixed hour every day to await the arrival of some unknown philanthropist who would endow his schemes for social regeneration. Étienne Cabet went further than any other early socialist to advocate a true communism. It is perhaps to be expected that these early and transitional figures thought less in terms of reconstruction through large-scale social engineering than they did in terms of regeneration by example; they advocated the formation of communities, which would live by socialist rules and principles and would point the way to what Owen called "the new moral world"; it was this characteristic that led Marx and Engels in time to dismiss them scornfully (and not altogether wrongly) as "utopian" socialists.

To find a true advocate of social engineering, one must turn to Count Henri de Saint-Simon, a down-at-heels aristocratic intellectual, who by way of a temporary enthusiasm for economic liberalism ended in a remarkable anticipation of modern technological society, in which bankers and entrepreneurs would replace the old aristocracies of landowners and lawyers and in which remuneration would be decided in accordance with the social input of each individual. Saint-Simon's influence was far-ranging; it affected both Thomas Carlyle and John Stuart Mill in England, and, by way of disciples who avoided the neoreligious and sexual crankiness of some of the French Saint-Simonians, helped to shape the structure of the French economy: by mid-century the Saint-Simonians had produced a number of bankers, industrialists, and engineers, the most famous being Ferdinand de Lesseps, whose imagination and entrepreneurial skill brought about the digging of the Suez Canal. But the Saint-Simonians also point to a strand in the socialist tradition that particularly concerned the great French liberal historian Élie Halévy: while socialism sought to carry further the liberating impulses of the French Revolution, it proposed to do so by means of a more stringent organization of society, thus giving new economic and administrative form to the apparent paradox of freedom and organization in the political theory of Jean-Jacques Rousseau.

These varied and fertile currents of socialist doctrine were brought together with certain even more basic elements in contemporary thought in one of the most remarkable and original syntheses in the history of the human intellect, the work of Karl Marx. Marx was born in Trier, in the Rhineland, in 1818, the son of an enlightened liberal Jewish lawyer, who had converted, for convenience and without conviction, to Lutheranism. Warmly encouraged at home, Karl Marx studied law at the University of Bonn and went on to the University of Berlin, where he became a philosopher or, more properly, an enthusiastic intellectual. In these years immediately following the death of G. W. F. Hegel, the great philosopher who had dominated the university, his thought was subject either to the unimaginative form-filling of epigones or to the raking criticism of rebellious disciples who still could not escape the forms that Hegel had imposed on German philosophy. Since the conservative implications of Hegel's thought were intolerable to his activist mind, Marx fell in with the latter group, but in turn saw most of their remedies as pretentious and unreal. The work of Ludwig Feuerbach, a relatively unoriginal materialist philosopher, suggested to Marx a way in which greater specificity could be brought to Hegelianism, as well as a justification for political action: the solution lay in rejecting Spirit as the motive force of evolution and replacing it with material circumstances, in short with economics, of which the spiritual realm was an inevitable product and reflection. The final amalgam was "historical materialism," a view and interpretation of history that received no definitive statement from Marx's own hand but that underlay his entire enterprise and that, to a historically minded century, lent a special conviction to the Marxian analysis and program.

The full development of Marx's system had to wait on his absorption of still other currents of thought. Supported at first by his family, then by his journalistic efforts, Marx soon earned a reputation as a violent radical and in 1843 was forced to leave Germany. Already fascinated by the French socialists, Marx went to Paris, where he plunged into the socialist ferment, not only in the realm of ideas (where he was severely critical) but in the realm of organization and action (where he was a great admirer). In 1844 he met Friedrich Engels, the prosperous son of a German merchant who represented his father's firm in England and who the next year was to make something of a reputation by publishing an analysis of the situation of the working classes in industrial England. Engels, a Hegelian radical, an admirable popularizer, and for the rest of his life the devoted friend of Marx and the expounder of his philosophy, focused Marx's attention more clearly on the analysis of the regnant economic system by the English economists, notably David Ricardo; and when Marx's activities made him an unwelcome guest, first in France, then in Belgium, he took refuge (like so many Continental revolutionaries) in London.

During his stay in Paris, Marx had moved to the extreme wing of radicalism, to communism, a term that at the time was used to distinguish the more radically democratic socialists from the moderates. As was inevitable in the later years of Louis Philippe's reign, he was deeply impressed by the potential for success that seemed to lie in violent insurrection, an insurrection carried out by a band of perceptive and determined men who would act on behalf of the proletariat. Marx had come to see the proletariat, in Hegelian terms, as the ultimate negation of bourgeois society, just as the bourgeoisie had been the negation of feudal society, but until the proletariat was fully prepared to live in the final communist society, the leaders would exercise a dictatorship, a "permanent revolution."

In time, when the last remnants of the bourgeoisie and bourgeois property had been eliminated, the coercive power would disappear—the state would wither away—and free association, true communism, would take its place.

These ideas were summed up in one of the most brilliant documents ever written, the *Communist Manifesto;* issued jointly by Marx and Engels, but primarily the work of Marx, the *Manifesto* appeared on the very eve of the French Revolution that broke out in February, 1848: it is a sketch of the historical dynamics that led to the triumph of bourgeois civilization, a celebration of the accomplishments of that civilization, a scathing denunciation of its cruelties and vices, and a call to action on the part of the proletariat to speed on the historical process: "The proletarians have nothing to lose but their chains. They have a world to win. Workingmen of all countries, unite!"

Notorious now throughout Europe, Marx arrived in England in August, 1849; thereafter, along with deep involvement in the sectarian politics of working-class radicalism, some pamphleteering, and some journalism, Marx's major activity was the construction of his vast economic treatise, *Capital,* the first volume of which appeared in 1867; the two remaining volumes, less well worked out, appeared only after his death. Again, Marx produced an astonishing synthesis, though the conviction it has carried and still carries must rest on the schematic brilliance of its historical insights rather than on the economics itself, for Marx projected the categories of the classical economists forward at precisely the time that other, bourgeois economists were exploding the very foundations of that economics. What is perhaps more to the point is that in his years in London Marx turned away from the insurrectionary emphasis of the *Manifesto* to demand the thorough preparation of the working class for its historic role, temporary cooperation with the bourgeoisie, the encouragement of trade-union activity, and the passage of social legislation: he became in short the prophet of democratic as well as of insurrectionary socialism, though he never doubted that one day revolution would provide the means of overturning the present system. Therefore, just as Marx had brought together a wide variety of social, economic, and philosophical reflection and prescription, so there descended from him an almost equal variety of socialisms. He was the prophet of social democracy as well as of insurrectionary communism —and he was also the principal inspirer of the new discipline of economic history and (through his class analysis) of equally fruitful work in the field of sociology.

Although in time the varieties of Marxism would come to claim the mantle of orthodoxy, in Marx's own lifetime his doctrines, both theoretical and tactical, were sharply contested. Three other socialist thinkers may stand for the main countercurrents.

Pierre Joseph Proudhon, the son of working people and largely self-taught, burst on the shocked awareness of Europe in 1840 with a tract that asked in its title *What Is Property?* and answered, "It is theft." Proudhon was a superb maker of phrases and paradoxes, as well as a scorching controversialist, and in effect this appalling assertion argued only that profit constituted exploitation; in fact, never able to escape his peasant background and certainly never able to think consistently and logically about economics, Proudhon was a defender of individual property and opposed the bourgeois system only because it was unjust and exploitative. The essential victory of the proletariat, which would inaugurate a just order of mutuality and cooperation, was to be brought about, not necessarily by revolution (a question on which he blew hot and cold), but gradually through the establishment of a system of free credit, to liberate producers from the tyranny of lenders and to allow them to meet each other's needs freely: it was a plan fundamentally opposed to the then fashionable democratic state socialism of the reformer Louis Blanc as well as to the communism of Étienne Cabet or, indeed, of the early Marx. Now Marx, who had praised Proudhon at first but could not get on with him, had little trouble in exposing his ignorant analysis of the classical economists (Marx devastatingly replied to Proudhon's treatise called *The Philosophy of Poverty* with a tract called *The Poverty of Philosophy*) or in ridiculing the Hegelian veneer that Proudhon gave to his work, a borrowing of the dialectic in which the contradictions were seen not as motive power but as descriptive oppositions of good and evil. But Proudhon's profoundly felt though illogical moralizing, his individualism, and his hostility to the state, as well as his deep involvement in French working-class organization, were vital legacies to the syndicalist and anarchistic variants of socialism in the later nineteenth and twentieth century, particularly in France, Italy, and Spain.

If in Proudhon the cosmopolitan Marx was fighting an ingrained French tradition, in Mikhail Bakunin he was fighting a romantic revolutionism that was profoundly Russian. Again, the two men were entirely antithetical as personalities, but they disagreed as well on the question of ultimate goals and tactics. The theoretical opposition was not complete: Bakunin acknowledged Marx's centrality as a socialist theorist, translated the *Communist Manifesto* into Russian, and contracted to translate *Capital* as well. But he opposed the centralization advocated by Marx, preferring small units to be given freedom to revolt in their own interests, and true to his conspiratorial and flamboyant nature, he stuck by the notion of the violent revolution that Marx had tacitly abandoned in favor of political action. Bakunin made a vital contribution to anarchistic movements and was a source of the special characteristic that came to mark some of them, terrorism.

The third member of the trinity of Marx's great opponents, Ferdinand

Lassalle, presents the most fascinating ambiguities. Not on the personal level, to be sure: here there could be nothing but hostility, after a brief initial collaboration, between the sober, respectable, scholarly Marx, and Lassalle, the intense, slapdash, self-dramatizing romantic who made himself famous in the 1840's defending the Countess von Hatzfeld against her husband and who got himself killed in 1864 at the age of thirty-nine in a duel over the beautiful Helene von Dönniges. Lassalle's unoriginal economics—he was famous for a reformulation of the English wages fund theory as the "iron law of wages"—hardly needed Marx's contempt; where the crucial opposition came was over Lassalle's intense German nationalism and over the question of political tactics. Lassalle was a believer in state socialism and in the last years of his life was in steady correspondence with Bismarck; he may, indeed, have indirectly inspired the state socialism to which that superb politician committed Germany in the 1880's. Marx, on the other hand, believed that the state must disappear. Lassalle was, moreover, the founder in 1863 of the first German socialist party, an ancestor of the great Social Democratic party that played so vital a part in German history until its extinction at the hands of Hitler in 1933. Although he had come to approve of political action as opposed to insurrectionism, Marx could not accept, as Lassalle did, political action that lay completely within the framework of the existing system or that gloried in patriotic nationalism. In 1869 a rival party, more orthodox, was founded; the two, finally unified in 1875, were subject to a steady stream of criticism from Marx and Engels.

The quarrels with the Proudhonians and Bakuninists were fought out in the stormy history of the International Working Men's Association (the First International), which was founded in London in 1864 and which ended, amid mutual recrimination, in the aftermath of the Franco-Prussian War and the Paris Commune of 1870–1871. The Second International, founded in 1889, was not so much an association of individuals and small groups as it was of great national parties, a confirmation of Élie Halévy's striking dictum that the ideological history of socialism came to an end with the publication of *Capital;* thereafter, he said, there was only the political history of socialism.

The founding of the great socialist parties occupied the last third of the century, beginning with Germany and ending with the formation of the Labour party in Great Britain in 1900–1906, although it did not become an avowedly socialist party until 1918. This politicization of socialism had profound effects on the social policy of European countries and on socialism itself. In country after country broad programs of social welfare legislation—factory laws; workmen's compensation; health, old age, and unemployment insurance—were adopted, in some instances at the promptings of conscience or broadened liberal theory (as in England), in others in response to the threat of labor and socialist organization or (as in Germany) as a Machiavellian device for undercutting it. But the spread of welfare and prosperity placed at further and further remove the possibility of imminent revolution and set some socialists at least, in the manner of millennarians in all times and places, to recalculating the prophecies. Of these recalculations, by far the most influential and attractive was the "revisionism" associated with the one-time orthodox Marxist Eduard Bernstein. It is possible to defend the paradox that Marx himself was the first revisionist in his turning away from revolutionary to political tactics; but Bernstein and his followers openly abandoned the goal of revolution in favor of a gradualist, political approach to social democracy, a heresy for which they were subjected to the most bitter attacks from those Marxists who fancied themselves the carriers of the true Marxist revolutionary heritage. But theoretical consistency was the last line of defense for orthodoxy against the manifest course of history, at least as it appeared in the late nineteenth century, and the self-evident spread of social equality and justice. And, European politics being what they were, the problem of political accommodation came to be presented in a particularly poignant form when the question arose, as it did for the French socialist politician Alexandre Millerand in 1904, of socialist participation with bourgeois parties in inevitable coalition governments.

Great Britain was spared most of these difficulties, in part because the theoretical constructions of Marxism held little appeal in the home of so many empirical and liberal philosophies, in part because the British trade-union movement was well established before any of the systematic social-isms were devised. Insofar as workingmen entered politics after 1870, it was largely as defenders of the pragmatic interests of labor, not as advocates of socialist reconstruction. Still, among some workingmen but more among middle-class intellectuals, certain idiosyncratic forms of socialism appeared. A variant Marxism was advanced in the Social Democratic Federation headed by the aristocratic and dictatorial stockjobber H. M. Hyndman, but in contrast stood the anarchism of the Socialist League, distinguished by the presence of the poet and designer William Morris, and the basically moral and religious socialism represented in the Independent Labour party, founded in 1893 by the working-class politician Keir Hardie. But the most famous of the English socialisms was that of the Fabians, headed by the remarkable partnership in historical scholarship and social engineering of Sidney and Beatrice Webb, and graced by the presence of the playwright Bernard Shaw and a host of distinguished intel-lectuals. Subject to intellectual schism, and undoubtedly elitist and pater-nalistic, the Fabians avowed a nonrevolutionary, gradualist policy to attain a highly organized democratic state socialism by way of scholarly demonstration, brilliant propaganda, and the permeation of established political organizations. Perhaps because the Fabians were so adept at self-advertisement, historians still argue about their exact role and about the success of the strategy of permeation; but the crucial role of the Webbs as inspirers (directly or by reaction) of two or three generations of English socialists and as architects of the socialism adopted by the Labour party in 1918 is not open to serious question.

Gradualism, an emphasis on legislation, and integration into established political processes inevitably provoked a reaction, particularly among trade-unionists who were experiencing greater and greater successes in organization and who, in the years immediately before the outbreak of the First World War, found more and more occasion to resort to direct economic action to gain their quite concrete ends. In France and throughout southern Europe a new heresy arose. Syndicalism, proceeding from Proudhonian theory and trade-union experience, emphasized an economy and state that would be organized on the basis of economic interests, following a revolution brought on by means of a general strike; a similar, antiparliamentary, but less extreme movement appeared in England in Guild Socialism, whose most distinguished representative was the dissident Fabian social philosopher G. D. H. Cole. The syndicalist movement, however, survived the war only as a legacy, as in the economic organization prescribed by the Fascists in Italy or in the British General Strike of 1926; it was replaced as a leftward force in the trade-union movement by communism. It would have been hard to see, however, from the vantage point of 1914 where a socialist victory would come from. The established socialist parties had in fact become respectable, and their ultimate bankruptcy was proved when, at the price of some defections, they each supported the war effort of their respective countries—the victory of nationalism over the class solidarity and cosmopolitanism for which Marx had stood.

Most believers saw Marxism as a doctrine suited to more advanced economies. Backward European countries spawned their own small socialist movements, chief among them the Russian socialist movement that grew up in opposition to reactionary agrarian populism, with excursions into anarchism and terrorism; the abortive revolution of 1905 against the deadly and inefficient czarist tyranny was in part socialist. It would have been difficult for most socialists, however—though Marx and Engels had anticipated the possibility at the very end of Marx's life—to predict that an overwhelmingly agrarian country with little industry and virtually no bourgeoisie would be the country to experience the first communist revolution and to present the principal socialist example to the twentieth century.

For Further Reading

Halévy, Élie, *The Era of Tyrannies: Essays on Socialism and War.*
Harrison, J. F. C., *Quest for the New Moral World: Robert Owen and the Owenites in Britain and America.*
Hobsbawm, Eric, *Primitive Rebels.*
Joll, James, *The Anarchists.*
Landauer, Carl, *European Socialism: A History of Ideas and Movements.*
Lichtheim, George, *Marxism: A Historical and Critical Study.*
————, *The Origins of Socialism.*
————, *A Short History of Socialism.*
Manuel, Frank, *The Prophets of Paris.*
Pelling, Henry, *A Short History of the Labour Party.*
Tucker, Robert C., *The Marxian Revolutionary Idea.*

12   The Antislavery Impulse in America

Few foreigners who visited the United States in the 1830's failed to note the inherent contradiction of a people who prided themselves in their equalitarian democracy, but who simultaneously kept subjugated the black sixth of their population. But the visitor had the advantage of detachment; he did not have to live with the consequences of their "peculiar institution." He could return home to muse upon a people who proclaimed themselves the vanguard of the modern world, even as they assented to the most ancient of man's systems of exploitation—slavery. For Americans who sustained the hypocrisy of preaching liberty and accepting slavery, the experience was often agonizing. "It is hardly fair for you to assume," wrote Lincoln to a southern friend, "that I have no interest in a thing which has, and continually exercises, the power of making me miserable." Trapped by a Constitution that legitimated slavery, many Americans struggled to reconcile their obligations as citizens with the maintenance of a labor system that crucified their consciences. Indeed, to be loyal to a nation that tolerated and in influential quarters even glorified slavery demanded a treason to conscience that was beyond the power of many.

Out of such conflicting emotions there gradually emerged a comprehensive antislavery movement. It was rooted in the intellectual currents of the eighteenth century, which by fusing the doctrine of man's natural rights and the law of God proclaimed slavery a monstrous injustice. Even before

A.D.   1777   Vermont ends slavery
        1804   New Jersey ends slavery
        1808   Slave trade ends
        1817   American Colonization Society established
        1820   Missouri Compromise
        1822   Denmark Vesey Conspiracy
        1829   David Walker *Appeal* published
        1831   *The Liberator* begins publication; Nat Turner rebellion
        1833   Britain ends slavery
        1836   Gag Rule
        1840   Liberty party formed
        1843   Repeal of Gag Rule
        1845   Texas annexed; Methodist Church splits along sectional
                lines
        1846   Mexican War; Wilmot Proviso
        1848   Mexican War ends; Free Soil party organized
        1850   Compromise of 1850
        1854   Kansas-Nebraska Act
        1857   Dred Scott decision
        1860   Abraham Lincoln elected; South Carolina secedes
        1861   Civil War begins
        1863   Emancipation Proclamation
        1865   End of Civil War, 13th Amendment ratified

independence had been achieved by the United States, a small but persistent group of Quakers denounced the "traffick of mens-body." Their opposition resulted from their interpretation of the New Testament. "Christ died for all," declaimed George Fox, "for the tawnies and for the blacks as for you that are called whites." The Quakers cataloged the moral and social consequences of slavery in words that were repeated with increasing frequency as the antislavery movement grew. The separation of families, the theft of the enslaved labor, the corruption of human values, all were inherent in slavery. It was a theme that Alexis de Tocqueville compressed into a single sentence: "It is easy to perceive that the lot of these unhappy beings inspires their masters with but little compassion, and that they look upon slavery, not only as an institution which is profitable to them, but as an evil which does not affect them."

What provokes assault invites defense. If the Bible legitimated an attack, so also it underwrote the justification of slavery. When the Missouri Compromise debate reached fever pitch in 1820, South Carolina's Senator Smith rumbled, "It is said that slavery is against the spirit of the Christian religion. Christ himself gave sanction to slavery. He admonished them to be obedient to their masters. . . ." To argue that the Bible restricted ownership of slaves to Israelites alone, as some abolitionists contended, led one Pennsylvanian to declare, "It would be pure heathenism to say, that ever God granted any thing as a privilege that was unjust in itself." Divine assent had universal implications.

The appeal to the Bible had subtle and explosive consequences. In a profoundly Protestant land like the United States, both supporter and opponent of slavery could eliminate moral doubt with an appropriate Biblical reference. If God is usually on the side of the largest army, in this debate, at least, he seemed to declare his neutrality.

The early criticisms of slavery were directed against a condition that had barely existed in North America in 1660. Introduced into the New World more than a century and a half earlier, it had arisen out of an elementary need for labor. The availability of free land lured away any workingman who could exercise a free choice. Anyone who wished to exploit the land on a large scale needed forced labor. As an Anglican priest explained, "to live in Virginia without slaves is . . . impossible." Thus the black slid into permanent subservience because economic necessity seemed to dictate it, and once slavery was established, a process of legitimation set in. A whole complex of laws codified the blacks' servile condition.

Although white masters preferred to believe their bondsmen relished, or at least tolerated, their condition, outbreaks of black violence, mainly sporadic, left them seemingly no choice but to build an effective police control. When colonial New York established special slave courts to try black infractions of the law, the governor attempted to explain the harsh procedures to London with the plea, "After the late barbarous attempt of some of their slaves nothing less would please the people." South Carolina accounted for its repressive code with the explanation that its slaves "are of barbarous, wild, savage natures, and such as renders them wholly unqualified to be governed by the laws, customs, and practices of this province." Black rebellion justified repression, and the need for repression proved black savagery. The white had built a self-legitimating system within which the black was hopelessly confined.

When independence was achieved in 1781, slavery was part of the American system, but so also was the soaring assertion of the Declaration of Independence that "all men are created equal." Thomas Jefferson, author of this hallowed phrase, harbored doubts on whether the principle applied to blacks. In his *Notes on Virginia,* he concluded: "This unfortunate difference of colour, and perhaps of faculty, is a powerful obstacle to the emancipation of these people." Abstractly committed to emancipation, he boggled at the prospect if the blacks were to remain within the body politic. "Among the Romans emancipation required but one effort," he wrote. "The slave, when made free, might mix with, without staining the blood of his master. But with us a second is necessary, unknown to history. When freed he is to be removed beyond the reach of mixture." The "stain" of racism marred the usually elevated tone of the great Virginian, but he was not alone, as the debates on the formation of the Constitution revealed.

When the call for an immediate end to the slave trade had been sounded at the Convention, Charles Cotesworth Pinckney, a South Carolinian aristocrat, stated flatly: "While there remained one acre of swampland uncleared in South Carolina, I would raise my voice against restricting the importation of negroes." With no less emphasis, he defended the permanence of slavery. "I am . . . thoroughly convinced . . . that the nature of our climate, and the flat, swampy situation of our country, obliges us to cultivate our lands with negroes, and that without them South Carolina would soon be a desert waste." In the resulting compromise, the importation of slaves was guaranteed until 1808, southern states were allowed to count three-fifths of their slaves in determining their congressional representation, and a fugitive slave law was promised. But the debate revealed the widely held conviction "that the States were divided . . . principally from . . . their having or not having slaves." The proudly conservative Pennsylvanian Gouverneur Morris spoke for a powerful strand of northern opinion. Slavery, he said, was "a nefarious institution . . . the curse of heaven on the States where it prevailed." The three-fifths compromise, he went on, "comes to this: that the inhabitant of Georgia and S.C. who goes to the Coast of Africa, and in defiance of the most sacred laws of humanity tears away his fellow creatures from their dearest connections & damns them to the most cruel bondages, shall have more votes in a Govt. instituted for protection of the rights of mankind, than the Citizen of Pa. or N. Jersey who views with . . . horror, so nefarious a practice."

Even as the federal Constitution was ratified, the antislavery agitation was achieving its first victories. Beginning with 1777, when Vermont, soon to become the fourteenth state, explicitly forbade slavery in its constitution, one northern state after another abolished slavery, a process which was completed in 1804 when New Jersey promulgated gradual emancipation. The revolutionary ferment, stirred by its espousal of the Rights of Man, had, at least north of the Mason and Dixon Line, adhered to principle. Colonial no longer, the new American sensed that to "persevere in this wicked practice," as one antislavery agitator argued, would lead "the world [to] call us liars and hypocrites." To redeem the revolutionary promise, slavery had to end.

From this starting point the agitation against southern slavery began, but the issue did not become critical until 1819 when the Missouri Compromise dispute arose. The fight to determine whether Missouri would enter the Union slave or free was won by the proponents of slavery, but in the compromise all the rest of the Mississippi Valley north of latitude 36° 30′ was closed to the peculiar institution. And whatever the settlement, the debate touched a raw nerve. Ex-President Thomas Jefferson proclaimed it "a firebell in the night," temporarily stilled but certain to ring again. Though President James Monroe thought the issue could be winked away by a compromise, John Quincy Adams, his Secretary of State, shared Jefferson's sentiments. "Much am I mistaken if it is not destined to survive his political and individual life and mine," he somberly commented. And he added dourly, "If the Union must be dissolved, slavery is precisely the question upon which it ought to break."

Powerful forces were gathering which would reopen the issue and sharpen its intensity until it swallowed up all other questions. Antislavery agitators who had placed their hopes in the moderate American Colonization Society suffered increasing doubts. The insistence upon making emancipation conditional upon expatriation to Africa, a point that commanded Jefferson's constant support, ran up against an insurmountable obstacle: few blacks evidenced a desire to retrace the journey from Africa, and sheer numbers made the enterprise implausible if not impossible. Outright abolitionists gradually increased their strength. In New England they published a *Black List* of northern congressmen who had had the temerity to support the Missouri Compromise and tried to wreak vengeance at the polls. Antislavery concealed a political potential that a quarter-century later would smash traditional alignments.

Outside the United States, British abolitionists under the militant leadership of William Wilberforce also attacked slavery. In 1833 the institution was finally abolished within the British Empire. Once Parliament had confirmed emancipation, the victorious antislavery leaders appealed to their American counterparts to emulate the British example. They gained a ready audience. "Let us imitate our British brethren," one abolitionist journal demanded, "and open the flood gates of light on this dark subject." Ralph Waldo Emerson spoke for many when he proclaimed the event "a day of reason; of the clear light. . . ." The transcendentalist philosopher, convinced of the efficacy of human progress, left no doubt of his expectations. "The Power that built this fabric of things," he said confidently, "has made a sign to the ages, of his will." Within the South, response to the British action was fearful, a harbinger of trouble. "It is not the fanatics at the North that the South fear," one South Carolinian admitted. "It is this abstract love for liberty, it is that the moral power of all Europe is against us." This fear was compounded guilt and the suspicion that their silent black gangs might someday rise in hideous rebellion.

Southern unease grew as the drum taps of abolitionist criticisms increased in tempo. Benjamin Lundy, Quaker born, had since 1821 used his journal, *The Genius of Universal Emancipation,* to lash out at the curse of slavery. In 1829, the free Negro David Walker published his chilling *Appeal . . . to the Colored Citizens . . . of the United States,* bluntly warning whites, "Some of you . . . will yet curse the day that you ever were born. . . . My [people] will yet root some of you out of the very face of the earth!" When, in 1831, a year after Walker's mysterious death, the Nat Turner rebellion brought savage and sudden death to sixty-two Virginia whites, Southerners had their worst fears confirmed. Although Nat Turner was caught and hanged, his memory lingered on, reminding slaveholders that behind black impassivity lurked hidden passions, awaiting only the chance to strike. One Virginian, after interviewing Turner in his death cell, commented, "I looked on him and my blood curdled in my veins."

The fears that permeated southern life were further reinforced when William Lloyd Garrison launched his antislavery paper, *The Liberator,* and rejected "moderation." Though he condemned the Turner uprising, he left no doubt of his own position. "Of all men living," he charged, "our slaves have the best reason to assert their rights by violent measures." It hardly mattered to southerners that Garrison's journal, two years after its first appearance, had fewer than 400 white subscribers, or that the bulk of his funds came from free blacks, or that, in 1837, Elijah P. Lovejoy, an abolitionist editor, was murdered in Alton, Illinois, while defending his press from a white mob. The fevered imagination of the South granted to all abolitionists a clarion voice. They read of Garrison's intemperate attacks and accepted as confirmed that his views held sway throughout the North.

Within the South, a handful of idealists, dismayed at the tightening repression of slaves, fled into northern exile. The Grimké sisters, Angelina and Sarah, embraced abolitionism. Angelina, soon to marry Theodore Weld, the spokesman for political abolitionism, in a plea to southern women to work against slavery remarked, *"God never made a slave,* he made man upright, his back was *not* made to carry burdens, nor his neck to wear a yoke, and the man must be crushed within him, before *his* back can be *fitted* to the burden of perpetual slavery." For her temerity, Angelina earned from the mayor of Charleston permanent expulsion from her native city. No less instructive was the experience of James G. Birney, a former slaveholder who emancipated his slaves and became an abolitionist. When he attempted to publish an antislavery journal, he quickly learned that in the South there existed freedom neither of the press nor of speech if either was directed at the sacrosanct institution of slavery. His reception in Cincinnati was no better. With the mayor looking on, a proslavery mob destroyed his press. As the administration of Andrew Jackson entered its final two years, the American scene revealed a profound inhospitality to antislavery sentiment.

On December 7, 1835, in his annual message, Andrew Jackson called upon Congress to prohibit the circulation through southern mails of "incendiary publications intended to instigate the slaves to insurrection." The postmaster of New York City had already refused to forward abolitionist tracts southward. John C. Calhoun, defender of southern minority rights, although preferring state action to federal censorship of the mails, recognized in the abolitionist movement an opportunity to unify southern opinion. By exaggerating the importance of abolitionists, Calhoun hoped to hold the South firm in support of slavery. Congress never complied with Jackson's request, but until the outbreak of the Civil War no southern postmaster delivered abolitionist mail. Northerners in general remained quiescent, their calm to be broken only with the adoption of the "Gag Rule" in 1836, which provided that petitions to Congress on the subject of slavery be automatically tabled. This brought into the antislavery camp ex-President John Quincy Adams, now a member of the House of Representatives. Outraged by this restriction of a fundamental liberty, he arose, time and again, to challenge the gag rule, and as frequently, he was silenced by his fellow members. But Adams, his long hostility to slavery now in the open, pushed endlessly "for agitation, agitation, agitation, until slavery in the States was shaken from its base." When, in 1843, the gag rule was finally repealed, the antislavery forces had scored a singular victory.

Whereas Garrison relied on "moral suasion," a new breed of anti-slavery agitators committed to the overthrow of slavery through political action had, in 1840, entered the struggle. With James G. Birney as their standard-bearer, they formed the Liberty party. But their bare 7,000 votes seemed piddling when compared to the millions who had rallied to the Whig and Democratic banners. The election convinced many abolitionists that only by working through the established parties could they achieve their objectives. Already within the Whig party a small but devout band, self-constituted as the Select Committee on Slavery and led by the gentle Joshua R. Giddings of Ohio, laid the foundations for the emergence of the Conscience Whigs. The Liberty party, broadened to include the whole spectrum of reform, increased its vote ninefold in 1844. Abolitionism in the mid-1840's was becoming increasingly pragmatic.

The issue of antislavery was steadily undermining established religious and political institutions. In 1844 the Methodist Church convened its annual conference at New York, and almost immediately bogged down in debate over slavery. When the weary delegates finally adjourned, Methodism stood on the verge of a sectional split, and within the year the Methodist Episcopal Church South had broken away from the parent body. Similar agitation split the Baptist and then the Presbyterian Church. From the pulpits of the nation increasingly came defense and denunciation of the peculiar institution. The tone of the preachments was increasingly harsh, as indicated by one northern Methodist preacher who declared: "Southerners tell us that slavery 'is a political, domestic, and religious blessing;' if so, why not enter into the slave-trade, wholesale and retail? go with armed ships, kidnap human beings by the thousand, bring them to America, sell them into perpetual bondage? . . . Tell them . . . that it is to make Christians of them that you buy and transport them to 'the land of the free and the home of the brave.' "

Within the two major parties, the future of slavery was inextricably intertwined with the issue of territorial expansion. The long agitation for the annexation of Texas, following the Texas Revolt against Mexico in 1835, culminated in the election of 1844. Neither Henry Clay, the Whig presidential candidate, nor Martin Van Buren, the leading Democratic contender, supported annexation, a situation which convinced proannexation Democrats that they had to block Van Buren. Skillfully they maneuvered to control the Democratic convention at Baltimore, first eliminating Van Buren and then nominating the dark horse James K. Polk. Polk won the election on a platform calling for expansion in Texas and Oregon. Texas entered the Union by joint resolution of Congress before his inauguration. His appointment of a cabinet of men who had pushed Texas annexation together with Polk's vigorous support of expansion into both Oregon and southwestwardly into Mexican territory precipitated a split with the Van Buren faction. Democratic unity was further fractured when after agreeing to a compromise settlement in Oregon, the President precipitated a war with Mexico over the issue of expansion in the Southwest. The antislavery charge that the South meant to expand its peculiar institution by any means at its disposal took on added plausibility.

Northern Democrats who supported the Mexican War disassociated themselves from the charge that they intended to extend the domain of slavery. When in 1846 Congressman David Wilmot, a Pennsylvania Democrat, moved in a proviso that slavery be outlawed in any territories obtained from Mexico, they flocked to support the proviso. Only a negative response in the Senate kept it from becoming law. Those who opposed the war denounced it in unbridled terms. It was, the Massachusetts General Court declared, "a war against freedom, against humanity, against justice, against the Union, against the Constitution, and against the *Free States.*" In a tongue-lashing speech, Congressman Abraham Lincoln accused Polk of aggression. "He is deeply conscious of being in the wrong," Lincoln said. "The blood of this war, like the blood of Abel, is crying to Heaven against him."

Final victory over Mexico in 1848, and the vast Mexican Cession, only deepened the sectional rift. Within the North a coalition of dissident Democrats and agitated Conscience Whigs, unwilling to accept the major party candidates, formed the Free Soil party and ran Martin Van Buren for President, with Charles Francis Adams, son of John Quincy, as his running mate. The Free Soilers polled 291,000 votes, enough to defeat the Democrat, Lewis Cass, and deny either party control of Congress.

A hard, bitter struggle shook Congress when it convened after the election. Whether to extend or confine slavery was the central question, and as Senator Thomas Hart Benton of Missouri gloomily complained, the capital was "almost in a state of disorganization—legislation paralyzed— distant territories left without government—insult, violence, outrage on the floors of Congress." The impasse was broken only upon the unexpected death of President Zachary Taylor, whose threatened veto of any concession to southern slaveholders had obstructed compromise. In the settlement that followed, Clay lent his prestige to a wide-ranging compromise largely contrived by Stephen A. Douglas of Illinois. California came into the Union free, but the future of slavery in the territories of Utah and New Mexico was left to local settlers. This system, called "popular sovereignty," had been introduced as a response to free soil. The slave state of Texas gave up its claim to part of New Mexico Territory in return for federal assumption of its bonded indebtedness. As a concession to the North, the slave trade was terminated within the District of Columbia, but in exchange a strengthened fugitive slave act was passed. This last measure quickly became a dead letter as one northern state after another passed personal liberty laws that made it almost impossible to implement the act, an ironic twist by which northern antislavery elements resorted to the southern strategy of nullification to frustrate federal action in defense of slavery.

Increasingly, northern members of Congress expressed antislavery views. Growing numbers of them espoused the doctrine of the "higher law," the argument that when the Constitution was at variance with the inherent rights of mankind, no man was obliged to uphold it. As southerners insisted that their slave property was entitled to protection in all federal territory, these northerners adopted Salmon P. Chase's reasoning that "the law of the Creator, which invests every human being with an inalienable title to freedom, cannot be repealed by any inferior law, which asserts that man is property."

The divisive impact of the Compromise of 1850 proved lethal to the Whig party. The bulk of the Democratic supporters of the Free Soil party returned to their traditional allegiance, with the result that the Democrats won a thunderous victory in the 1852 presidential election. Briefly the antislavery agitation was muted. However, this momentary lull ended abruptly in 1854 when Stephen A. Douglas introduced the Kansas-Nebraska Act, a plan to divide the region west of Missouri and Iowa into two territories and allow popular sovereignty to determine whether or not slavery should be introduced.

Foes of slavery denounced this as an "enormous crime." Free Soil had come thunderously alive. Within months meetings were held throughout the North setting into motion the organization of the Republican party, dedicated to the restriction of slavery to the states where it already existed. This Republican policy was energetically expounded by speakers like Senator Charles Sumner of Massachusetts, who called for "the overthrow of Slave Power" and the ultimate goal of opening "the gates of Emancipation" in the slave states.

The struggle over slavery now approached its climax. At stake was nothing less than the control of the federal government. The issue was joined in Kansas, where antislavery and proslavery partisans fought bloody battles in their efforts to control the territory. Attempts by the Democratic administration to remove Kansas from the political arena by admitting it to the Union with slave property protected resulted in a party rupture, when Senator Douglas, well aware of the potency of the Free Soil issue in the North, insisted upon the maintenance of popular sovereignty. He understood that to abandon this policy would terminate any chance of winning northern support for his presidential aspirations. When the Supreme Court, seeking to take the issue out of politics, announced in the Dred Scott case (1857), "Congress has no rightful power to prohibit Slavery in the Territories," antislavery elements were outraged.

As the voters went to the polls in 1860, the long agitation over slavery had brought the nation to the brink of civil war. Everyone understood that the Republican candidate, Abraham Lincoln, was unalterably opposed to the expansion of slavery into the territories. To the plea of Alexander H. Stephens of Georgia for a word of reassurance to the South, Lincoln replied that his administration had no intention of interfering with slavery where it already existed. "I suppose," he added soberly, "this does not meet the case. You think slavery is *right* and ought to be extended; while we think it *wrong* and ought to be restricted. That I suppose is the rub." And so it was. To accept the Republican position was to admit that slavery was wrong, a concession which, once made, would have led to an assault upon slavery where it already existed, not merely where it might exist in the future. Rather than accept such a prospect, the South seceded, went to war, and lost.

When peace finally was restored in 1865, slavery was gone, its demise soon confirmed by constitutional amendment. Black Americans were also assured by the Fourteenth and Fifteenth Amendments of their civil rights. But the black American was soon to learn the sad truth that constitutional guarantees are frail reeds upon which to rely when such guarantees go contrary to popular prejudice. With slavery abolished, a new issue arose. The black abolitionist Frederick Douglass posed it eloquently when he asked, "Do you mean to make good to us the promises in your constitution?" More than a century later, no American knew for certain what the final answer would be.

For Further Reading

Barnes, Gilbert Hobbes, *The Antislavery Impulse, 1830–1844*.
Duberman, Martin (ed.), *The Antislavery Vanguard: New Essays on Abolitionists*.
Filler, Louis, *The Crusade Against Slavery, 1830–1860*.
Quarles, Benjamin, *Black Abolitionists*.
Zilversmit, Arthus, *The First Emancipation: The Abolition of Slavery in the North*.

13   Unification Movements

Until the middle of the nineteenth century, nationalism, though an active force in Europe, had achieved very limited successes. Especially in mid-Europe, the Metternichian order continued to prevail; to contemporaries, the revolutions of 1848 appeared to have been utter failures. The map of central Europe in 1850 was not appreciably different from the map drawn at Vienna in 1815.

This map, however, was radically revised in the course of the next two decades, most significantly with the emergence of two states, Italy and Germany—perfect examples of the success of nationalism. This great transformation took place during the period of the Second French Empire. The President of the Second Republic, Prince Louis Napoleon, soon Napoleon III, Emperor of the French, was sympathetic to nationalism everywhere. This sympathy, however, came into conflict with French national interest, which had traditionally fostered the political fragmentation of mid-Europe. Thus Napoleon III's policy was, not surprisingly, tortuous, and would prove a failure for himself and for France. He could not control events in Italy or in Germany.

The legacy of ancient Rome is one of the main strands of European civilization, but from the fall of the Roman Empire to the nineteenth century Italy was little more than a geographical expression. The long medieval period, and Italian association with the Holy Roman Empire, had created another legacy, that of divisiveness and of local strength; if the feeling of Italian unity and the desire for its political renewal persisted through the centuries, as the works of Dante and Machiavelli attest, they did so largely at the cultural and literary levels. When modern national monarchies began to emerge, rival Italian states became their political pawns; Italy was the battleground of French and Spanish armies and diplomats, and later, especially during the period of the French Revolution and Napoleon, of the Austrian Hapsburgs.

The impact of Napoleon I on Italy was considerable; it is to him that the origin of a conscious and active Italian nationalism can be traced, whether by imitation of or reaction to French rule. In 1815, in Italy as elsewhere, the Congress of Vienna restored the old order, and the Hapsburg acquisition of the Kingdom of Lombardo-Venetia confirmed Austrian predominance in the entire peninsula. Metternich was the willing guardian of these arrangements, which he identified with the Hapsburg interest.

A.D.   1792–1815   The French Revolution and Napoleon; political rearrangements in central Europe; wars of liberation
1815   Settlement of Vienna
1815–1848   Italian Risorgimento; Metternichian system
1819–1844   German Zollverein
1846   Pius IX pope
1848   Piedmontese Statuto
1848–1849   Failure of revolutions in central Europe; Austro-Sardinian wars
1852   The Danish Duchies; London Protocol; Cavour prime minister of Sardinia
1854–1856   Crimean War; Sardinia joins in 1855
1856   Congress of Paris
1858   Plombières agreement between Napoleon III and Cavour; Franco-Sardinian alliance
1859   War between Austria and France and Sardinia; Armistice of Villafranca
1860   Collapse of the Italian structure; Garibaldi's expedition
1860–1861   Insurrection in Syria; French expedition; Statute of the Lebanon
1861   Proclamation of the Kingdom of Italy
1862   Bismarck minister president of Prussia; union of Moldavia and Wallachia under Alexander Cuza
1863   Polish insurrection; Alvensleben Convention
1864   War of Prussia and Austria against Denmark; cession of Schleswig and Holstein by Denmark
1865   Gastein Convention between Austria and Prussia; Biarritz meeting of Napoleon III and Bismarck
1866   Austro-Prussian War; Treaty of Prague; Italy acquires Venetia
1866–1868   Cretan revolt
1867   North German Confederation; Austro-Hungarian *Ausgleich*
1868–1870   Hohenzollern candidacy to the Spanish throne
1870–1871   Ems dispatch; Franco-Prussian War
1871   Proclamation of the German Empire at Versailles; Treaty of Frankfurt; annexation of Alsace-Lorraine

Italy faced added difficulties. Rome was the seat of the papacy and around it had grown the States of the Church, a state among Italian states. Yet it was endowed with a unique character. The papal argument—not an illogical one—was that the pope needed territorial sovereignty for the proper, unfettered discharge of his spiritual role. In any case the fate of the papacy was of international importance since, when threatened, the pope could seek the support of Catholic opinion everywhere.

Italians were overwhelmingly Catholic, and some of them thought they had found a way of reconciling their national aspirations with their religious allegiance: let the Italian states form a federation headed by the pope. In his *On the Moral and Civil Primacy of the Italians,* published in 1843, the priest Vincenzo Gioberti (1801–1852) clearly expounded the hopes of Italian liberal nationalists of this persuasion.

Others held more radical views. Giuseppe Mazzini (1805–1872) was a universal nationalist, a believer in free association of free peoples, among whom Italy would furnish leadership by example. Mazzini would have made a tabula rasa of all existing Italian regimes and set up a republic in their place. An ineffectual plotter and an exile during most of his life, he was yet a great influence on the future of Italy. The hopes and writings of such men set the climate of the Risorgimento, an effort to secure the "rebirth" of Italy. This movement was in large measure confined to the educated segment of society; the masses, most of them illiterate peasants, were passive bystanders. They justified the later quip: "We have made Italy; all that remains to do is to make Italians."

Italian hopes for unity had still another root—power politics. Among Italian states, only the Kingdom of Sardinia—also known as Piedmont—could claim real independence. There were many who thought that its unique position endowed Sardinia with the mission of leading the rest of Italy to freedom and unity. It was certainly clear that the making of Italy could only be an anti-Austrian operation; from his point of view, Metternich was quite right to detest and fear Mazzini.

It is in the context of these forces that the events of 1848–1849 operated. When Pius IX became pope in 1846, some of his measures gave rise to hopes for a liberal leadership on his part. But the revolutions of 1848, particularly the short-lived Roman Republic of which Mazzini was one of the leaders, made liberalism anathema to him. Thereafter he consistently denounced and opposed the ways of the modern world as the road to perdition. The Roman Republic was actually destroyed by French intervention, and France became the mainstay of the pope's position, somewhat reducing Austrian influence in Italy.

By late 1848 it was clear that the approaches of Gioberti and Mazzini had failed. There remained the third possibility: Sardinian-Piedmontese leadership. The initial surge of nationalist enthusiasm that swept the whole peninsula had resulted in war against Austria, under the leadership of the Piedmontese. The latter scored some successes at first, since the Austrians faced difficulties elsewhere, but Austria retrieved the situation and re-established control in Italy after the defeat of Piedmont in July, 1848. A renewed attempt in 1849 led to the same result—another Piedmontese rout.

Only British and French diplomatic intervention saved Piedmont from the consequences of this defeat. It suffered no punishment, and was even able to resist Austrian pressure and retain its constitution, the Statuto, of 1848.

The events of 1848 had yet another and decisive result: the emergence of Cavour as prime minister of the Kingdom of Sardinia. Camillo Benso di Cavour (1810–1861) belonged to the generation, and shared the ideals, of the Risorgimento. In contrast to Mazzini, Cavour was a practical man, aware of the active forces of his time and keenly interested in technological innovation; his general outlook was that of contemporary English liberals. After the political reorganization of Piedmont in 1848, he entered the government, and soon rose to its head, to remain there virtually without interruption until his death in June, 1861.

Cavour ranks as one of the outstanding European statesmen of the nineteenth century, the equal of Bismarck. Different from Bismarck in personality and in his liberal predilections, he resembles him in his manipulative skill. His objective was the modernization of the state: the encouragement of industry and the improvement of finances, administration, and the army. In addition, Cavour believed in "a free church in a free state," and had little confidence in the slogan *Italia farà da sè*—Italy will manage alone.

There was sympathy for Italian national aspirations in France and in England. But the British would not supply the necessary bayonets, and Cavour therefore procured them from France by reconciling Italian and French interests. While he was assisted by Napoleon III's natural sympathies, his success is a measure of his diplomatic skill.

Cavour brought Sardinia into the Crimean War, a seemingly far-fetched policy, which gave him an opportunity to air the Italian situation before the European powers at the Congress of Paris in 1856. While few listened to his claim that the need for reform in Italy was a European question and that reforms were the best way to forestall revolution, he now set about cultivating the French in earnest. His first success was the agreement, or plot, he contrived with the French emperor in July, 1858, at Plombières: France and Sardinia would maneuver Austria into war; the hoped-for victory would result in a rearrangement of the Italian structure.

Austria would be evicted from Italy, her holdings joined to Sardinia to constitute a Kingdom of Northern Italy. The Kingdom of Naples and the Papal States would be left unmolested; the rest of the peninsula would be merged into a central unit, possibly with a French prince at its head. Then the four units would federate under the pope's presidency. What made this scheme acceptable to France was the prospective enhancement of her influence at the expense of Austria's, the safeguarding of the pope's position —French Catholic opinion could not be ignored—and France's acquisition of Savoy and Nice.

After Plombières, Napoleon III had second thoughts and hesitated, for war with Austria might raise international complications. But Cavour managed to overcome his doubts, and the Plombières agreement was formalized into a defensive alliance in December. It remained only for Cavour to maneuver Austria into the position of agressor. Austria obligingly walked into his trap, in April, 1859, declaring war over a relatively minor dispute. Franco-Sardinian forces were victorious, though not without hard fighting. However, fearing larger European complications— Prussia had mobilized—Napoleon accepted an armistice at Villafranca, a compromise by which Austria would yield Lombardy alone. Sardinia had little choice but to accept the *fait accompli,* and its results were registered in the Treaty of Zurich the following November.

Cavour might be disappointed, even incensed, but it was too late to limit the effects of the war to the cession of a province. The time was ripe for the whole Italian structure to topple. While north central Italy was in ferment, clamoring for annexation to Sardinia, Giuseppe Garibaldi, the romantic knight of liberty, launched from Genoa the picturesque adventure of his Thousand Red Shirts; he landed in Sicily in May, 1860. His filibustering expedition may fairly be described as a joyous war. Sicily overrun, Garibaldi crossed the straits to the mainland; he entered Naples in September. Garibaldi was a colorful, romantic enthusiast, an appropriate symbol of Italian nationalist feeling, but he was no diplomat. The complications that would have resulted from his proceeding to Rome, as he would cheerfully have done, were obvious enough; there were French bayonets in Rome.

Cavour, who had resigned after the compromise of Villafranca, was back in office by this time, and fully understood the situation. A new treaty with France in March, 1860, superseding the alliance of the preceding December, had sanctioned the union of the north central states, the Duchies, and the Papal Legations with Piedmont; Napoleon, embarrassed by the awkwardness of Villafranca, was anxious above all for a termination of the Italian uncertainties. But he insisted on an independent pope, even if in a much reduced domain. Cavour proceeded with alacrity and determination. To forestall complications in Rome, a Sardinian army marched into the Papal States from the north; bypassing Rome, it met the forces of Garibaldi, who, as a good patriot, turned over his conquests to the King of Sardinia. This, in effect, was the making of Italy; formal proclamation of the Kingdom took place on March 17, 1861. Cavour lived just long enough to see the final crowning of his work. The new Italy joined the ranks of the powers, not quite certain whether she was the smallest among the great or the greatest among the small.

Yet Italy was incomplete; Venetia was still in Austrian hands and the pope still reigned in Rome. There was irony in the fact that the making of Italy at this particular point was the result of the war with Austria, a war which could not have been waged successfully without French arms. But in Italian eyes Villafranca had been a betrayal, and now it was French arms again which alone prevented the incorporation into Italy of the most Italian of cities.

It was less than a decade before these anomalies were redressed. In 1866 Italy joined Prussia in war against Austria. Though she herself did poorly in the war, she created a useful diversion of Austrian forces and was able to share in the fruits of Austria's final defeat: she acquired Venetia, leaving but a small irredenta (described by the subsequent cry for *Trento e Trieste*) which was finally obtained after the First World War.

As for Rome, a renewed Garibaldine attempt on the city in 1867 brought a French force again to protect the pope, but when France found herself at war with Prussia in 1870, she withdrew her forces. On September 20, against only token resistance, the Italian army entered Rome, which became the capital of Italy. Yet these triumphs were marred by a sense of uneasiness. The manner in which Italy acquired Venice and Rome, riding the coattails of Prussian success in both instances, left a legacy of inferiority feelings which repeatedly influenced the behavior of Italy as a national state.

The Germans, like the Italians, were a distinct people. Like them, too, they desired national unity for cultural reasons, and their nationalism drew inspiration from the romantic movement of which Germany was one of the original centers. The German equivalent of Italy's ancient Rome was the past glories of the Germanic people. In both cases, the impact of the Napoleonic era triggered the beginnings of active political consciousness.

There was no pope in Germany who might appeal to universal opinion for personal assistance. But the Germanies had long been a part of the Holy Roman Empire, itself the assertion of a universal idea. That empire was never so substantial as the Roman Church; even its name was finally abolished by Napoleon I. But though its successor, the German Confederation, created in 1815, could hardly claim universality, it rested on more than merely national foundations. Its head was the Austrian emperor, whose Germanic and Bohemian domains were included in the Confederation. This led to awkward conflicts, and it was inevitable that the Hapsburgs (and Metternich while he lasted) should be staunchly opposed to the assertion of the principle of nationality which could mean no less than the destruction of the Hapsburg empire.

Among the German states, Prussia alone had achieved the status of great power. The rivalry between Hapsburgs and Hohenzollerns was well established; but the intrusion of nationalism gave it a new turn, which, given the ethnic composition of the Hapsburg state, could only work to Prussia's advantage. History had produced particularism within the purely Germanic world, but it was less acute than the particularism engendered by the enormous diversity of the peoples under Hapsburg rule. Munich and Vienna may have felt no special love for Berlin, but they shared the same culture, whereas the Czechs and Hungarians were trying to revive distinct cultures of their own.

The revolutions of 1848 were deeply felt in the Germanic world, but, as we know, the old order triumphed, and the dilemma of definition, the choice between Grossdeutschland and Kleindeutschland, which beset the Frankfurt Assembly, remained unresolved. The Germans did not produce a Cavour in 1848, but the Italian success had an impact on Germany. Prussian mobilization during the war of 1859 had hastened its end, and the continuing uncertainties of the international situation made Prussia pay increased attention to military matters. Army reform and reorganization led to a demand for credits which the Prussian Diet would not grant, in part because the proposed reorganization of the army had political implications. The deadlock continued for a time until King William was persuaded by Albrecht von Roon, his minister of war, to make Bismarck his chief minister. The year was 1862.

Otto von Bismarck, Cavour's junior by five years, came, like Cavour, from the landed gentry. He had entered the diplomatic service and gained valuable experience in Frankfurt (where he observed the events of 1848), in St. Petersburg, and in Paris. His judgment of 1848, characteristic of his consistent outlook, was expressed in one of his most famous statements, made before the budget commission on September 30, 1862: "Not through speeches and majority resolutions are the great questions of the day decided—that was the great mistake of 1848 and 1849—but through blood and iron."

Bismarck's way out of the impasse of 1862 was of the simplest: if the Diet would not appropriate credits, he would dispense with legality. The interesting thing is that he succeeded so easily. In any event, what mattered more to him than the limited financial issue was the larger political one.

The first step in Bismarck's program was to settle matters with Austria; after that, like Cavour, he would observe events, and seize, or possibly create, further opportunities. Settling matters with Austria meant not its destruction but its reduction to the Hapsburg domain proper. This would mean the end of the German Confederation, a result not likely to be achieved without war. Bismarck's aims dictated his means: in order to wage a successful war with Austria two things were necessary—an adequate military force and the isolation of the conflict.

Favored though he was by circumstances, Bismarck's diplomatic maneuvering can only be described as masterful. Above all, he had to secure the good will of Russia and France. Czar Nicholas I had entertained friendly feelings toward Austria—witness his intervention in Hungary in 1849—but his successor, Alexander II, resented Austria's hostility at the time of the Crimean War. Then, in 1863, the Poles rose in rebellion. As thirty years before, no one came to their assistance, but while Britain, France and Austria sent the czar advice (which only irritated him) Bismarck offered cooperation. The episode gave Bismarck the opportunity of replacing a Franco-Russian with a Prusso-Russian amity.

Dealing with France was a more delicate operation. Nevertheless, at his meeting with Napoleon III at Biarritz in October, 1865, Bismarck dangled before the French emperor vague prospects of compensations, and came away with a reasonable assurance of at least initial French neutrality. Napoleon made the erroneous though not unreasonable calculation that a conflict between Austria and Prussia would be a protracted affair which would place him in the position of arbiter. Finally, in April, 1866, Bismarck concluded an alliance with Italy. Bismarck was now ready for the showdown. The Duchies of Schleswig and Holstein, the latter wholly German, the former partly Danish, were ruled by the King of Denmark, although Holstein also belonged to the German Confederation. Attempts by the Danish king to integrate the Duchies more closely into his other possessions, and complications growing out of the question of succession, had already produced a minor flare-up in 1848. That had been adjusted through the intervention of the powers in the London Protocol of 1852. But the question revived ten years later. Although it was in part a clash between Danish and German nationalism, Bismarck chose to pose as the defender of existing international arrangements in order to enlist Austrian support.

The result was a joint Austro-Prussian war against Denmark, whose outcome could only be the defeat of the Danes left unassisted. The Duchies were jointly ceded to Austria and Prussia. As with Cavour in 1859, Austria walked into Bismarck's trap: the Gastein Convention of 1865 for the administration of the Duchies was contrived by Bismarck with a view to fostering dissension between Prussia and Austria.

This dissension flared up into open war in June, 1866. The efficient Prussian military machine performed in accord with Bismarck's expectations. Other German states played no significant part in the conflict owing to the rapidity of operations, and the Battle of Sadowa, on July 3, while a close engagement, ended in a Prussian victory which settled the conflict. In the Treaty of Prague in August Bismarck demanded only one thing of Austria, but that was highly important: acceptance of the dissolution of the German Confederation. The empire of Austria would henceforth be confined to the Hapsburg domain.

Prussia's rapid victory led to a drastic reorganization of mid-Europe in 1867. The Austrian Empire became Austria-Hungary, the very name an acknowledgment of Hungarian parity with Austria—a success of Hungarian nationalism. The German states south of the Main were left to proceed as they wished without interference, while a North German Confederation was created. This new entity, dominated by Prussia, constituted a simplification of the earlier political structure. In Prussia proper Bismarck ironically indulged in the luxury of securing a bill of indemnity which legalized his unconstitutional rule. In view of his triumphs, even most of his former opponents endorsed this bill. Who would insist on doctrinaire objections in view of the outcome? Thus the curtain fell on the first act of the story of German unification: whatever one might think of the methods of the stage director, the performance had been without a doubt masterful.

The outbreak of the Austro-Prussian War had come as no surprise; its brevity had. As early as May, during the course of a debate in the French Corps Legislatif, Louis Adolphe Thiers had given a highly pessimistic, but as it turned out wholly correct, forecast of the future course of events. In a sense Sadowa was a French as much as an Austrian defeat, for that battle destroyed the calculations of Napoleonic policy: French attempts to secure from Bismarck some compensation after his victory were pathetic.

Yet Napoleon persisted. He was increasingly under attack at home for the failures of his foreign policy; his ill-contrived attempt to establish a puppet regime in Mexico under the rule of the luckless Maximilian had ended in ignominious failure. He felt he must achieve some compensatory success; almost anything would do. He suggested the Bavarian Palatinate, a part of Belgium, an alliance with Bismarck in turn. Bismarck never flatly rejected these proposals, but instead collected from the French ambassador incriminating memoranda that could be put to good future use. In 1867, negotiations for the purchase by France of Luxembourg from the Dutch king appeared promising until a storm was raised in the North German Reichstag. Bismarck, no stranger to the negotiations, pleaded helplessness in the face of aroused German national feeling, and the proposed deal fell through.

Nor were the prospects very promising that an intra-German equilibrium—North German, South German, plus an Austrian unit—within the larger European equilibrium would prove durable. Bismarck had no desire for war with France for its own sake, but he came to the correct conclusion that the completion of German unity would constitute so far-reaching an alteration of European power relationships that France would not let it take place passively. If there was to be war with France, Bismarck would adopt the same strategy as against Austria: effective use of the splendid Prussian military machine combined with isolation of the conflict.

The opportunity arose from an unexpected quarter, revolution in Spain, one of the consequences of which was a search for a new ruler. One candidate was a Hohenzollern prince, and his candidacy produced a very strong reaction in France. It was abandoned, but, not content with this minor diplomatic success, France sought to push her advantage. Instead, Bismarck turned the situation to Prussia's advantage with a crude but effective trick. Benedetti, the French ambassador, had discussed the Hohenzollern candidacy with William I, the Prussian king, at the bathing resort of Ems. The discussions had been entirely courteous, but Bismarck took his king's telegraphic report of the interviews and so doctored and condensed it as to make them appear a hostile and mutually insulting encounter. This fed the bellicose demands of the war parties in both countries, and in July, 1870, the French declared war. This made France technically the aggressor and gave Bismarck what he wanted: France stood alone.

At the same time, Bismarck held the Russians and the British in line. He enticed the Russians with prospects of support of their demand that parts of the Treaty of Paris (1856) demilitarizing the Black Sea be abrogated; he fed British suspicions of French designs by leaking details of French approaches concerning Belgium. The Austrians and Italians were soon pacified—by Prussian military successes. Within six weeks of the outbreak of war, in September, 1870, at Sedan, the Prussians compelled a French army to surrender. Paris held out for some months longer, and it was not until May, 1871, that the belligerents officially made peace at Frankfurt. The settlement imposed an enormous indemnity on France, and gave the new German Empire Alsace and part of Lorraine.

The new German Empire came into existence several months before the Peace of Frankfurt. On January 18, 1871, in the palace of the French kings at Versailles, King William was proclaimed German emperor; the locale of the ceremony, perhaps unwisely chosen, was nonetheless symbolic, expressing simultaneously the unification of Germany and its rise to first place among the Continental powers.

Unlike Italy, still claimant to an irredenta, Germany contained a number of non-German people: some Danes, a considerable larger number of Poles, and, most significant for the future, many Frenchmen in Alsace and Lorraine. Germany's annexation of these provinces introduced a festering sore in European relations, for it was regarded in France, and elsewhere, as a moral wrong. True, the people of Alsace were Germanic, and it had not become the property of Louis XIV until the seventeenth century. Yet by 1870 the overwhelming majority of Alsatians considered themselves French. The historian Heinrich von Treitschke's contention that they were really German, and that they should be made to understand this, if necessary by force, illustrates the degree to which nineteenth-century nationalistic aberrations could go.

Treitschke's view also illustrates the difference between two antithetical interpretations of nationality. Treitschke himself saw nationality as a fundamental, unchangeable fact, ultimately rooted in biological origins. Against this was the French and American, or democratic, view: nationality is essentially a matter of personal allegiance; a man is a Frenchman, a German, an American, or anything else, if he chooses to consider himself such. In this view nationality is not a fixed condition but a cultural phenomenon. Needless to say, long membership in a group or locale, common language and traditions, crystallize certain cultural characteristics: that is the basis of the ethnic variety of Europe. Yet, as American nationalism shows, nationality can rise from a synthesis of various ethnic strains.

The time lag in the emergence of nation-states in central Europe as compared with western Europe was an important historical fact, fraught with various consequences. For Italy and Germany, nationalism had been a unifying factor, bringing together scattered fragments. Considering the evolving technology of the day, the formation of larger political units seemed, certainly from the economic standpoint, a desirable development. At the same time, nationalism obviously had a disintegrating effect on multinational empires. The Austro-Hungarian *Ausgleich* of 1867 pointed in two opposite directions. On the one hand, what Hungarians had done might be emulated by others, opening up the possibility of a multinational state and justifying the observation that if Austria had not existed it should have been invented, for the Hapsburgs had played a useful role in Europe. Similarly, Switzerland was a living example of the harmonious and effective integration of various ethnic groups. But there was the opposite possibility: attempted suppression, as when the Hungarians breached the Croat constitution of 1868. Beginning with the *Ausgleich,* and for the remaining half-century of its existence, the Dual Monarchy grappled with the problem of subject nationalities, which, collectively, constituted a majority of the empire. Solving this fundamental issue was basic for Austria's survival.

Ottoman decadence, which the passage of time did not mitigate, was another source of strain. The theocratic foundations of the Ottoman state, in which law was based on religious affiliation, were ill suited to modern conditions, which call for territorial civil law, applicable to the confines of a state. In the Balkan dependencies, mainly Christian, the nationalist virus was making steady inroads, and the Crimean War further loosened the Turkish hold on the Balkans. Despite this, the Ottoman state was formally admitted to the Concert of Europe; the great European powers guaranteed its integrity and placed it under an implicit collective European protectorate.

The effects of this policy were soon felt in the Principalities of Moldavia and Wallachia, where the powers substituted their collective right of supervision for the exclusive right hitherto held by Russia. The Principalities desired to unite, and Europe allowed them identical, though still formally separate, administrations. The simultaneous choice of Alexander Cuza as ruler in both provinces in 1859 was the prelude to what happened three years later, when the Sultan agreed to the fusion of their two legislatures: Rumania had in effect been born, though still for a time subject to certain obligations to the Porte.

Nationalism thus was a unifying force for the Principalities; at the same time, from the Turkish point of view, their growing independence meant the loosening of Ottoman control. The same applies to Greece, which persistently strove to extend its domain to the Greek-speaking areas of the Balkans, to the Aegean islands, and in particular to Crete, which was in a state of endemic revolt against Turkish rule. Like the Hapsburg state, the Ottoman state was destined to ultimate disintegration into its distinctive ethnic parts.

The Russian situation was different: the Russians, with the Ukrainians, constituted the overwhelming majority of Russia's component peoples. But in the process of westward expansion initiated by Peter the Great, Russia had come to absorb Finns, Letts, Latvians, and Lithuanians along with a much larger Polish contingent. Among these people only Polish nationalism was vigorous—the final extinction of the Polish state was little more than half a century old. Czar Alexander II managed to split the Polish movement: his restoration of pre-1830 conditions was acceptable to moderates. But when in January, 1863, he attempted to deal with irreconcilables by drafting them into the army, an insurrection broke out in Warsaw. The rebels were subdued, but Polish nationalism, although rendered impotent for a time, was not destroyed.

Without a doubt the most significant achievement of nationalism during the nineteenth century was the redrawing of the map of central Europe, where it produced two large powers, Italy and Germany. These two new states adopted different internal organizations: the Italians wiped out all preexisting units, extended the Piedmontese constitution to the whole country, and made Italy a centralized entity on the French model.

The Germans adopted a less radical federal constitution, but the sheer dimensions, power, and population of Prussia inevitably gave her a dominant position in the whole. Besides, Germany had been made through Bismarck's blood-and-iron methods. In 1871 Bismarck's prestige stood high, though the legacy of his methods would weigh heavily on the future course of his creation. While he sincerely strove to keep the peace of Europe after 1871, the significant fact that Germany increasingly became the foremost power of the continent meant that first through Bismarck's active leadership, later through the more flamboyant policy of William II, Germany would determine the course of Europe's destiny.

Thus 1871 was a landmark. Apart from the emergence of Germany as a united country, a fact fraught with such heavy consequences for the future, there was a change in the effects and the tone of nationalism in the latter part of the century. In southeastern Europe, and to a lesser degree in Russia, nationalism became a disintegrating force, powerfully contributing to the outbreak of the First World War. But also, especially in the areas where it had been successful, it was increasingly appropriated by conservative elements, given to manifestations of intolerance and aggressiveness. Overflowing its original European confines, it even became associated with that characteristic activity of the latter part of the nineteenth century, an unprecedentedly vigorous imperial expansion.

For Further Reading

Darmstaedter, F., *Bismarck and the Creation of the Second Reich.*
Marriott, J. A. R., *The Eastern Question.*
Smith, D. Mack, *Cavour and Garibaldi, 1860.*
Taylor, A. J. P., *The Hapsburg Monarchy, 1809–1918.*

Toward Disintegration

14 Imperialism in Africa

At the beginning of the nineteenth century the interior of Africa was still almost wholly isolated from the rest of the world. The slave trade, by its nature, discouraged penetration by foreigners, since the slaves were brought to the coast for sale, and potential buyers did not need to go into the interior. No diamond or gold strikes, such as occurred later in the century, lured prospectors inland, African kings and chiefs looked askance at white men entering their lands, and missionaries trying to proselytize mostly died, since no cures had yet been found for diseases like malaria, yellow fever, and sleeping sickness. On those parts of the coast where slave forts and trading posts existed, the resident Europeans lived precariously and by local African permission.

Along the wide belt of the Sudan running from Cape Verde to the Horn lay a series of states, many of them of great antiquity. In the middle Senegal valley and in the mountains of northern Guinea were the Fulbe-dominated theocracies of Futa Toro and Futa Jallon. In the Niger Bend, the great empires of medieval times had given place to numerous successor states, of which the chief were Segu, Ka'arta, and Masina. East of Masina lay the city-states of Hausaland. In the Lake Chad region the kingdom of Bornu controlled the area west of the lake and the sultanate of Bagirmi the lands to the east. Between Chad and the Nile ruled the sultans of Wadai and Darfur, and on the Nile itself the Funj sultanate of Sennar was the leading political authority, though its ruler had recently been compelled to give up his northern province of Nubia to nomad invaders. All these states except Segu and Ka'arta had Muslim rulers. The only Christian state in the northern half of Africa at that time, Ethiopia, had lost the unity it possessed in the Middle Ages, and an emperor without power was the nominal head of a country rent by rivalries among provincial warlords and subject to repeated attacks by Galla nomads to the south. In the forest zone of

A.D.	1805	Accession of Muhammad Ali, pasha of Egypt
	1820	Egyptian conquest of the Sudan
	1830	French occupation of Algiers
	1833	Abolition of slavery in the British Empire
	1836–1837	Great Trek in South Africa
	1859–1860	Spanish-Moroccan war
	1861	British annexation of Lagos
	1869	Opening of Suez Canal
	1872	Internal self-government in South Africa
	1873–1874	Anglo-Ashanti war
	1876	Founding of International African Association; European control assumed over Egyptian finances
	1882	British occupation of Egypt; Makoko Treaty (Congo)
	1884–1885	Declaration of German African protectorates; Berlin West Africa Conference
	1885	Founding of the Congo Independent State; fall of Khartoum and death of General Charles Gordon
	1886	Discovery of gold on the Witwatersrand; Anglo-German East African boundary agreement; grant of charter to Royal Niger Company
	1889	Italo-Ethiopian Treaty of Wichale; grant of charter to British South Africa Company
	1890	Anglo-German African boundaries agreement; British protectorate over Zanzibar and Pemba; "Pioneer Column" to Rhodesia
	1893 ff.	French conquest of Dahomey
	1894	British protectorate over Uganda; French occupation of Timbuktu
	1894 ff.	French conquest of Madagascar
	1895	Jameson Raid in the Transvaal; British protectorate over East Africa (Kenya)
	1896	Battle of Aduwa; British occupation of Ashanti
	1896–1897	Revolts in Matabeleland and Mashonaland
	1898	French defeat of Samori Touré; Battle of Omdurman and "Fashoda Incident"
	1899–1902	South African (Boer) War
	1900–1903	British occupation of Northern Nigeria
	1905–1907	Maji-Maji Rising (German East Africa)
	1912	French protectorate over Morocco

West Africa the chief states were Ashanti (in modern Ghana), Dahomey, and Oyo and Benin (in modern Nigeria). A cluster of strong kingdoms, Bunyoro, Buganda, Ankole, Karagwe, Rwanda, and Burundi, had grown up in the area of the Great Lakes of East Africa. In the savanna country south of the Congo basin were the states of the Luba-Lunda peoples, ruled by the Mwata Yamvo and the Mwata Kazembe, while the kingdom of the Mwene Mtapa (in modern Rhodesia), first encountered by the Portuguese in the sixteenth century, still retained some of its former power, though hard pressed by the rival Rozwi state of the Changamires.

The rulers of these states were for the most part unconcerned with the wider world around them, yet they were not unfamiliar with that world's products. On the West Coast goods exchanged for slaves had for centuries included a wide variety of European manufactures, guns, gunpowder, cloth, and iron bars. The Sudanic states conducted an extensive trade across the Sahara with North Africa and Egypt, bartering slaves, leather goods, and kola nuts for weapons, horses, foodstuffs, and holy books. Merchants like the Dyula and Hausa of West Africa and the Nyamwezi and Yao of East Africa moved from marketplace to marketplace along trade routes many hundreds of miles long. Thus, when penetration by Europeans began, the intruders encountered well-organized kingdoms and chieftaincies, which were militarily strong, often highly centralized, with complex bureaucracies and established commercial and diplomatic procedures.

The banning of the Atlantic slave trade, agreed to by all but a few European states during the first two decades of the nineteenth century, signaled a new approach to tropical Africa. The trade in slaves could not be halted at once, but the abolitionists hoped it would gradually be replaced by "legitimate" trade. Naval patrols, mainly British, harassed illegal slavers, Christian missionary activity increased, the hinterland began to be systematically explored, and coastal chiefs were persuaded to accept protection and, in some cases, financial compensation in return for abandoning the slave trade and ceding small stretches of territory to one or other of the European powers. Palm oil, produced in many parts of Africa but particularly in the Niger delta, became an important export, and attempts were made to encourage the growing of cotton and groundnuts. Missionaries and traders found that they functioned more effectively when European consuls and gunboats were within call, and European influence gradually increased along the coasts.

These developments did not mean that much more of tropical Africa was being ruled by Europeans in 1880 than had been the case in 1800. A basis for later imperial competition, however, had been laid. This was especially true in West Africa, where commercial spheres of influence and areas of "informal empire" were coming into existence. The British were

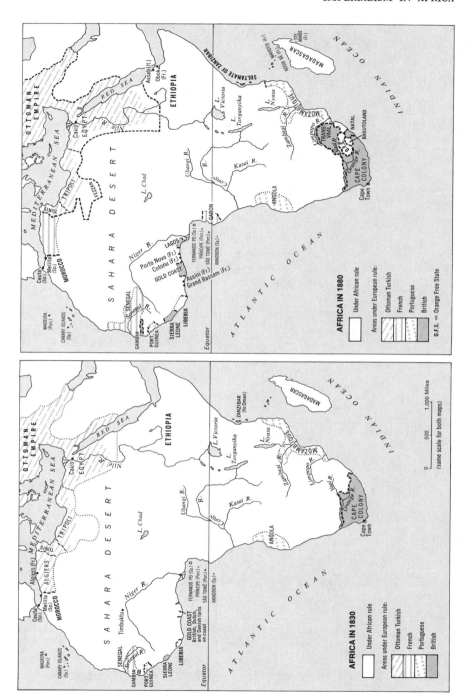

beginning to regard the lower Niger basin as their own—Lagos had been annexed as a British crown colony in 1861—and the French had begun a drive up the Senegal valley in an effort to make that region profitable through control of the gum trade.

In two parts of the continent actual European colonization took place. Following the French conquest of Algiers in 1830, undertaken more for reasons of prestige than to gain territory, a long war ensued between the French army and the indigenous Berbers. When the French eventually won this war, they turned Algeria into a colony of settlement, closely tied to metropolitan France. French influence also increased in Morocco, Tunis, and Egypt. In South Africa, dissatisfaction with British rule led large numbers of Boer farmers to break out of Cape Colony in 1836–1837 and establish their own independent republics, the Orange Free State and Transvaal. These changes in the far north and far south of the continent did not directly affect the situation in the tropical areas, but they heightened economic rivalries generally and raised many new problems of strategy and security for the European powers involved.

Nevertheless, it is doubtful that Britain, France, and Portugal, the states with the greatest holdings in Africa in the early 1880's, would have wished seriously to extend them if other powers had not intervened. It was the entry on the scene of two entirely new participants, Leopold II of the Belgians and Germany, that precipitated what has become known as the "Scramble for Africa." In 1882, moreover, the British occupied Egypt. This action was undertaken to safeguard the Suez Canal and the route to India, but it angered and alarmed the French, who regarded Egypt as belonging to their sphere of influence. Within three decades from 1884, when the competition for territory began in earnest, the entire African continent except for Ethiopia and Liberia was brought under one form or another of European rule.

The precise reasons why Europe rushed into Africa after having neglected it for so long have been much debated. The industrial nations, it has been said, needed new lands in which to invest their surplus capital, and knew that this capital would flow only into territory that Europeans controlled. On the other hand, only a small amount of capital was actually invested in Africa, even after the colonial regimes had been established, because speculators found Canada, Australia, Latin America, and other non-African areas more attractive. The attitude of the imperialists at the time, however, was clear. They may have been mistaken about Africa's overall economic potential, but in the 1880's and 1890's they unquestionably regarded the continent as a prize worth contending for—"ce magnifique gâteau africain," as Leopold II once called it—and took steps accordingly. Many imperialists were convinced that only by overseas ex-

pansion could their country's future place in the world be secured; some
Frenchmen, for example, hoped to recoup in Africa in the nineteenth century what their ancestors had lost in India in the eighteenth. The ambitions
of career-minded soldiers also played their part; the conquest of the French
Sudan and Sahara was masterminded not in Paris but by French army
officers on the spot. Finally, all the imperial powers were influenced by
what has been called the "turbulent frontier." Empires have a way of
extending themselves; to the imperial or colonial official it often seemed
that the occupation of an area adjacent to his own was all that was needed
to ensure prosperity for traders, security for missionaries, and peace of
mind for himself. The resulting annexations and extensions of spheres of
influence were often authorized by the official's home government after the
event. Frequently this was done not as a sign of approval of the official's
conduct, but because the alternative, to disavow his actions and recall him,
might cause loss of prestige and diplomatic embarrassment.

When Henry Morton Stanley returned from his journey down the
Congo in 1877, he offered his discoveries to Britain. The British declined,
and King Leopold, who had long sought an outlet for his imperial ambitions, saw a unique opportunity. He took Stanley into his service and
employed him to build a road from Stanley Pool on the Congo to the sea.
(Without proper communications the interior could not be exploited because of impassable rapids on the lower river.) Stanley's activities alerted
the French, on whose behalf another explorer, Savorgnan de Brazza, proceeded to sign treaties with the ruler of the Bateke kingdom on the north
bank of the Congo, adjacent to the territory Leopold was hoping to control. Leopold then instructed Stanley to sign up as many chiefs as possible
on the south bank to offset the advantages Brazza had won for the French.
These actions stimulated a flurry of treaty making along the West African
coast as far as Nigeria and Dahomey. In the lower Niger, too, relations
between the British and French were deteriorating because of monopoly
policies being pursued by Sir George Goldie's United African Company
(later the Royal Niger Company) against competing French firms.

The second newcomer to the African scene was Germany. Pressure
from commercial interests and colonial enthusiasts at home and a desire to
drive a diplomatic wedge between France and Britain in Europe persuaded
Bismarck to abandon his earlier opposition to overseas expansion. During
1884 and 1885 German protectorates were declared over four sections of
the African coast not yet claimed by other powers. Southwest Africa, the
East African coast between Mozambique and the future Kenya, and Togo
and Cameroun in West Africa all became German.

Portugal, as a relatively weak colonial power with most to lose if the
competition for Africa became serious, now proposed the calling of an

international conference to discuss the principles which should guide the recognition or rejection of claims to African territory. The idea was taken up by Bismarck, and a conference on West Africa met at Berlin from November, 1884, to February, 1885. It was attended by all European states with interests in the continent and also by the United States and the Ottoman Empire. Its decisions, formalized by the Berlin Act of 1885, recognized Leopold's authority in the Congo, which became the Congo Independent State, declared the basins of both the Congo and the Niger rivers free trade areas, and asserted the intention of all signatories to suppress slavery and promote civilization. Of greatest importance, however, were two provisions of the act which laid down the procedures to be followed by imperial and would-be imperial powers. From now on, acquisitions of terriery would have to be formally announced, and would not be recognized internationally unless the claiming power could demonstrate that the regions were being effectively occupied. Thus, although the Berlin West Africa Conference was not summoned to carve up Africa, it did in fact give the signal for partition. The doctrine of effective occupation introduced a new element of urgency. No longer was it sufficient for an imperial power to point to long-standing claims to possession; such claims, if they were to be acknowledged by others, had to be supported by the placing of men actually on the ground.

The first phase of the partition of Africa was characterized by the deployment of relatively small European forces and, with some exceptions, by equally minor African resistance. Many kings and chiefs ceded lands and granted mineral rights without fully comprehending the significance of their actions. Some certainly hoped that, once the mysterious piece of paper on which their unwelcome visitors set so much store had been signed and handed over, the white men would go away. Of course the result was a rapid increase in the area of the continent subject, if only nominally for the time being, to Europe. In West Africa, the French increased their influence in Guinea, the Ivory Coast, Dahomey, and Gabon, and continued the drive they had begun in the 1860's up the Senegal valley into the Sudan. The British engaged in extensive treaty making in the lower Niger basin, secured control of the coast from Cameroun to Lagos, occupied Ashanti, took over the Northern Territories of the Gold Coast, and extended protection to the interior of Sierra Leone. In East Africa, agreements between Britain and Germany in 1886 and 1890 recognized Zanzibar, Uganda, and Kenya as belonging to the British sphere, and Tanganyika (then including Rwanda and Burundi) as German. In Central Africa, following the declaration of the Bechuanaland Protectorate in 1885, Cecil Rhodes's British South Africa Company dispatched a column to take over Southern Rhodesia in 1890, and this action was soon followed by the establishment of

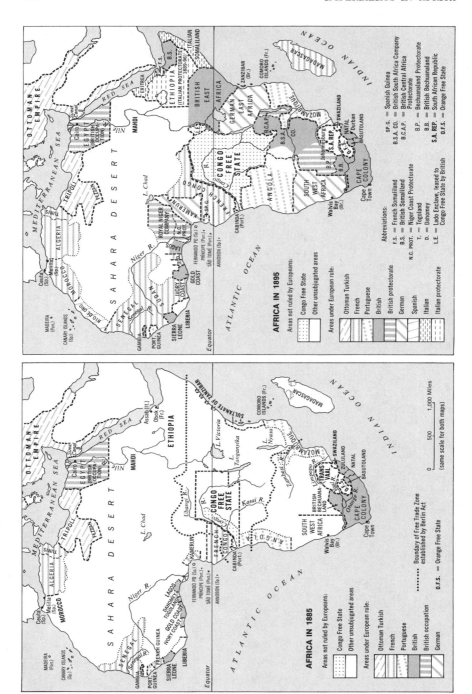

British protectorates over Nyasaland and Northern Rhodesia. In the Congo, the authority of the Independent State was extended inland. The Italians, belatedly infected by the imperialist spirit, installed themselves in Eritrea on the Red Sea.

However, during the second phase of the partition, which began about 1895, the extension of European control met increasingly bitter African resistance. Many Africans, realizing for the first time that the imperialists intended to stay, wanted to get rid of them. Some chiefs, learning by the experience of their neighbors, fought against annexation more violently than they would probably have done if their turn had come first. Yet the most important cause of growing hostility between African and European was the behavior of the imperialists themselves.

The setting up of colonial administrations, the payment of the salaries of colonial officials, soldiers, and police, the building of roads, railroads, bridges, and harbors, the financing of boundary commissions to survey frontiers decided on in Europe without proper geographical knowledge of Africa—all these activities cost a great deal of money and the necessary funds had to be provided. Home governments were willing, for a time, to make "grants-in-aid," but imperialism was not a form of philanthropy; all new colonies were expected to pay for themselves as soon as possible. Before the "Scramble" small coastal forts and settlements had struggled along financially on revenues derived from customs and excise duties. Now this source of funds, always meager because of the smallness of African purchasing power, had to be rapidly and drastically augmented. The colonial governments therefore turned to raising money by direct taxation. Hut and poll taxes forced many Africans to work for wages or grow cash crops to earn tax money, and when a man had no money, he could be made to give his labor instead. Corvée or forced labor systems became widespread in early colonial Africa. The obligation to work without pay, provided the tasks assigned were light and did not take a man away from his own district, did not necessarily provoke resentment. If, for example, a district officer instructed a chief to turn out the village young men to cut a path through the bush, the order did not go against established custom and was usually accepted. But when labor was recruited on a large scale, and when the conscripted workers were employed (sometimes in conditions of virtual slavery, as in the Congo) to build railroads, work plantations, and collect jungle products, resentment against the system became intense. Probably the two gravest injustices of early imperialism in Africa, and those which aroused the most anger among Africans, were this type of forced labor and the permanent expropriation of land by white settlers, such as occurred before the "Scramble" in South Africa and Algeria and in Southern Rhodesia and Kenya after it.

In the last years of the nineteenth century, therefore, and in the early years of the twentieth, wars in Africa became longer, more destructive, and more bitter. The French had to struggle hard to master Dahomey and Madagascar, and met strong resistance in the Western Sudan from the Tukolor Empire and from powerful warlords like Samori Touré and Rabeh. The Germans fought savage wars against the Herero in Southwest Africa and against the Maji-Maji rebels in Tanganyika. The British had to contend with Matabele and Mashona uprisings in Rhodesia, with the Hut Tax War in Sierra Leone, and with the Ashanti Revolt of 1900. Although they conquered the Sokoto Empire of Northern Nigeria without great difficulty, they encountered much stiffer resistance from the Ibos of Eastern Nigeria. All these and other contests the imperialists won, helped mainly by their superior weapons, in particular the machine gun, and by their better organization and resources. In one case, however, African resistance triumphed. The Italian attempt to enforce a protectorate over a newly unified Ethiopia collapsed after the defeat of an Italian army by the forces of the emperor Menelik II at the Battle of Aduwa in 1896.

In the eastern Sudan a special situation developed. The revolt of Muhammad Ahmad (the Mahdi) against Egyptian rule which led to the capture of Khartoum and the death of the Egyptian-appointed governor general of the Sudan, Charles Gordon, in 1885, endangered the security of the Upper Nile. A British army under General Horatio Kitchener accordingly invaded the Sudan, and in 1898 defeated the army of the Mahdi's successor, the Khalifa, at the Battle of Omdurman. Soon afterward a French force, led by Commandant Marchand, which had marched across Africa from the West Coast, confronted Kitchener at Fashoda. For several months the issue of peace or war between British and French in Africa hung in the balance, but in the end the French backed down, and the Sudan became an Anglo-Egyptian condominium.

The African war that caused the heaviest casualties, however, and in many ways marked the climax of imperialism in the continent was not fought by whites against blacks but among the whites themselves. This was the Anglo-Boer War in South Africa. In the last quarter of the nineteenth century the independence of the Boer republics began to be threatened by an influx of immigrants. These uitlanders, as the Boers called them, most of whom were British, were attracted to the northeastern part of South Africa by the discovery of diamonds at Kimberley in 1869 and of gold on the Witwatersrand in 1886. Cecil Rhodes, as prime minister of the Cape and a heavy investor in South African mining, favored the annexation by the Cape government of the Boer republics. The Jameson Raid, an attempt by Rhodes in 1895 to prod the uitlanders of the Transvaal into taking over its government by force, was a fiasco, and Rhodes fell from power. But the

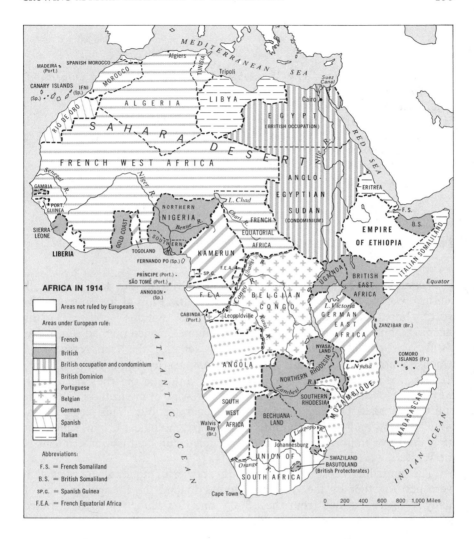

British imperial cause was sustained by the high commissioner to South Africa, Sir Alfred Milner, supported by some members of the British home government. Milner deliberately provoked war with the Transvaal, and hostilities began in 1899. The Boers of the Orange Free State fought alongside the Transvaalers, and the war dragged on until 1902, leaving behind it a legacy of mistrust and bitterness between Boer and Briton that the passage of time has only partially removed. Following the Peace of Vereeniging, which brought the war to an end, the whole of South Africa became part of the British Empire.

For Further Reading

Betts, Raymond F. (ed.), *The "Scramble" for Africa: Causes and Dimensions of Empire*.
Collins, Robert O. (ed.), *The Partition of Africa: Illusion or Necessity*.
Oliver, Roland, and Atmore, Anthony, *Africa Since 1800*.
Robinson, Ronald, and Gallagher, John, *Africa and the Victorians: The Climax of Imperialism*.

15   American Imperialism

The American venture into political imperialism in the late nineteenth century was the central fact in the changed relationship of the nation to the world. Imperialism—as old as the history of nations—contains many meanings, but as the economist Joseph Schumpeter once pointed out, it has always carried the implication of aggressiveness, "the true reasons for which do not lie in the aims which are temporarily being pursued." For Americans the aim was never clearly stated, although the rhetoric of high purpose which included such phrases as "the work of civilization" and "the uplifting of alien peoples" intrigued the general public. This sense of national mission and pride, obviously of deep psychological origin, may have been the most important single cause of nineteenth-century imperialism in the Western world.

The impelling sense of duty and the powerful national energies that were tied together by the zeal for colonies shaped the foreign policies of many Western nations from the 1860's on. Englishmen—the undisputed pacesetters—often boasted that "the sun never sets on the British Empire." Rival Europeans tried to explain that this phenomenon owed something to the fact that "the Lord wouldn't trust the British in the dark"; but when other nations expanded their horizons, the British Empire inevitably was the standard and the model.

Unquestionably many Americans were influenced by the arguments for acquiring colonies that drifted out of Europe in the late nineteenth century. These arguments, whatever their true character, were geared to the interests of industrial men—factory owners and factory workers alike. The appeal to national prestige permeating the seductive phrases of the publicists for imperialism ideally suited the outlook of enterprisers reaching for

A.D.   1867   Alaska purchased
        1887   Pearl Harbor acquired
        1898   U.S.S. *Maine* destroyed; McKinley's war message; Battle
               of Manila Bay; Battles of El Caney and San Juan Hill;
               Spanish fleet destroyed; Hawaii annexed; Treaty of
               Paris (ratified 1899), ending war with Spain; Puerto
               Rico, Guam, Philippine Islands acquired
        1902   End of Philippine insurrection
        1904   Panama Canal Zone acquired on lease
        1917   Danish West Indies purchased (renamed Virgin Islands)

---

raw materials to supply their industrial plants and for markets in which to sell their manufactured goods.

The economic arguments for acquiring colonies offered in the insistent propaganda were not so much justifications as rationalizations for action. The direct beneficiary of imperialism was not the business community as a whole, but only a fortuitously placed coterie that included shipbuilders, shipping magnates, the manufacturers of cheap alcoholic beverages, and the importers of tropical products like copra, rubber, cocoa, and coffee. This is not to suggest that no other groups profited: for example, the uniform and flag makers and the manufacturers of equipment for railroads and other heavy construction often made money out of colonies. But the benefits accruing to these capitalists were only marginally important to them.

The activities of Christian missionaries were as influential as those of the publicists in the making of modern imperialism. The "opening up" of inaccessible regions, a product of the increasing range of European mercantile activity and scientific curiosity, as well as of improved technology, created unexpected opportunities for Christian endeavor. The rapid urbanization of the industrial countries found church leaders unprepared and ill equipped to deal with new social problems of vast magnitude. Thus, the work of saving souls in distant places, besides appealing to the passion for adventure always alive in the population, supplied a substitute for religious energies frustrated or paralyzed at home.

The notions of "civilization" and "savagery" which were catchwords used by Christian missionaries had not yet been blurred by anthropologists

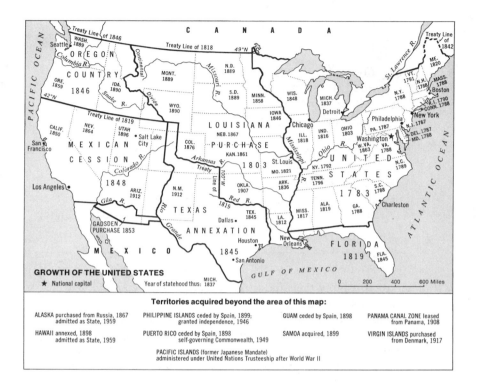

GROWTH OF THE UNITED STATES

★ National capital   Year of statehood thus: MICH. 1837   0   200   400   600 Miles

Territories acquired beyond the area of this map:

ALASKA purchased from Russia, 1867   PHILIPPINE ISLANDS ceded by Spain, 1899;   GUAM ceded by Spain, 1898   PANAMA CANAL ZONE leased
    admitted as State, 1959   granted independence, 1946   from Panama, 1908

HAWAII annexed, 1898   PUERTO RICO ceded by Spain, 1898   SAMOA acquired, 1899   VIRGIN ISLANDS purchased
    admitted as State, 1959   self-governing Commonwealth, 1949   from Denmark, 1917

PACIFIC ISLANDS (former Japanese Mandate)
administered under United Nations Trusteeship after World War II

whose rise, incidentally, was in part an unintended by-product of imperialism. Armed with modern weapons as well as with the Bible and missal, missionaries found that their somewhat unwilling "hosts" lacked the capacity to defend their beliefs any better than they could defend their lands. And what passed for success in proselytizing the faith was often, in fact, for the colored populations involved, a way of gaining access to a superior technology.

Ancient and flourishing cultures, pursuing goals other than material gain, some of them incomprehensible to Western men, were shattered under the hammer of modern imperialism. In the process, peruked judges, ladies in white frocks sipping scotch-and-soda on the irrigated lawns of "white men's" clubs, the extravagant pomposities of nationalism, and rigid crop-production quotas imposed upon "natives" baffled and infuriated conquered peoples around the world.

The American drive for colonies matured with sudden force in the 1890's, after a desultory build-up in the generation following the Civil War. The first interest in owning faraway lands was, in some respects, the contribution of William Henry Seward. As Secretary of State under Lincoln and Johnson, Seward dreamed of the American eagle spreading its protective shadow alike over the warm waters of the Caribbean and the frozen wastes of the north. Like John Quincy Adams, the formulator of the Monroe Doctrine, whom he regarded as his mentor, Seward envisioned American expansion also in the Pacific—to those places, as Adams once put it, "where the strange roads go down." Still, most Americans of Seward's day did not share his enthusiasm for colonies; they had too much under way on their own soil: the physical and political reconstruction of the nation, the completion of the transcontinental railroads, the search for solutions to the problems of social disorganization produced by rapid industrialization. Aside from the acquisition of Alaska in 1867, Secretary Seward enjoyed no imperial triumphs. But as Europe's advocates of imperialism gained plausibility and stature, like-minded Americans began to find an enthusiastic reception. To engage in colony seeking could give a nation goals and ideals loftier and more inspiriting than the selfish, sordid purposes of spoilsmen and businessmen.

The American voices that responded to these arguments had many characteristics in common. Some had studied in Europe and absorbed the new "liberalism" on its native soil. Many were well-born and ostentatiously "gentlemen" who felt themselves congenial with aristocratic English society—a feeling not shared by the general population—and they respected Germany, a newcomer in the family of nations (though predominant in nineteenth-century scholarship). Above all, this rising group of Americans accepted as axiomatic the moral and intellectual superiority of white Anglo-Saxon Protestants over every other human type, and they allowed this view to inform their social and political attitudes. At home, the idea of racial superiority gave them political leverage on the urban immigrant masses. Abroad, it gave direction and focus to their longings for an American empire. Self-assured and full of energy, these striving men found leaders in politicians like Henry Cabot Lodge and Theodore Roosevelt, the poet-politician John Hay, and the clergyman Josiah Strong. The movement toward imperialism produced a "philosopher" too: Alfred Thayer Mahan, a naval officer with a gifted pen, who formulated a doctrine for naval expansion that appealed to steel manufacturers and diplomats as well as to the young idealists.

To the mass of Americans the last years of the nineteenth century presented many frustrations, including periodic economic depressions, a loss of a feeling of community in the large cities, the appearance of an industrial proletariat, and the rise of great monopolistic corporations seemingly immune to governmental control. Men and women feeling trapped by these powerful forces could find emotional compensation in overseas triumphs for their country. The conquest of "primitive" peoples might offer such perplexed Americans a basis for rebuilding their morale by resuscitating their faith in their power to shape the world. And if one kind of response to fear is to become a bully, an imperialist policy could restore the courage of millions.

The United States entered the ranks of the imperial nations in the early 1890's. A revolution against Spain was ravaging the island of Cuba. Supporting the *insurrectos* with money and advice, Americans did not at first envision official United States involvement. Yet the course of the Cuban struggle gradually enlarged the public sympathy in the United States for the beleaguered rebels, who seemed to millions of Americans comparable to the patriots of 1776. As emotions and concern rose in the United States, the idea of helping to expel Spain at last from the hemisphere gained converts rapidly.

The United States had not fought a foreign war in more than half a century; the memory of the Civil War was fading, and a new generation of young men felt ready for trial by battle. The "New Navy" constructed in the 1880's and 1890's was spoiling for action. President McKinley, who as a soldier in the Union army had seen the terror and horror of war, struggled manfully to keep the peace. By the spring of 1898, though, Congress stood on the verge of declaring war on Spain without a formal request from the White House, and the President capitulated to the pressure on him.

When, in April of 1898, war finally came, the outcome seemed by no means a preordained conclusion. Many feared a Spanish attack on the big eastern cities. But strident, jingoistic newspapers, particularly those published on the Atlantic coast, made the war generally popular. The "official" heralds of expansion, including many Senators, gave it a noble purpose: it would fulfill the nation's "destiny." Although some Americans recognized that Spain was not a very powerful foe ("If only Germany could be persuaded to come in," Commodore George Dewey had yearned privately), some astonishing military and naval luck protected the United States forces from a protracted encounter, if not from defeat itself.

Dewey's fleet in Pacific waters subdued the Spanish squadron in the Philippine Islands in a day, and other military and naval units demolished Spanish power in the Caribbean only slightly less swiftly. By the late summer, Spain had been crushed. The United States had become an imperial power with interests, proudly called "overseas possessions," including, besides the Philippines, the islands of Guam and Puerto Rico. New national heroes like Dewey (shortly to be an admiral) and Theodore Roosevelt (shortly to be President) proclaimed the new day.

Yet despite its enthusiasm for war, the nation was not of one mind about imperialism. Taking seriously the announced principles of the Republic, that "all men are created equal," and that governments exist at the "consent of the governed," many leading Americans took their stand against acquiring colonies and demanded that the nation turn off from the imperialist path. Some of these people, to be sure, were motivated chiefly by hostility to dark-skinned "alien races," but others, the morality of the issue aside, feared the pride of power that had been the ruin of so many strong nations in the past.

These anti-imperialists could not prevent the seizure of Spain's colonies, and many were angry as well as disappointed. Within a few years, however, the mood of the 1890's began to change. Except for the Canal Zone in Panama and the tiny Virgin Islands, the United States took no other lands. Cuba, in fulfillment of a pledge by Congress, was allowed to run its own affairs almost immediately—although the United States retained Guantanamo as a naval base on a long lease and exerted a powerful influence on the Cuban economy. Filipino patriots, believing that the Americans had come to the Philippines only to help them fight the Spanish, took up arms against their erstwhile "ally," precipitating a bloody insurrection not put down until 1902. When peace returned, a civil government was established, with the object of eventually granting full independence to the islands. This promise, reaffirmed by a succession of Presidents, was finally redeemed in 1946. Puerto Rico moved by comparable steps toward greater self-government; in 1952 it was granted commonwealth status, a political position poised uneasily between independence and statehood. Of the other important colonies, Hawaii, annexed in July, 1898, became the fiftieth state during the Eisenhower administration, and Guam, a poorhouse of the Pacific, remains under the administration of the Department of the Interior.

The United States never developed a coordinated colonial policy, and the public never acquired a taste for the pomp of empire. Perhaps Americans espoused imperialism too late, after the trappings of imperial power were already frayed even for the British in India. Perhaps, too, the cherished Revolutionary War traditions of Americans quickly reasserted themselves after the aberration of the 1890's. In Latin America especially, the enormous economic pressures generated by an expanding American capitalism kept the nations of the region in a state approaching vassalage and roused deep local resentments; according to their own lights, though, Americans did the best they could by their conquered peoples and by their neighbors, undertaking to inculcate American political principles in them, and to lead them on the road to economic development. Still, the sanitary engineering the United States introduced in its possessions may have been the most significant accomplishment. This immense labor, moreover, was profoundly symbolic: like Lady Macbeth, Americans seemed to cry, "Out, damned spot!" as if by a Herculean effort they could wash out the stain of having transgressed the unalienable rights of other peoples.

For Further Reading

Beisner, Robert L., *Twelve Against Empire: The Anti-Imperialists, 1898–1900*.
Freidel, Frank, *The Splendid Little War*.
LaFeber, Walter, *The New Empire*.
May, Ernest R., *Imperial Democracy*.
Pratt, Julius W., *The Expansionists of 1898*.
Wolff, Leon, *Little Brown Brother: America's Forgotten Bid for Empire Which Cost 250,000 Lives*.

16   China Under the Impact of the West

The history of China from the Opium War of 1839–1842 to the Revolution of 1911 is the story of the disintegration of a great and proud civilization. In the face of unrelenting pressures from the Western powers and devastating rebellions in the interior, the Chinese political and intellectual elite and the Manchu rulers clung tenaciously to the ideals and institutions that had preserved China for 2,000 years. But the failure of these ideals and institutions to meet the unprecedented threat from abroad eventually had to be conceded. It was a long and agonizing process, and in the end the slowness of the Chinese response determined the drastic nature of the final reaction—impossible to imagine in 1839: the end of dynastic rule and the repudiation of the whole Confucian social and intellectual tradition.

The first clash between China and the West, the Opium War, was a minor affair compared with what was to come, but it exemplified the fundamental conflict between two vastly different civilizations which was to last for more than a century. The immediate issue was trade. To the Chinese official, merchants were parasites, men motivated solely by material gain who exploited the labors of others and produced nothing of value. Foreigners were barbarians, ignorant of the ethical precepts that were the foundation of the civilization of the Middle Kingdom. It followed that foreign traders were particularly despicable, and that foreign trade should be closely supervised. By 1757, foreign sea trade was confined to Canton. The foreign merchants in Canton were frequently exasperated by the restrictions on trade and the aloofness of Chinese officials, who dis-

A.D. 1839–1842 Opium War
     1850–1873 Taiping and other rebellions
  1860's–1870's Self-Strengthening movement
     1894–1895 First Sino-Japanese War
       1898 Hundred Days of Reform, under K'ang Yu-wei
       1900 Boxer Rebellion
       1905 Civil service examinations abolished
       1910 Annexation of Korea by Japan
       1911 Revolution of 1911

---

dained to deal with them directly. But high profits made the conditions tolerable.

In the last half of the eighteenth century, as tea became the national drink of England, the British came to dominate the Canton trade. To balance the import of tea, large quantities of opium, shipped from India, were eventually required. In the 1820's the Ch'ing government became alarmed, both because of the debilitating effects of the drug on the populace and because of an exaggerated estimate of the silver leaving China to pay for it. In 1838 Peking decided to crack down: the death penalty was prescribed for anyone dealing with opium in any way. A high official, Lin Tse-hsu, was dispatched to Canton to enforce the prohibition and to ensure that trade was conducted within the confines of existing regulations.

The English merchants and the British superintendent of trade in Canton saw the situation quite differently. For them, the issue was not the opium; it was that loftiest of civilized principles, freedom of trade. The "unreasonable" restrictions on trade and the haughty attitude of Chinese officialdom were intolerable, especially to Englishmen, and would have to be changed.

Since neither side was inclined to compromise on fundamental issues, and both sides were determined to use force if necessary, friction was inevitable. When Lin Tse-hsu stopped trade, confiscated and destroyed the opium held by foreign firms and refused to pay compensation, tension became acute. In November, 1839, a Chinese fleet exchanged volleys with British men-of-war near Canton. Thus began the Opium War, and a century of defeat and humiliation for China.

In the sporadic engagements that followed, British ships and guns demonstrated their superiority again and again, but the Ch'ing court refused to concede that the Celestial Kingdom was at the mercy of barbarian fleets, and so the war dragged on until 1842. Finally, with great reluctance, the Manchu government was forced to sign treaties that ceded Hong Kong to Great Britain, opened five coastal ports to trade, established a low, fixed tariff rate, and granted extraterritorial rights to foreigners in China. Through the most-favored-nation clause, the benefits of these and later treaties were extended to any nation that signed a treaty with China.

These were the first of many treaties—"unequal treaties," as they came to be called—imposed on China by foreign powers. For a time, the government evaded implementation of the Opium War treaties, but after defeat in another war (1856–1860), China was forced to comply with the provisions of these treaties, and in addition to legalize the opium traffic, to open other ports and the Yangtze River to trade, to permit the propagation of Christianity in the interior, to grant diplomatic recognition to foreign states on the basis of equality, and to permit foreign states to station resident ministers in Peking. China was thus forced to conduct her foreign relations according to European standards.

But there were far greater immediate problems facing the government than the foreign warships at China's gates. In the years from 1850 to 1873, China was convulsed by the most devastating rebellions of her long history. The largest of these, the Taiping Rebellion, resulted from a combination of tensions that had previously engendered rebellions and new ideological and economic forces from abroad. The leader of the Taiping, or Heavenly Kingdom of Great Peace, Hung Hsiu-ch'üan (1812–1864), came from a poor family of a minority group in south China. The emotional strain of repeated failures in the civil service examinations caused Hung to have visions, which were influenced by ideas from Protestant missionary tracts he had picked up in Canton. Hung came to believe that he was the younger brother of Jesus Christ, whose mission on earth was to rid China of evil demons—Manchus, Taoists, Buddhists, and Confucians. He went forth preaching a doctrine that combined traditional Chinese ideas with half-digested notions from the Bible.

Hung's teachings and his iconoclastic crusades against Confucian temples brought him into conflict with the local gentry. By 1851 he and his followers were in open rebellion. The small band was swollen by transport hands who had become unemployed owing to the shift in internal trade routes after the Opium War had opened new ports to foreign trade. And as Taiping expeditions roamed over large areas of southern and central China, they were joined by large numbers of peasants. Nanking was captured and made the capital of the Heavenly Kingdom, and for a decade much of the Yangtze valley was under Taiping control.

Although Taiping political and military organization and leadership were poor, imperial armies were generally ineffective against the rebels. But from the earliest stages of the rebellion gentry-led local militia demonstrated their ability to withstand Taiping forces. The Manchu government, always apprehensive of the latent strength of regionalism, was reluctant to surrender authority to the provinces, but eventually it had no other choice than to permit the formation of regional armies, led by prominent local gentry, as the only means of subduing the rebels. Furthermore, in order to finance the new armies, provincial officials were permitted to tax internal trade, and to use the receipts within their province.

Thus, the rebellions were vanquished not by the Manchu central government, but by the Chinese gentry, who saw the Taipings as a threat to the Confucian tradition and the existing social structure. The gentry leaders who emerged and rose to high office as a result of the rebellion were conservatives. The most prominent, Tseng Kuo-fan, was a top graduate of the civil service examinations, who exemplified the best in the gentry tradition. Tseng led the suppression of the Taipings, and in the following years he and similar regional leaders quelled the Muslim and other rebellions in northwestern and southwestern China.

The rebellions caused great death and destruction. Even before peace was restored, the immense task of reconstruction was begun. In the 1860's and 1870's the new leaders undertook a program not only of rural rehabilitation but also of "Self-Strengthening" to counter the foreign threat. Intelligent men, they saw that the West knew how to build excellent weapons, ships, and railroads; good Confucians, they believed that the ancient Chinese ideals of social harmony and the institutions that embodied these ideals were superior to European civilization. Western technology was to be used to strengthen China in order to preserve the traditional social order. To implement this program, arsenals and shipyards were built in several ports, and Western language schools and translation bureaus were established to enable Chinese to study Western science and technology. Although Self-Strengthening was essentially a conservative program, many among the scholar-official class viewed even these moderate innovations with hostility.

The limited achievements of the Self-Strengthening movement were insufficient to brace China against renewed foreign encroachment, which was climaxed by disastrous defeat in the Sino-Japanese War of 1894–1895. Despite diplomatic intervention on China's behalf by Germany, France, and Russia, the Japanese terms were harsh: a huge indemnity (three times the annual revenue of the Chinese government), the right to build industries in treaty ports, cession of Taiwan to Japan, and recognition of the independence of Korea, which was annexed by Japan in 1910.

The defeat by Japan was followed by new demands from the European

powers for special privileges. Fear that China would be partitioned impelled some Chinese to insist on far-reaching reforms. The most prominent
of these reformers, K'ang Yu-wei, argued that if China was to be strengthened and saved, government institutions had to be altered. To many this
was profoundly immoral, for it would be unfilial for the emperor to modify
the institutions established by his ancestors. But according to K'ang, even
Confucius had been a reformer who had advocated the creation of new
institutions to suit the changed circumstances of his own times. If Confucius could reform institutions, then so could K'ang. In 1895 K'ang led
more than 600 examination candidates, in Peking for the metropolitan
examinations, in submitting to the throne a lengthy memorial urging
radical reforms. The memorial disappeared somewhere in the conservative
bureaucracy and never reached the emperor. But by 1898, the emperor had
been impressed by K'ang's ideas and summoned him to the capital. Edicts
announcing sweeping reforms were promulgated: the government bureaucracy was to be revamped, sinecures abolished, modern industry encouraged, the army reorganized, and Western subjects given more attention in
the schools.

The edicts were not implemented. Conservative Confucians and refractory bureaucrats dominated the government apparatus. To some, K'ang's
theories were heresy; others saw their careers threatened. Moreover, real
power lay in the hands not of the young emperor, but of his wily and
bigoted aunt, the xenophobic Empress Dowager, who had been the power
behind the throne for a generation. With ease, she forced the emperor into
retirement, and the "Hundred Days of Reform" came to an end. K'ang and
some of his supporters fled into exile, while others insisted on remaining to
die as martyrs. The attempt to adapt Confucianism to the modern world
and to modernize China under the auspices of the monarchy had failed.

Two years later, with the connivance of the Empress Dowager and a
few reactionary officials, one last attempt to exorcise the foreigners was
made, this time by a disorganized mass of superstitious peasants, known as
the Boxers. The rabble entered Peking and besieged the foreign quarter.
But peasants who thought they possessed magical powers were no match
for the well-armed foreign troops who marched to Peking and lifted the
siege. Meanwhile, Russian units occupied Manchuria to protect "public
order" and Russian interests. They did not leave when the disorders had
been quieted. In a few years, Japanese influence began to replace the
Russians in Manchuria, and for a half-century after the Boxer Rebellion,
Manchuria lay beyond the control of the government of China.

Even the Empress Dowager learned the lesson of the Boxer Rebellion:
China had to modernize. Under the direction of Yüan Shih-k'ai, an able
military commander, the army was enlarged and strengthened with Western

weapons and organization. Railroads were built. A constitution and a cabinet were promised in an attempt to gain confidence in the government. More Western subjects were introduced into the educational system, and in 1905 the civil service examinations were abolished, sundering the institutionalized tie between the Confucian classics and the imperial system that had endured for more than 1,000 years. A Confucian education was no longer the prerequisite for a government career; this signified the imminent extinction of the Confucian-educated gentry elite.

The reforms were too late to save the dynasty. In 1908 the emperor and the Empress Dowager died, and a two-year-old boy succeeded to the throne under a regency. Yüan Shih-k'ai, now almost surely the most powerful man in China, and a potential threat to the dynasty, was forced into retirement. Concessions were made to stem growing provincial dissatisfaction with the central government and the Manchu house. But reform was no longer enough. Revolution was on the agenda.

Since the turn of the century, small bands of anti-Manchu revolutionaries had been fomenting uprisings, especially in south China. Outbreak after outbreak failed to gain support and was suppressed, but the revolutionaries persisted. Their most prominent leader was Sun Yat-sen, a Christian who had been educated in Western schools in Hawaii and Hong Kong; his rather crude political theories, which envisioned a new China founded on what he termed the Three People's Principles—Nationalism, Democracy, and People's Livelihood—were largely derived from Western political and social thinkers.

Sun was in America on a fund-raising tour when, on October 10, 1911, a revolt of the army garrison in the city of Wuchang set off the revolution that toppled the Ch'ing. The city fell to the revolutionaries, and in the next two months most southern and central provinces declared their independence of the central government. The Ch'ing court recalled Yüan Shih-k'ai from retirement. Yüan agreed to return to office—on his own terms. He was made prime minister and given command of the crack northern army. There was no real coordination between the newly independent provinces, and the revolutionaries were poorly organized. But the loyalty of some governmental units was doubtful, and although by late November the revolutionaries were on the defensive, Yüan did not commit his forces to a final test of strength. He had other plans. When Sun Yat-sen returned to China and was proclaimed president of the Republic by the revolutionaries, Yüan entered into negotiations with him. Sun agreed to resign the presidency in Yüan's favor if Yüan would arrange the abdication of the Manchu monarch and declare his support of republicanism. The Manchus had no choice. In February, 1912, the infant emperor was dethroned and given a comfortable pension to live within the Imperial

Palace. The Ch'ing had lost the Mandate of Heaven, and China embarked on a half-century of turmoil.

For Further Reading

Fairbank, John K., *The United States and China.*
McAleavy, Henry, *The Modern History of China.*
Schwartz, Benjamin I., *In Search of Wealth and Power: Yen Fu and the West.*
Wright, Mary C., *The Last Stand of Chinese Conservatism: The T'ung-chih Restoration, 1862–1874.*
———, ed., *China in Revolution: The First Phase, 1900–1913.*

17   India Under British Rule

The political unification of India in the first half of the nineteenth century and the rise of nationalism in the second half were linked in a multitude of ways with the new forces and ideas that were reshaping the Western world. Warren Hastings saw the conquest of territory in India in the 1780's as balancing British losses in the New World, and during the French revolutionary wars the danger of the spread of Jacobin ideas was seriously debated in Calcutta. France's European preoccupation during the Napoleonic wars made possible the spread of British power in India without a challenge from any European rivals. The impact of the new inventions for the manufacture of textiles was felt in India within a decade of their introduction in England. Jenner's method of smallpox vaccination was widely used in India during the first years of the century, and an experimental telegraph line was constructed in 1839. Indians petitioned for freedom of the press in 1823, arguing that they were "secured in the enjoyment of the same civil and religious privileges that every Briton is entitled to in England." Later, the writings of Giuseppe Mazzini were translated into Bengali, and the nationalist movements of Europe, particularly the unification of Germany and Italy, provided examples and illustrations for Indian writers.

Neither expansion nor the spread of Western ideas had been looked upon with favor in the early period of British rule. East India Company officials in London and the British Parliament had opposed the wars that added to the Company's territories, and the Indian Act of 1784, the first important constitutional document of modern India, had declared that conquests in India were "repugnant to the wish, the honor, and the policy of

A.D.   1757   Battle of Plassey; sack of Delhi by Afghans

1761   Marathas defeated at Panipat by Afghans and Mughals

1765   Grant of *diwani* to East India Company by Mughal emperor

1784   Pitt's India Act

1786–1793   Lord Cornwallis governor general

1792   Ranjit Singh comes to power

1793   Permanent Settlement in Bengal

1798–1805   Lord Wellesley governor general

1799   Defeat of Tipu Sultan of Mysore

1817–1819   Final war against the Marathas

1828–1835   Lord William Bentinck governor general

1835   Resolution on use of English for higher education

1839   Death of Ranjit Singh

1839–1842   First Afghan War

1843   Annexation of Sind

1849   Annexation of Punjab

1853   First railway line opened

1857–1858   Rebellions and army mutinies

1858   Power transferred from East India Company to Crown

1880–1884   Lord Ripon governor general

1885   Organization of Indian National Congress

1892   India Councils Act

1899–1905   Lord Curzon governor general

the British nation." As for Western ideas and values, Company officials were convinced that the only possibility of maintaining British power in India, as well as the most moral course of action, was to maintain, with a minimum of interference, the existing laws and customs of the Indians.

The injunction against territorial conquests was never very seriously observed, however, and during the governor-generalship of Lord Wellesley (1798–1805) a series of wars brought most of the coastal regions and the Gangetic plain up to Delhi under direct British control. Wellesley's defense of his policy, used in one form or another throughout the century to justify conquest, was based upon his reading of the Indian and international situation. If Britain did not control India, France or Russia would; peaceful relations were impossible with Indian rulers, since "a restless spirit of ambition was characteristic of every Asiatic government"; the replacement of the misgovernment of the native rulers by the good government of the British carried its own moral justification; and finally, once the country was reduced to order, trade and commerce would prosper. Perhaps the basic cause of expansion was simply the political situation in India and the challenge this presented to restless, imaginative men like Wellesley. The point has already been made that one of the stress lines of Indian history is the tendency of a strong government, especially one based in the Gangetic plain, to expand, and the Bengal government was following this pattern. Some territories were annexed outright, becoming part of what was known as British India. Others were brought under control through a system of subsidiary alliances which left local rulers with considerable internal control in their territories, at the price of abandoning all claims to carry on relations with other Indian states. A second burst of expansion took place in the period from 1815 to 1825, when the Marathas were finally defeated and much of Burma was annexed. Then, after a pause to consolidate these gains, a new forward movement began, leading to a war against Afghanistan in 1839 which ended in a disastrous defeat for the British. But the Sind, the lower valley of the Indus, was annexed in 1843, and the Punjab, the last important Indian territory outside British control, was conquered in 1849.

The policy of not interfering with Indian laws and customs was challenged by representatives of two of the most potent intellectual and social forces of early nineteenth-century England, the Evangelicals and the Utilitarians. For the Evangelicals, the duty of the British government to bring about change in social customs was clear: Christians should actively seek to introduce Western light and learning into the darkness and ignorance of Hinduism. For the Utilitarians, India offered scope for social change through legal reform and the construction of a rational system of administration and jurisprudence. These pressures were greatly strengthened by

INDIA IN 1798

British territory

.... Approximate boundaries

0   100   200   300   400 Miles

the enthusiastic response shown to Western ideas of change and improvement by a small but very influential group of Indians in Bengal. Ram
Mohan Roy, the most notable of these men, pleaded with great eloquence
for the introduction of Western science and technology and for the ending
of what he regarded as social evils born of superstition, such as caste, child
marriage, and suttee, the practice of widows immolating themselves on
their husbands' funeral pyres.

Out of these divergent pressures came thirty years of effort, from about
1825 to 1855, to achieve what was known as "material and moral
progress" through legislation, administrative reforms, and the introduction
of the fruits of Western technology. The result, in general terms, was the

political unification of India and the creation of a modern state. The elements involved are very disparate, and their effects were noticeable through changes in the administrative structures rather than in any widespread transformation of society, but a listing of them indicates something of their significance for the fabric of Indian life.

One of the directives of the Charter Act of 1833, the parliamentary legislation that provided for the continuance of the East India Company as the ruler of British India, was that "a general system of judicial establishments and police, to which all persons whatsoever . . . may be subject, should be established . . . and that such laws as might be applicable in common to all classes . . . should be enacted." This common law code for all citizens was never fully achieved, but its articulation points to one of the areas in which Western power perhaps made its profoundest impact. Indian law, whether under Muslim or Hindu rulers, had been particularistic, taking into consideration religious affiliation and personal status. At first the British had sought to follow existing practices in both civil and criminal law, but the introduction of law courts in the late eighteenth century modeled on British practice inevitably altered the application of the laws. It was recognized that criminal law must follow Western precedents, and a penal code which would be applicable to all subjects was drafted in 1837. Civil law procedures were made to conform to English usage, and although in cases touching upon such matters as inheritance, property rights, or marriage, the customs of particular religious and caste groups were followed, there was nevertheless a general movement toward the Western understanding of law as universalistic. Authority moved from caste and village groups to the law courts, creating strains that slowly made themselves felt throughout the traditional society. In another direction, Western legal practices tended to solidify caste customs: once they were used in court, they became binding precedents, losing the flexibility that they had had throughout history.

One of the first tasks that the British confronted was the establishment of a system of land revenue collection. Lacking detailed knowledge of the Mughal system, and without sufficient experienced personnel, they decided in 1793 to recognize the old Mughal tax farmers and district revenue officers as the actual owners of the soil in Bengal and to fix their taxes in perpetuity. The Permanent Settlement thus created a class of landlords, or zamindars, who, it was hoped, would provide stability in the countryside by supporting the government to whom they owed their existence. On the whole, the Permanent Settlement fulfilled this expectation, but it was not applied in the new areas that came under British control, for it had a number of major weaknesses. In fixing the landlords' taxes in perpetuity, the government had deprived itself of the right to profit from the increasing value of land, yet it had not provided any protection for the peasants, whose rents could be raised at will. Nor did the Bengal zamindars improve their properties on the model of their eighteenth-century English counter-parts; many were unable to adjust their habits to the inexorable demands of the new government that taxes be paid in full and on time, and as a consequence were forced to sell their lands. Elsewhere the government either made arrangements to collect the land tax directly from the culti-vator-owner, as in Madras, or from village communities, as in the Punjab. The actual tax demands were probably less than under previous govern-ments, but collection was more regular, and there was less chance of using stratagems to avoid payments, which had to be made in cash. It is difficult to sense the quality of life in rural India at this time, but one gets the impression that while more secure than in the previous century, it was also pervaded by a vague disquiet as the new power reached down to the village level.

The use of legislation to institute social change began during the gov-ernor-generalship of Lord William Bentinck (1828–1835). The most dramatic example of this was the law passed in 1829 forbidding suttee. The frequency of this practice had been much exaggerated, but the ques-tion of its abolition assumed great importance because it constituted a clear invasion by government of an area guarded by religious sanction. Bentinck recognized this, but argued that in making moral decisions the rulers must consult their own consciences, not those of their subjects. This provided a guideline for other legislation. Action was taken to suppress female infanti-cide, slavery, and human sacrifice, which was common among the primitive people of Orissa.

Of a different order, but of great social significance, was the decision made by Bentinck's administration in 1835 to support higher educational institutions that used English, rather than an Indian language, as the medium of instruction. This move was opposed by the older generation of British officials who saw in it one more attempt to transform Indian society by interfering in its deepest intellectual and religious concerns, but it re-ceived eager support from other powerful interests. Many officials argued that the language of government must be the language of the rulers; the Evangelicals saw English as the medium for introducing a true understand-ing of the world; and, above all, Indians like Ram Mohan Roy saw English as the key that would open the door of the future of India.

These changes in administrative and social patterns were helped, as was the whole process of political unification, by the improvement of internal communications. Much of this took place during the energetic, modernizing administration of Lord Dalhousie (1848–1856). Twenty-five hundred miles of telegraph lines were completed by 1855; the Grand

Trunk Road linked Calcutta with northern India; and railway construction was begun. The impact of the new technology had been felt at an even earlier period in external communications: the first steam vessel arrived in India from England in 1826, and a steam-powered vessel was launched at Calcutta in 1828.

One of the most controversial aspects of nineteenth-century Indian history is the economic impact of Western rule, but a number of generalizations can be safely made. One is that trade and commerce responded to new conditions more extensively than industry. Another is that the creation of a market economy was an important factor in political unification. Calcutta, Bombay, and Madras were essentially nineteenth-century cities, which were linked to each other and their hinterlands through banking, insurance, and government.

Throughout the century India had a favorable balance of payments, brought about by a world demand for such products as jute, hides, oilseeds, and wheat, and a lack of internal demand for foreign goods. Both foreign and domestic capital investment throughout most of the century was in commercial enterprises relating to these basic agricultural products, not in industries based on the new technology. As part of the free trade economy of Great Britain, India had no tariffs to protect new industries, and this, combined with the lack of internal markets, was probably the major barrier to industrial growth. The result was that throughout the nineteenth century the rapidly increasing population pressed more and more heavily on the land instead of finding outlets in urban areas.

Two formal institutions channeled the innovative forces that were producing political unification and social change: the army and the bureaucracy. The East India Company administered India until 1858, but long before, its power had passed to the British Parliament, which in effect reigned through a governor general. In theory, the governor general was a despot, but in fact his power was circumscribed by Parliament, the system of laws under which he operated, and above all, by that unique bureaucracy, the Indian Civil Service, which consisted of approximately 1,000 British officials who were appointed from England, at first through patronage and after 1854 through competitive examinations, and who held all the senior posts in the Indian government. The exclusion of Indians from executive posts had been one of the results of the administrative reforms carried out in the 1790's by Lord Cornwallis, and the first Indian member of the civil service was not appointed until 1869. Below the top level, almost all the thousands of posts in the bureaucracy were held by Indians, but none of these positions had either the glamour or the prestige of the civil service, entrance into which became the symbol of Indian political aspirations. British India was divided up for administrative purposes into

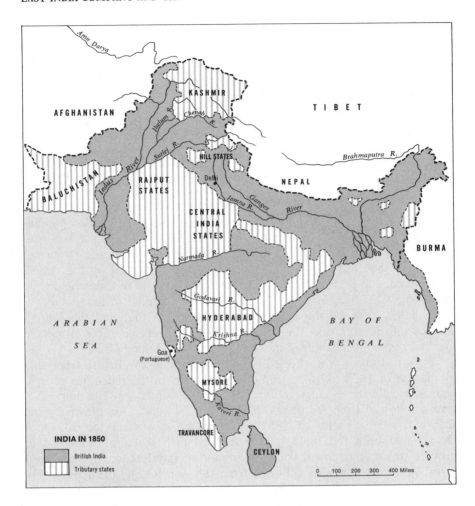

districts, each with a population of about a million, and the district officer, who was almost always a civil servant, had a large degree of autonomy. Even a very energetic governor general could not make much headway in instituting measures that were not popular with the district officers, who prided themselves on knowing India, in contrast to the governor general, who seldom had any knowledge of conditions before coming to India and who generally remained in office for only five or six years.

Of the role of the army in creating a modern state in India surprisingly little is known, but the contrast between the functions and nature of the small, disciplined British military force and that of the Mughals is great. It was a professional army of never many more than 200,000 men, made up of approximately two-thirds Indian and one-third British soldiers, all the officers being British. These officers were frequently used in administrative capacities, but British rule in India was a civil, not a military, despotism, and the political authorities always asserted their control over the army. The prestige of the army was very great, however, and a mystique that glorified the courage and loyalty of the Indian soldiers, no less than the British troops, was a vital element in the self-confidence that characterized British rule in India.

Faith in the loyalty of the Indian soldier was shaken (though not destroyed) by the uprisings which began in the most trusted regiments of the Indian army in 1857. During the summer of 1857 the British lost control of large areas of the Gangetic plain, including the key cities of Delhi, Lucknow, and Cawnpore. The uprisings among the civilian population were frequently led by members of the dispossessed ruling classes who were making a last desperate bid to regain their power. An important element of their appeal was that the new changes initiated by the British were intended to destroy the old religious traditions and to force the people to become Christian. Since the rebellions were centered in areas only recently taken over by the British, not in the areas that had the longest contact with foreign rule, this argument had considerable effect on people uncertain as to the meaning of the changes that were taking place.

Most of India was unaffected by the uprisings, so the British were able by the end of 1858 to isolate and destroy the last of the rebellious groups, and outwardly the country returned to normal conditions. But important results followed from the upheaval. The general conclusion drawn by the British from the events of 1857 was that the movement toward social change had been too rapid, and that henceforth the aim should be to provide stable government with a minimum of interference in social concerns. A curious paradox followed from this conclusion: the government turned increasingly for support to the most conservative elements of the society, and looked with suspicion upon the English-educated groups in the great port cities that had most enthusiastically identified themselves with the British during the uprisings.

The result was estrangement in the last decades of the century between the intellectuals and the government. In Bengal especially there was a growing demand that those Indians who were, in Macaulay's famous phrase, "Indian in blood and color, but English in taste, in opinions, in morals and in intellect," should be allowed to participate in the administration the British had created. To men like Surendranath Banerjea, who became in the 1870's perhaps the best-known Indian of his time, the right to such participation had been earned not only through their acquiring Western knowledge but by their ready acknowledgment that British rule had been beneficial for India. A response to this demand came during the administration of Lord Ripon, the governor general appointed by Gladstone in 1880. A greater measure of freedom for the press and the creation of corporations for local self-government indicated the direction in which the British Liberals wanted to move, but the attempt to remove existing restrictions on the trial of Europeans by Indian judges provoked a storm of opposition from many officials as well as from the British business community in India. The legislation was withdrawn, and after Ripon's departure in 1884 the government moved away from his policy.

The widespread resentment caused by the British community's ardent defense of discriminatory laws, along with the expectations fostered by Gladstonian liberalism, led to the formation of various organizations intended to provide forums for the expression of Indian opinion. Most of these were local and short-lived, but the leaders of a number of them combined in 1885 to form what became known as the Indian National Congress. From the beginning the Congress spoke for an influential section of the new professional classes created by British rule—college teachers, lawyers, journalists, doctors—as well as for the students who were beginning to crowd into the colleges. It was this remarkable organization, perhaps unique among nationalist movements for its longevity as well as for its identification with the aspirations of the people, that dominated Indian political and social thinking during the twentieth century.

For Further Reading

de Bary, William T., et al. (eds.), *Sources of Indian Tradition,* Vol. II.
Seal, Anil, *The Emergence of Indian Nationalism.*
Spear, Percival, *India, Pakistan, and the West.*
Woodruff, Philip, *The Men Who Ruled India.*

18   Darwin and Freud

What Newtonianism had been to the eighteenth century Darwinism was to be to the nineteenth: the pivotal point in a crisis of faith and in a whole series of profound revaluations in philosophy and social thought. It animated scientists seeking truth and imperialists seeking colonies. It is, of course, always possible to overstate the novelty of Darwin's ideas; for at least a century and a half before the publication of his *The Origin of*

A.D.   1798   T. R. Malthus publishes *An Essay on the Principles of Population*

          1801   Lamarck publishes *Système des animaux sans vertèbres*

          1809   Charles Darwin is born

          1820   Herbert Spencer is born

     1830–1833   Charles Lyell publishes *Principles of Geology*

          1848   Darwin's theories are fully developed in unpublished papers

          1856   Sigmund Freud is born

          1859   Darwin publishes *The Origin of Species*

          1862   Spencer publishes *First Principles*

          1871   Darwin publishes *Descent of Man*

          1882   Darwin dies

          1897   Freud discovers essential principles of psychoanalysis; undertakes his self-analysis

          1899   Freud publishes *The Interpretation of Dreams*

          1905   Freud publishes *Three Essays on the Theory of Sexuality*

          1909   Freud, in the company of Jung, visits the United States to lecture at Clark University

          1910   Founding of the International Psychoanalytical Association; Jung president

     1911–1913   Falling out of Freud with Jung and Adler, mainly on issue of infantile sexuality

       1923 ff.   Freud publishes *The Ego and the Id;* period of the last works, including *The Future of an Illusion,* and *Civilization and Its Discontents*

          1939   Freud dies

Species in 1859, rationalist criticism had struck hard and wounding blows at Christianity, undermining not only its teaching of revelation and the miraculous but also the idea that its morality provided the only sound basis for human conduct. A belief in changing species and in evolutionary development had been made familiar to educated men by a long line of speculative thinkers dating back to the previous century, whose tradition is evoked by the names of Buffon, Lamarck, and Charles Darwin's own grandfather, Erasmus Darwin. Geology, the most popular of the sciences in the first half of the nineteenth century, had prepared many people to understand that the world was much older than it appeared in Biblical chronology.

It is true that most geologists confined themselves to descriptive accounts of physiography and fossils, but in 1830 the first volume of Charles Lyell's *Principles of Geology* set forth in fresh and impressive terms an old theory, known as Uniformitarianism. According to Lyell, the geologic history of the earth had been a slow, uniform, orderly development brought about by the accumulation of constant small changes. This was, of course, profoundly at odds not only with the prevailing view among scientists but with the Biblical version of the creation and the flood. Cautious as Lyell was about the theological implications of his own findings, his authority weighed heavily toward a new view of the antiquity and history of the earth that was consistent with the evolutionary idea. Finally, religion was shaken from another quarter, the development of Biblical criticism, which flourished particularly in Germany. With their critical examination of Biblical texts, the new scholars threw into doubt the received version of the origins of the Bible, dwelled on its many inconsistencies, and encouraged the impious eighteenth-century view that it was not the product of divine inspiration but the work of many fallible human beings. By the middle of the nineteenth century it was quite possible, even for a pious man, to think about the natural world in a fashion uninhibited by the ancient Biblical cosmology; and indeed in some areas of science serious work was possible only after the scientist had discarded what we would today call the tenets of fundamentalist religion.

Still, Darwin himself was stunned by the implications of his own work, as they gradually became clear to him. Let us remind ourselves of the basic elements of his theory of natural selection, which was first drawn up in an unpublished paper of 1848—eleven years before *The Origin of Species*. First, as Malthus and Spencer had done before him, Darwin observed that within each species more organisms are constantly generated than can be nourished and supported by the environment. Second, the rapid rate at which living forms increase produces a constant struggle for existence, a competition for food and other means of survival. Third, some variation of

physical type always occurs within a species. Thus not all organisms are
equally equipped for survival: those whose variations are better adapted to
the environment in which they must live are the ones that survive and
reproduce themselves. Fourth, the offspring of these survivors inherit their
favorable variations. Finally, the accumulation of these small favorable
variations over a very long period of time introduces such changes of type
that a new species emerges. On the strength of this theory, and of a study
of the distribution of animal forms on the face of the earth, one could draw
up a hypothetical picture of the development of complex forms from
simple ones, a picture of evolutionary change beginning with rudimentary
forms and ending with man. In 1871, with *The Descent of Man,* Darwin
made it painfully clear that his theory embraced human origins as well as
others, and disturbed many people who had been able to consider the idea
of changes in all the other species.

It is hardly surprising that many religious people should see Darwinism
not primarily as a scientific hypothesis but as a formidable challenge to
revealed religion. Such challenges had been experienced before: as we have
seen, the skepticism of the Enlightenment had left its mark; and the
philosophes' favorite theology, the natural religion of Deism, had been set
up as a competitor to the revealed religion of traditional believers. Darwinism, of course, went beyond natural religion in its own disturbing implications; it undermined the old view of nature as a stable framework of
structures contrived as a rational and unchanging unity by God. And after
Darwin the implications of this threat were to be pushed still further, as
men argued that natural science could be applied to all the affairs of man
and society as well as to nature, and indeed that the methods of natural
science were the *only* methods by which anything could be learned about
man and society.

It is important to recognize that men and women reacted to the threat
of Darwinism in various ways. Some were panicked at the thought of a
complete loss of religious faith to be followed, it was assumed, by a complete loss of morality. Others believed that a new and enlarged, and in
many ways more imposing and more consoling, view of God and nature
would finally emerge (like the clergyman who, reading Darwin's account of
the devices by which orchids survived, exclaimed, "O Lord, how manifold
are Thy works"). Some scientists, like Darwin himself, refrained from
attacking the Bible. Others, like his friend Thomas Huxley, the primary
publicist and promoter of evolutionism, believed that the victory of science
depended upon vigorous combat. "Extinguished theologians," he wrote, "lie
about the cradle of every science as the strangled snakes beside that of
Hercules." It would be too much to say, as some nineteenth-century rationalists did, that there was a "war between religion and science." There

was much conflict, to be sure, but there were too many effective diplomats on both sides to permit the tension between faith and inquiry to break out in general war; there were too many scientists who agreed that no matter what they learned about the universe it would always be possible to find God behind it, too many liberal clergymen and theologians who conceded that in this enlightened age the lines of the traditional, literal-minded Biblical faith had to be reformed and to give way to that even grander and more complex conception of God and nature that they thought they saw emerging from the new science.

That there was a net loss of faith one can hardly doubt. Others must have followed a course similar to that Darwin reported:

. . . I had gradually come, by this time, to see that the Old Testament from its manifestly false history of the world and from its attributing to God the feelings of a revengeful tyrant, was no more to be trusted than the sacred books of the Hindoos, or the beliefs of any barbarian. The question then continually rose before my mind and would not be banished,—is it credible that if God were now to make a revelation to the Hindoos, would he permit it to be connected with the belief in Vishnu, Siva, etc., as Christianity is connected with the Old Testament. This appeared to me utterly incredible.

By further reflecting that the clearest evidence would be requisite to make any sane man believe in the miracles by which Christianity is supported,—that the more we know of the fixed laws of nature the more incredible do miracles become,—that the men at that time were ignorant and credulous to a degree almost incomprehensible to us,—that the Gospels cannot be proved to have been written simultaneously with the events,—that they differ in many important details, far too important as it seemed to me to be admitted as the usual inaccuracies of eye-witnesses;—by such reflections as these, which I give not as having the least novelty or value, but as they influenced me, I gradually came to disbelieve in Christianity as a divine revelation. . . . This disbelief crept over me at a very slow rate, but was at last complete. The rate was so slow that I felt no distress, and have never since doubted even for a single second that my conclusion was correct.

Whereas Darwin looked upon the loss of faith as a possible anguish which he had happily been spared, Huxley saw the loss of faith as a necessary part of the combat. "I am very glad," he wrote to another biologist, "that you see the importance of doing battle with the clericals. . . . I desire that the next generation may be less fettered by the gross and stupid superstitions of orthodoxy than mine has been. And I shall be well satisfied if I can succeed to however small an extent in bringing about that result."

Over the perspective of a longer span of time, however, much of the trial and torment aroused by the challenge of Darwinism to religion appears to be one version of a recurring and never resolved struggle. In the seventeenth century—to go back no further—a struggle between traditional faith and the avant-garde criticism of miracles had been vigorously waged; this battle was repeated, in new variations, during the height of the eighteenth-century Enlightenment; and again in the Darwinian era. Each time, one may believe, there was a net loss of faith. But each time too, the lines reformed, with differing religious responses. In our own time, a modernist Christianity, fully at home with Darwinism, has survived; and it coexists with what we have come to call fundamentalist Christianity, which is still based upon Biblical literalism. For many enlightened men of the nineteenth century the faith in Christianity was replaced, or at least supplemented, by a new and stronger faith in progress—for evolution was all too simply construed to imply progress. Darwinism became a doctrine, for many an optimistic one, of social advancement.

The effect of Darwinism on social thought was almost as profound as its effect on religion. Darwin's thought won its sway over science at a time when conservatives were looking for new and more authoritative answers to democracy and liberalism, when spokesmen of private capitalism were trying to resist the encroachments of the national state, when the prophets of nationalism were seeking justifications for national self-assertion, and when imperialists were justifying the work of extending their dominance over less favored races. Hence the ideas of evolution and natural selection were absorbed into Western thought in the midst of arguments over competition and collectivism, laissez-faire and state control, democracy and liberty, nationalism and imperialism.

Social thinkers found it easy to translate Darwin's main hypotheses into social categories. The struggle for existence became economic competition or war; survival became economic or military predominance; the idea of inheritance of variations was further evidence of necessary human inequality; adaptation to environment was elevated to a social as well as a biological value. Many thinkers took the whole scheme of development to be a promising analogue of social progress; some writers indeed concluded that the mechanisms of natural selection were the chief means, perhaps the only means, of securing that progress. Even the conception of geological periods of time came to serve as a model for society: long periods of time would be necessary to bring about any social change, conservative theorists argued, just as it had taken eons to produce the highest forms of animal life. Therefore, all schemes for rapid reform fly in the face of nature.

Soon, however, opponents of these thinkers were able to point out that the Social Darwinists had got themselves into serious difficulties. It had proved to be all too easy to construct analogies between society and nature, but these pointed in all different directions. It was easy to look upon the life of men in society as a constant struggle, but not so easy to interpret the meaning of the struggle. Which, in fact, were the struggling units? Individual men, groups, business firms, tribes, races, nation-states? It made a great deal of practical difference how this question was answered. A social theory built upon the struggle of individuals would require one response, a social theory built upon the struggle of groups, another. The struggle of individuals seemed analogous to economic competition, that of tribes or races analogous to war. But, many writers argued, if war is the true equivalent of the struggle for existence in nature, then solidarity among the individuals in the warring tribes is necessary for the survival of the group. And, if so, how could one tolerate the competitive struggle among individuals which would be certain to destroy such solidarity?

Understandably, a whole generation was thrown into confusion by such problems. Some thinkers, notably Herbert Spencer, compounded the confusion by trying to have it both ways. As an individualist, Spencer was all for severe competition, and let the devil take the loser. But as an advocate of an organismic theory of the state, he seemed to give away most of his individualism—the parts of an organism can hardly be said to engage in a competitive struggle with one another. Karl Marx and his followers complicated matters by trying to take Darwinism away from both the individualists and the nationalists. The real natural struggle, they insisted, was between classes. Marx thought, as he put it, that Darwinism gave him a basis in natural science for the class struggle in history. Later social scientists concluded that the important struggle to consider was not among individuals, nations, or classes, but among institutions, habits, and types of character. But this took them a long way from Darwin.

At bottom, Darwinism was put to two basic and mutually antagonistic uses: first, it was placed into the service of conservatism, industrial capitalism, and laissez-faire by men like Herbert Spencer in England and William Graham Sumner in the United States. When Sumner said in the 1880's that "the millionaires are a product of natural selection, acting on the whole body of men to pick out those who can meet the requirement of certain work to be done," he laid down the essential tenet of this point of view. In due course the spokesmen of reform had little difficulty in demonstrating the pseudoscientific character, as well as the smugness, of such statements. Spencer himself, near the close of his lifetime, sadly admitted that the hopes of the Social Darwinian philosophers had not been justified. In 1893 he wrote: "The doctrine of evolution has not furnished guidance to the extent I had hoped. Most of the conclusions, drawn empirically, are such as right feelings, enlightened by cultivated intelligence, have already sufficed to establish."

The second phase of Social Darwinism was the racist-militarist phase,

militarism

particularly influential on the Continent, though visible also in the Anglo-American world. As early as 1872 Walter Bagehot, the English economist, concluded in his *Physics and Politics* that those nations which are strongest tend to prevail and that in certain marked peculiarities the strongest are the best. Other writers, particularly in central Europe, raised the Social Darwinian tenets to a much more strident militarist creed. "War," wrote the German Marshal Helmuth von Moltke, combining evolutionary science with religion, "is an element of the order of the world established by God. Without war the world would stagnate and lose itself in materialism." This view of the matter was repudiated by most thinkers even before the terrible bloodletting of the First World War; and after the war it had no support among serious thinkers anywhere. There was, however, a reawakening of Social Darwinism in the ideologies of the Fascists, expressed both by Mussolini and by Hitler. "The stronger has to rule," Hitler proclaimed. "Only the born weakling can consider this as cruel. The fight for daily bread makes all those succumb who are weak, sickly, and less determined." With its harsh militarism and its genocidal mania, twentieth-century totalitarianism seemed like a ghastly caricature of the relatively innocent ideas of the nineteenth-century Social Darwinians, and its history suggests that this form of Social Darwinism could recur as a serious strain in human thought only with a grave lapse of humankind into barbarism.

rational excuse for desires

The writings of Charles Darwin, well or ill understood, had a profoundly unsettling effect on men's perception of themselves. Some decades after him another scientist, Sigmund Freud, developed a psychology that would be even more unsettling. As Darwin had expelled man from his privileged place in nature, Freud expelled reason from its privileged place in human nature. Today, more than thirty years after Freud's death, the world is still assimilating (often distorting and vulgarizing, but always invoking) the revolutionary ideas he first articulated in 1899–1900 in *The Interpretation of Dreams*.

Freud was born in 1856, in the Moravian town of Freiberg, the son of a Jewish merchant. As a small boy he moved with his family to Vienna, a city he loved and hated; he was to live and work there down to 1938, the year before his death, when the Nazi seizure of Austria compelled him to seek refuge in London. Freud early displayed a sturdy talent for science and an inordinate ambition for greatness. "I am not really a man of science," he later said of himself, "not an observer, not an experimenter, and not a thinker. I am nothing but by temperament a *conquistador*—an adventurer, if you want to translate the word—with the curiosity, the boldness and the tenacity that belong to that type of being." The remark, though instructive, is rather unjust: curiosity, boldness, and tenacity Freud had in abundance, and needed for his radical, unpopular, shocking theories, but he disciplined these qualities with an iron will and a superb technical competence to enlist them in his search for a science of man.

It was a slow, time-consuming, often disheartening search: Freud did not discover the central principles of psychoanalysis until the late 1890's, when he was in his early forties. After he completed his medical training he began to specialize in neurology and wrote some meritorious papers on the physiological origins of nervous diseases: his first book, published in 1891, was on aphasia. But his ambitions were wider than this. Studying with pioneers in psychopathology—with physicians like Josef Breuer in Vienna and Jean Martin Charcot in Paris—Freud began to develop, in the early 1890's, remarkable hypotheses about the origins of hysteria and related nervous disorders. It is a heroic story: his most cherished guesses turned out to be untenable, but then, in 1897, the *annus mirabilis* of psychoanalysis, Freud turned defeat into victory, and used the very hypotheses he could no longer defend as the foundations for the theory he *could* defend. He had been impressed by the tales his female patients were telling him with remarkable consistency: all these hysterics, it seemed, had been sexually assaulted by their fathers. For some time Freud had already been conjecturing that anxiety neuroses must be traced back to some sexual experience, and now his patients were providing him with specific evidence of such an experience: incestuous seduction. But by mid-1897 his confident assumption collapsed under the weight of contradictory evidence. For a time, as he remembered it later, he felt "helpless bewilderment." He thought that his technique of inquiry was correct, and he continued to think that sex must have a decisive part in the origins of hysteria. Besides, as a strict scientific materialist, Freud could not doubt that every effect must have a cause. There was a moment, he confessed, when he "would gladly have given up the whole thing," but he persevered, sustained by the reflection, which came at last, "that, after all, one has no right to despair because one has been deceived in one's expectations; one must revise them. If hysterics trace back their symptoms to fictitious traumas, this new fact signifies that they create such scenes in phantasy, and psychical reality requires to be taken into account alongside actual reality." This was one quality that made Freud into the great scientist he was: his willingness to permit reality to impose itself on him.

All of Freud's central discoveries were contained in his reflections of these months in 1897, if often in still rudimentary form: the powerful role of the sexual drive in man's psychic economy, infantile sexuality, the distorting work of memory and fantasy, the need for interpretation, and the existence within every human being of a large subterranean realm: the unconscious. Later that year, in the summer, Freud took another step that

would serve to confirm his guesses and supply him with a technique at once
of interpretation and of therapy: he began his self-analysis.

This courageous act has often been praised, and justly so. "It is hard
for us nowadays to imagine how momentous this achievement was," Ernest
Jones, Freud's one-time associate and later biographer, has written, "that
difficulty being the fate of most pioneering exploits. Yet the uniqueness of
the feat remains. Once done it is done forever. For no one again can be the
first to explore these depths." It was the act of a conquistador, glorying in
the absence of a map. Since this was the first psychoanalysis ever conducted, Freud had to develop his own techniques as he went along. The
discoveries that other, earlier searchers into the self had made were interesting and important, but they had been fitful, occasional; they did not
build on one another. Freud now worked systematically, exploring every
avenue that opened before him, always on the scientific assumption that
there are no accidents in mental life. He investigated his dreams, and
traced his feelings to their source; indeed, the very obstacles in the way of
self-understanding—the resistance, as he came to call it—became meaningful material open to study, to be incorporated in Freud's emerging
portrait of the human mind.

Freud was taking great risks with his self-analysis: the erotic and
hostile wishes he uncovered within himself were terrifying, and he could
not know just what kind of person he might become as he delved into
himself, deeper and deeper. But the results of three or four years of
analysis were enormously gratifying and doubly so: Freud found it possible
to arrive at psychological laws; to generalize, on the basis of his own
discovered feelings—especially his jealousy of his father and desire for his
mother, the celebrated Oedipus complex—and then, as a personal bonus,
he discovered that his neurotic symptoms had gradually disappeared.
Understanding of a very profound kind, it seemed, was the way to psychological health.

The first public result of Freud's self-analysis—though not the last,
since he faithfully continued that analysis for the rest of his life—was *The
Interpretation of Dreams*. It was this book, more than any of his others,
that exhibited Freud's daring. He was, after all, a physician, and the notion
he was here espousing, that dreams yield meanings, had been for ages the
property of the uneducated and the semiliterate, of peasant women and
servant girls who studied dream books to discover what kind of husband
they might catch or children they might have. Freud, of course, had no
such concerns. For him, dreams were part of mental life, of particular
value because they gave a kind of privileged access to the unconscious. In
sleep, resistance to one's most deeply hidden desires is relatively weak, and
they will emerge, as dreams. But even in sleep, censorship is at work,

distorting and recomposing these wishes into bizarre shapes. Hence interpretation becomes necessary.

The Interpretation of Dreams is a milestone on the long road to the science of man, but for years the world passed it by without a glance: it took a decade, after the scanty first printing of 600 copies had been sold out, before a second edition appeared. Freud continued his work undeterred, certain that he was on the right track, and sustained by his own theories which taught him *why* the world resisted his insights: they were unwelcome, psychologically easier to deny than to face. For about twenty years, Freud elaborated his central views with only minor amendments; he published case histories notable for their lucidity; he delivered and published introductory lectures on psychoanalysis, quite as lucid; he applied his theories to ordinary experiences, like forgetting, or slips of the tongue, in a relatively popular book, *The Psychopathology of Everyday Life;* and he summed up his ideas on infantile sexuality in *Three Essays on the Theory of Sexuality,* which appeared only to confirm the already widespread impression that Freud was a dirty man with a dirty mind. Who else could attribute lustful desires to innocent babies—and for their parents at that! Freud's denigrators did not realize that he had been anything but pleased by his discovery of infantile sexuality. He was, in this as in so much else, a man of his age; his scientific probity alone had compelled him to affirm and to publish what had at first repelled him.

While the official world of Austrian and German psychology continued to treat Freud with studied contempt and elaborate silence, Freud's sense of isolation gradually diminished, as he found supporters and disciples. A small society, devoted to the discussion of Freud's discoveries, was formed in Vienna; from abroad, enthusiastic admirers like C. G. Jung, Ernest Jones, Sandor Ferenczi, and others began to correspond with Freud, and then to work with him. In 1909 Freud made a memorable visit to the United States—which, despite receptive audiences, he cordially disliked. And the following year, after much preparation, an International Psychoanalytical Association finally came into being.

Inevitably with a discipline as new, as unusual, as close to speculation and sheer eccentricity as psychoanalysis, dissension soon emerged. Those who had occasion to know Freud well found him ready to discuss and happy to acknowledge the contribution of others, but he was, naturally enough, inflexible about his major theories, especially about infantile sexuality, which, it seemed, other psychologists found particularly obnoxious. The first of several important defectors was Alfred Adler, who developed a version of "depth" psychology that practically dispensed with the unconscious and substituted what he called "masculine protest"—aggressiveness—for infantile sexuality. The second, and in the long run more important, defector was the Swiss psychiatrist Jung, a brilliant, highly intuitive, but erratic theorist, for whom Freud had developed a strong affection and on whom he had pinned high hopes. Jung turned away from the scientific materialism of Freud toward mysticism and mythology, and formed an influential school of his own. His evolution—or so it seemed to Freud—was mainly designed to avoid the harsh truths on which Freud had insisted. "Anyone who promises to mankind liberation from the hardship of sex," he wrote to Jones, "will be hailed a hero, let him talk whatever nonsense he chooses." Reluctantly, Freud entered the battlefield of polemics: in 1914, free from false modesty, he published a "History of the Psychoanalytic Movement" in which he reiterated his claim to being the founder and most authoritative interpreter of psychoanalyis. The specter of rival sects, each claiming equal authority, distressed him, and he used all the resources of his vigorous style to exorcise it.

Despite these factional struggles, despite the hardships that World War I and its hungry aftermath imposed on Freud and his followers, Freud himself continued to construct and reconstruct his psychology. In the 1920's, when he was in his late sixties, he clarified his theories of anxiety and developed his topography of the mind—the id, ego, and superego—specifying their respective functions in man's mental geography. In addition, he wrote a series of brief but brilliant essays that applied his radical ideas to social psychology, prehistory, and social theory. These were explorations, frankly labeled, but securely grounded in Freud's theories; they offered psychoanalytical views of culture and of history. Perhaps the most wide-ranging of these explorations was *Civilization and Its Discontents* (1930), an essay in which clear-eyed pessimism struggled with a modest confidence in the future. For Freud civilization is an arena of inescapable conflict between the wishes of individuals and the requirements of society. Individuals want to gratify their desires—to act out their aggressions, satisfy their erotic urges, or achieve tranquillity. Since society must frustrate many of these desires for the sake of order, men in civilization must learn to postpone or to relinquish much of what they most want. Civilization compels men to conform to social norms by imposing on them both external restraints and the equally effective internal restraint, the conscience. Civilization means limitation, total freedom means barbarism, and the two are forever in conflict. It follows that civilization must make men unhappy and that civilization is always precarious, always threatened by the impulses it represses: "The price of progress in civilization is paid by forfeiting happiness through the heightening of the sense of guilt." Which would win in the end—love or death? Freud did not claim to know, but he was not without hope. "Men have brought their powers of subduing the forces of nature to such a pitch that by using them they could now very easily exterminate one another to the last man. They know this—hence arises a great part of their current unrest, their dejection, their mood of apprehension. And now it may be expected that the other of the two 'heavenly forces,' eternal Eros, will put forth his strength so as to maintain himself alongside of his equally immortal adversary." In the light of events that Freud witnessed in his last years—the rise of Fascism, the triumph of Nazism, the purges in the Soviet Union—his tentative optimism seemed, if anything, not tentative enough.

By the 1920's and even more the 1930's, Freud's ideas and, often, his vocabulary, had entered the mainstream of Western civilization. The number of patients undergoing psychoanalysis grew considerably, though it remained small, for the treatment—a single person meeting the analyst several times a week for years to recount his dreams and explore his free associations—was both expensive and by its very nature restricted to the few. But many influential and articulate persons—novelists, journalists, professors—subjected themselves to it and began to use its ideas in their own work. Gradually, too, psychoanalytical ideas invaded academic disciplines like sociology, anthropology, and political science, and gained measurable influence over educational theory, over art and literature. In addition, and much to the dismay of responsible psychoanalysts, the notions of analysis—repression, complexes, Oedipal feelings—lent themselves admirably to parlor games. While the profession of psychiatry, most philosophers, and much of the general public remained hostile, and while many continued to treat psychoanalysis as a fad, a fraud, or a new religion, the movement made distinct progress in the public consciousness. In some respects, perhaps, it suffered quite as much at the hands of its friends as at those of its enemies: rival schools carried on their debates in public, and the "revisionist Freudians," notably Erich Fromm and Karen Horney, greatly reduced the Freudian emphasis on infantile sexuality and the inevitable paradoxes of culture to stress social determinants of neuroses and seek a possible alliance with reformist or revolutionary social theories like Marxism. Worse than that, rash interpreters hastily applied notions borrowed from Freud to offer explanations of art or of historical personages— areas into which Freud and his most faithful followers had ventured only on occasion and with great caution—and even to construct a new philosophy. Freud himself strenuously denied that psychoanalysis was a *Weltanschauung:* it was, he insisted, part of the general scientific view of the world, nothing more. He considered it wholly incompatible with mysticism, with supernatural explanations of the world—with all authoritarian systems of explanation. Referring to science generally, he once wrote: "Science is no illusion. But it would be an illusion to suppose that we could get anywhere else what it cannot give us." This statement applies splendidly to psychoanalysis—the branch of science that Freud literally created.

The present state and probable future of psychoanalysis are hard to assess. Since Freud's death, his daughter Anna Freud, Heinz Hartmann, and such theorists as David Rapaport have developed and clarified, but only slightly modified, his theories. Without doubt, the Freudian revolution was one of the greatest upheavals that Western man has experienced. Freud dethroned reason for the sake of reason—he laid bare the subterranean powers of the passions so that men might understand and master them. While his teachings incidentally contributed to the sexual revolution that seems to have swept the West since World War I, his doctrine was never directed at the elimination of all repression, but at the reduction of crippling pressures on man. Necessary pressures were to be retained. "Where id was," he said, "there shall ego be." Whatever may become of individual ideas that Freud advanced, his general achievement will last as long as rational civilization.

For Further Reading

DARWIN

De Beer, Sir Gavin R., *Charles Darwin.*
Eiseley, Loren C., *Darwin's Century.*
Hofstadter, Richard, *Social Darwinism in American Thought, 1816–1915.*
Moorehead, Alan, *Darwin and the Beagle.*

FREUD

Costigan, Giovanni, *Sigmund Freud: A Short Biography.*
Jones, Ernest, *Sigmund Freud: Life and Work.*
Rieff, Philip, *Freud: The Mind of the Moralist.*
Sachs, Hanns, *Freud: Master and Friend.*

19   The Great Powers to the Verge of War

The Pax Britannica of mid-century was undoubtedly British but far from peaceful, either in Europe or outside it. Between the Paris Commune of 1871 and the Balkan Wars of 1912–1913, though fighting was endemic in the rest of the world, Europe experienced only one small war and two revolutions, all confined to its margin in the reactionary empires of Russia and Turkey. Yet no one talks of a Pax Germanica. Perhaps the very horror of the catastrophe of 1914, following a decade of mounting tension, makes us too ready to submerge earlier diplomatic crises and war scares in a

A.D.		
	1867	Second Reform Act in Great Britain
	1871	Proclamation of William I as Emperor of Germany; Russia denounces the Black Sea clauses of the the Treaty of Paris (1856)
	1871–1875	Gradual emergence of Third Republic in France
	1873	Onset of agricultural depression in western Europe
	1876	"Bulgarian atrocities" committed by Turks in suppressing a revolt
	1877	Russo-Turkish War begins
	1878	Treaty of San Stefano; Congress of Berlin
	1879	Alliance of Germany and Austria
	1881	Czar Alexander II assassinated
	1882	Germany, Austria, and Italy form Triple Alliance; British invade and occupy Egypt
	1884	Third Reform Act in Great Britain
	1884–1885	Berlin Conference (on Africa)
	1886	Introduction of First Home Rule Bill in British Parliament; its defeat followed by splitting of Liberal party
	1887	Reinsurance Treaty between Germany and Russia
	1888	Death of William I; accession of Frederick III; death of Frederick III; accession of William II
	1890	Bismarck dismissed
	1893–1894	Franco-Russian Alliance
	1898	Fashoda Crisis; first Germany Navy Law begins naval race with Great Britain
	1899	First Hague Peace Conference; Boer War between Great Britain and Transvaal begins
	1902	Anglo-Japanese Alliance; Treaty of Vereeniging ends Boer War
	1904	Anglo-French Entente concluded
	1904–1905	Russo-Japanese War
	1905	First Moroccan Crisis
	1905–1906	Russian Revolution
	1906	Algeciras Conference
	1907	Second Hague Peace Conference; conclusion of Anglo-Russian Entente
	1908	Austrian annexation of Bosnia and Herzegovina

1911   Second Moroccan Crisis
1912–1913   First Balkan War
1913   Second Balkan War
1914   Assassination of Archduke Francis Ferdinand at
            Sarajevo; Austrian ultimatum to Serbia; Russian
            mobilization; German and French mobilization;
            Germany declares war on Russia; Germany de-
            clares war on France; following German invasion
            of Belgium, Great Britain declares war on Ger-
            many
1915   Italy enters the war on the Allied side

---

vague impending sense of doom. But to do so is to lose perspective and to
miss what may have been most important in the life of late nineteenth-
century Europe. In those years more and more western Europeans came to
know prosperity and security. Despite the intensification of nationalistic
feelings and the competition implied by increasingly protectionist national
economies, Europe built up a practical internationalism. The gold standard
was universal. It was possible to travel from one end of Europe to the other
without a passport. And the industrial diplomacy of the giant firms that
came to dominate the national economies evolved a system of agreements—it is tempting to say treaties—as conducive to peace as any creation of the foreign offices. The Hague Conferences of 1899 and 1907
successfully codified the laws of war and gave birth to the idea of an
international court. That they failed to secure the peaceful settlement of all
international disputes should not reduce them to aberrations in a world
bent on war: they grew out of an experience of peace unparalleled in the
history of Europe and from a desire to prolong and improve it.

Contemporaries were not aware that the years around 1870 were the
watershed that they have come to appear to historians. The balance of
power was unshaken as the ruling concept of diplomacy. The League of the
Three Emperors, descended from the old Holy Alliance of 1815, was
dutifully resurrected and then re-resurrected, surviving almost to the end of
the eighties. That nobler creation of 1815, the Concert of Europe, survived
as well. Gladstone invoked it in 1871 to ratify Russia's unilateral denunciation of the neutralization of the Black Sea, imposed on her in the Treaty of

EUROPE IN 1914

□ European Allied countries in World War I
▓ The Central Powers in World War I
⋯ Neutral countries

0   200   400   600 Miles

Paris of 1856. The powers met again in 1876 and 1878 to try to settle the Eastern Question; another conference in 1884 imposed rules on the partition of Africa; and a faint echo of the Concert could be heard as late as 1906 when the powers met at Algeciras to sort out the Moroccan imbroglio.

It took time to appreciate the international implications even of such obvious changes as the emergence of Italy and Germany as unified states or the crushing defeat of France, no longer the threat to peace she had been under the two Napoleons. In the years immediately after Sedan some right-wing French leaders dreamed of reconquering the lost provinces of Alsace and Lorraine, and in the eighties and nineties the French displayed more initiative than any other European nation in the colonial game. But that was by way of compensating for a formidable decline: Bismarck encouraged the French in Africa to keep them in good temper on the northeastern frontier. And whereas the French menace had been the cornerstone of Bismarck's defensive diplomacy in the seventies, by the eighties it was more likely to be pulled out to serve his tactical needs: when that insub-

stantial demagogue General Boulanger stirred French political waters in
1886–1889, Bismarck used the reminiscence of Bonapartism to secure the
election of a complaisant Reichstag that would pass an army law he was
finding it difficult to carry. But not everyone was so perceptive as the
Chancellor.

If any Englishman saw the years around 1870 as a turning point, it was
probably because Gladstone was pursuing a foreign policy whose stated
grounds lay not only in a novel estimate of the national interest but in that
high moral sense that so moved or outraged English voters, depending on
their party. But in fact realistic assumptions governed most essentials of
Gladstone's policy, and when Disraeli returned to office in 1874, even the
old gestures were revived. Sending the fleet to Besika Bay in 1877 to
overawe the Russians, or the special train made ready to carry Disraeli
away when the Congress of Berlin, the next year, showed signs of going
against his wishes, were both splendid instances of Palmerstonian bravado.
Again, change can be discerned in the eighties. Under Lord Salisbury after
1886, British foreign policy became a technically brilliant rear-guard
action, and Salisbury is said to have been delighted with the Chinese ambassador who addressed him as the representative of one declining empire to
another. In the nineties, Britain's old self-imposed isolation was reinforced
by the determined hostility of the whole Continent; by the time of the Boer
War, the dimmest minister could not be unaware of that. In the same
decade the British public developed the alarming conviction that the country was being flooded with German goods—the high level of imports
natural to a prosperous country had just been made evident by an indirectly protectionist measure requiring that imported goods be labeled with
country of origin. In another ten years, the armaments race had made it
clear to everyone that the real threat lay in Berlin.

Immediate sweeping changes were to be found about 1870 in internal,
not foreign, policies. All the west European powers had to cope, for example, with pressing problems of industrial change. Here France fared
least well. She was short of coal in any event, and losing Alsace and
Lorraine deprived her of rich deposits of iron ore that could at last be
exploited thanks to the discovery of a process for neutralizing the phos-
phorus they contained. French industrial output increased little, despite
some brilliant inventions. Even more alarming, the country that had once
been the most populous in Europe remained virtually stationary in population; its birth rate remained stubbornly low. In Britain the industrial situation was ambiguous, combining notable progress in some sectors of the
economy with a sharp relative decline in world position and profitability
among the basic manufactures of the Industrial Revolution; notwithstanding a fairly steady, if modest, rise in output and a marked rise in well-being

among the working classes, men talked of a "great depression." Industrial Germany, on the other hand, moved ahead in great leaps, a performance owing much to a superb ability to turn science to productive ends.

All three nations, moreover, faced an agricultural crisis. Railways, steamships, and refrigeration made it possible for the vast new productive areas in Russia, North America, and Australia to sell grain and meat in the European market for lower prices than those needed to sustain the high-cost agriculture of western Europe. French farmers had to bear the added burden of the phylloxera, a disease that came near to destroying France's wine industry in the 1870's. Both Germany and France responded with tariff protection; smaller ·nations like Denmark even improved their position by specialization. But Britain, tied emotionally and institutionally to the free trade so advantageous to her in mid-century, could not accept protection. So, though some sectors of British agriculture (dairying and market gardening among them) prospered, the fall of wheat and meat prices speeded the breakup of rural society and undermined the economic foundations of the landed oligarchy, which at about the same time had to face the first fundamental political challenge to the continuance of its old supremacy.

The Western nations had, similarly, to absorb major constitutional changes. In default of a viable monarchical alternative, the French had backed into the Third Republic in the mid-seventies, an outcome to which the French right, firmly entrenched among the peasantry as well as in key national institutions like the Church and the army, was never reconciled. Politically, a multiplicity of parties made parliamentary government highly uncertain; policy appeared to be in a state of constant flux. But these tendencies to instability were counteracted by the strength of a centralized bureaucratic administration, and the dominance of cabinet making by various shades of radicals meant that politics oscillated, not violently from left to right and back, but less dramatically about the center. In the end policy changes were not so much matters of irreconcilable principles as of emphasis and personal style. This stability was reinforced by a strengthening of the republican spirit. The crucial question was education, for eradicating the power of the Church there would eliminate a major citadel of right-wing influence. The so-called laic laws of 1882 were aimed at securing a secular system of primary and secondary education; the late eighties and nineties even saw a "Ralliement," an attempt (encouraged by the new liberally inclined Pope Leo XIII) to bring the Church to support the Republic and to heal the breach in French opinion. Then, at the end of the nineties, the country was again split apart by the Dreyfus case: a Jewish bourgeois army officer had been convicted on trumped-up charges of espionage; defended by the left and execrated by the right, Dreyfus

became the touchstone of political loyalty—and of nearly everything else—
for a generation. There was a resurgence of the old republican anticlerical-
ism. In 1904 religious orders were forbidden to teach, and secular education became obligatory; in the following year a new concordat with the
Vatican brought about the definitive separation of church and state.

A similar pattern was to be found in Italy. The temporal power of the
papacy was destroyed when Rome was at last occupied in 1870, at the very
time that the pope's infallibility in questions of faith and morals was being
proclaimed by the first Vatican Council. The papacy's steadfast refusal to
exchange recognition of the new Italian state for recognition of its own
privileged status within the Vatican worsened social divisions. The flux of
parties, owing less to ideas and more to men, was far more unsettling
than its analogue in France, while administrative centralization was prevented from attaining the French level of success by a stubborn regionalism,
reinforced by the economic backwardness of much of the country. Least
successful of the Western nations in solving her constitutional problems,
Italy remained of little account in European affairs.

In Germany, Bismarck also faced—or created—a struggle with the
Roman Catholic Church. The Liberals, with whom he was in uneasy
alliance in the seventies, called it the Kulturkampf. But Bismarck was not
motivated by Liberal ideology. Rather he was fighting the intrusion into
politics of the Center party, a specifically Catholic party with sympathetic
ties to Catholics in Austria, Poland, and France. But the Kulturkampf was
less important as a weapon against encirclement than as a phase of
Bismarck's war on his political enemies: as the Center party had succeeded
the Liberals, whom he had pursued so implacably in the 1860's, so it was
in turn succeeded by the Social Democrats; in 1877 Bismarck abandoned
the Kulturkampf, leaving the Center party strengthened and political
Catholicism as a political fact that has survived in German life to the
present day. This political jousting suggests that Bismarck's basic problem
was not the preservation of a constitution, as in France, but the preservation of his own power: the complicated federal structure on which his
power rested was useful as long as it worked. But for all its success in
neutralizing his enemies and competitors at home and abroad, Bismarck's
system contained a fatal flaw: responsible only to the emperor, he could be
dismissed by the emperor. It happened when Bismarck's willing if sometimes restive accomplice William I was succeeded in 1888—leaving out of
account the three-month reign of Frederick III—by the young William II,
who was determined to assert himself, and forced Bismarck to resign in
1890. The highly artificial machine could not be worked so well by the
lesser men who were heirs to Bismarck's power.

The English constitution easily absorbed a succession of fundamental alterations—the enfranchisement of urban workingmen in 1867, the secret ballot in 1872, nearly universal male suffrage in 1884, and a drastic re-working of parliamentary representation the next year. The civil service was effectively reformed, and Parliament was brought under tighter execu-tive control, made necessary by the imperatives of increased legislation and consistent, programmatic appeals to the electorate. But Britain came close to political paralysis over Ireland. A short-lived ration of autonomy given to that agrarian, Catholic nation in the late eighteenth century had been extinguished by the Act of Union of 1800. Once Daniel O'Connell had won the battle for "Catholic Emancipation"—the right of Catholics to sit in Parliament and to hold office—in 1829, he began to agitate for repeal of the Union. The apathy that followed the terrible famine of 1845–1846—which killed nearly a million and drove another million abroad—led some Englishmen in the 1850's to think that the Irish problem had been solved by a cruel providence. But the famine lent a new dimension to Irish bitter-ness, and in the sixties and seventies the old land agitation was revived and a new drive to independence was launched by the Fenians, both move-ments secret and violent. The moderate answer to this extremism was Home Rule—not separation but autonomy in internal matters—fought for in Parliament in the eighties by an Irish party, superbly disciplined and led by Charles Stewart Parnell. It had proved hard enough for English opinion to accept the land reforms carried by Gladstone to provide some security for the hard-pressed Irish tenants; to accept even a partial severing of the political tie was unthinkable. Indeed when the Conservatives at the end of the century turned to a different kind of land reform and by subsidized land purchase created an Irish peasant economy entirely unlike the capitalist agriculture of England, their avowed intention was "to kill Home Rule by kindness." Gladstone's attempt to carry Home Rule in 1886 split the Liberal party, a second attempt failed in the Lords in 1893, and the third, successful attempt in 1914 was carried by the Liberals only after the powers of the House of Lords had been reduced and at the risk of civil war between the Catholics and the Protestant minority in the northern Irish province of Ulster, fully backed by much of English Conservatism.

Finally, the western European nations had increasingly to reckon with the growth of public opinion. Statesmen had once been able to act without constantly looking over their shoulders, except to the known or usually predictable pressures of a king, a court, or a small aristocratic class. The French Revolution, emerging working-class movements, and liberal nation-alism had helped to break up this old dispensation; after 1870, with the spread of education and literacy, the multiplication of newspapers, and the new complexity of social and economic life, all was in confusion. Even an authoritarian ruler like Bismarck was not untouched by the problem of public opinion, as he showed in his efforts to neutralize Pan-Germanism or in his reluctant concessions to the new German taste for colonies. In Great Britain, public opinion plunged from one emotional orgy to another—now protesting the massacre of Bulgarians by Turks, now cheering the heroic stand of the same Turks against the Russians, crying for vengeance for General Gordon's death at Khartoum, or rioting in rather ugly joy over the relief of Mafeking during the South African War. Great Britain was not unique, only advanced. In time, this uncertain force would be better understood and controlled, even used by demagogues with technical resources far beyond those of their pale ancestors. In the years between Sedan and Sarajevo, public opinion lends a fitful appearance to the age.

Below this troubled surface there were, of course, important basic shifts in attitude, among them a growth of racial thinking and of anti-Semitism in particular, a tendency to regard irrationalism and violence as norms, a flight from politics. For the most broadly symptomatic of these changes, one would probably turn to the gradual eclipse of mid-century liberalism by a resurgent conservatism on the one hand and an emergent socialism on the other. It was encapsulated in the confrontation of the Bismarckian state and German social democracy, both so alien to the liberalism of 1848; with the growth of syndicalist doctrines, it added a new dimension to the endemic split in French society. In Great Britain, the home of classical liberalism, the middle classes, their major ambitions gained, retreated from their old radicalism to the Conservatives; the Liberal party, though out of power for most of the twenty years after 1886, was to some extent freed by this desertion to become more radical, but after the brilliant Indian summer of social reforms enacted between 1906 and 1911, it fell victim to the war and to the very English socialism of the Labour party after 1918. In every country in western Europe to some degree, this polarization seemed to threaten dissolution in the years just before 1914, and men on both sides thought that when war came socialism might cut across national lines and lead soldiers to lay down their arms rather than fight in a capitalist war. But the mercurial nature of public opinion asserted itself again, and nationalism triumphed after all.

However greedy their colonial ambitions or intricate their diplomacy, the Western powers were committed to peace. England was isolated, France too weak to fight, and Germany "satiated." Beyond that, as beneficiaries of industrialism and the machinery of the nation-state, they stood to lose most from war. Ironically, the initiative lay with three powers surviving from an older imperial, preindustrial world. One of those powers, Turkey, an empire in name only, had long been transmuted into the "Eastern Question": what would happen to his holdings when "the Sick Man of Europe" died at last? In Austria-Hungary, tension between the

German and Magyar parts of the Dual Monarchy was compounded by the bitter quarrel of each of them with important minorities, Czechs or Croats. But while Austria-Hungary was making the transition from empire to question, she, like Turkey, was propped up because the Western powers knew of nothing better to take her place. Only the Russian autocracy showed signs of moving into the modern industrial world, with the help of massive infusions of Western capital, more and more of it French. Yet after the assassination of Czar Alexander II in 1881, the autocracy grew worse under his incompetent successors and their reactionary advisers. Russia's rulers could not be unaware of the movement of public opinion. But they would yield nothing to the desire for reform growing among the increasingly frustrated intelligentsia or to the idiosyncratic Russian socialism; they learned little even from their resounding defeat by Japan in 1904 or the abortive revolution of 1905. They responded only to old traditions like anti-Semitism or to the newer, though uneven, enthusiasm for Pan-Slavism. Russia did not make the transition from empire to question: war and revolution destroyed her.

These three empires ringed the Balkans. There Turkey was in retreat: her European provinces had broken away or were doing so by reproducing Western nationalism. Only occasionally would she try, violently, to reassert her suzerainty. In the Balkans Austria-Hungary could find an outlet for her commerce and capital. A forward movement, moreover, might bring her compensation for her loss of German leadership at Sadowa and prevent the formation of a large southern Slav state, a particularly threatening prospect, given Austro-Hungarian troubles with Slav minorities at home. In the Balkans Russia had two steady concerns—to erect a barrier against Austrian aggression and to assure that the Straits at Constantinople, commanding entry to the Black Sea, remained in control of a power that, if not friendly, was at least weak. But when she was seized with Pan-Slavic enthusiasm, Russia could go further and assume her old role as patron of her fellow Slavs and of the Orthodox Church. If the Balkans were, as the old saw has it, the powder keg of Europe, the danger of explosion lay not so much in the conscious, criminal wielding of a firebrand as in the flickers of spontaneous combustion arising from decay.

Rebellions in the Turkish provinces in 1875 provoked terrible massacres in Bulgaria. A European conference called in 1876 to impose reforms on Turkey got nowhere, and the following year Russia declared war. Turkish power proved far more resilient, and Russian armies far less efficient than expected; still, having staggered through to a victory of sorts by 1878, Russia demanded the creation of a "Big Bulgaria"—partly to bolster her sagging prestige, partly to provide a viable alternative to Turkish misrule—that she had agreed not to support the year before. Russian ministers were divided about the Pan-Slav implications of the Treaty of San Stefano; this provided an opportunity for Disraeli to reassert his pro-Turkish policy, now that Gladstone's anti-Turkish campaign had been momentarily neutralized by the Turks' heroic stand at Plevna. The main result of the ensuing Congress of Berlin was the partition of Big Bulgaria: one part, called Macedonia, was returned to Turkish misrule and more atrocities in the nineties; the remainder was broken into Bulgaria proper and Eastern Rumelia, though the two were reunited without serious protest seven years later. The British initiative, taken so dramatically at Berlin, was not maintained. In 1879, Gladstone's novel "Midlothian Campaign"— a minister had never before carried his case to the country—once more roused British voters against Disraeli's forward policy; but Gladstone's own government after 1880 was so divided that no clear line could come from the Liberals, and thus the way was opened for Salisbury's greater realism after 1886.

The nation that emerged from Berlin with its prestige most enhanced was Germany, although Bismarck had gained nothing but a reputation as an "honest broker." In 1879, to provide a firmer basis for the security he had gained opportunistically, Bismarck launched the first of the alliances that were to be the forms determining official and popular thinking about European alignments for a whole generation. His explicit alliance with Austria-Hungary was mildly reinforced in 1882 by the addition of Italy to create the Triple Alliance: Italy got some badly needed prestige, and there was a not very impressive exchange of promises of Italian neutrality in case of an Austro-Russian war and of German help for Italy in a French war. But Bismarck had no intention of alienating Russia, though the Alliance was clearly directed eastward. In 1881 he secretly revived the League of the Three Emperors, and when it expired in 1887 concluded a bilateral "Reinsurance Treaty" with Russia. When Bismarck fell in 1890, his successors at once refused to renew the unpopular Russian agreement; only then did Austria's strong confidence in German support begin to have some foundation in fact.

Bismarck's system for German security gained not only from his own skill but from the rupture of whatever tacit understanding existed between Britain and France when Britain unilaterally occupied Egypt in 1882. Bismarck neatly capped this estrangement by covertly encouraging the French to pursue an active colonial policy. With his own reluctant colonial enterprises, he thus helped to force Britain into the un-Palmerstonian necessity of adding more and more responsibilities to secure her traditional goals, protecting the route to India and isolating the Boer Republics in South Africa. But the occupation of Egypt had two further consequences for Europe. As the French could not allow themselves to be isolated, they edged, with whatever degree of republican discomfort, into an alliance with Russia, concluded in 1892–1894 and firmly sustained by rapidly growing French investment; the Triple Alliance was thus confronted with the beginnings of an opposing bloc. And now that Britain was firmly entrenched in Egypt, her superintendence of the Eastern Mediterranean could be conducted from there (and from Cyprus, which she occupied in 1877). The old need to prop up Turkey fell away, leaving Turkey open to German penetration.

Although in the 1890's the western European powers were primarily concerned with Africa and the Far East, the decade was a watershed in European diplomacy. Bismarck's fall in 1890 gave the working of German foreign policy to men without his percipience or skill. The British, to escape their isolation, began to look less than ever across the Channel and more across the ocean—to the growing Commonwealth of her self-governing colonies; to Japan, with whom she concluded an alliance in 1902; and, of most importance in the long run, to the United States, with whom a tacit alliance began to emerge as the two countries settled the last of the disputes that had kept them at loggerheads throughout the nineteenth century. Britain remained a European power, of course, but her new relationships with France and Russia, worked out from 1904 to 1907, were approached gingerly by settling outstanding conflicts (for example, delimiting Russian and British spheres of influence in Persia) and by military conversations. There was thus the risk that the Triple Entente, based on largely secret, certainly informal understandings, was likely to be seen as weaker than in fact it was.

Yet another element transforming European diplomacy was military. The wars of mid-century and the stunning German example brought home to Europe's statesmen the possibilities of modern warfare. Except in England, European nations relied increasingly on universal military service to provide manpower for their armies. This widening of the military net was paralleled by a growing professionalization among officers, particularly in the high commands, where the crucial invention was the general staff of the Germans; copied elsewhere (the British again resisting until the new century), it made possible long-range planning for mobilization and strategy against all eventualities. Supported in writings of military and naval theorists and by the work of publicists and historians caught up in the new enthusiasm, the professional soldiers became a powerful pressure group, far more regularly influential in government than military men had usually been before. Basic to this new military thinking was a revolutionary technology resting on rapid scientific development (in chemistry in particular) and on the growth of the heavy industry required to produce armaments and that in turn required them for its own perpetuation and profitability.

Although there was steady improvement in small arms and artillery, and although European armies broke through to new ideas in training, military engineering, and logistics (especially in the use of railways), the most striking technological changes affected the world's navies. The mine, the torpedo, and the submarine were all developed in these years and were to become major weapons in the future. But between 1890 and 1914 men's imaginations were captured far more fully by warships. The old wooden ships of the line, little changed for centuries, had given way in mid-century to ironclads; now there appeared a whole range of specialized ships—destroyers, cruisers, and battleships—protected by steel armorplate, propelled by triple-expansion steam engines and later by steam turbines, and equipped with fire power unimaginable a generation before. In 1898 William II and his chief naval adviser, Admiral Alfred von Tirpitz, launched, against considerable domestic resistance, a naval building program designed to bring the German navy into approximate equality with the British, who replied in turn. Reformed and expanded armies, the naval race, and the novel problem of an unceasing technological obsolescence sharply distorted traditional government policies, not only in strategic and diplomatic planning, but in finance. The need to meet vast expenditures, added to the demands of increasing social services, dictated levels of taxation unthinkable in the nineteenth century. That barrier broken, the resources of the modern leviathan state were there for the asking.

From about 1905 tension rose steadily in Europe, partly a result of the arms race, partly a consequence of an increasingly frenetic insistence by Germany on her claims as a world power. Once in 1905 and again in 1911, the Germans asserted their "rights" in the somewhat surprising locale of Morocco, a French sphere of influence under the terms of the Anglo-French entente; the earlier confrontation raised the prospect of Franco-German hostilities for the first time in thirty years, and the threat of war in the second was taken most seriously in Great Britain. But it was in the Balkans that the fuse was laid. In 1907, a revolution took place in Turkey, though the Young Turks proved immediately that they could do little more to solve Turkish problems than the deposed sultan. The revolution gave Austria-Hungary the chance formally to annex Bosnia and Herzegovina, which she had occupied since the Congress of Berlin as a hedge against the expected expansion of Serbia into the possibility of a southern Slav state that so troubled imaginations in Vienna. In 1912, when Turkey was further embroiled in a war with Italy over Italian designs on Libya, the Balkan states of Serbia, Greece, Bulgaria, and Montenegro united against Turkey, in the end limiting her to a tiny European foothold about Constantinople. But the victorious allies fell out, and in 1913, following a Bulgarian attack, Serbia and Greece were joined by Rumania to defeat Bulgaria and to make territorial gains for themselves.

The two Balkan wars provide a new context for the competing ambitions of Russia and Austria-Hungary, the latter perhaps especially dangerous from the blow to her prestige by the victories of the Balkan states. Bismarck had often said that the Balkans were not worth the bones of a single Pomeranian grenadier; now his successors, mesmerized for years by the prospects of a Berlin-to-Baghdad railway, found them well worth the living presence of Liman von Sanders, a general at the head of a military mission to Turkey, which was rapidly becoming a German protectorate. The Russians had been content to have the Straits controlled by a weak sultan; they could not be indifferent to their domination by Germany. Moreover, the Russians were forced into supporting Serbia in order to maintain a neutral buffer against any possible Austrian expansion. For their part, the Austrians continued their harassment of the Serbs. Not content with their Bosnian coup of 1908, in 1913, they conjured up an independent Albania to block Serbia's outlet to the Adriatic. The pretext they wanted for still further action arose on June 28, 1914, when the Archduke Francis Ferdinand, heir to the Austro-Hungarian throne, was assassinated at Sarajevo by a member of a secret society of Serbian nationalists.

Austria-Hungary at once consulted her principal ally. Germany, apparently willing to satisfy Austrian ambition and to see the Serbian problem solved by running the risk that the war could be contained, gave her ally a free hand. Although Serbia's reply to the Austrian ultimatum was an almost complete surrender, the Austrians deemed it insufficient. Their declaration of war on Serbia forced the Russians to reply, in an attempt to force Austria to back down, with a partial mobilization, made general on July 30. This triggered German mobilization the next day. Then, having failed to get guarantees of neutrality from Russia's ally France, Germany declared war on her on August 3. Germany's long-established western strategy committed her to strike at France through Belgium; her refusal to respect that neutrality, demanded in a British ultimatum, brought Britain into the war on August 4. Only Italy, whose ties to the Central Powers had progressively weakened, kept neutral, to enter the war (well rewarded) on the side of Britain and France in 1915. Since 1879 the developing alliance system had worked to keep the peace. Now, with that one exception, it continued to work perfectly. Once the switches were pulled in Vienna and Berlin, mobilizations followed in sequence, like an expertly engineered set of electrical relays, and the lights went out all over Europe.

For Further Reading

Albertini, Luigi, *The Origins of the War of 1914.*
Brogan, D. W., *France under the Republic (1870–1939).*

Ensor, R. C. K., *England, 1870–1914.*
Fischer, Fritz, *Germany's Aims in World War I.*
Lafore, Laurence, *The Long Fuse: An Interpretation of the Origins of World War I.*
Langer, William L., *The Diplomacy of Imperialism.*
Taylor, A. J. P., *Bismarck: The Man and Statesman.*
———, *The Struggle for Mastery in Europe, 1848–1918.*

The Great World War: 1914-1945

20   World War I

[handwritten: Jean Jaures & an active socialist 3rd minority]

With what innocence, with what enthusiasm, did the Europeans of 1914 respond to the tocsin! No one foresaw even the contours of the disaster ahead, and most people welcomed the war as a great patriotic adventure. After a decade of worsening crises and a spiraling arms race, they had come to expect a final showdown, but after decades of peace, they had forgotten what war was like and few had an inkling that a modern war would multiply the terrors of earlier conflicts. Europeans marched off to battle with something close to exultation, proud in their patriotism and certain of their cause, confident of a victorious end in a short time. It was the last time in our civilization that war could be greeted in this fashion.

Patriotic exultation had been preceded by the solicitous efforts of all governments to save the appearances of peacefulness, to make it seem as if the enemy were also the unprovoked aggressor. None had pursued this policy of deception with more cunning or under greater difficulties than the German government, and nowhere was the appearance of fighting a defensive war more important than in Germany, where the Social Democratic party, with its avowed pacifism, represented a third of the electorate. Indeed, international socialism, pledged to oppose all imperialist wars, became the first victim of the war. Its most attractive leader, the French Socialist Jean Jaurès, was assassinated at the end of July, and socialists everywhere felt their national allegiance far more strongly than their commitment to international class solidarity. Socialist backing of the war made possible that instantaneous closing of national ranks—epitomized by the formation in France of the *union sacré*—that promised the adjournment of political conflicts for the duration of the war. In the passion of the moment, all parties and all classes pledged their full support to the nation, in what everybody expected would be a short, decisive testing *moment.*

At the beginning of the war, the sides were fairly evenly balanced. In a

A.D.   1914   German declaration of war on Russia; German declaration of war on France; British declaration of war on Germany; Battle of the Marne

          1915   *Lusitania* sunk by German submarine, 139 Americans lost; Italy enters war on Allied side; Dardanelles operation

          1916   British Parliament passes conscription; Battle of Verdun; Hindenburg appointed chief of staff with Ludendorff as quartermaster general; Lloyd George becomes prime minister of Great Britain

          1917   Germany notifies U.S. that unrestricted submarine warfare will begin the next day; provisional Russian government established under Prince Lvov; Nicholas II abdicates; U.S. declares war on Germany; mutinies in French army; beginning of ill-fated Brusilov offensive; German Chancellor Bethmann Hollweg forced to resign and succeeded by Dr. Michaelis; real power in hands of Hindenburg and Ludendorff; beginning of Italian disaster at Caporetto; Bolshevik Revolution; Clemenceau becomes prime minister in France; Bolshevik Russia concludes armistice with Central Powers

          1918   Russia signs Brest Litovsk Treaty, ceding Poland, Lithuania, Ukraine, etc.; Germans begin great spring offensive in the west; Foch named commander in chief of Allied forces in France; first major, successful American engagement at Château-Thierry; Second Battle of the Marne; successful Allied counteroffensive in the west; Bulgaria receives armistice; new German government of Prince Max von Baden asks President Wilson for armistice based on Fourteen Points; armistice with Turkey; Allies sign armistice with Austria-Hungary; Germany accepts armistice and hostilities cease everywhere

short war, the Central Powers, with the German army as the backbone of their strength, would enjoy certain advantages. They were poised for action, and their interior lines of communication allowed for the quick transport of troops and equipment. The Allies held potential advantages in a long war: the vast manpower of Russia and the great naval superiority of England that guaranteed free access to foreign, especially American, supplies. In such intangible matters as leadership and morale, the great contestants—Germany, France, and England—were evenly matched, at least at the beginning.

German strategists had long hatched meticulous plans for a lightning war and for nothing else. In August, they set them in motion. By attacking France through Belgium, they expected to capture Paris from the west and to break French resistance in a matter of weeks. The Russian front, meanwhile, was to remain virtually undefended, until, after France's defeat, the bulk of the German army could be sent eastward, to crush the czarist armies. For four weeks, the German advance proceeded like clockwork, as Belgian defenses crumbled and French armies retreated.

In early September, German troops were within sight of Paris; the Germans, however, had weakened their right flank. They had changed their minds about Russia, and sent troops to the eastern front, while the French rallied for the defense of their capital. With magnificent, if costly, gallantry, they counterattacked, and the miracle of the Marne, as it came to be called, threw German troops back and ended the threat to Paris. Fighting then shifted to the northwest, with each side aiming to outflank the other; the Germans also hoped in the process to capture the channel ports, thus depriving the British army of its vital supply routes. The British bore the brunt of this savage "race to the sea," and denied the Germans this strategic prize as well.

Even after the Marne, the German people could comfort themselves; on the eastern front, they had won gigantic victories, notably at Tannenberg, victories they wrongly credited to the genius of Hindenburg, and which had weakened, but not destroyed, the Russian army. Everywhere German troops stood triumphant on enemy soil. But the decisive victory had eluded them, and would elude them forever. Six weeks after the outbreak of the war, most German leaders realized that their chances for winning a clear-cut victory had virtually vanished. The Allies, injured but intact and resolute, faced a Germany that had won enough in those early weeks to reject a peace that did not bring them large gains but not enough to impose its own terms on a world of enemies. The tragedy was that neither side could win.

The losses in those early weeks of fighting had been monstrous, especially to the British and French, whose casualties then and for the rest of the war consistently outran those of the Germans. The young elite of each army had been decimated, and the great blood bath which was to destroy so many talented Europeans had begun in earnest. The cost of a long war should have been clear to all, but war enhances man's capacity for self-delusion.

By the end of 1914, the western front had become stabilized, and the vast armies stretching from the Channel to the Alps dug themselves in, built trenches behind barbed wire, with a narrow gap between lines, known as no man's land. In trenches that were wet and crawling with rats, millions of soldiers huddled together, battling alternately monotony and death. Never before had so many soldiers faced each other in such futility, terrorized by the all-powerful machine gun which made every offensive action, every patrol, a death trap.

There were apparently no alternatives, no ways of escaping this bloody stalemate. Yet strategists devised many ingenious ideas and clever projects. The Germans, for example, sought to attack their enemies from behind, by fomenting revolution in the Near East or India or even Ireland. New weapons were invented; the Germans introduced zeppelins for bombing raids and poison gas for land attacks, forgetting that prevailing westerly winds would vitiate all but initial successes. Lloyd George championed armored vehicles, later known as tanks, and pushed their construction, despite Kitchener's sneer: "A pretty mechanical toy; the war will never be won by such machines." How was it to be won?

Two traditional means remained to be tried: the winning of new allies and the opening of new fronts. Diplomats on both sides worked on remaining neutrals. In September, 1914, Turkey joined Germany and Austria, not unexpectedly, thus blocking Allied access to Russian ports in the Black Sea. A few months later, the Allies persuaded—or bribed—Italy to enter on their side, in violation of her treaty obligations but in pursuit of her *"sacro egoismo,"* her immense annexationist appetite. The greatest neutral, the United States, admonished by its President to remain neutral in thought as well as deed, became an ever more important supplier of food, weapons, and credit to France and Britain, who controlled the sea. Germany's efforts to use her few submarines to cut off English supplies proved risky because, as the sinking of the *Lusitania* in 1915 showed, effective submarine action entailed the loss of neutral lives and evoked the threat of American retaliation. The English blockade of Germany also violated neutral rights—and humanitarian scruples—but took no American lives and hence aroused less opposition. Still, the submarine proved an enticing new weapon to the Germans, and her military leaders ceaselessly urged its unrestricted use.

There were some leaders in England, notably Winston Churchill, who

agitated for the opening of a new front that would break the western stalemate. After months of wrangling, an expedition for the capture of the Dardanelles Straits was launched; if it had been successful, it would have separated Turkey from the Central Powers and provided much-needed help for Russia. But staggering incompetence ruined the enterprise, and very nearly eclipsed Churchill's fortunes. Years later, he still viewed it as the decisive turn to disaster: "Thereafter events passed very largely outside the scope of conscious choice. Governments and individuals conformed to the rhythm of the tragedy, and swayed and staggered forward in helpless violence, slaughtering and squandering on ever-increasing scales, till injuries were wrought to the structure of human society which a century will not efface, and which may conceivably prove fatal to the present civilization."

The main reason for the failure of Gallipoli had been the unwillingness of Anglo-French military leaders to do anything that might weaken the western front. They—and their German opponents—were mesmerized by that front, certain that the next time around, "with one more push," they could achieve a breakthrough and regain mobility. To that hope were sacrificed millions of men. Even on ordinary days, when all was quiet on the western front, many soldiers died on useless reconnaissance missions, while for the rest, the monotonous and debilitating routine remained unbroken. Both sides launched gigantic offensives as well, but at best these gained a few useless square miles, at the cost of tens of thousands of casualties. The French launched such futile attacks in 1915, and the next year both sides resorted to a strategy of attrition, hoping to wear down the enemy. In February, 1916, the Germans attacked Verdun, a stronghold of strategic and symbolic value. They assumed the French would defend it at all costs, that French armies would be bled white, and that German losses would be lower. For four months the battle raged. The French held Verdun, at an immense price to themselves—and to the Germans. Allied losses were always heavier than those of the Germans, but the Germans had another front to contend with. In the west, men were sacrificed to a military Moloch without reason, without intelligence, and without compassion. War had lost what glory it once possessed, and terrified men were killed by machinery that human reason had devised but could no longer control.

In the east, the war wore a more traditional guise. Armies moved over large tracts of land, hoping and sometimes succeeding in trapping or encircling enemy formations. In 1915, the Central Powers were everywhere successful, and Russia was deprived of her Polish possessions, leaving Germany and Austria quarreling over the spoils. In 1916 Russian Commander Aleksei Brusilov launched a counteroffensive which attested and strained Russian resiliency and by its failure hastened the final collapse of czardom. The eastern front never acquired the horrid glamour of the western front; the territory was unfamiliar and the fighting less gruesomely novel. But it determined the shape of things to come for more than half a century; the Russian revolutions would have been unthinkable without the prior breakdown of Russian life owing to the war.

In fact, the war imposed a tremendous burden on all belligerent societies, and the universal response to this new burden was a degree of social regimentation undreamed of in earlier decades and centuries. The anticipated short war had become protracted and total—the first war in history that deserved the epithet. Since there was no precedent, there was no master plan of regimentation—only step-by-step innovation and improvisation in order to mobilize, clothe, feed, and equip millions of combatants, to maintain production when manpower was short and raw materials scant, to feed the civilian population and keep up their morale. Problems were innumerable, and bewildering in their intricacy and unexpected interrelatedness. In the early months of the war, the British carried on under the motto "Business as usual," while the German High Command was stunned when a great industrialist, Walther Rathenau, asked what provisions had been made for the stockpiling of raw material. War as usual, war as it had been taught at Sandhurst or St. Cyr or the Kadettenschule, was dead. The Great War, to paraphrase Georges Clemenceau, France's fiery premier, was too complicated to be left to the soldiers.

Under the duress of war, the modern Leviathan was born. The State— so exquisitely circumscribed by decades of liberal theory and practice— suddenly assumed new powers over realms hitherto deemed immune from its control. The State as night watchman, as the English myth had it, now became the mobilizer of men and property, the commander of economic life, the censor of men's expressions, and the manipulator of men's minds. All this took place while traditional politics were adjourned, and while dissent was often denounced as unpatriotic, so that governments could assume these new powers with a minimum of struggle or opposition. Indeed, as governments began not only to conscript their male citizenry— this was novel only in England, where conscription was adopted in 1916—but to impose rationing, to control prices, to allocate labor and resources, their own powers over against parliament greatly increased. War socialism, as the Germans called the new statist regimentation, went hand in hand with war dictatorships, and even in democratic countries like England and France, parliaments lost much power. Lloyd George entered office in December, 1916, and Clemenceau in November, 1917; in July, 1917, the seemingly moderate German chancellor, Bethmann Hollweg, had to surrender power to a thinly disguised military dictatorship under Ludendorff and Hindenburg. In Russia, on the other hand, where autocracy had been the rule of centuries, the government's gross inefficiency stimulated demands for some measure of parliamentary control. In all countries, however, the freedom of individuals contracted. This was assumed to be temporary, but the prewar balance between individual liberty and public authority would never be restored.

Civilians everywhere sacrificed comforts and suffered deprivations; soldiers suffered incomparably more, but at least the common terror at the front bred a kind of camaraderie that sustained their spirits. Soldiers and civilians alike lived under the shadow of sudden death, lived with the fear that their lives or the lives of those close to them might suddenly be snuffed out in one of those futile battles in what gradually appeared to be an endless war. By winter, 1916, the enthusiasm of August, 1914, had long since turned into a grim, sullen mood, relieved by bursts of mordant cynicism.

Governments did their best to whip up ever fresh enthusiasm for the killing, and in the process received ample help from the established classes.

The chauvinistic cant that poured from press and pulpit was meant to rouse flagging spirits to new sacrifices. The techniques of propaganda, borrowed from prewar modes of advertising, became so important in the hands of governments that one English wit spoke of "propagandocracy" as the new type of rule. Wartime propaganda became ever cruder and uglier: it started with the theme "love your country and defend it" and gradually turned to "hate your enemy and kill him."

Allied minds were poisoned by atrocity stories about the Huns mutilating bodies of Belgian children, and German minds by horror tales about English greed and hypocrisy that were responsible for the war and the starving of innocent women and children. Truth was devalued along with life, and hardly a voice was raised in protest. The guardians of God's word led the martial chorus. Total war came to mean total hatred, though perhaps least of all among soldiers, because they knew that the enemies across the trenches were fellow pawns.

The systematic poisoning of men's minds by paroxysms of nationalism —which at the time Corporal Adolf Hitler found most impressive and worthy of emulation—further obstructed the search for peace. As the war dragged on, as the vilifications of the enemy mounted, appetites increased and war aims became more grandiose in order to justify past and future sacrifices. "They shall not have died in vain" became the monstrous slogan by which the war was escalated, and the still living were led to ever greater slaughter—to justify the already dead. Could those who had died, thinking they were defending their country, be justified by others dying for some new annexation? Thus the war fed on itself, and governments became prisoners of their own propaganda.

The definition of war aims proved divisive among and within nations. The French demands were deceptively reasonable: they wanted the restoration of Alsace-Lorraine—which only a defeated Germany would yield; the English vowed to destroy Prussian militarism and terminate the German threat to the European balance of power. Colonial gains would be incidental rewards. Germany harbored the most ambitious war aims which would in fact have established her as the hegemonial power in Europe— hence a world power in England's place. The heart of Germany's programs—different groups embraced different varieties of avarice—was the establishment of a Central European Confederation, dominated by a victorious Reich. Many Germans thought of this new order as establishing in the twentieth century a Pax Germanica to replace the Pax Britannica. Whether flamboyant or seemingly reasonable, the war aims of the belligerents ruled out a compromise peace such as the pope or President Wilson hoped to mediate. The appetite grew with the eating—or, this time, with the dying.

The escalation of war aims had political origins and consequences. By and large, the traditional right in Europe propounded harsh war aims, hoping that visible, national gains would redound to the prestige and profit of the upper classes. German industrialists were vehement exemplars of this combined greed and fear. The European left was far more diffident, and a steadily growing minority of socialist militants demanded a peace without annexation or indemnity that would put an end to "the imperialist war." The suspicion that the war was being continued to serve class ends began to spread among radicals and working-class groups, particularly in Russia and Germany—in the very countries where the lower classes had to bear the brunt of mounting hardships, such as inflation, with wages lagging far behind the rise in prices, malnutrition, and the worst form of class warfare—the fight for bread. This suspicion and the daily experience of inequality fostered a new socialist militancy, which in Germany, for example, led to a schism among socialists and the founding of the Independent Socialists, a radical antiwar party. In neutral Switzerland, Russian exiles led by Lenin and radical socialists from other countries vowed to turn the imperialist war into a revolutionary struggle, to end the war by first ending capitalist oppression, as they called it. By 1916 the national unity that had swept across Europe in August, 1914, was shaken; in 1917 that unity collapsed in one country and was severely tried in all others.

In retrospect, 1917 looms as one of the decisive years in the history of European civilization. For in that year, the old system collapsed as America's entry into the war signaled the end of the more or less autonomous European states-system and the Bolshevik Revolution signaled the beginning of a new revolutionary challenge to Europe's social order. In 1917 Wilson and Lenin appeared simultaneously on the scene and faced each other across a prostrate Europe. In a sense both had been called forth by the challenge of German power; neither would disappear with its destruction. The implications of America's entry and Russia's revolutionary secession were not evident at first; they became clear gradually, as for half a century of disaster Europe fitfully suffered from the constellation that dominated 1917: German power, Bolshevism, and the intermittent need for an America that was by unpredictable turns too remote and too close.

These three elements were strangely intertwined from the beginning. Without the direct challenge of German power, embodied in her declaration of unrestricted submarine warfare, the United States would not have entered the war. Gratuitously, Germany's ruling classes, made arrogant by their victories and frantic by the elusiveness of victory, provoked their own nemesis: the Allies would never have been able to defeat Germany without American help. German power also paved the way for Bolshevism: indirectly, by precipitating the collapse of czardom and of its immediate, liberal successors, and directly, by transporting Lenin from Switzerland to the Finland Station, and by supplying Bolshevism with subsidies. Ludendorff's hope to use Lenin, and Lenin's to use Ludendorff, was but an early example of that collaboration between right and left extremists which was to prove so debilitating to political stability in the ensuing half-century. In 1917, Germany drew short-term advantages both from unrestricted submarine warfare and from her support of Bolshevism. The long-term advantages accrued to her enemies. The Germans, however, were not the only ones to stumble onto tactics that would defeat the very ends they were to serve: the politics of Europe had become so obscure, so filled with blinding hatreds and uncertainties, that clarity in political thought and action was virtually unattainable. The very pace of events suddenly outstripped the power of comprehension.

The beginning of 1917 saw a great intensification of hardships for all belligerents. Food shortages in England, Germany, and Russia worsened perceptibly, and people were alarmed that chronic malnutrition might turn into famine. In Russia, the workers first struck because of the breakdown of supplies; once out on the street, they demanded the end of czarism itself, and no group, not even the army, thought that Nicholas was savable. A provisional, bourgeois government was organized and vowed to fight on, but radical pressure forced it against its will to promise to seek a "peace without annexations and indemnities." War weariness spread in the East as in the West, where the stalemate continued bloody and unbroken. The much-heralded spring offensive of the French ended in failure and widespread mutinies. For the first time anywhere, the military's principal virtues, discipline and obedience, were flouted by exhausted and disillusioned men who, having lost their faith in their officers, refused to return to the trenches. Their new commander, Henri Philippe Pétain, went on the defensive: "I will wait for the Americans and for tanks." In Germany, there were wildcat strikes and some naval mutinies. War weariness—and the suspicion that the war was continued only for reasons of national greed—inspired an upsurge of left-wing militancy.

The greatest socialist victory came in Russia, where the Provisional Government's offensive ended in total disarray. Lenin's Bolsheviks seized power and demanded an immediate peace. France and England, close to collapse themselves, recognized that the Bolsheviks intended to desert them militarily and subvert them politically. The socialist agitation everywhere for an immediate revolutionary peace was most stimulated by the Bolshevik victory; it was only Wilson's promise of a liberal peace, based on national self-determination, that enabled the moderate left in the other belligerent countries to continue to support the war.

From the fall of 1917 to the following spring, the Germans had it all their own way, and they imparted some of their new energy to their lagging ally, Austria. In October, the Austro-German armies inflicted a monumental defeat on the Italians at Caporetto—a defeat that years later Mussolini's aggressive antics still sought to exorcise. At Brest Litovsk the Germans dictated a Carthaginian peace to the stunned Bolsheviks who had expected succor from their German comrades and instead saw most of industrial Russia torn from their hands. In March, 1918, Ludendorff, having shifted all but a million men from the east, threw the German armies into a series of offensives in the west that repeatedly broke through Allied lines. So precarious was their position that the Allies, who for three years had fought under separate and often poorly coordinated commands, finally appointed a French general, Ferdinand Foch, as supreme commander. By July, the Germans were once again across the Marne and within 35 miles of Paris. But this time, they quickly succumbed to Allied, including American, counterattacks. Weary, without reserves of men or supplies, they began a retreat which—if the Allies had had more strength or self-confidence—could easily have been turned into a rout.

Defeat threatened Germany's allies as well. Anglo-French offensives in the Near East and the Balkans—offensives that were not unrelated to imperialist aims—brought the Ottoman Empire and Bulgaria close to disaster. The tremors were felt farther north, and as Allied troops advanced in southeast Europe, the Austro-Hungarian monarchy, long plagued by internal strife, finally disintegrated into its national components. The Czechs and Slovaks, the Poles, the Hungarians, and the Yugoslavs proclaimed their independence. The venerable empire which, as Trotsky put it maliciously, "had long before hung out a sign for an undertaker, not demanding any high qualifications of him," ceased to exist. The Central Powers were crumbling at last—faster indeed than the Allies had thought possible.

In late September, Ludendorff precipitously demanded the creation of a democratic government that should immediately appeal to President Wilson for an armistice. The choice of Wilson was deliberate and cunning. His moral ascendancy in Europe was such that the Germans could hope that he would break Allied vindictiveness and insist on a "soft peace." For the moment, American power was the arbiter of Europe; Wilson told the Germans that they must first rid themselves of the imperial dynasty and told the Allies that they must grant Germany an armistice on the basis of his Fourteen Points. Weeks passed, until Foch finally presented the Germans with the terms of a harsh armistice. They had no choice but to accept, and on November 11, 1918, at eleven in the morning, the fighting stopped. Europe experienced its last day of universal rejoicing. The agony was over.

But life could never be the same. The very fact that the peace conference in Paris was dominated by a non-European, Woodrow Wilson, who had won the hearts of Europeans as no leader of their own ever had, symbolized the tremendous changes that the war had wrought in Europe. The physiognomy of Europe had been decisively altered, and historians have been debating ever since whether the war created or merely accelerated these changes. It certainly created the conditions for change—witness the Bolshevik Revolution: Bolshevism, long nurtured in prewar thoughts and antagonisms, could never have triumphed without the war.

The war had brought immense changes and taken an incalculable toll of European life. It is relatively easy to measure the material cost: the homes and factories destroyed, national economies exhausted, existing assets wasted, currencies ruined by inflation, and national debts acquired that a few years before would have been unimaginable. The total cost of the war has been estimated at $350 billion—the dollar reckoned at 1918 value. Europe's place in the world economy was impaired beyond recovery; two new giants, America and Japan, had been making colossal strides, while Europe bled.

The human cost is harder to assess. More than 10 million Europeans had died in battle—as well as 115,000 Americans. At least twice that number had been wounded, many of them left to live out their lives as cripples. Thereafter, millions of mutilated men walked the streets of Europe as reminders of the ravages of war. France lost half its men between the ages of twenty and thirty-two—and others suffered almost as much. But numbers fail to tell the full story. Among the dead was the promise and flower of Europe's youth. The potential leaders of the 1920's and 1930's had been decimated, as thousands of men of recognized talent died alongside others whose talents and genius would remain undiscovered forever. In those futile charges across no man's land, junior officers and young volunteers were mowed down first: nearly 20 per cent of all Oxford University men who served in the war were killed. Of 346 students of the École Normale Supérieure mobilized, 143 never returned. Even Europe, with its historic abundance of talent, could not suffer such losses without greatly impoverishing its future.

And what of the millions that finally returned from the trenches—to families that had been living in dread of their not returning? Their collective outlook, their moral expectations, had changed radically. The war, as one veteran turned historian put it, had scorched the minds and character of a generation. To many the war had been a discovery of violence, a lust for violence even in their own selves, that nothing in the genteel, repressed world of before 1914 had prepared them for. "Most men, I suppose, have a paleolithic savage somewhere in them. . . . I have, anyway," wrote a gentle English scholar about his experience in the trenches. In other ways, too, that earlier world had been thoroughly discredited. It had been discredited by the bloody bungling of incompetence, by the failure of leadership, by the greed of war aims, and by the hollow claims of church and state. The rough "deference" for church, fatherland, and social superiors that still existed in 1914 was hopelessly compromised four years later. Superiors had been proven inferior, and the old notion that there was a rough equivalent between performance and reward, that there was a social order that made sense, this too had broken down. What was to take its place? What faith would claim the disillusioned? The immediate reaction of many was a hunger above all for peace and "normalcy," though not a few, particularly among the defeated peoples, thirsted for the renewed glories of military companionship. The war left a legacy of cynicism and skepticism as the dominant mood, and a spiritual thirst for action among others.

Yet, even Europe's worst catastrophe brought hope and betterment to some. The war hastened the development of egalitarian democracy and brought new benefits to long-suffering minorities. By the end of the war, nationalities long oppressed attained their independence. During the war, women's rights had been more generally acknowledged, as it became clear that women's capabilities were fully as necessary to society as were men's. Religious minorities were further assimilated into national societies, and cherished prejudices were suspended, at least for the duration. In central Europe, for example, Jews, needed in wartime, were rewarded with greater privileges. The full integration of trade unions into national life greatly advanced the rights and expectations of labor. "A country fit for heroes" was Lloyd George's promise to the English, and the drabness of postwar performance contrasted ill with the new deal that had everywhere been expected.

Europe had suffered too much to honor its pledges, to satisfy the aroused expectations of millions of its citizens. Victor and vanquished alike were too enfeebled to build material conditions that would protect and promote the precarious stirrings of a new democracy. The war had not only immeasurably weakened the old order; it weakened the forces that could have built a new order as well. Despite the resiliency of man, despite brave beginnings, Europe proved incapable of dealing with this tangled legacy of war and revolution. Everywhere, in Europe and elsewhere, in Russia, the United States, the great Asian powers, the end of war did not bring peace.

For Further Reading

Churchill, Winston, *The World Crisis.*
Cruttwell, C. R. M. F., *A History of the Great War.*
Marwick, Arthur, *The Deluge.*
Mayer, Arno J., *Political Origins of the New Diplomacy, 1917–1918.*

21   The Russian Revolution and the Stalin Era

At a distance of more than half a century the Russian Revolution of 1917 appears as an enigmatic Janus: one face looking back to the classic revolutions of modern European history; the other looking to the future, to the turbulences and upheavals of the non-European world that so marked the second third of the twentieth century. Like its revolution, Russian history, too, seems to live in two worlds. In much it has followed general European patterns of development, though at its own tempo and with its own accent. But Russia has always stood on the borders of Europe; more than half its vast territory lies in Asia. Mongols, Turks, and Chinese as well as Poles, Swedes, and Germans have been its neighbors. Therein lies much of the fascination of Russian history and of the Russian Revolution: for good or ill they have spanned the European and non-European worlds.

This dualism lies at the root of much of the controversy about Russia in its age of revolution, an age extending roughly from the revolt of 1905, which shook the czar's throne but did not topple it, through the years of Stalin, who converted revolutionary Russia into a world power, the Soviet Union. From the European perspective a twentieth-century Russia ruled by an autocrat—Nicholas II, a man bearing many resemblances to such ill-fated earlier monarchs as Charles I of England and Louis XVI of France—was an evident anachronism bound to undergo vast change if it was to survive. At the same time, the example of Bismarck's Germany suggested that Russia, too, could warp its way into an age of industrialization, mass politics, and rational administration without necessarily undergoing the throes of violent political and social turmoil. From the non-European perspective this very challenge, confronting a sprawling, still poor, still largely agrarian country, was precisely a foreshadowing of the strains and dislocations that were to disrupt nearly every non-European society forced to cope with the problems of modernization and industrialization.

Although these contrasting perspectives must enter into any assessment of the Russian Revolution's place in general history, the actual course and outcome of the revolution itself were decisively influenced by two specific, and seemingly contingent, events: the outbreak of the First World War in the summer of 1914 and the arrival of Lenin (real name Vladimir Ilich Ulyanov) in Russia in April, 1917. The foreign policy of Imperial Russia undoubtedly played an important part in determining that the war

A.D.   1904   Outbreak of Russo-Japanese War
          1905   "Bloody Sunday," beginning of 1905 Revolution
          1914   Outbreak of First World War
          1916   Murder of Rasputin
          1917   March 8–15, "February Revolution"; April 16, Lenin
                 returns to Russia; July 16–17, "July Days"; Sept.
                 9–14, Kornilov Affair; Nov. 7, Bolshevik seizure of
                 power: "October Revolution"
          1918   Treaty of Brest-Litovsk with Germany
     1918–1920   Civil war and foreign intervention
          1921   Kronstadt mutiny; beginning of New Economic Policy
          1922   Stalin named Secretary General of Communist Party
          1924   Death of Lenin
          1926   Zinoviev, Trotsky, and Kamenev removed from Polit-
                 buro
          1928   Adoption of First Five-Year Plan
          1929   Bukharin ousted from Politburo
          1934   Assassination of Kirov; beginning of Great Purges
          1936   Stalin Constitution approved
          1939   Ribbentrop-Molotov Pact
          1941   German invasion of U.S.S.R.
          1953   Death of Stalin

should come about when it did and how it did, but in respect to domestic Russian affairs the war was a calamity from without. It seems likely that the old order was approaching a serious, possibly mortal, social and political crisis, but a revolutionary denouement was perhaps not inevitable. In a country belatedly groping its way to new forms of government and social organization—with a new parliament, the Duma, which had yet to prove itself, with a discontented peasantry in uncertain transition from old communal structures, with a satisfactory formula for the treatment of the numerous non-Russian nationalities still to be devised, with the rapidly expanding industrial centers trying to accommodate the influx of raw workers from the countryside—the fearful strain of sustaining a war against the most powerful army in the world led to disaster. Initially, the war caused the Russian people to rally in defense of the fatherland, and their military record was by no means one of unrelieved disaster. They fought a full-scale war for nearly three years. Still, the circumstances surrounding the astonishingly rapid and total collapse of the czarist regime in a single week of mounting disturbance in Petrograd (from March 7 to March 15, 1917) are virtually all related to the war, whatever the deeper sources may have been: open disaffection in the upper ranks of Russian society over what was deemed wretched, even treasonous, mismanagement of the war; the disruption in the bread supply to the capital, owing in part to an overtaxed transportation system; war-inflated industries with vast masses of unseasoned workers; and, perhaps most decisively, a capital glutted with ill-trained and undisciplined troops in replacement regiments, less than anxious to be sent to the front. The czar fell in March, 1917, not through palace coup or revolutionary plot or peasant uprising, but because the impingement of the war on Russian society, at top and bottom, had created a highly explosive situation in the center of the empire.

The war not only occasioned the fall of the czar, it also destroyed the short-lived Provisional Government of Aleksandr Kerenski, which sought to play the caretaker until such time as a constituent assembly should determine the future form of the Russian state. The role of "moderates" in a period of deepening revolution is always difficult, and one may wonder whether any government could have dealt adequately with the host of domestic issues created by the disappearance of the old order. But certainly Russia's continued involvement in the war exacerbated the sequence of crises the Provisional Government faced, and contributed mightily to the harsh polarization of political life in the summer of 1917 and to the eventual isolation of that government, assailed from both left and right. It was hard for the Provisional Government to withdraw from the war. The implications of such a step—the fair likelihood of a general German victory with a consequent hegemony over Europe—were daunting. Still, the Provisional Government might have defended its own front and resisted the temptation to demonstrate its vitality in the summer of 1917 by mounting an attack which failed and simply worsened matters. Whatever the alternative, the war, partly by its direct effect, partly by diverting energy and attention from other urgent problems, served to extend the chaos and push Russia to the social and political disintegration so poignantly depicted in Boris Pasternak's *Dr. Zhivago*.

Thus, the breakdown in 1917 was intimately associated with the vicissitudes of the Great War. And while this external calamity upset Russia's domestic equilibrium, there was at least a symbolic connection between this last of the classic European revolutions and the general catastrophe that overtook European power politics. A whole historical epoch reached tragic climax in these two experiences.

The contingency associated with the next phase of the Russian Revolution was, however, of a quite different kind. If Lenin had been unable to make his way from exile in Switzerland to Russia in April, 1917 (and it required the cooperation of the Germans, who were understandably eager to promote disorder in Russia), it seems unlikely that the Bolsheviks would have been able to seize power on November 7, 1917, and if the Bolsheviks had not done so at that time and in the way they did, the course of Russian history could well have been quite different.

The Provisional Government was probably fatally weak by the late summer of 1917, but what was to succeed it was problematic: possibly pure anarchy might ensue, perhaps Russia would break up into small units, perhaps (what most Russians either feared or hoped for), a military dictatorship might emerge. Or perhaps a left-wing coalition including the Bolsheviks (an eventuality Lenin fought desperately to avoid) might have resulted. Unlike the breakdown of an established order, the appearance of a new system or structure in the midst of chaos is by its nature a highly contingent matter; accidents of timing and personality can play a decisive role. Lenin ranks among those rare individuals in history who achieved a result that would not have come about through the "normal" play of politics, or through unilateral group action, or through the efforts of any other identifiable character on the scene. (Even Trotsky was of the opinion that Lenin was the indispensable man.)

Lenin's role is not easy to define precisely. Born in 1870 in a small town on the Volga to parents of comfortable circumstances, Lenin received a good education and, in the tradition of the time, moved into the ranks of the radical intelligentsia. Early in his career, however, there appeared a steely, uncompromising quality to his revolutionism that was to mark him off from most Russian radicals. His own synthesis of German Marxism and the Russian revolutionary tradition consistently aimed at forging the most effective revolutionary instruments. He fought against liberalism, revisionism, compromise, anything that might dampen the revolutionary impulse. The party he created (named the Bolsheviks after the split with the Menshevik faction of the Russian Social Democratic movement in 1903, and renamed the Communist party immediately after the 1917 revolution) was designed to serve as a vanguard of disciplined professional revolutionaries operating within a tightly controlled organization.

The instrumentalities Lenin had worked so hard to create before 1914 served him well, but perhaps better after the 1917 revolution than during it. During the critical months between March and November, 1917, the Bolsheviks were not particularly well organized—perhaps more so than the other parties, but still subject to the confusions and uncertainties of that frenetic year. Lenin and his followers played no significant role in the fall of the czar, for most of them were in prison or in exile. Joseph Stalin and Lev Kamenev were initially inclined to offer guarded support to the Provisional Government, and when Lenin, in the late summer of 1917, announced to his comrades from his hiding place in Finland that the time had come for armed insurrection, he alarmed them by his rashness. Two of his closest associates, Kamenev and Grigori Zinoviev, openly broke with him. Organizational genius does not seem to be the clue to Lenin's success at this particular point.

Rather it would appear that Lenin's great achievement in 1917 lay at the level of political instinct. First, immediately upon his return to Russia he strongly opposed any expression of confidence in the Provisional Government. By this unqualified stand he put himself in a unique position to profit when sentiments began to polarize with the deteriorating situation. Second, he immediately sensed the vulnerability of the Provisional Government when it came into conflict with General Lavr Kornilov, who was trying to reestablish order and discipline. Lenin recognized that growing peasant disturbances made it impossible for counterrevolution to assemble the countryside against the unruly cities.

These insights provided the key to Lenin's victory in November, 1917. The course by which this victory was achieved, however, was remarkably circuitous and included many forces over which he had no control; these were times of flux and accident. Two myths must be dispelled. Lenin did not ride to power on a mighty revolutionary upsurge channeled and directed by the Bolshevik party. Russia in the autumn of 1917 was breaking apart; a strange sense of emptiness, almost of vacuum, permeated the atmosphere. Not that the Bolsheviks were an insignificant minority; while they received only one-quarter of the vote in the elections to the Constituent Assembly held shortly after their access to power, their areas of strength were strategically located in the cities. It should also be noted that the vote in this unique free expression of Russian political sentiments was overwhelmingly for "radical" parties. Moreover, the Bolsheviks by October, 1917, dominated the workers' and soldiers' (though not the peasants') soviets, the somewhat irregularly elected representative bodies that sprang up throughout Russia in the wake of the March Revolution. Still, the myth of a massive revolutionary tidal wave is only a myth. The counterimage of a carefully planned, skillfully executed Bolshevik coup d'état is also false. As Bolshevik documents of the time make only too clear, the overthrow of the Provisional Government was neither well planned nor well executed. On the very eve of the seizure Lenin was frantically uncertain about the intentions and actions of his own Central Committee.

Yet, through a combination of governmental weakness, Bolshevik strength among the workers and troops in Petrograd, and the force of Lenin's demonic will to revolution, the Bolsheviks came to power and, as was apparent from the outset, not as the instrument of the soviets but as their masters, and not in coalition with the other radical parties, the Mensheviks and the Social Revolutionaries. The Bolsheviks took over the throne of the czars as autocrats.

Such was Lenin's tour de force of November, 1917. The term tour de force carries overtones of sleight of hand, of something not quite real. Much of Russia's subsequent history has been a playing out of the implications of that extraordinary event, successive stages in a continuing effort to bring Lenin's singular achievement into a reasonably harmonious relationship with the realities of Russia and the world. First, the seizure of power in Petrograd had to be extended into effective sovereignty over all Russia. This occupied the remainder of Lenin's lifetime. Second, this new revolutionary entity had to face the tough demands of life, economics, and power politics. It was Stalin's role to hammer out solutions of a sort to these demands. Third, there was the need to reconcile the internal contradictions produced by Lenin's revolution and Stalin's creation. This seems to have been the basic task of Stalin's successors.

Although the Bolsheviks quickly won control of the most important cities, it took them three years of bitter civil war to subdue the broad reaches of Russia. Casualties in the 1917 revolution had been relatively light, but the civil war exacted a fearful toll: battles without prisoners, organized terror and unorganized marauding, Red against White, village against city, nationality against nationality. Entire towns were depopulated. Inevitably, widespread famine followed.

Though they were on the brink of defeat in 1918 and again in 1919, the Bolsheviks enjoyed several advantages and profited from several bits of good luck. By moving the capital to Moscow early in 1918 they could defend interior lines in the heart of old Muscovy, whereas their opponents had to operate on Russia's vast periphery. The major threats came in sequence; the Bolsheviks never had to meet all opponents at once. The German threat evaporated in November, 1918. Thereafter French, British, Japanese, and American forces were in remote areas, and their efforts were generally half-hearted, ill-coordinated, and frequently at cross purposes. Moreover, the numerous domestic enemies of the Bolsheviks were never united and were frequently in open conflict. The military mistrusted the socialists; the Volunteer Army in the south was at odds with the Ukrainian nationalists, who had their own troubles with the Poles and with local peasant partisans. While the peasants resisted Bolshevik squads seeking grain, they also feared that the victory of the Whites would mean the return of the landlords. An effective and durable coalition of any of several sets of opponents could have crushed the Bolsheviks. But of course these antagonisms were an integral part of the confusion that had descended on Russia.

In addition, the Bolsheviks enjoyed a quality of leadership, most notably in the persons of Lenin and Trotsky, that their enemies could not match. It was a broken-backed struggle, often a sordid and horrible one, but it did prove the temper of the new rulers of Russia, who demonstrated that when survival was at stake they were more than visionaries, agitators, or theoreticians of revolution. Many of the grimmer features of the Soviet system emerged in those years, most notably the terror and xenophobia; implicit perhaps in Lenin's will to bring socialism to Russia by main force, they became manifest in the rigors of the civil war and foreign intervention.

These early years also witnessed a rash of extreme economic and social experiments, usually lumped under the term "war communism": the nationalization of industry, state control over labor, centralized management of the economy, state distribution of goods, and an effort to get away from a money economy. Although these steps were later rationalized as measures imposed upon the Bolsheviks in prosecuting the civil war, they certainly reflected some of the more utopian visions entertained by Lenin and his associates.

The Bolsheviks won the civil war, but they ruled a land bled white, facing famine and the prospect of a peasant convulsion. One of Lenin's important gifts, unusual in a revolutionary, was his ability to stop for a breathing space, and even to retreat. He forced through the bitter treaty of Brest Litovsk with Germany in early 1918 against the violent opposition of more sanguine comrades who thought Russia capable of leading a revolutionary war. He inaugurated the New Economc Policy (NEP)—a major retreat involving a partial return to a market and monetary economy— again with opposition from comrades who considered this the Thermidor of the revolution. But Robespierre had been executed in the French

Thermidor; Lenin and the Bolsheviks remained in power. The revolution had been neither defeated nor discredited; its ideology had not been called in question. The revolution was in this sense still open-ended.

In his last two years of active life, before the strokes that left him helpless until his death in January, 1924, Lenin wrestled with the problem of stabilizing and healing an exhausted nation without backsliding into old habits. As his powers faded he voiced his anguish at the retrograde trends he saw: the faltering élan, the reappearance of the old spirit of bureaucratic Russia, the ugly revival of chauvinism. At the end these fears tended to focus on the figure of Stalin, now coming rapidly to the fore.

Josif Vissarionovich Dzhugashvili, who took on the revolutionary name of Stalin, was born in Georgia in 1879. An early follower of Lenin, he played an important though not decisive role in 1917 and in the civil war. Viewed by his colleagues as a man of action rather than a theorist, he was at home in organizational and operational matters. He became general secretary of the Central Committee of the Communist party in 1922. From this strategic position he outmaneuvered his rivals and became undisputed master of Russia by the late 1920's.

Although Stalin came to the top through adroit manipulation of the party machinery and continued to use manipulation, laced with terror, throughout his long rule, he could not have become or remained master of Russia had he been nothing but an organization man or an executioner. He also had a policy, somewhat primitively and ambiguously expressed in the phrase "Socialism in one country." By the time of Lenin's death Russia seemed to be faced by two unacceptable alternatives. The prospects of an immediate world revolution were fading. To press forward on this front, as Trotsky advocated, promised only to destroy what was left of an exhausted Russia. On the other hand, the retreat to NEP seemed to threaten a return to old ways. Stalin cut through this quandary by proclaiming that, whatever happened in the outside world, Russia could proceed toward socialism on its own, through its own efforts and will.

This determination, which flew in the face not only of the Marxian view of history and economics but also of common sense, carried important implications. It required a massive and concerted assault on reality; any normal play of political and social forces would not suffice. And while Stalin has been described as a great realist there was undoubtedly a dark corner of his mind—the same dark corner that created the horrors of Stalinism—which saw reality as something to be created by his own will.

The abrupt and violent turning point came in 1928–1929, with the wholesale collectivization of agriculture and the inauguration of the first Five-Year Plan. While it is a debated point, it does not appear that the NEP had exhausted its potentialities, although it had run into some difficulties.

However, to continue the program threatened to undermine the role of the Communist party as the unique guiding force in Russia. There is an intimate connection between the twists and turns by which Stalin gained control over the party and the shift in economic policy that precipitated the forcible collectivization of the peasantry.

This shift has been termed a "revolution from above." It was certainly a revolution in that it rapidly, and permanently, altered the face of Russia. Millions of peasants were forced into collective farms; vast and incredibly ambitious plans were applied to the entire economy. The initial efforts had disastrous effects: agricultural production declined, livestock were killed off, an unnecessary famine hit several regions. Nevertheless, despite some brief pauses and retreats, the drive went on, guided and impelled by Stalin. The Communist party was by now merely his personal instrument.

The totalitarian regime that emerged in the 1930's has been interpreted by some as a necessary if highly unpleasant means to achieve rapid industrialization. Agriculture, the argument runs, had to be made to provide a collectable surplus, whatever the cost to the peasants; the workers had to labor more intensely than they would normally; the political system, and especially the coercive apparatus of police and courts, had to enforce these measures; and the party had to be an unfaltering executor of Stalin's commanding impulse. But this interpretation reverses cause and effect. The decision to mount an economic offensive in such circumstances was itself totalitarian.

Probably the most bizarre and baffling episode of the Stalin years was the period of the Great Purges, extending from 1934 to 1938. Triggered by the assassination of a leading Communist (in which Stalin himself may have had a hand), it soon extended to a settling of Stalin's accounts with former opponents, a virtual wiping out of Old Bolsheviks, and ultimately to a murderous purge even within the Stalinist ranks. Millions of people, Communists and non-Communists, were caught up in this nightmare of arrest, torture, slave labor camp, and execution. Stalin killed more Communists than any right-wing or fascist dictator ever did. He had more at hand.

Although amenable to rational analysis, the purges displayed neither objective nor subjective rationality. The liquidation of party factionalism, the prophylactic extirpation of real or potential traitors, the clearing of avenues of advance for a new party elite—all these explanations are at best marginally relevant. Even the picture of a terror apparatus out of control, devouring everything in sight including its own agents, while doubtless true at some levels, is not satisfactory. Stalin was able to call a halt rather abruptly before the fabric of Soviet society disintegrated. The ultimate explanation lies in the brooding, paranoid personality of Stalin. He saw enemies everywhere, and doom descended on any person, group, or even nationality which came under his suspicion.

Yet Stalin's actions occurred in a social setting. Purely maniacal actors are normally strait-jacketed. Stalin's distorted reality was after all a reality, partially inherited from the Russian past, significantly derived from Lenin's revolution, and partly brought into being by Stalin himself.

That Stalinism, for all the insanity of the purges, was still in touch with the real world, domestic and foreign, was demonstrated by Russia's ability to withstand the Nazi invasion of 1941. The "excessive excesses" of Stalinism exacted their cost in the war with Hitler. The purges did not strengthen the Red Army (its general staff was decimated in 1938), any more than collectivization heightened the patriotism of the Russian peasantry, or enforced Soviet nationalism led to loyalty among the Ukrainians. On the other hand, the savagery of the Nazi invasion and occupation of the Soviet Union in 1941–1943 does not explain the extraordinary powers of resistance and endurance displayed by the Russian people. Stalin had taken up Lenin's revolutionary tour de force and created a social mechanism capable of meeting the severe test of war.

While the Soviet Union was still dedicated to the ideals of the revolution, in many respects it was their antithesis: the inegalitarianism of Russian life (demonstrated, for example by increasing wage differentials), the appearance of a new Russian nationalism (marked by the resurrection of such figures as Ivan the Terrible and Peter the Great), the vast expansion of the bureaucracy (not a hint that the state would "wither away"), and the permanent institutionalization of terror (a quite different thing from revolutionary violence)—in all these respects the Soviet Union showed little resemblance to the goals of Marxism.

Perhaps these deformations were a necessary stage; perhaps the way to a freer society was open once the test of war had been survived. So many Russians thought. But Stalin was not willing, or not able, to entertain such thoughts. To some extent he was a victim of his own system, which certainly developed its own powers of self-perpetuation. The breakdown of the Big Three alliance and the onset of the Cold War provided a rationale for continued austerity and repression, but it is doubtful that this was really the cause. In some measure age played a part; in his last years Stalin was notably unreceptive to innovation. But basically, Stalin simply did not believe that there was any other way to run Soviet society, to advance toward Communism, and, ultimately, to see it victorious on a world scale.

Consequently, postwar Russia was forced to undergo new rigors. The Communist ideology, which had been overshadowed by nationalist themes during the war, came back in full force. There was renewed emphasis on the party, although it never really recovered from the bloodletting of the late 1930's. The command economy continued to give highest priority to industrial production, especially to areas of greatest military relevance. The consumer and the peasant stayed on short rations; indeed, at the time of Stalin's death the level of agricultural production still lagged behind that of 1913. Writers, artists, and musicians were brought under ideological constraint in the name of "socialist realism." The forced labor camps continued to receive their quotas, and important sectors of the economy were manned by unfree labor. Within the Communist party itself the pervading fear, never fully dissipated since the Great Purges, became more pronounced. In 1949 a number of prominent officials were liquidated—the so-called Leningrad Affair. As Stalin's health declined, his morbid suspicions increased, and on the eve of his death in March, 1953, a replay of the Great Purges seemed imminent.

But Stalin died. He had achieved much, at hideous cost, but he died. He was one of the most fearsome rulers of all time. It has been observed that the fate of newly created states or political systems often hinges on the presence of an able successor to the founder; without someone to translate his triumph into an ongoing system all may collapse. Surely the Lenin-Stalin sequence was one of the most formidable in recorded history. Just as the Communist victory in the Russian Revolution could scarcely have occurred without Lenin, so the conversion of this victory into a reality that would neither deny the victory (though it might pervert it) nor succumb to the drift of events was Stalin's singular achievement.

Yet for all its awesome massiveness, its effort to achieve a monolithic, totally integrated society, Stalinism did not, and could not, arrive at a stable equilibrium. By main force Stalin beat down domestic and foreign opponents; he was able, to a degree hitherto thought not possible, to shape whole economies, whole peoples, to his will. He institutionalized the precepts and principles of Marxism-Leninism-Stalinism, rendering them free of individual vagary to an astonishing degree. But Stalin could not reproduce himself, and his principal lieutenants, fighting among themselves, were in mortal terror lest they become victims. The immediate response to the death of Stalin was the search by the elite of the system for some assurance that they, their careers and lives, would not be in constant jeopardy. The problem was not so much operating the Stalinist system without Stalin as rendering the system less perilous to those close to the center of power. This search inevitably opened the way to much broader issues which have constituted the central challenge to post-Stalin Russia. Khrushchev contended with these and failed; they are still before the present rulers of the Soviet Union, men who rose to the top through the tough and unattractive Stalin school of advancement, men with an acute instinct for personal and political survival but without a notable sense of imagination.

Thus, out of Lenin's ambiguous achievement, a "socialist" revolution imposed by the Communist party on ill-prepared Russian soil, Stalin forced into being a political, economic, and social system capable of surviving the harsh atmosphere of this century (while contributing singularly to its harshness) and even of presenting itself as a plausible model for other societies. But how, in the long run, was this system to come to terms with its own internal, self-generating contradictions and conflicts? Old Russia was dead; there could be no Restoration. By the time of Stalin's death Russia could admit its past, even glorify selected parts. Could it build creatively from it? The industrial Western world had been the enemy for half a century; Soviet history and Soviet pride would not permit any simple acceptance of the virtues of "capitalist-imperialist" ways. Post-Stalin speculation in the West about prospects for "convergence" of the two systems offered little of relevance to Russia's problems. In the last third of the twentieth century the great challenge for the Soviet regime must be to seek a resolution of its revolutionary inheritance that would do less violence to the individual, who has problems enough adapting to the promises and perils of the contemporary world.

For Further Reading

Chamberlin, W. H., *The Russian Revolution.*
Deutscher, Isaac, *Stalin.*
Rauch, Georg von, *A History of Soviet Russia.*
Ulam, Adam B., *The Bolsheviks.*

22   The United States: Prosperity and Depression

The factory whistles and church bells that sounded the news of the armistice on November 11, 1918, signaled the end of a remarkable interlude in American history. The participation of the United States in World War I lasted but nineteen months; yet in that short period, the country underwent a number of "Europeanizing" experiences. For the first time, the national government, acquiring some of the character which European theorists gave to "the State," intervened directly in the American economy. It allocated resources, regulated prices, supervised cartels, ran the railroads, even commandeered factories. For the first time, too, American troops crossed the Atlantic to take part in an Old World conflict. Three weeks after the war ended, the American President, Woodrow Wilson, broke still another

A.D. 1918 End of World War I
      1919 U.S. Senate rejects League of Nations treaty; Red Scare;
            18th Amendment (Prohibition) ratified
      1920 19th Amendment (Women's Suffrage) ratified; Republi-
            cans returned to power; census reveals U.S. predomi-
            nantly urban
      1922 Nine-Power Treaty
      1928 The Big Bull Market; Kellogg-Briand Pact
      1929 Wall Street crash
      1932 Election of Franklin D. Roosevelt: Democrats new
            majority party
      1933 Bank crisis; beginning of New Deal; the Hundred Days;
            recognition of U.S.S.R.
      1935 Second Hundred Days; Social Security Act and welfare
            state; first neutrality legislation
      1937 Sitdown strikes; Constitutional crisis; recession
      1938 End of New Deal reforms
      1939 Outbreak of World War II in Europe

----

precedent by traveling to Paris to traffic with diplomats from foreign chancelleries on the shape of the postwar world.

But the war experience proved short-lived. For too many Americans it had been a wrenching upheaval. The war did not really head the nation in new directions; instead, the administration lost little time in dismantling the machinery of the mobilization. And when Wilson returned from Versailles with a treaty that included a League of Nations, the Senate rejected it. Disillusioned with the fruits of war, frightened by the spread of Bolshevism in Europe, the United States in 1919 turned in on itself. In the frenzy of the Red Scare it sought to exorcise all European ideas; in doing so, it released the psychic frustrations built up by the war through assaults on radicals and unionists.

The presidential election of 1920 confirmed the rising mood of isola-tionism and conservatism. The undistinguished Republican nominee, Sen-ator Warren Harding of Ohio, insisted that the country needed "not nostrums but normalcy." He denounced revolution, agitation, experiment, and internationalism, calling instead for "serenity," "equipoise," and old-fashioned nationalism. Woodrow Wilson, seriously ill, wanted the election to be a "great and solemn referendum" on the League, but both parties muddled the question, and in the campaign Harding made full use of his exceptional talent for taking a simple matter and rendering it obscure. With the electorate swollen by millions of new women voters (the Nineteenth Amendment was ratified that summer), Warren Harding won a landslide victory.

Two days after the election, Harding announced that the League was "now deceased." The United States had come out of the war as the preeminent world power, but for the next two decades the country, with rare exceptions, followed a policy of withdrawal. Blithely ignoring the economic dislocations wrought by the war, the government insisted that its European allies pay their debts to the last penny. It raised mountainous tariff barriers, thus further hampering international trade. In 1922 at a conference in Washington, the United States negotiated a naval disarmament pact with the great powers and a Nine-Power Treaty guaranteeing the integrity of China and maintaining the Open Door, but these agreements set up no machinery for enforcement. Even more meaningless was the Kellogg-Briand Pact of 1928 in which nations renounced war as an instrument of national policy. By its failure to assume a more creative role in foreign affairs, the United States helped ensure that the two decades following the war would be nothing more than a "long armistice."

The 1920 election marked an end, too, to an era of progressive government. The Republican leaders of the decade were committed to minimal interference with business and to the Whig doctrine of the weak president. No one looked more a great statesman than Warren Harding, who, it was said, "needed only a toga to complete the illusion that he had come out of the ancient world." Yet few men less equipped for the task ever held so high an office. Harding's speeches were so devoid of ideas and so graceless in form that they reduced his critics to despair. The poet e. e. cummings alleged that "beautiful Warren Gamaliel Harding" was

> the only man or child who wrote
> a simple declarative sentence with seven grammatical
> errors. . . .

Harding is remembered chiefly for the scandals that disgraced his brief tenure. When as a consequence of his role in the Teapot Dome oil scandal, Secretary of the Interior Albert Fall was sentenced to the penitentiary, it marked the first time that such a fate had ever befallen a cabinet officer.

When Harding died in 1923, he was succeeded by Calvin Coolidge, a man with the instinctive resistance to change of a Vermonter who never went west. Coolidge reduced the role of his office to one almost of insignificance. "The kind of government that he offered the country," wrote the satirical essayist H. L. Mencken, "was government stripped to the buff." Coolidge's subordination of the government to business reflected the national admiration for corporation leaders like Henry Ford and the conviction that such men were wiser and infinitely more valuable to society than public officials. "Our business intelligence has so far outgrown our political intelligence that it looms like a white lily on a stagnant pool," commented one writer. "Are we approaching a millennium," asked an editorial in *Life,* "in which visible government will not be necessary and in which the job of running the world will slip away from obstructive politicians and be taken over by men trained in the shop?"

Yet even in the 1920's the state continued to grow relentlessly. A host of new government agencies sprang up: the Bureau of the Budget, the Grain Futures Administration, the Federal Radio Commission. In large part, this expansion resulted from demands by business groups which paid homage to laissez-faire but insisted on government favors to advance their own interests. The president of the National Association of Manufacturers remarked: "It is unthinkable that a government which thrives chiefly upon its industries will withhold from them for a single unnecessary moment the protection which they so sorely need and deserve."

"Never before, here or anywhere else," wrote the *Wall Street Journal,* "has a government been so completely fused with business." Federal regulatory agencies fell under corporation control. Secretary of the Treasury Andrew Mellon, under whom, it was said, three Presidents served, pushed a tax policy which benefited the rich. Both the Attorney General's office and the Supreme Court dealt heavy blows against the labor movement, which in these years declined markedly in strength. The Court invalidated two child labor acts, sanctioned yellow dog contracts, and struck down an anti-injunction law and a minimum wage statute for women.

The public's admiration of business rested on the stunning performance of the economy in these years. Between 1921 and 1929, as mechanization accelerated economic growth, industrial output nearly doubled. The pace-setting automobile industry (the number of cars in use almost tripled in a decade) was responsible for a number of subsidiary developments, including the building of a vast highway network which knitted the nation together and the burgeoning of suburbs from Shaker Heights to Beverly Hills. Reflecting the contagious optimism of these years, stock prices went up, up, and then up again; during the Great Bull Market in the summer of 1928, industrials climbed 110 points. Yet the structure of prosperity had weak underpinnings. Five per cent of the population received one-third of the income, and 25 million families—more than 87 per cent of the nation—lived on less than $2,500 a year.

Most Americans were impressed less by the frailty of the economy than by the marvelous new products it spewed forth. It was about 1920 that mechanization took possession of the American home. Countless new electrical appliances caught the public fancy: first, toasters and irons; then vacuum cleaners; then stoves; then refrigerators. At the same time, mass entertainment, especially radio and the Hollywood dream factory, became a major American industry. In 1920 the first radio station opened in Pittsburgh; ten years later there were nearly 13 million radios in American homes, by 1940, 52 million. Businessmen created a vast home market by developing new consumer products and by whetting the consumer's appetite through novel techniques of advertising, salesmanship, and installment buying.

In these years the New Middle Class, from the advertising man to the office machine clerk, moved to the center of the stage. The white-collar worker found himself in growing demand in an economy increasingly concerned with merchandising and distribution. This produced subtle alterations in the national character. The country was fast moving toward a Veblenian society in which styles of leisure and consumption determined status. Thrifty Poor Richard ceased to be the nation's culture hero. "The credit mechanism has made the Ant a fool and the Grasshopper a hero," one commentator observed.

The census of 1920 revealed that for the first time in the nation's history a majority of the population lived in urban areas, and the society of the twenties showed the increasing impact of metropolitan influence. Much of the attention of the decade concentrated on the world of the city: the jazz of New Orleans and Chicago, the soaring skyscraper, the brassy flapper. The literature of the period, too, focused on the experience of young men from "Gopher Prairie" or "Winesburg, Ohio," who had come to the big city; the novelist F. Scott Fitzgerald arrived in New York, he wrote, "like Dick Whittington up from the country." City-bred writers, far removed from the villages of Whittier and Twain, explored the asphalt world of Langston Hughes's Harlem and James T. Farrell's Chicago.

The antics of loose-living Hollywood stars projected on village screens distressed rural Americans, and so did the "revolution in morals" loosely associated with the name of Sigmund Freud. The swiftly rising divorce rate was cause for further alarm: the Democratic presidential nominee in 1920 had been divorced in 1911 and had remarried in 1917; he had children by both wives; nonetheless he won the nomination. Yet rural attitudes toward the metropolis were ambivalent; the city was viewed both as a den of evil and as an alluring bazaar of pleasure. By punishing urban institutions, the rural American could also suppress his own sinful fantasies.

The countryside scored an early victory in its war with the city through the ratification in 1919 of the Eighteenth Amendment, which prohibited the manufacture, sale, or transport of alcoholic beverages. The rural, Protestant, old-stock culture found in prohibition a way to impose its abstemious, work-minded style of life on the leisure-loving, loose-living city. One prohibitionist claimed: "Our nation can only be saved by turning the pure stream of country sentiment and township morals to flush out the cesspools of cities and so save civilization from pollution." Prohibition was deeply resented by city dwellers; Mencken complained that it had caused suffering comparable only to the Black Death and the Thirty Years' War. In the cities, the illegal liquor traffic often fell into the hands of gangsters; in Al Capone's Chicago, more men died violent deaths each year than in all of Great Britain.

The rural white Protestants, who for so long had been the unchallenged leaders of the nation, chalked up a number of other triumphs. Congress drastically restricted immigration and imposed a quota system to preserve America as an outpost of Anglo-Saxony. In the South, fundamentalists secured state laws banning the teaching of Darwinian evolution. More extreme elements organized the Ku Klux Klan, another vehicle of rural values, which waged war against Catholics, Jews, Negroes, foreigners, and all the forces of "metropolitan morality" which were creating "modern Sodom and Gomorrahs."

The politics of the 1920's centered less on liberal-conservative disputes over economic policy than on the resistance of rural and small-town America to the growing influence of the metropolis, as witness the division in the 1924 Democratic convention between the forces of the urban Northeast and the rural South and West that made possible Calvin Coolidge's landslide triumph over his disrupted opponents.

In 1928 Al Smith became the first Roman Catholic and the first spokesman of the Newer Americans to win the presidential nomination of a major party. Rural Protestant America perceived Smith's candidacy as a threat to national traditions. A leading Republican dry declared: "The stability and continuation of our democratic form of government depends on keeping in the political saddle what we used to call the frontier and what today we call Main Street; the virile, clean-minded, middle class mentality." Smith was soundly defeated, largely because the Republican candidate, Herbert Hoover, was the nominee of the majority party in a time of prosperity. But the cultural issues raised by Smith's candidacy also shaped the vote, as Hoover broke the Democratic hold on the Solid South.

When Hoover took office in March, 1929, the Republican party was at its zenith. Not once since the election of Franklin Pierce in 1852 had a Democrat entered the White House with a majority of the vote. Hoover spoke for the Old Order of individualism and Protestant morality but also for the New Era of corporation leadership and modern technology. Men had come to believe that they had achieved "a permanent plateau of prosperity." In his inaugural address, the new President claimed: "In no nation are the fruits of accomplishment more secure."

Just seven months later, the crash of the stock market shattered these illusions. In the next three years, the bottom dropped out of the economy. By 1932, American industry was turning out less than half its 1929 volume, and new investments had fallen from $10 billion to $1 billion. Blue chip stocks tumbled, General Motors from 73 to 8. As crop prices plunged downward, the farmer was driven to the wall. On a single day in April, 1932, one-fourth of the state of Mississippi fell under the auctioneer's hammer. One observer commented: "We seem to have stepped Alice-like through an economic looking-glass into a world where everything shrivels. Bond prices, stock prices, commodity prices, employment—they all dwindle."

In three years, national income was cut in half, and the number of unemployed soared to some 15 million. Thomas Wolfe wrote of the winter of 1930–1931 in New York: "I saw half naked wretches sitting on park benches at three in the morning in a freezing rain and sleet: often I saw a man and a woman huddled together with their arms around each other for warmth, and with sodden newspapers, rags, or anything they could find over their shoulders." At the end of 1931, a Philadelphia relief authority announced: "We have unemployment in every third house. It is almost like the visitation of death to the households of the Egyptians at the time of the escape of the Jews from Egypt."

The longer the depression persisted, the more it threatened to engulf everyone. "Anybody sinks after a while," commented one jobless man. "Even you would have if God hadn't preserved, without apparent rhyme or reason, your job and your income." Detroit's relief rolls, Mayor Frank Murphy told a Senate subcommittee, embraced doctors, lawyers, ministers, and "two families after whom streets are named."

Hoover attempted to meet this disaster with the ideas of the Old Order: faith in business leadership, trust in voluntary endeavor, and emphasis on action by local governments. To be sure, he assumed responsibilities that no President had undertaken before. But he placed his main reliance on budget-balancing and the staples of classical economics. When his Federal Farm Board boldly intervened in the economy to shore up farm prices, the program proved a dismal failure, because no restrictions were placed on production. Despite mounting evidence of privation, Hoover refused to sanction federal aid to the unemployed. A man hitherto known as a Great Humanitarian for his relief efforts in World War I, a leader identified with government intervention in the economy in wartime and with public works planning, Hoover during the depression displayed a rigidity which made him appear callous. Perhaps never in our history has a President entered office with such high expectations and left in such ill repute.

By the spring of 1932, the country faced a relief crisis. New York City, with payrolls down more than $80 million a month, was spending only $4 million a month on relief and had 25,000 emergency cases on its relief waiting list. Chicago separated families and sent husbands and wives to different shelters. Houston announced: "Applications are not taken from unemployed Mexican or colored families. They are being asked to shift for themselves." The vice-chairman of the Mayor's Unemployment Commission of Detroit saw "no possibility of preventing widespread hunger and slow starvation . . . through its own unaided resources."

As the depression deepened, the country came to question both the claims of business leaders and the worth of the capitalist system. Nothing seemed so severe an indictment of capitalism as the phenomenon of want in the midst of plenty. At a time when many lived on the edge of starvation, Montana wheat was left standing uncut in the fields, bushels of apples lay rotting in Oregon orchards. The breakdown of the market system and the social irresponsibility of business leaders produced a loud chorus of disapproval. The Methodists condemned the American industrial order as "unchristian, unethical, and antisocial"; the Episcopal *Churchman* pronounced capitalism "rotten to the core"; and the editor of the *Catholic World* denounced capital's treatment of labor as "worse than that accorded an animal."

This sorry state of affairs placed Hoover and the Republicans in an extremely vulnerable position. The Democratic party made the most of its opportunity by naming as its presidential candidate in 1932 the popular governor of New York, Franklin Delano Roosevelt. Although Roosevelt offered few specifics, he scored an emphatic victory in the November election, capturing 42 of the 48 states. The Democrats also won their biggest margin in the House since 1890, their largest majority in the Senate since before the Civil War. The election displaced the Republican party as the nation's majority party, and made possible a marked change of emphasis in American policies. As Hoover himself asserted: "This election is not a mere shift from the ins to the outs. It means deciding the direction our nation will take over a century to come."

During the four-month interregnum between Roosevelt's election in November, 1932, and his assumption of office on March 4, 1933, the economy plunged downward, and in the last three weeks of Hoover's term, the financial illness that had plagued the country took a critical turn. In the previous three years, more than 5,000 banks had collapsed, burying 9 million savings accounts in the debris. Now banks in every part of the country folded. On the morning of Roosevelt's inauguration, the president of the New York Stock Exchange mounted the rostrum to make a momentous announcement: the Stock Exchange was closing down. The decision symbolized both the disintegration of the nation's financial system and the surrender of initiative from Wall Street to Washington. By the morning of Roosevelt's inauguration, every state in the Union had closed its banks or permitted them to operate only on a restricted basis.

Moving swiftly to deal with the financial crisis, the President summoned Congress into special session, halted transactions in gold, and proclaimed a national bank holiday. When Congress convened on March 9, in an atmosphere tense as wartime, the administration submitted a bill validating a wide range of presidential powers over banking, and arranging for the reopening of banks with liquid assets and the reorganization of the rest. At 8:36 P.M., less than eight hours after the bill had been introduced, President Roosevelt, at a room in the White House littered with piles of books and pictures of the new tenants, signed the first measure of the New Deal. Three days later, FDR delivered the first of his "fireside chats" over the radio to reassure the nation about the safety of savings accounts. When the banks opened the next day in the twelve Federal Reserve cities, deposits far outnumbered withdrawals. The crisis was over. Roosevelt had vastly extended the sphere of government action, and yet he had left the financial institutions of the country essentially intact.

Thus began the historic "Hundred Days." Between March 9 and June 16, when Congress adjourned, a period of precisely one hundred days, President Roosevelt sent fifteen separate messages up to the Hill, and Congress enacted all fifteen proposals. No Congress in history had ever adopted such a panoply of legislation. During the Hundred Days, Roosevelt functioned under a kind of constitutional dictatorship which resembled such World War I governments as the Sacred Union in France, the Lloyd George coalition in Britain, and the Burgfrieden in Germany. Unlike such administrations, it was not a coalition government but a Democratic party operation. Nor was opposition ever stifled, nor did Congress ever become a rubber stamp. Yet the sense of crisis blunted partisanship and made it possible for FDR to have his way in almost every instance.

Few of the institutions of the 1920's could survive the test of hard times. Prohibition, which gave to the twenties much of its distinctive character, was doomed by the victory of the Democrats, with their big-city support. Before the year was out, the thirty-sixth state had ratified the Twenty-first Amendment, which repealed the Eighteenth Amendment.

The jovial reception accorded to the end of prohibition symbolized one of the most important contributions made by Roosevelt: the return of a sense of national confidence and the end of the gloom and torpor of the

Hoover years. Two weeks after the decisive new President took office, the spirit of the country seemed changed beyond recognition. "The people aren't sure . . . just where they are going," noted one business journal, "but anywhere seems better than where they have been. In the homes, on the streets, in the offices, there is a feeling of hope reborn."

The bank crisis resolved, prohibition repeal under way, a new spirit of confidence in government achieved, Roosevelt felt free to undertake the more difficult tasks of recovery and reform. The spearhead of his recovery program was the National Industrial Recovery Act, an omnibus law which made concessions to a number of different groups. Businessmen were authorized to draft industry-wide agreements, called "codes," which would be exempt from the antitrust laws but supervised by the government. Section 7(a) of the act guaranteed workers the right to collective bargaining and stipulated that the codes should set minimum wages and maximum hours. In addition, the law provided for $3.3 billion in public works. One Congressman charged that the measure was the product of Roosevelt's intellectual advisers, "fresh from the academic cloisters of Columbia University, and with the added inspiration of all they have learned in Moscow." Yet the act represented less a triumph of government planning than a willingness to permit business, free of the threat of antitrust prosecution, to negotiate industry-wide pacts controlling price and output.

To meet the farm crisis, Congress approved the Agricultural Adjustment Act, authorizing a project which one New Dealer called "the greatest single experiment in economic planning under capitalist conditions ever attempted by a democracy in times of peace." The law levied a tax on processors of agricultural commodities, and paid the farmer who agreed to restrict production a subsidy based on "parity," which would give him the same level of purchasing power he had had before the war. A companion Farm Credit Act made possible the refinancing of farm mortgages. Yet not until Roosevelt's second term did the government do anything, however modest, to aid the most depressed members of the farm community— sharecroppers, tenant farmers, and migrant laborers (vividly portrayed in John Steinbeck's *The Grapes of Wrath*). Roosevelt's farm program resulted in an unprecedented involvement of the government with the American farmer. William Faulkner later wrote: "Our economy is not agricultural any longer. Our economy is the federal government. We no longer farm in Mississippi cotton fields. We farm now in Washington corridors and Congressional committee rooms."

Roosevelt also heeded the ancient cry of the farmer for cheap money. Although his first steps, notably an Economy Act which slashed government salaries and soldiers' pensions, had been severely deflationary, he recognized the need for early action to boost prices. The President wanted to develop a carefully controlled inflation, but soft-money men from the South and West compelled him to go further. He took the nation off the gold standard; experimented with gold-buying, to raise prices; and, reluctantly, also undertook silver purchases. But by 1934 he had lost most of his interest in money manipulation, which had succeeded in halting deflation but had otherwise yielded little, and thereafter he fought a rear-guard action against the strong inflationist wing in Congress.

The NIRA, AAA, and managed currency constituted the New Deal's main recovery efforts, but even in his first weeks in office, the President was working toward a different aim: reform of the nation's financial system. In May, 1933, Congress approved Roosevelt's recommendation for federal regulation of securities. The following year, it brought the stock exchange under national control and created the Securities and Exchange Commission to administer the new regulations. The Glass-Steagall Act of 1933 separated investment from commercial banking and provided for a controversial innovation, government insurance of bank deposits, which turned out to be a brilliant success. In 1935, the Congress of the Second Hundred Days enacted a banking law, which centralized control of the Federal Reserve System, and the Public Utilities Holding Company Act, which leveled holding company pyramids. Well before the end of Roosevelt's first term, the country, which had once regarded Wall Street as the power center of the nation, had shifted its attention to Washington. As one writer noted, the front page of the newspaper had become "more important to the businessman than the market page, and the White House Press conference of vaster import than the closing prices of the New York Stock Exchange."

The Holding Company Act climaxed a 29-month campaign by the federal government to expand its influence in the electric power field and to initiate new conservation programs. The Tennessee Valley Authority, created in 1933, plunged the government into the generation of hydroelectric power and a series of experiments in planning for a region the size of England and Scotland. The Public Works Administration (PWA) helped construct such mammoth dams as Grand Coulee and Bonneville in the Pacific Northwest and Fort Peck in Montana. Even more dramatic was the work of the Rural Electrification Administration, set up in 1935. When Roosevelt took office, nine out of ten American farms had no electricity. Under the stimulus of the REA, by 1950 nine out of ten farms enjoyed the benefits of electric power. The New Deal also accomplished an enormous amount in the physical rehabilitation of the country, especially in soil conservation, and in coping with the prolonged drought which turned a large section of the Great Plains into a dust bowl. The Civilian Conservation Corps (CCC), another product of the Hundred Days, put thousands of young men into the forests to feed wildlife, count game, clear camping grounds, and above all, to plant trees.

Both the CCC and the PWA helped meet one of the most demanding problems Roosevelt faced—relief for the unemployed—but neither proved as important as the Federal Emergency Relief Administration created in 1933 to channel federal money to the jobless through state and local agencies. To head the FERA, the President named the dynamic New York social worker Harry Hopkins. A half hour after he left the White House, Hopkins set up a desk in the hallway of a government building, and in the next two hours "spent" $5 million. By the end of 1934, more than 20 million persons—one out of every six in the nation—were receiving public assistance.

In 1935, Congress voted nearly $5 billion for work relief. Hopkins directed the spending of most of this money for public works such as hospitals, schools, and airports under the aegis of a new agency, the Works Progress Administration. Determined to make use of the special skills of white-collar workers, and especially men and women of artistic talent, Hopkins created under the WPA a Federal Theatre, a Federal Writers' Project, a Federal Music Project, and a Federal Art Project; these agencies found employment for painters like Stuart Davis and writers such as Ralph Ellison. The National Youth Administration gave part-time jobs in the next eight years to over 600,000 college students and more than 1.5 million high school pupils.

In part as a consequence of these relief activities, the New Deal also took unprecedented steps in housing. The Home Owners' Loan Act of 1933 made it possible to save tens of thousands of homes from foreclosure. The following year, Congress set up a Federal Housing Administration which, by guaranteeing mortgages, enabled Americans to borrow money on reasonable terms to buy a new home or repair an old one. In the next three years, the FHA gave home-improvement loans to a million and a quarter people. The government sponsored more than a hundred model communities, some of them subsistence homesteads, and created "green-belt" towns which sought to combine the best in urban and rural living. Most important, especially after the establishment of the United States Housing Authority in 1937, the administration assumed responsibility for clearing slums and erecting projects to house the poor.

Although Roosevelt and his Secretary of Labor, Frances Perkins, the first woman cabinet member, did not intend to use government to foster unionization, organized labor benefited from the humanitarian emphases of the New Deal. Under the leadership of John L. Lewis, United Mine Workers' organizers told coal miners: "The President wants you to join." When the American Federation of Labor proved unsympathetic to the attempt to enroll workers in the mass industries, Lewis led a number of unions out of the A. F. of L. and created what would be known as the Congress of Industrial Organizations (CIO). The CIO's campaign received a boost when in 1935 Congress enacted the National Labor Relations Act; the Wagner Act, as it was called after its sponsor, Senator Robert Wagner of New York, forbade employers to interfere with union efforts at organization and empowered a National Labor Relations Board to enforce these prohibitions and to conduct plant elections. Yet labor learned that, even with a friendly government, it had to take the initiative if it was to break the resistance to unionism in the big industries. In 1937, it found an effective weapon in the sitdown strike; by March of that year, almost 200,000 workers—opticians, milliners, clerks, farm hands, even wet-nurses—were sitting down at their jobs somewhere in the country. Before the year was out, such titans as U.S. Steel, General Motors, and General Electric had capitulated, and the attempt to organize workers in the factories, frustrated for so many years, had scored a stunning success.

Of all the welfare measures of the New Deal, the most significant was the Social Security Act of 1935, which created a national system of old age insurance, set up a federal-state program of unemployment insurance, and authorized federal aid to the states, on a matching basis, for care of dependent mothers and children, the crippled, and the blind and for public health services. Republican Senator Daniel Hastings typified conservative response to Roosevelt's proposal when he stated: "I fear it may end the progress of a great country and bring its people to the level of the average European." But most Congressmen believed that such action had been too long postponed; decades earlier, European countries had provided for security against the perils of old age and joblessness in an industrial society.

The New Deal came a long way toward creating a welfare state. It accepted responsibility for aiding millions of unemployed; took at least preliminary steps to deal with the problem of rural poverty; engaged the government directly in clearing slums; focused national attention on the impoverished "one-third of a nation"; set federal standards of minimum wages and maximum hours; wiped out sweatshops and child labor; and set up a system of social security. The First Lady, Eleanor Roosevelt, whose career reflected the growing importance of women in politics, played an important role in nurturing the government's humanitarian concerns. "Government has a final responsibility for the well-being of its citizenship," Roosevelt declared. "If private co-operative endeavor fails to provide work for willing hands and relief for the unfortunate, those suffering hardship from no fault of their own have a right to call upon the Government for aid; and a government worthy of its name must make fitting response."

By 1936 the sorts of issues that had concerned the country in 1932 seemed as far removed from contemporary reality as the tariff debates of Calhoun and Webster a century earlier. Under Roosevelt, the government was engaged in a spectrum of activities—documentary films, Indian art, shelterbelts—that was different not merely in degree but also in kind from almost anything Washington had ever undertaken before. Just four years earlier no one could have anticipated that the government would be running its own circus, supporting Jackson Pollock's painting, paying farmers not to raise peanuts, attempting to regulate the brassiere industry, sending bookmobiles through the Tennessee Valley, patronizing the ballet, and teaching the Pine Ridge Sioux how to milk goats.

Before the New Deal, most Americans did not conceive of the national government as an agency that acted directly on them. By the end of Roosevelt's second term, it was affecting the everyday life of people in countless ways. Millions survived wholly because of relief payments. Others cashed Social Security checks or drew unemployment insurance benefits financed in part by the federal government. Millions of farmers cast ballots in AAA referendums, and factory workers voted in NLRB elections. Suburbanites lived in FHA-financed homes, and city dwellers in mammoth U.S. housing projects. Schoolchildren ate hot lunches provided by the federal government, college students received monthly NYA checks from Washington, and the WPA taught more than a million illiterates to read and write. At the beginning of the decade, the nation's primary loyalties were still to local and state governments. But local units of government proved unable to cope with the crisis, and by the end of the decade, it seemed natural to center one's attention on Washington.

To staff the new federal agencies, Roosevelt turned to university-trained experts. Save for a brief moment of glory in the wartime agencies in 1917, this new class of administrators did not make its appearance in the national arena in large numbers until the 1930's. Roosevelt made use of a "brain trust" in the 1932 campaign, and when he took office he combed the campuses for professors and authorized them to decide a range of economic questions. "On a routine administration matter you go to a Cabinet member," observed a reporter, "but on matters of policy and the higher statesmanship you consult the professoriat."

Roosevelt also succeeded in legitimizing this expansion of governmental power, although only after a fierce struggle. In the spring of 1935, the Supreme Court invalidated the National Industrial Recovery Act. Early in 1936 it held the AAA's processing tax to be unconstitutional. By a series of further decisions, the tribunal wiped other New Deal and state laws off the statute books. In retaliation, the President in 1937 sought to "pack" the Court with six additional justices. Congress balked, but in the course of the battle, the Court reversed itself, and sustained such New Deal laws as the Social Security Act and the Wagner Act. After the "revolution of 1937," there was almost no act of Congress in the area of economic regulation that the Court would not sanction.

Roosevelt and his political chieftains exploited the opportunity offered by the depression to establish the Democrats as the country's new majority party. The foundation of the new coalition was the support of the urban masses. In 1936, Roosevelt captured 104 of the 106 cities in the United States with 100,000 or more residents. Especially significant in this urban alliance were ethnic voters and organized labor. In 1932, most Negroes, still wedded to the party of Lincoln, had backed Hoover; in 1936, they switched emphatically to FDR. Although no civil rights legislation was adopted under the New Deal, unemployed Negroes received a large share of relief payments and other benefits and Roosevelt appointed men such as Robert Weaver and women like Mary McLeod Bethune to his "black cabinet." Labor in 1932 made almost no contribution to the Democratic cause; in 1936, the Mine Workers gave the party nearly half a million dollars, the largest donation from any source.

With 523 electoral votes to Alf Landon's 8, Roosevelt won reelection in 1936 by the largest margin in more than a century. The President swept so many Democratic Congressmen into office with him that a number of the newcomers had to sit on the Republican side of the aisle. A Chicago Democrat later reflected: "Franklin Roosevelt was the greatest precinct captain we ever had. He elected everybody—governors, senators, mayors, sheriffs, aldermen." Roosevelt would win two more terms in the White House, and even after he was gone, the Great Depression and the New Deal would leave its mark on the political alignments of the postwar world.

Yet for all the achievements of the New Deal, it failed to make much headway in its most important assignment: ending the depression. To be sure, this was a most formidable task. By the time Roosevelt took over, the economic structure had been so badly damaged and the morale of investors so shattered that even at best slow progress could be expected. New Deal policies resulted in a quick spurt in the spring of 1933, but for the next two years, little advance was made. Encouraging gains began in mid-1935. By the spring of 1937, the nation had finally risen above 1929 levels of production. But in August, 1937, a sharp recession struck, from which the country only painfully recovered. As late as 1939, ten years after the Wall Street crash, some 10 million were unemployed.

Although critics denounced Roosevelt as a profligate spender, the economy behaved so sluggishly chiefly because the New Dealers failed to appreciate the importance of deficit spending in bad times. Roosevelt felt almost as strongly as Hoover that an unbalanced budget was sinful. Not until 1938, and then only to a limited extent, did the President adopt the recommendation of British economist John Maynard Keynes to employ fiscal policy to achieve recovery. Moreover, for all the social measures of the New Deal, the basic pattern of distribution of income remained virtually unchanged. In May, 1940, Secretary of the Interior Harold Ickes noted in his diary: "This is our weakness. The New Deal has done a great deal during the last seven years, but we have not been able to force from those who own and control the preponderant part of our wealth the social and economic security that people are entitled to." Only with the coming of World War II, which sharply accelerated government spending, did the country once more enjoy full employment and effect a modest redistribution of income. Since the Roosevelt era, the severity of recessions has been mitigated by the stabilizers created by the New Deal, but the economy has never achieved full employment without the stimulus of military spending.

By the end of 1938, the New Deal had lost its impetus as a force for social reform, and Roosevelt was compelled to direct much of his attention to problems of foreign policy. Even before he took office, the post-Versailles world was disintegrating. When, in September, 1931, Japan invaded Manchuria, it demonstrated that neither the League of Nations Covenant, the Nine-Power Treaty, upholding the territorial integrity of China, nor the Kellogg-Briand Pact, outlawing war as an instrument of national policy, would suffice to contain a power bent on conquest. Hoover, when called on to enforce the Kellogg and the Nine-Power pacts, replied that they were "solely moral instruments." In Roosevelt's first week as President, the Reichstag granted absolute power to Adolf Hitler, and for the rest of his life FDR had to cope with the menace of totalitarianism. During Roosevelt's first term, Mussolini's forces would invade Ethiopia, Germany would march into the Rhineland, and both powers would convert Spain's civil war into a testing ground for the greater war that was to come.

Although by instinct and experience a Wilsonian internationalist, Roosevelt believed that he had to concentrate on pulling America through the crisis, and his first actions veered in an economic nationalist direction. When he began to consider a different course, isolationist and pacifist opinion left him little room to maneuver. Congressional isolationists insisted on an embargo on the sale of war material to belligerents, and they refused to grant the President the discretionary power he requested to decide whether an embargo should be applied, and, if so, to which nation. A series of neutrality laws, designed, as critics noted, to keep the United States out of World War I, tied Roosevelt's hands, and he was reduced through most of his first two terms to futile moralizing. By the summer of 1936, the President seemed to have surrendered altogether to the isolationists and pacifists. "We shun political commitments which might entangle us in foreign wars; we avoid connection with the political activities of the League of Nations," he asserted. Both the President and Congress were conforming to public opinion; in March, 1937, a Gallup poll (another innovation of the 1930's) reported that 94 per cent of Americans favored a policy of staying out of all wars instead of preventing these wars from erupting.

In other parts of the world Roosevelt had more maneuverability than he did with respect to western Europe. He implemented a "Good Neighbor" policy toward Latin America, "recognized" the Soviet Union, and negotiated reciprocity agreements which modified the high Hawley-Smoot tariff of 1930. In the Far East, where he also had a freer hand, he was more sympathetic than Hoover had been to the ideas of Henry Stimson, who sought to restrain the Japanese; yet, like Hoover, he and his associates opposed strong measures against Tokyo. "Then if moral ostracism is ineffective, how can we implement the Kellogg Pact?" asked Joseph Grew, ambassador to Japan. "Certainly not by force of arms, which would be contrary to the very principle for which the Kellogg Pact stands," Grew replied.

But by 1939 Roosevelt and many of the men around him had come to feel that the United States must make some contribution to halting fascist expansion, and they began to extend limited kinds of help to Britain and France. In September, 1939, the German invasion of Poland would set off a chain of explosions that would involve the United States ever more deeply in the spreading war. Little more than two years later, the United States would be fighting the war it had vowed never to fight. It would enter that war a vastly different nation from the country that engaged in World War I—more industrialized, more committed to the ways of the city, more cosmopolitan, less deferential to business leadership, more aware of the possibilities of the welfare state, more responsive to the demands of labor and of various ethnic groups, and, as its role in the creation of the United Nations would shortly demonstrate, much more willing to assume a role in world affairs commensurate with its power.

For Further Reading

Bernstein, Irving, *The Lean Years.*
Leighton, Isabel (ed.), *The Aspirin Age.*
Leuchtenburg, William E., *Franklin D. Roosevelt and the New Deal, 1932–1940.*
————, *The Perils of Prosperity, 1914–32.*
Schlesinger, Arthur M., Jr., *The Age of Roosevelt.*

23   Modern China

The fall of the Ch'ing was a real revolution, perhaps the first in Chinese history. Dynasties had been overthrown before, but no emperor had ever been succeeded by a president. With the Ch'ing traditional concepts of legitimacy, above all the hereditary principle, disappeared. Henceforth, China was to be a republic.

This was not immediately apparent. President Yüan Shih-k'ai's idea of what was best for China was far from revolutionary. In Yüan's view, China needed a strong executive, and this led him to the conclusion that he should establish a constitutional monarchy. One after another, possible rivals—the cabinet, the young political parties, and the parliament—were subdued by Yüan in the first years of his rule.

Yüan's acceptance in 1915 of the Japanese Twenty-one Demands, which granted far-reaching economic privileges to Japan in China, damaged his reputation as China's strong man, but did not deter him from his intention to establish a monarchy. But when Yüan launched his campaign to become emperor, he found little support. Opposition from the provinces and, more important, from military leaders, including some of Yüan's own subordinates, caused the monarchical movement to collapse, and in 1916 Yüan died a broken man.

For the next decade Chinese political life was dominated by Yüan's former subordinates and other militarists who had acquired power in the provinces after the revolution. The regionalism that had begun with the Taiping Rebellion now reached its final stage. China became a kaleidoscope of satrapies at the mercy of the warlords, each strong enough to control and exploit a few districts or a province or two, none powerful enough to eliminate his rivals. There was a central government in Peking, recognized by the powers, but its authority did not extend beyond the territories held by the armies of the warlords who formed it, and its composition changed with the frequent shifts in the balance of military power in north China.

With few exceptions, the warlords stood above all else for their own self-interest. In this they were symptomatic of the time, for, as the Confucian ethic, the traditional social fabric, and central political authority continued to disintegrate, there remained no higher principles compelling loyalty, no cohesive force to hold society together. In the words of Sun Yat-sen, China resembled "a sheet of loose sand." For a time it seemed that

A.D. 1912–1916 Yüan Shih-k'ai first president of the Republic of
            China
      1919 May Fourth Movement
      1924 Reorganization of the Kuomintang
      1926–1928 Northern Expedition, and reunification of China un-
            der the Kuomintang
      1934–1935 Chinese Communists' Long March
      1937–1945 Second Sino-Japanese War

----

military power alone was strong enough to maintain order. But order was impossible in a country divided among contending mercenary armies, and so the warlords were eventually superseded by new political parties inspired by constructive programs and possessing disciplined armies—the Nationalists, then the Communists.

First, new ideological foundations had to be discovered. As during the late Chou and the Six dynasties, intellectual life was stimulated by the disintegration of political authority. The abolition of the examination system and the expansion of Western education spurred the search for new values to replace the discredited intellectual tradition. Adam Smith, John Stuart Mill, Dickens, Darwin, Spencer, Ibsen, and Tolstoy were translated and discussed. Several thousand students went to Europe, America, and Japan to get a closer view of the modern world. Most became convinced that the West had much to offer China. One of these, Hu Shih, who took a Ph.D. at Columbia in 1917, urged that colloquial Chinese replace the archaic classical style as the national literary language to facilitate the spread of literacy and Westernization. Others extolled individualism, women's rights, democracy, and science, and denounced Confucianism and the traditional family system. When these new ideas combined with nationalism, a new and powerful historical force was born.

This happened in 1919. In early May of that year it was learned in Peking that the Versailles Peace Conference had awarded former German rights in the Shantung peninsula to Japan. Indignation—at the powers, at Japan, and at pro-Japanese "traitors" within the Peking government—led to a demonstration of some 3,000 Peking students on May 4. The arrest of hundreds of the students only inspired more to join the protest. Within days the fever had spread to other cities. Students organized and demonstrated, workers struck, and merchants closed their shops as gestures of solidarity with the patriots. A nation-wide boycott of Japanese goods began. The government was helpless, and for a brief time it became evident that armed force was not the ultimate source of political authority. The cabinet fell. Nationalism had made a triumphant entry onto the political stage.

The students and professors who had participated in the events of May emerged as the intellectual leaders of the nation and used their new-found eminence to propagate their ideas. Within a few years more than 400 new periodicals appeared, filled with articles in the colloquial style about the Western world and the regeneration of China. No aspect of tradition was sacred, from Confucius and the most venerated legends of antiquity to arranged marriages and footbinding. Anarchism, Liberalism, Materialism, Pragmatism, German Idealism, Art of Art's Sake, Socialism, and the newest of all, Bolshevism, all found advocates. Some ideas took organizational form, in labor unions, literary societies, and political parties, including a small Chinese Communist party founded by Westernized intellectuals in 1921. The periodical press carried lengthy polemics about the ability or inability of science to solve all problems of human existence, and over the relative merits of Chinese and Western civilizations. One general conclusion soon became apparent: most educated Chinese now looked to the West, not to China's past, for their ideals.

The new ideas were invigorating, but they were also a source of frustration, for foreign privilege and warlord rapacity remained, and the gap between the imported ideals and Chinese realities was all too obvious. The ironies of this situation were a common theme in the fiction of the twenties, most especially in the trenchant satire of China's greatest modern writer, Lu Hsun. To the perspicacious it was clear that ideals alone could not save China; only force could root out the warlords and compel the foreigners to relinquish their privileges.

It was Sun Yat-sen who found a way to give the new nationalism military power. Over the years, Sun's requests for aid had been rejected by Japan, Great Britain, and the United States, but in 1923 Soviet Russia agreed to support him. Under the guidance of Soviet advisers, Sun's political party, the Kuomintang (Nationalist party), was reorganized along the lines of Bolshevik "democratic centralism." Military assistance, in the form of advisers and matériel, was also supplied by the Russians. A party military academy was founded at Whampoa, in the outskirts of Canton. There, under Commandant Chiang Kai-shek, officer candidates were trained in military science and indoctrinated in party ideology, which under Russian influence now included anti-imperialism and nationalization of major industries. The new party constitution and program and a united front with

the infant Chinese Communist party were approved at the First National Congress of the reorganized Kuomintang in January, 1924, in spite of opposition from the party's right wing. Although the Kuomintang never became as efficiently regimented as its Leninist model, for many years it was superior in numbers, organization, discipline, and zeal to any other political group in China. By the time of Sun's sudden death in March, 1925, the Kuomintang controlled Canton, and had extended its influence into surrounding Kwangtung province.

Soon after Sun's death came another outburst of indignation at China's humiliating condition. In May and June, foreign police in Shanghai and Canton fired on student and worker demonstrations protesting the treatment of Chinese workers in foreign-owned factories. A number of the demonstrators were killed, and antiforeign feeling soared. Organized and led by the left wing of the Kuomintang and the Communists, and supported by Chinese businessmen, workers struck in Shanghai, Canton, Hong Kong, and other cities. The Hong Kong strike, which lasted well over a year, and a widespread boycott of British goods damaged British trade. Under similar leadership, in a number of southern provinces the peasant movement gathered momentum, and in some areas progressed from hostility against warlords and foreigners to confiscation of land from landlords. This upsurge of revolutionary nationalism help to sweep the Kuomintang to national power in the following months.

By mid-1926, the Whampoa Military Academy had graduated several thousand officers, the Nationalist army numbered about 100,000, including many units absorbed from warlord armies, and the party itself had something like 200,000 members. To Chiang Kai-shek it seemed time to fulfill Sun Yat-sen's ambition to reunify China through a military expedition against the powerful northern warlords.

Within the Kuomintang there were two closely related issues to be resolved: Who was to succeed Sun Yat-sen—Wang Ching-wei, the leader of the party's left wing, or Chiang Kai-shek, the commander in chief of the Nationalist army? And how far was the revolution to go? The antiforeign strikes had proved injurious to Chinese business, and in general the worker and peasant movements were becoming a cause of considerable uneasiness among Chinese businessmen and landlords, many of whom had connections with the Kuomintang.

Chiang settled both issues by allying himself with conservative elements, within and without the Kuomintang. With their support, he turned against those fomenting social revolution, crushed the Communist-led labor unions in Shanghai, where they were strongest, and split with the Russians, the Chinese Communists, and the Kuomintang left wing. Without an army, Wang Ching-wei and the left wing disintegrated. The Communists instigated several uprisings, all futile. The Russians quietly returned home. The power struggle temporarily retarded the progress of Chiang's "Northern Expedition," but it soon continued triumphantly northward through one province after another, culminating in the capture of Peking in June, 1928, and the formal submission of the northern warlords. Chiang was now paramount within the Kuomintang, and head of the newly proclaimed Nationalist government in Nanking. By the end of 1928, the new government had been granted diplomatic recognition by most of the foreign powers, with the United States in the lead.

The Nationalist government was formally the government of all China, but its direct influence was largely confined to the central and lower Yangtze provinces, which, along with the coastal ports, especially the great metropolis of Shanghai, provided its main sources of support. The land tax, the most important source of revenue, remained in the hands of provincial officials, many of whom were warlords who had nominally submitted to the new government, but who in reality were virtually autonomous within their territories. During the decade from 1928 to the outbreak of the Sino-Japanese War in 1937, such militarists occasionally joined and rose against the Nanking government, but they were no serious threat, and in the process of suppressing these revolts the central government extended its authority into new areas.

After Chiang's split with the Communists, the government cracked down on the party, driving many members from the cities to the countryside, where the party was to gain the understanding of rural China crucial to its eventual victory. In 1931 a "Soviet Republic" was established in Kiangsi province, but by 1934 the attacks of government armies forced the Communists to abandon Kiangsi, and they embarked on the epic Long March to the northwest, through 6,000 miles of the most difficult terrain in China. Only 30,000 of the original 90,000 reached their destination a year later. During the march a new group of tough and resourceful leaders emerged, headed by Mao Tse-tung.

Meanwhile, the Nanking government was slowly modernizing China. A provisional constitution and a modern law code were promulgated, and although both remained paper legislation in many respects, they were steps forward. The army was strengthened. Progress was made in public health, industry, transportation, irrigation, and flood control. Education continued to develop rapidly, particularly on the higher levels, although the infusion of Confucian precepts into the Kuomintang ideology taught in the schools was a sign of the regime's growing conservatism, and alienated many students and Westernized intellectuals. The currency reform of 1935 resulted in financial stability for a few years, before wartime inflation set in. In foreign affairs, tariff autonomy, lost in the Opium War treaties, was regained, providing the government with a valuable means of increasing revenue. Other onerous provisions of the "unequal treaties" were not abolished until 1943.

The threat of Japanese aggression was never absent. Nationalist troops had clashed with Japanese units as early as 1928. In 1931, the Japanese army took over Manchuria, in the next year the puppet Manchukuo regime was inaugurated at Mukden, and in the following years Japanese pressure on north China steadily increased.

In spite of growing popular demand to resist Japan, Chiang adhered to a policy of eliminating internal enemies, primarily the Communists, before confronting China's powerful external foe. But in December, 1936, when Chiang flew to the northwest to compel enforcement of this policy on recalcitrant subordinates, he was held captive by them until an agreement to halt the civil strife was reached. The hard-pressed Communists welcomed this change, and so when the war with Japan began in July, 1937, there was some semblance of national unity.

The war had two important internal political consequences. The Japanese assault drove the Nationalist government inland from Nanking to Chungking in the southwest, severing it from its former sources of support in the coastal cities and Yangtze provinces. Although Chiang gained in personal prestige as the leader of the national resistance, the eight years of warfare left the Kuomintang and the Nationalist government considerably weakened and widespread corruption, which continued after the war, alienated many earlier supporters of the regime. The Communists, on the other hand, exploited the opportunity to extend their influence into rural areas over large parts of central China, which Nationalists had been forced to abandon, but which the Japanese were unequipped to administer. Through mobilization of the peasantry around a program of resistance to the foreign invader and moderate agrarian reform, designed to appeal to a broad stratum of the rural population, the Red army grew from about 90,000 in 1937 to almost 900,000 at the end of the Second World War, while in the same period the membership of the Communist party increased roughly from 40,000 to 1,200,000. Thus in 1945, although the Nationalists were still vastly superior in numbers and equipment, Mao Tse-tung had sufficient strength to challenge Chiang Kai-shek. The stage was set for the final and decisive contest for the mastery of China.

For Further Reading

Chow, Tse-tsung, *The May Fourth Movement: Intellectual Revolution in Modern China.*
Grieder, Jerome B., *Ha Shik and the Chinese Renaissance.*
Sharman, Lyon, *Sun Yat-sen, His Life and Its Meaning: A Critical Biography.*

24 Modernizing Japan

The Meiji Restoration of 1868* is a convenient event from which to date the beginning of Japan's rapid transition to a modern society. To be sure, some aspects of modernization had earlier origins. Recent historians have pointed out that late Tokugawa society provided a better base for modernization than was previously supposed, more affluent, less rigid in social stratification, and with a higher level of popular education. The shogunate had made an initial commitment to technological modernization in the

---

* Meiji was the name of the calendrical era proclaimed in that year. Later it became the posthumous name of the reigning emperor (1867–1912). The implication of the word "restoration" was not primarily the return of the imperial dynasty to power, but rather the return of the country to some earlier moral condition from which rule by military families had presumably been a deviation.

A.D.   1868 New imperial government established at Edo, re-named Tokyo

1871–1876 Basic policies of centralization and liquidation of caste privilege

1873 Universal military conscription; dispute over Korean invasion resolved in favor of peace faction

1877 Satsuma Rebellion

1881 Date set on constitution and parliament

1889 Promulgation of Meiji Constitution

1890 First session of Imperial Diet

1894–1895 Sino-Japanese War

1904–1905 Russo-Japanese War

1915 Japanese attempt to assert political and economic dominance over China (Twenty-one Demands)

1918 Cabinet of Prime Minister Hara, first to be headed by a member of the House of Representatives

1930 World depression reaches Japan

1931 Mukden Incident, leading to Japanese conquest of Manchuria

1932 Abandonment of party cabinets

1936 Abortive "February Mutiny"

1937 Incident at Marco Polo Bridge brings all-out war with China

1941–1945 Japan at war with Western allies

fields which it recognized as essential for national defense, though the actual accomplishments in industrialization and military preparations up to 1868 were very slender. The significance of the Restoration was that it brought to positions of leadership a new group with sufficient youth and vision to try new ways of action. Specifically, some of the group perceived the particular impediments in society that would have to be removed if modernization was to be accelerated. Two of these were among the most persistent and characteristic features of traditional Japanese society: political decentralization and caste privilege.

The political system immediately after the Restoration was not unlike that under the shogunate. The emperor and his government fell heir to the holdings of the Tokugawa shoguns, but much of the country continued to be semiautonomous domains of the daimyos. The imperial government lacked the power to tax these lands, or even, in the absence of a true national army, to exercise normal police and administrative powers over them. Centralization took the form of a voluntary return of domain land registers by the great western han, followed by a not quite so voluntary program of the same kind for all of the other domains. All of the territory of the country was then reorganized into prefectures, units of provincial administration strictly accountable to the central government.

The initial acts of the Restoration had left the ancient condition of class privilege little impaired. The daimyos were still daimyos; the samurai were still samurai; the peasants and urban commoners were still legally bound to their occupations and localities. Government leaders came to realize that national strength required the broad participation in public life by all classes on a merit basis, and this led them to their most revolutionary reform: the abolition of class qualifications for political or military office, with the concomitant abolition of the pensions and all other caste marks of the samurai. Social rationalization—or at least the firm national commitment to it—was furthered by a reform of agricultural policy: agricultural land was reappraised in terms of cash value instead of estimated annual yield, enabling the government to levy taxes on it that were constant in terms of money. A peasant's real property had been legally inalienable, but was now "freed" (i.e., made subject to sale or foreclosure) in the interests of economic rationalization.

Simultaneously other modernization policies were initiated. The government began to build telegraph lines and a railway system (100 miles of track being laid before 1880), supported by a loan from Great Britain of one million pounds. The central government fell heir to the factories and mines that had belonged to the shogunate and added to them. Industrialization was rigorously planned from the start, strategic industries taking first priority, followed by industries such as textiles that could be used as capital accumulators in foreign trade, and only last by industries specifically for domestic consumption. A modern army and navy were created, with universal military conscription (1873) and a general staff system modeled on that of Prussia (1878).

One major aim of the new government was the recovery of diplomatic equality, that is, revision of the unequal treaties that Japan had been forced to conclude with the Powers before the Restoration. Westerners based their extraterritorial rights on the contention that the Japanese legal system was inefficient and cruel. The Japanese commenced a program of wholesale legal reform, using foreign advisers.

The revolution of early Meiji attests to forthright, able leadership. In law the head of the new government was Emperor Meiji, but he was an adolescent at the time of his accession, and the traditional seclusion of his office made him at most a ratifying, rather than a deciding, figure in the politics of his time. The group actually in control was an oligarchy of men who had proven their mettle in the struggle against the shogunate. Most were from the great western domains that had overthrown the Tokugawa, and the remainder were mostly political activists among the imperial court caste (*kuge*). Despite desertions from the original group by dissenters and the addition to it of younger protégés, the oligarchy had remarkable cohesion and continued to dominate the administration until well into the twentieth century. An internal policy dispute of 1873 (over a quixotic scheme to invade Korea) left as survivors in the central government a group united on goals of international cooperation and internal improvements. That group was almost wholly comprised of former retainers of the Chōshū and Satsuma domains.

The Satsuma Rebellion of 1877 was the most serious of several uprisings by regional samurai bands protesting the abolition of the domains and dispossession of the samurai. The victory of the central government was decisive, demonstrating the superiority of its new citizen army and further strengthening the control of the oligarchy. But opposition to the oligarchy did not cease; in fact it became broader in extent, though less violent in means. The most characteristic form of that opposition from the late 1870's on was the movement for parliamentary institutions, and its first great accomplishment was the establishment of an elected national assembly in 1890.

The belief that Japan should eventually have representative institutions of some kind was widespread. It was in fact part of the craze for all kinds of Western traits, and even members of the oligarchy shared it to some degree. Their consistent position in the 1870's, however, was that the people lacked experience in politics, and that the necessity of rapid modernization would continue to demand authoritarian control for the foreseeable future. Against that view, a group of dissidents organized political action associations—the first political parties—whose aim was to break oligarchic control and inaugurate parliamentary government. The founders of the democratic movement were for the most part former Restorationists who had become disaffected with the government. Their initial objective was not mass egalitarian democracy, but the better representation of the samurai and of local interests. Only gradually did Japanese liberalism become a truly popular cause.

In 1881 the liberal campaign embarrassed the government into making the promise that a constitution would be promulgated eight years hence. The actual drafting of the document was secret and undertaken entirely by the conservatives in the oligarchy. It is not surprising, therefore, that the text which emerged was at best a compromise between liberal and authoritarian principles. It established a bicameral legislature, the Imperial Diet, to meet for the first time in 1890, but the powers of the lower house, elected by limited suffrage, were balanced by those of a House of Peers. Parliamentary power did not extend to certain matters (e.g., the governance of the army and navy) deemed imperial prerogatives, and was severely restricted even over budgetary appropriations.

In form the 1889 Constitution was described as a gift from the emperor, who was therefore regarded as beyond its control. The practical implication of that doctrine was that ultimate state power would continue to rest with any group, such as the existing oligarchy, which enjoyed imperial confidence or which could plausibly claim to speak for the emperor. The chief administrative organ under the throne was a cabinet without responsibility to the parliament, and it tended, with other major civil and military offices, to be manned by the oligarchs or their appointees.

No description of the authoritarian features of the Meiji government or of the opposition to it from outsiders should disguise the fact that the dominant popular mood of late-nineteenth-century Japan was one of ebullient, hopeful self-congratulation for the new paths on which the leaders had set the nation's course. Though some samurai resented the loss of privilege, many others welcomed the opportunities that a rapidly modernizing society gave them. Opposition to the government was sometimes directed against slowness of change. This is nowhere clearer than in the case of popular attitudes to foreign relations. The most important issue in early Meiji was revision of the unequal treaties, and here the almost universal public sentiment was that the government was insufficiently forthright in obtaining it from the Powers. Where relations with other Asian countries were concerned, the public consistently supported a more expansionist, nationalistic policy than the government was willing or able to pursue. Each of the three victorious wars that Japan fought between 1894 and 1918 was popular; each succeeding peace was unpopular because it failed to secure the territory, indemnification, or other gain that the public thought the country was entitled to.

Korea was the main issue in the Sino-Japanese War of 1894–1895 and the Russo-Japanese War of 1904–1905. In the first Japan acquired Formosa and the Pescadores, and made China relinquish her claim to suzerainty over Korea's foreign relations. In the second she won Southern Sakhalin and a concession on the Manchurian coast (including Dairen and Port Arthur), and as a by-product also gained a protectorate over Korea that was extended to outright possession in 1910. In the First World War Japan participated on the side of the Allies. She took advantage of the Powers' involvement in the war by attempting, in the famous Twenty-one Demands (1915), to establish a position of economic and political dominance on the mainland, and was rewarded in the Versailles Treaty with the former German colonial possessions in the North Pacific and on the China coast that she had taken in the fighting.

The generation between the opening of the Diet and the First World War saw internal maturation of several kinds. From this period on, Japan was an industrial power, though the population continued until after the Second World War to be predominantly rural. Education spread, and so did popular concern with national affairs. An incipient social movement created the first labor unions and the first socialist parties. Of far greater immediate importance was a change in the character of the older, main-line party movement. Having gained their rudimentary objectives of a constitution and parliament, liberals next turned to a campaign for broader participation in government by means of responsible party cabinets on the British model. For a decade or so after 1890 the Diet and political parties were dominated by men of such sentiments, but the executive of the government was just as securely dominated by the oligarchs and their protégés, who were opposed to party government. Bit by bit the two factions reached a compromise. Liberal leaders like Ōkuma Shigenobu and Itagaki Taisuke accepted invitations to sit with the oligarchs in the cabinet; oligarchs like Itō Hirobumi accepted leadership in political parties. All agreed that the future should bring a closer relationship between the executive and legislative branches. From about the turn of the century the aging first-generation oligarchs retired from titular executive positions, but retained considerable power behind the scenes in a semiofficial body known as Genro (Elder Statesmen). It was this group who determined the choice of a prime minister and other executive officers, and they turned with increasing frequency to party leaders.

In most of the years from 1918 to 1932 there were party governments—cabinets whose prime ministers and most other members belonged to the majority party in the House of Representatives, even though this had not yet been accepted as a regular constitutional procedure. During these years there was considerable hope from Japanese liberals that Japan was about to become democratic in its domestic institutions as well as peace-loving and cooperative abroad. That a disastrous career of authoritarianism and expansionism, war and defeat, intervened before that dream became possible was a great tragedy for Japan, for which a complex interaction of internal and external causes is responsible.

Public disenchantment with liberalism and party government was one contributing factor. Many associated the parties with opportunism and corruption. Some of the policies adopted by party governments were inept or unpopular. In 1930, for example, the cabinet of Prime Minister Hamaguchi Yūkō was blamed for economic disaster when the deflationary fiscal policy it had adopted to stabilize the international value of the yen coincided with the general world depression and priced Japanese goods entirely out of the world market. The same cabinet was also castigated by chauvinists for concluding the London Naval Disarmament Treaty.

If liberal institutions seemed doomed to frustrating failure, the tactics of rightists and militarists seemed all too often to get things done. The Mukden Incident of September, 1931, an instance of military direct action without the prior knowledge of the civilian government, led to an easy conquest of all of Manchuria. Not only did the army gain glory from this incident. An army-controlled state in Manchuria (ostensibly the independent Empire of Manchukuo) also provided a testing ground for military rule and controlled economy.

Extremist agitation sometimes took the form of assassinations of civilian leaders in politics or business, and in one incident, the attempted coup of February 26, 1936, a wide spectrum of moderate and conservative figures, including advisers to the emperor and antimilitarists in the armed services, were marked for liquidation. The army itself restored discipline, but exacted from frightened moderates a greater share in the government than before. Party cabinets had been abandoned in 1932; succeeding cabinets were made up of a variety of bureaucratic elements, with the army in increasing control.

Japanese foreign policy through the decade had the primary aim of protecting and extending Japan's economic and political interests in the Far East. In 1933 the frontiers of Manchukuo were extended through military means, and in 1935 further areas of northeast China were placed under Japanese surveillance. In July, 1937, a skirmish between Chinese and Japanese troops at the Marco Polo Bridge near Peking at last brought the two countries to war. Japan quickly took the coastal areas and leading cities, but the Chinese held the hinterland, where they stood off the Japanese for eight years.

The Western democracies opposed each new step in Japan's expansion.

Growing friction with them caused the Far Eastern crisis to become part of a world confrontation between fascism and its enemies. Japan joined the Rome-Berlin Axis in 1940 more from the perception that she shared common foes with the European fascists than from any fundamental community of positive goals. The pact further deepened American hostility, yet the United States still permitted the export of strategic materials to Japan until the following summer, fearing that to embargo them would only trigger Japanese seizure of new sources of supply in Southeast Asia. When Japan did occupy Indochina, in prelude to further thrusts southward, America responded with a general embargo. In ensuing negotiations aimed at reducing the tension the two sides made mutually incompatible demands: Japan, that the United States recognize her position in China; and the United States, that Japan withdraw from China. The Pearl Harbor attack of December 7, 1941, was a preemptive strike, based on the premise that the United States was already irrevocably committed to resist those actions of Japan's in East Asia that had by then become the unalterable conditions of her national policy.

For Further Reading

Beasley, W. G., *The Modern History of Japan.*
Fairbank, John K., Edwin O. Reischauer, and Albert M. Craig, *East Asia: The Modern Transformation.*
Reischauer, Edwin O., *Japan: The Story of a Nation.*
Tsunoda, Ryusaku, William Theodore de Bary, and Donald Keene, *Sources of Japanese Tradition.*

25   Nationalism in India

In a carefully phrased announcement to the British Parliament in August, 1917, the Secretary of State for India declared that the policy of the British government was to work for "the increasing association of Indians in every branch of the administration, and the gradual development of self-governing institutions, with a view to the progressive realization of responsible government in India as an integral part of the Empire." This emphasis on gradualism is a reminder that the roots of Indian nationalism were in nineteenth-century constitutionalism and liberalism, and that the cataclysmic forces released by the First World War and the Russian Revolution

A.D.   1905 Partition of Bengal
          1906 Founding of Muslim League
          1909 Morley-Minto Reforms
          1912 Delhi made capital of India
          1917 Announcement by British Parliament of responsible government as goal for India
          1919 Montagu-Chelmsford Reforms
          1920 M. K. Gandhi becomes leader of Indian National Congress
          1921 First Noncooperation Movement
          1927 Simon Commission
          1930 Civil Disobedience Movement
          1935 Government of India Act
          1937 Inauguration of provincial autonomy
          1939 Congress ministries resign on war issue
          1942 Last civil disobedience movement; August uprisings
          1946 Negotiations for transfer of power
          1947 Lord Mountbatten governor general; partition and independence

---

worked upon a nationalism whose course was already largely determined. The preoccupation of Indian nationalism was always with political, not social, solutions, and the common description of its culmination in 1947 as a "transfer of power" is exact. A social transformation had been neither promised nor expected; such social change as was necessary would follow, it was widely believed, from the transfer of political power from an alien to an indigenous elite.

Such a belief was consonant with the demands of the early nationalist leaders. As was noted previously, the men who organized the Indian National Congress had as their aim participation in the existing administrative structure that the British had created, not control of the mechanism of government, and certainly not its destruction. Almost without exception they were men who had made careers through social structures that were products of the modernizing impact of the west. Dadabhai Naoroji (1825–1917) was a businessman who became a member of the House of Commons; Surendranath Banerjea (1848–1925) founded a newspaper and a college; G. K. Gokhale (1866–1915) was a teacher of English. The early resolutions of the Indian National Congress define the concerns of both the leadership and their following: easier entrance into the Indian Civil Service, the tiny, all-powerful pinnacle of the bureaucracy; expanded membership in legislative councils; protective tariffs; and a decrease in military expenditure. Change would come about as the Indian intelligentsia made known both the needs of India and their own ability to share in the task of rule with the British, since, as Naoroji put it, "the genius of the British people is fair play and justice."

Almost from the very beginning of the nationalist movement there were those who challenged this faith in the British, arguing that no imperial power would act generously, and insisting that the Indian people should not be mendicants for power in their own homeland. The most influential exponent of this view was B. G. Tilak (1856–1920), who in his Marathi and English newspapers eloquently reminded his readers that in leaders like Shivaji, the Marathi chieftain who had defied the might of the Mughal empire, and in the ancient glories of Hinduism, the people of India had traditions of greatness upon which they could draw for strength.

This appeal to the Hindu past made explicit the tensions that had always been latent in the nationalist movement. The advocates of Western education, social reform, and constitutional gradualism, who styled themselves moderates, were dependent upon the examples and the ideals of the British; the forces of reaction were represented for them by India's own traditions. Over against the moderates were men like Tilak, whose wholehearted acceptance of the Hindu heritage freed them from this ambiguity about their past, permitting them to make a self-confident appeal that gave their nationalism a Hindu vocabulary and Hindu symbols. They proudly accepted the title of "extremists" the moderates bestowed on them.

This emphasis created, or perhaps more accurately, brought to the surface, another tension: an overt hostility between Muslims and Hindus. Sir Syed Ahmed Khan (1817–1898), the leader of modernizing forces in Indian Islam, had argued that the democratic, representative institutions sought by the Indian National Congress would make Indian Muslims a permanent minority, and Tilak's appeal to a Hindu past as the basis of nationalist sentiment sharpened such fears.

Another element of tension came with the increasing emphasis by Tilak and others that violence, not constitutional gradualism, might be necessary for achieving India's freedom. In Bengal, Aurobindo Ghose (1872–1950) preached a passionate identification of the sacrifice required by the nation with the blood offerings made to Kali, the Mother Goddess. Tilak's revivalism and Ghose's mysticism were strengthened in 1905 by the Japanese victory over Russia. By using the West's own weapons, Japan, it was argued, had triumphed over the power Britain had feared for a century.

For the first time since 1857, the British were confronted with the politics of violence, expressed in sabotage and political assassinations.

The working out of the tensions within the nationalist movement emerged in a number of developments. In a struggle for control of the Indian National Congress, the Moderates won an uneasy victory in 1907, but at the price of losing the dynamism imparted to the movement by the passionate logic of the extremists. A group of Muslims responded to the growing concern with India's political future by founding the Muslim League in 1906 for the protection of Muslim interests. The British response to the violent expressions of nationalism was a campaign against the extremist leaders which included the jailing of Tilak, the suppression of newspapers, and the execution of a number of young men found guilty of sabotage and political assassinations. But at the same time an attempt was made to satisfy what were regarded as justified political aspirations through the constitutional act of 1909, known as the Morley-Minto Reforms, which gave the right to vote for members of the legislative councils to an electorate defined by a property franchise. But even the most moderate leaders of the Indian National Congress denounced the 1909 act for one of its provisions: the creation of special constituencies for Muslims. For Indian nationalists, this recognition of religion as a criterion of citizenship was a deliberate attempt by the British to create dissension between the two religious communities. On the other hand, the leaders of the Muslim League regarded it as minimal protection for Muslims from the dangers inherent in the electoral process, and they saw the Congress attack on the act as anti-Muslim in its motivation.

While the First World War was on the whole remote from Indian concerns, it led to a considerable realignment and readjustment of political forces. India's entrance into the war was taken as a matter of course in 1914, and the general acquiescence of the population is suggested by the reduction of British troops in India to 15,000 and the raising of a volunteer Indian army of 1,300,000 men. Economically, the war led to a rise in agricultural prices because of the increased demand for Indian goods, and the shortage of imports gave Indian manufacturers an opportunity to compete with foreign goods for the first time. In politics, the moderates in the Indian National Congress supported the war effort, but other groups began to question the identification of British and Indian interests that had for so long been the basis of political discussion. Indian Muslims had been inclined to regard British rule as the necessary countervailing force to Hindu nationalism represented by the Congress, but events in the Middle East, especially the war against Turkey, raised doubts in the minds of many Muslim leaders about the soundness of this alliance. A small but highly articulate group of Muslims began to argue that Muslim interests could best be safeguarded by Muslim participation in the Indian National

Congress. Among these leaders, known as "nationalist Muslims," were Maulana Azad, Zakir Husain, later President of India, and, for a brief period, M. A. Jinnah, founder of Pakistan. Within the Congress itself, Tilak and the other leaders who had been regarded as extremists in the early years of the century were assuming the position of elder statesmen, and their place as proponents of radical solutions was taken by groups who advocated, and plotted, the violent overthrow of British rule. Many of the revolutionary leaders had fled to exile in the United States, and from there they attempted, with limited success, to get help from Germany for armed insurrections in India.

The declaration in Parliament in 1917 was the British response to these varied political changes, and it was followed by constitutional changes in 1919 known, from the secretary of state and the governor general, as the Montagu-Chelmsford Reforms. The fundamental element of the new constitution was the creation in the provinces of what became known as dyarchy: responsibility for certain aspects of government was handed over to popularly elected ministers, while an appointed governor maintained final authority. No basic changes were made in the central government, but a greatly enlarged franchise gave some form of political representation to 8 million people.

The promulgation of the new constitution, with its provision for political parties to form provincial ministries, faced the leaders of the Indian National Congress with a momentous choice. While there was almost universal denunciation of what seemed to be the niggardly installment of responsible government, the Congress leaders were deeply divided over the question of participation in the elections to be held in 1920. The moderate leadership argued for full acceptance of the reforms; the old extremists, who now occupied a far less radical position in the political spectrum, wanted to use the elections as an occasion to attack the government; the new revolutionaries were calling for violence. The government, frustrated by the reception of the reforms and fearing an outbreak of violence, matched the movement toward responsible government with the passage of legislation, the Rowlatt Acts, that provided for the arrest and imprisonment of political agitators without trial. In this atmosphere of mutual resentment and distrust in April, 1919, an army officer in Amritsar, in the Punjab, opened fire on a political gathering which had been called in defiance of a government order, killing at least 400 and wounding more than 1,000. It was this incident which set the stage for the emergence of Mohandas K. Gandhi as the dominant figure in the nationalist movement.

Gandhi was already a famous man, highly respected by the British as well as the Indians for his work in South Africa on behalf of Indian immigrants in their struggles against discriminatory laws. He had given his full support to the British during the war and at first had been inclined to urge acceptance of the new constitution, but he abandoned this position in 1920. The failure of the British to punish the officials responsible for the Amritsar Massacre, combined with his assessment of the weakness of the divided and fragmented Indian National Congress, had convinced him that a radical departure in nationalist aims and strategy was needed, and in 1920 he persuaded the Congress to adopt a resolution urging noncooperation with the government.

In addition to withdrawing the Congress from participation in the elections, the noncooperation resolution of September, 1920, called for a boycott on foreign goods, the renunciation of all British titles, a refusal to attend government schools, and, ultimately, a refusal to pay taxes. All of these activities were to be carried on without violence, for the heart of Gandhi's campaign was that change in the political order would be produced through the withholding of cooperation, rather than through negotiation, compromise, or coercion. This point is worth special emphasis, since Gandhi's aims were never very clear. The British complained that each time the government made a concession Gandhi would shift his ground, but Gandhi's actions were intelligible from his strategy of noncooperation and his metaphysics, which held that truth could not be embodied in any formula but needed continual restatement in action. The title of his autobiography, *My Experiments with Truth,* is thus a clue to both his methods and his aims. Insofar as Gandhi's intentions can be summed up, he seems to have pursued two general ends: the withdrawal of the British on India's terms, not theirs; and the fostering of a spirit of nationhood defined by self-respect.

To assign to Gandhi the role of creator of Indian independence is to misread the events of modern Indian history; the main thrust of nationalism had already made itself felt, and Gandhi's work probably did not either greatly hasten—or delay—the actual date of the transfer of power. His real achievements were of another order: on one level, the reorganization of the Indian National Congress to make it responsive to central control while reaching down into the life of the nation; on another, the maintenance of a considerable degree of unity between the moderate constitutionalists and the revolutionaries; and, above all, the identification of the nationalist movement with the concerns of the masses. Through the use of symbols— homespun cloth, the spinning wheel, his own renunciation of the modes of Western living he had once followed—he dramatized his cause with a success perhaps without parallel in modern politics. The fasts to the death, the boycotts, the appeals for nonviolent action, all helped to create a national self-awareness among a people in whom it had been notably lacking.

In addition to the Gandhian theme, two other lines of development characterize Indian political life between the wars. One is the growing separatism among the Muslims; the other is the modification of the constitutional reforms of the 1919 Act. The rapprochement between the Indian National Congress and the Muslim League, which had begun in 1917 when the leaders had reached a rather tentative agreement on such matters as special representation for Muslims, was strengthened by Gandhi's enthusiastic support of the Khilafat movement. This was based on the resentment many Indian Muslims felt at the dismemberment of the Ottoman Empire under British auspices at the end of the World War, but the abolition of the Caliph by the Turks themselves undercut this emotional appeal, and by the mid-twenties the Muslim League moved into definite opposition to the Congress. The Hindu religious vocabulary in which Gandhi articulated his positions added to the growing estrangement. The Indian National Congress protested that it was an all-inclusive secular organization, but inevitably its definition of Indian culture and history, by emphasizing Hindu values, aroused fears among the Muslims, who constituted a quarter of the population. The position taken by genuine secularists like Jawaharlal Nehru, that religion is not a basis for nationality, was a denial of much that was fundamental to the Islamic understanding of the nature of the state and the community. Insofar as the British fostered, as Indian nationalists claim they did, the antagonism between the two religious communities, it was by sharing the Muslims' predilection for the primacy of religion as a determining factor in national identity. Given that assumption, many officials undoubtedly used the antagonism to rationalize the need for British rule. But probably the fundamental cause of the divergences between the aims of the Indian National Congress and the Muslim League was, in simplest terms, the possibility open to Jinnah and the other Muslim leaders of creating an alternative nationalist movement and, ultimately, although not through long-range planning, of a separate state. Every nationalist movement is marked by internal tensions and struggles for control; India's historical experience pointed almost irresistibly to the creation of rival movements by extremely able and ambitious men.

The constitutional modifications and revisions of the twenties and thirties were partly responses to nationalist pressures, but they were not the result of negotiations and compromises. The Simon Commission, appointed in 1927 by the British government to report on the working of the dual system of responsibility initiated in 1921, was fiercely criticized by the leaders of the Indian National Congress on the grounds that it did not have any Indian members. This occasioned a new noncooperation movement, but in the end, with the help of moderate Indian liberals, many of whom had broken with the Congress, a new constitution was introduced in 1935. Dyarchy was abolished, and the provincial ministries were given enlarged powers and a very real measure of autonomy. Less change took place in the central government, for the governor general retained most of his powers.

At first the Congress stated that it would refuse to cooperate with the new constitution, but the attraction of office for men of ability and ambition, combined with a realization that a policy of unbending refusal to accept partial solutions was leading the Congress into sterility, forced a change in policy. The Congress was elected to office in eight of the eleven provinces, showing that it was in fact what it had long claimed to be: the representative of the majority of the Indian people. The Muslim League won no comparable victories, but by this time M. A. Jinnah had assumed its leadership, and it became in effect the parliamentary opposition as well as the spokesman for Muslim nationalism.

The outbreak of the Second World War brought an end to the cooperation in the political process by the Indian National Congress. When the British government refused to grant India a larger measure of independence immediately in return for support of the war, the Congress ministries resigned in the provinces where they had formed governments, and in August, 1942, Gandhi announced that a new campaign of civil disobedience would begin with the purpose of making Britain leave India. The government responded by jailing all of the Congress leaders. Most of them remained in jail until the end of the war, but by 1945 British political circles generally recognized that a devolution of power in India was inevitable.

The urgent problem was to find a constitutional formula which would be acceptable to both the Indian National Congress and the Muslim League. The Congress party demanded a strong central state and emphasized its commitment to a parliamentary system with universal suffrage. The Muslim League, as an opposition party, did not have to state its aims so precisely; Jinnah, who by this time was its unquestioned spokesman, insisted that such a unitary state was utterly unacceptable to India's 100 million Muslims. Negotiations centered, therefore, on defining a form of government that would permit enough provincial autonomy to satisfy the League's insistence on areas which would be controlled by the Muslims while maintaining the unitary national authority the Congress wanted. The resolution of the impasse was the decision to partition India, granting the Muslims a homeland and the Indian National Congress a strong central state where citizenship would be without religious reference.

Until the summer of 1947 perhaps none of the leaders on either side, including Jinnah, really believed that partition was inevitable, and for the Congress the decision was a defeat for its long struggle to become the successor to the undivided British inheritance in India. Indian nationalism

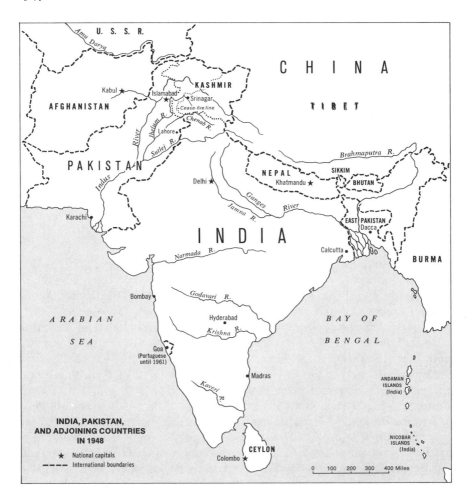

INDIA, PAKISTAN,
AND ADJOINING COUNTRIES
IN 1948

★ National capitals
- - - - International boundaries

had predicated a unity which was rooted in the soil of India, and its most eloquent spokesman had insisted that Indian nationality transcended the diversities of regions, races, and religions which were so conspicuous a feature of Indian history. Partition was so complete a denial of this passionately held belief that Pakistan was long regarded as *India irredenta* by important political elements in Indian politics. The Pakistan response to this attitude was a sense of unease at not being accepted as a state that had a right to existence, thus adding to the many problems that necessarily exacerbated relations between the two nations carved out of a single political and economic unit.

For Further Reading

Gandhi, M. K., *The Story of My Experiments with Truth.*
Menon, V. P., *The Transfer of Power in India.*
Nehru, Jawaharlal, *Towards Freedom.*
Sayeed, Khalid B., *The Political System of Pakistan.*
Tinker, Hugh, *India and Pakistan.*

26   Europe Between the Wars

The peace settlement worked out in Paris during the eighteen months that began in January, 1919, demands comparison to the thoroughgoing alteration of the European structure ratified at Vienna a little more than a century earlier. The kings and aristocrats who had set the style at Vienna were gone; in their place were a legion of bureaucrats and technical advisers and a largely new breed of statesmen. The experts seemed necessary: the problems at Paris were far more extensive and challenging. At Vienna the negotiators could deal with a Europe of recognizable shape, where nations that had been nations were viable still, and where such complexes as Italy and Germany needed no more than judicious reshuffling or rationalization. At Paris, though there was far more knowledge for the experts to draw upon, there was no such firm base on which to build. Save for Russia, which in 1917 had withdrawn into revolution and the humiliating Peace of Brest Litovsk, the victorious Allies survived as nations, but they were exhausted, deeply shaken by the terrible losses of life and by the internal convulsions that had racked both economy and society. On the losing side, there was only flux—revolution in Germany, disintegration in the Hapsburg and Ottoman empires and on the borders of Russia. The peacemakers had not so much to redraw the map of Europe as to create it anew.

It proved necessary in Paris, as at Vienna, to cut through the irreconcilable interests and the hangers-on by confining decisions to a small group; in time even the Council of Ten gave way to the Council of Four. Of those four, Vittorio Orlando of Italy (who did not speak English) had the least impact; the main outlines of the settlement were determined by Georges Clemenceau of France, David Lloyd George of England, and Woodrow Wilson of the United States. Only Clemenceau would have been compre-

A.D.   1919 Treaty of Versailles signed; Treaty of St. Germain with Austria; Treaty of Neuilly with Bulgaria

              1920 U.S. Senate rejects League of Nations; Treaty of Trianon with Hungary; Treaty of Sèvres with Turkey

              1921 New Economic Policy inaugurated in U.S.S.R.

              1922 Mussolini's March on Rome; Fascists take power

    1922–1923 Washington Naval Conference

              1923 French occupation of the Ruhr; Treaty of Lausanne with Turkey; Adolf Hitler stages Beer Hall Putsch in Munich

              1924 Lenin's death

              1925 Locarno Treaties

              1926 General strike in Great Britain; Stalin establishes control in U.S.S.R.; Imperial Conference defines nature of British Commonwealth of Nations

              1928 Pact of Paris, Kellogg-Briand Pact, "outlawing war"

              1929 Lateran Treaties between Italy and the papacy; stock market collapses in New York, ushering in worldwide depression

              1930 Reichstag election marks emergence of Nazis as major party

              1931 Incident at Mukden provides pretext for beginning of Japanese occupation of Manchuria; defeat of Labour party in general election, followed by formation of a National Government (a coalition) in Great Britain

              1932 Japanese occupation of Shanghai; Reichstag elections, from which Nazis emerge as largest party but without a majority

              1933 Hitler becomes chancellor in Germany

              1934 Purge of Nazi party

              1935 Italy invades Ethiopia

              1936 Germany reoccupies the Rhineland; Spanish Civil War begins

              1938 Germany takes over Austria; Munich Conference

              1939 End of Civil War in Spain; nonaggression pact between Russia and Germany; Germany invades Poland; Great Britain and France declare war on Germany

EUROPE
AFTER WORLD WAR I

German Republic

TERRITORIES LOST

by Germany

by Austria-Hungary

by Russia

by Bulgaria

E = Eupen-Malmédy   R = Ruhr District   S = Saar Region

hensible to the men of Vienna: tough-minded and even cynical, he was utterly devoted to the interests of France and equally determined to protect her against a recurrence of the devastation that the German war had brought. Wilson was at the other extreme: highly moral and rigid, determined to sweep away the old diplomacy, he was a political scientist increasingly isolated from the public opinion at home on which his success had ultimately to depend. Lloyd George, unlike Wilson a consummate politician, had just emerged from a general election, overwhelmingly victorious but ultimately compromised by his heavy reliance on Conservative support. He had played his part in a viciously anti-German campaign that suited the mood of the country; at the conference, however, he was all suppleness and the most responsive of all the leaders to Germany's claims as a great power. Perhaps Talleyrand would have understood him, but Talleyrand had spoken in 1815 for the defeated power: there was no one to speak for Germany in 1919.

The treaties with Germany and Poland were signed on June 28, 1919: there followed, over the next year, the treaties of St. Germain with Austria, Neuilly with Bulgaria, Sèvres with Turkey, Trianon with Hungary, and other treaties with lesser states. But the treaty with Germany, the Treaty of Versailles, fixed the main lines of the settlement; when it was completed, the Council of Four could abandon its work to other hands. Disarmed and stripped of her colonies, Germany had to return Alsace and Lorraine (which she had got in 1871) to France; she also gave up other bits and pieces of territory to Belgium and Poland, including the Polish Corridor which thereafter split East Prussia from the rest of Germany; and she faced the prospect (not confirmed by events) of losing still more through the vote of the inhabitants in plebiscites; the Rhineland was to be occupied by the Allies for fifteen years. Beyond paying the costs of the occupation, Germany had to make substantial restorations and compensations and was saddled with an enormous bill for reparations which her weakened economy had little chance of meeting. Added to the many potential grievances that were, understandably enough, built into the treaty, Germany was made to confess her responsibility for the war; this unfortunate clause, now given some diplomatic if not moral authority by historians, helped to compromise the treaty not only in German eyes but in those of many Allied citizens as well.

Any peacemaking tries to prevent the defeated powers from starting another war. But in 1919 a new device was put forward to check war and settle disputes, an institution far more positive and sophisticated than the periodic congresses of the old Concert of Europe or the vague and suspect Holy Alliance of Czar Alexander I. This was the League of Nations, set up on a model largely worked out during the war in Great Britain. The League was ultimately to fail in its grandest ambitions, in part because of the quick withdrawal of the United States into isolation, symbolized by the Senate's refusal to accept the Covenant of the League as a provision of the Treaty of Versailles. But the League was not hopeless from the start—some small disputes were effectively settled, and the Secretariat and its ancillary organizations opened a new era in international administration.

The statesmen at Vienna had not recognized and so did not need to cope with the problem of nationality, a problem that became the leitmotif of the history of the nineteenth century. At Paris the principle was fully recognized, and the negotiators seized the unparalleled opportunity to carry it through by creating "succession states" from the wreckage of the Austro-Hungarian Empire, by careful redrawing of national boundaries, and by resort to decisions as to national allegiance through plebiscites. But the two greatest geographical inventions of the settlement—Czechoslovakia and Yugoslavia—were themselves multinational states, ridden with tension and under constant threat of disintegration, like the empire from which they had sprung. A boundary line or a majority vote cannot disentangle mixed populations, and in some instances the need for compensation or insurance against new aggression left populations of clear nationality detached from their homeland, a problem particularly severe among the Germans. Still other countries saw portions of their territory taken away in the interests of minorities now seen as nationalities. So the peace settlement not only created minority problems in every country in central and eastern Europe but left a powerful irredentist spirit that threatened the peace from the moment of its completion.

Outside of Europe, three principal concerns deserve attention. Turkey, of course, lay in both Europe and the Near East. Greece and Italy had enforced claims against Turkey by occupying portions of her territory, and in Turkey a revolutionary movement led by Mustafa Kemal, ultimately fatal to the traditional forms of Ottoman rule, arose to drive out the invaders and to convert Turkey into a modern state on the European model. The Turkish pursuit of the Greeks, stopped at Chanak in 1921 by British forces, made it perfectly clear that the Turkish settlement foreseen in the still unratified Treaty of Sèvres had to be redone. In 1923 the Treaty of Lausanne confirmed the sovereignty of Turkey over the Straits and gave her a foothold in Thrace on the European continent. But she abandoned any claims to the Arab states that had been taken from her in the war and that had been carved up into spheres of influence by secret agreements between the English and the French. Some of these essentially artificial states were erected as independent kingdoms; others were given as "mandates" to the two European powers as, so to speak, temporary colonies. But dynastic ambitions were supplemented by only an incipient nationalism. Ironically, in the Balfour Declaration of 1917, Great Britain promised to create a national home for the Jews in the very heart of the Arab world, in what was to become the British mandate of Palestine; thus Britain, the principal patron of Arab independence, provided the major stimulus to the emergence of Arab nationalism as a real and explosive force.

The device of the mandate was also used to bring the former German colonies in Africa and Asia under the government of the victorious Allies, with Britain and Japan as the principal administering powers; in these areas of the world, too, nationalism was barely discernible and would not for thirty years begin to undermine this temporary European rule. But in a third, highly advanced non-European sector—Japan, the United States, and the British dominions, whose increasing autonomy was recognized by separate representation at the Peace Conference and in the League—there lay an immediate challenge, economic, political, and cultural, to the dominance of Europe. The United States retreated into its shell, to be sure, but Japan emerged from Paris unsatisfied, and the dominions, with one exception refusing to back the British stand at Chanak, went forward to establish themselves gradually as independent nations, tied at last by little but sentiment to the mother country, an arrangement defined and sanctified as the Commonwealth of Nations in 1926 and 1931. Ireland, the most rebellious and hostile of Britain's former colonies, won dominion status in 1922 and seized every opportunity to reduce even the appearance of a connection, although independence was not formally attained until 1949. For twenty years the victorious European nations could continue to fancy themselves the great powers they had once been. But the next world war would not be concluded by a primarily European settlement.

Even in Europe the Versailles settlement failed to work. Morally compromised among the defeated by its real or imagined injustices, and among the victorious by subtle and sophisticated criticism of some of its provisions, it was never given sufficient time. The new European nations were not always viable politically or economically, and, in the immediate aftermath of the war, some of the great powers were shaken by discontents that manifested themselves in new forms of government, as in Italy, or in abortive coups, as in Germany in 1919 and 1920. France had failed to get the guarantee she had wanted in the Treaty of Versailles against German resurgence; she had also been denied the collective security arrangements promised by the United States and Britain. Determined to get the reparations that Germany could not pay, France occupied the heavily industrial Ruhr Valley in 1923. The occupation provoked passive resistance from the German workers and inevitable clashes; moreover, a runaway inflation almost overnight destroyed the value of German money and threatened other currencies as well. Both sides drew back; the change was signaled by

the succession to power in France and Germany of the pacific Aristide
Briand and Gustav Stresemann. In 1924, under the so-called Dawes Plan,
a scaled-down scheme of reparations payments was worked out, and the
United States began to promote investment in Germany to make possible
the production that had to underlie fulfillment of the plan, although investment was not as intelligently directed as it might have been. An effort in
that year to promote collective security through arbitration procedures in
the League, the so-called Geneva Protocol, came to nothing, but in 1925 a
series of treaties signed at Locarno by the various European powers
brought partial German acceptance of the Versailles terms, the reintegra-
tion of Germany into the European system, German membership in the
League, and a general exchange of guarantees. In the glow of the "Locarno
spirit," many of the postwar tensions dissolved; the new spirit reached its
apogee in 1928 when the Kellogg-Briand Pact "outlawed war." Retrospec-
tively, the gesture seems as ill-founded as the Holy Alliance, though its
purposes were more beneficent; yet the ambition bespoke the weariness of
Europe and its determination to escape from tragedy. No one could then
quite imagine the collapse that would shatter the European system again
and create new tensions that would end in another war.

In the twenties at least, men could be pardoned for not reading correctly the signs of approaching disaster. It is true that the economy of
Europe was in a parlous state. All the combatant nations emerged from the
war with their industrial plant and transportation facilities seriously run
down, their capital resources depleted, and the relations between labor and
management subject to new and puzzling strains, not least because of the
rapid growth of Communist sympathies in some European trade-union
movements; to these problems, France and Belgium, in particular, had to
add the rebuilding made necessary by the physical destruction of the war.
Currencies had been dislocated, and the entire machinery as well as the
traditional channels of international trade were disrupted: a preoccupied
Europe saw some of its best prewar markets lost to the United States and
Japan, and European businessmen showed less determination than they
might have done to recapture their primacy. Pent-up civilian demand fed
a brief postwar boom, which quickly evaporated; it led men to think
for a time, however, that the prewar economy might be restored, and
it stimulated both the destruction of wartime controls, which might have
helped moderate the unfortunate effects, and capital investment in traditional but no longer highly profitable sectors of industry. The collapse in
turn led businessmen and governments to excessive caution and promoted
the raising of tariff walls that further cut down the possibilities of international trade on which the health of the economy (not to mention reparations) depended. The state of economic knowledge had simply not advanced to a comprehension of or solutions for an economy, international

or domestic, that could no longer depend on the self-regulating mechanisms of the nineteenth century. Still, despite the disaster of the inflation of 1923, there was gradual recovery. By the mid-twenties, currencies were largely stabilized, and the gold standard—that sacred cow of old economic thinking—resumed its sway. Much of the wartime wastage and destruction had been made up, and the prosperity of the newer industries—automobiles, aircraft, electricity, radio communications, chemicals—not only pushed forward a general recovery of the economy but, in increasing degree, changed the quality of life in the more advanced nations. Synchronized with the relaxation of international tensions in the Locarno period, this diffusing prosperity created a sense of confidence that proved, in the event, dangerously misplaced.

The international monetary system of the twenties no longer rested on the extensive reserves of gold and securities that had characterized the prewar system; rather, it was supported by a fabric of loans, with the United States as the principal lender. When in 1928 the unhealthy boom in the United States showed signs of faltering, followed by a decline in domestic demand and the psychologically destructive stock market collapse in October, 1929, American investments were recalled and then disappeared, and one after another national economy fell in the wake of the American disaster. By the early 1930's, every major advanced economy— except that of Russia—was in deep trouble, marked by a drastic fall in production and by widespread unemployment. The gold standard was nearly universally abandoned, the state intervened in the economy in ways unthinkable only a few years before, and industry itself undertook some long-overdue rethinking of its structure and priorities, although, given the psychologically demoralizing circumstances, that rethinking looked more toward contraction and sharing a limited market than toward the restoration of intelligent and healthy growth. The recovery of the late thirties was sparked, ominously, by the growing business of rearmament.

To hindsight the twenties show a similar undermining of the political arrangements of Europe. The war, in Wilsonian rhetoric, had been fought to make the world safe for democracy, and the forms of government in the new states, and above all in the Weimar Republic in Germany, suggested that that noble purpose had in fact been accomplished. But German democracy, handicapped by the apolitical attitude that had almost always characterized German intellectuals and by a steady barrage of destructive criticism from its enemies, was compromised for many more of its citizens by its origin in defeat, while in other countries, notably Poland and Hungary, the immediate postwar instability led ultimately to the establishment of regimes that might be in form democratic but that were in essence highly authoritarian.

The sharpest turn in this rightward direction was taken in Italy, where economic chaos, wounded nationalism, and frustrated ambition led to rapidly growing support for the Fascist movement headed by Benito Mussolini, a former socialist journalist. After some political successes, in 1922 Mussolini led the "March on Rome," to claim and be given political power. His regime had two faces. It relied in part on naked force, expressed in the organized ruffianism of the "Black Shirts," the destruction of trade unions, censorship of the press, the repression of dissent, and a growing tendency to regiment all of society. At the same time, much in the new regime was welcome to powerful parts of Italian society. The long-standing hostility between the Roman Catholic Church and the Kingdom of Italy was brought to an end in the Concordat of 1929. Mussolini's early liberalism in economic matters gave way after the abrogation of the old constitution in 1925 to the "corporative state" that took form over the next several years; this industry-by-industry organization of the economy—owing something to early twentieth-century syndicalist ideas—could be seen both as a means of gaining national efficiency and as a way of avoiding the destructive conflicts of labor-management relations under a freer system. Although the workers and, above all, the peasants gained least from the Fascist system, some effort was made, paternalistically enough, to confer social benefits, and it was possible for observers from more securely democratic countries to look benevolently on the Fascist experiment.

That this favorable judgment was possible for Frenchmen and Englishmen suggests a decline in the democratic impulse in the two countries that had given democracy its modern forms. In both nations, but particularly in France, the twenties were marked by a turning away from political commitment or interest. To some extent, the rejection of politics grew out of disgust with the war the politicians had made, but that disgust had simply exacerbated a current of political disillusion clearly evident before the war. The greater personal freedom that had burst on the Western world during and after the war—a breaking down of old conventions, sexual liberation, a frank hedonism—despite its enormous benefits to the quality of some individual lives and, above all, to the arts, could be read as indicating a loss of national or public purpose, a purpose that had been still recoverable when the nations went to war with near-unanimity in 1914 but that seemed now beyond recapture. Growing freedom and prosperity could mean, moreover, that many of the problems that had commanded political attention before the war had been solved and that the postwar problems were too complex and remote to bring ordinary men into political action, the more so when it was easy to assume cynically that they were beyond solution. It is not hard to understand, in such a situation, how forms of government (to borrow Alexander Pope's phrase) might be something for which only fools would contest. But forms revealed substance, and the substance, once made manifest, could be utterly subversive of the prosperity and the way of life that had been won at such cost and with so little promise of permanence.

Nothing reflects the ambiguities of the western European attitude toward politics more clearly than the strange role played throughout the twenties and thirties by the Soviet Union. During the civil war that followed the Revolution in 1919 and 1920, small Allied forces were in action around the edges of Russia, at first to prevent the Germans from taking the utmost advantage of the swift and complete Russian surrender, then in ill-judged and futile support of some of the anti-Bolshevik forces. At the same time, the victorious Bolsheviks eagerly set about fomenting the revolution many of them expected momentarily in more advanced countries; the Third International was founded to promote international communism and, incidentally, created in the West a standing fear of subversion. Despite these tensions, the early twenties saw a relaxation in relations with Russia, paralleling the adoption of the New Economic Policy in Russia itself and the calculated "liberalism" of Lenin's last years. Although there was much criticism of the policy, the Western powers were disinclined to go to war to save the eastern frontiers arranged in the peace settlement and that stood as perhaps the worst grievance of the Germans. Into this chink in the wall was built a strange cooperation between Russia and Germany, old enemies who thus bought time and release from pressure to forward their own internal development; the collaboration was made official in the Treaty of Rapallo in 1922. Other nations in the West soon recognized the Soviet government, although in Britain, for example, diplomatic relations were broken off again for a time. But after Lenin's death in 1924, and with the emergence of Stalin as the victor in the struggle with Trotsky for supreme power, Russia turned inward once more.

The course of Stalin's Russia posed a challenge difficult to comprehend. The forced drive to industrialization and collectivization in agriculture, the grisly and dramatic purge trials in the 1930's, and the ruthless elimination not only of political or military leaders who had fallen foul of Stalin's plans or megalomania but of hundreds of thousands of lesser people—notably the kulaks, rich peasants who had done well under the NEP but who were an obstacle to collectivization—brought home to European minds and consciences the full impact of totalitarian rule. When the response was not incomprehension or numbness, it was almost certain to be ideological. Men of the left, inspired by the Revolution and enamored of the seemingly rapid and certain Russian path to economic and social progress, obediently followed the twists and turns of Soviet policy, which had long since subordinated international communism (and the Communist parties in other countries) to Russian national ends; to men on the right, there was the bogey of Bolshevism, as pervasive as the fear of Jacobinism after 1815. On the one side the cry was "no enemies to the left"; on the other, only a plea of anti-communism was needed to forgive any authoritarian regime, however dreary or despicable.

The thirties were punctuated by crises, played out against a background of economic disaster, that even now, in their very appearance of inevitability, recall the sense of doom that lay over that troubled decade. In 1931 Japan marched into Manchuria and began her long, systematic effort to turn China into a client state; the League of Nations protested but had no force to bring to bear, and Japan showed her contempt for censure by simply resigning from the League and going on with her conquests. Meanwhile, in Germany, the Weimar Republic was tottering to its fall. With Gustav Stresemann's death in 1929 began a new era of political instability, heightened by the economic collapse that was worse in Germany than in any other European country. Seeking both security and scapegoats, German voters turned away from the mistrusted, even hated, republic, some to the extreme of communism, many more to the National Socialist (Nazi) party, which promised a Germany purged and regenerated.

The leader of the Nazis was a former Austrian house painter, Adolf Hitler, whose wartime experiences (he was a corporal) had turned him into a bitter and fervent nationalist. Like the Fascists in Italy, he exploited the growing taste for violence through the organization of his "storm troopers," and increasingly he found his major scapegoats in the Jews, a prosperous minority more fully assimilated into German society than perhaps any other society in Europe, though anti-Semitism was an old strain in German life and thought. Beyond this, Hitler's progress could be summed up in the main as anti-Versailles and anti-Communist. In 1923 he attempted a putsch in Munich, a miserable failure that seemed to doom his tiny party as Hitler himself went to prison. After his release, however, he slowly and systematically built up his political strength, depending on his effective mob oratory and on a simplistic analysis of causes and remedies for Germany's troubles, an analysis that became suddenly more persuasive after 1929. In 1930, the Nazis got more than 6 million votes and 107 seats in the Reichstag; in July, 1932, with 230 seats, they became the largest party in the legislature. The successive elections were part of a series of complicated parliamentary maneuvers aimed at keeping Hitler out of power. But the Social Democrats, the party that had given the strongest support to Weimar but which had precipitated the political crisis by withdrawing from the "Great Coalition" in 1930, were unimaginatively led and offered no visible alternative. The Papen government, in office from July to December, 1932, attempted to conciliate and use the Nazis only to be denied Hitler's cooperation; the next chancellor, General Kurt von

Schleicher, considered strong measures to break the Nazi movement but could not carry with him the aged president, Field Marshal von Hindenburg. Although—and perhaps because—the Nazis' representation in the Reichstag had dropped in the November elections to 196, Hindenburg installed Hitler as chancellor on January 30, 1933. Hitler asked for and got new elections that, under systematic terrorization, gave him (with some minor allies) a bare majority; he used it to suspend the constitution, and for the remainder of the Nazi era, the country was ruled by decree. All parties but the Nazi party and all trade unions were eliminated, censorship and propaganda were used intensively to mobilize opinion, and violence continued (visited even upon the Nazis themselves in the purge of 1934), compounded by the outright rejection of most of the rational, civilized, and intellectual values of which nineteenth-century Germany had in many ways been so remarkable an exemplar: in their place were put mystical evocations of a barbaric German past and idealization of the intuitional leader. The drive for "racial purity" was taken up in earnest in decrees of 1935 and 1938; and the S.S.—Hitler's elite corps within the army—and the Gestapo, the secret police, were used to bring the entire country under subjection. The Nazis' social program was at best piecemeal; the success the regime needed was to be found in adventure abroad.

Throughout the Weimar period, both government and army had connived at evasion of the limitations imposed on German militarism by the Treaty of Versailles. Shortly after coming into power, Hitler withdrew from the League and announced that he would undertake rearmament openly in defiance of the Versailles restrictions, for which no one in the West was willing or able to fight. Although it was four or five years before the German army was fully ready for war, Hitler was able to get his way in Europe by improvisation and bluff, certain that England and France would not fight.

In 1935, however, attention was distracted from Germany by Mussolini, who had managed until then to hold back his ambition to create a new Roman Empire dominating the Mediterranean. On the pretext of a border incident he launched from Eritrea and Italian Somaliland an invasion of Ethiopia. Although the Ethiopians had beaten the Italians at Aduwa in 1896—a stain Mussolini was eager to wipe out—they were no match for this new invasion. Nor was the League of Nations, which condemned the Italian action and launched its first and last venture with sanctions. The vital sanction on oil was withheld, however; Italy had declared that the oil sanction would mean war, and, again, the British and French were not prepared to take the risk. To be sure, a shift in public opinion in favor of collective security and even willingness to fight for the League had taken place in England; but France was crucially preoccupied with the German threat and troubled by grave domestic instability; her wily foreign minister Pierre Laval was dedicated to maintaining the "Stresa front," a flaccid agreement of 1934 by which the British and French hoped to secure Mussolini as a benevolent neutral, if not as an ally, in their posture toward Hitler. An agreement, secretly made in 1935 between Laval and the British foreign minister Sir Samuel Hoare, called for the handing over of much Ethiopian territory to appease Mussolini; when the news of the agreement leaked out, whatever good intentions the League had were undercut, and it was only a matter of time until Ethiopia was reduced to colonial status.

In 1936 a civil war broke out in Spain between the defenders of the recently established republic, supported by left-wing sentiment around the world and to some extent materially by Russia, and the nationalist forces under General Francisco Franco, supported by both Italy and Germany. For three years the war ground on, with terrible cruelties on both sides, again presenting an issue of conscience to the world. Although the Spanish Civil War had no central importance in the diplomatic history of Europe, it was of the first moral and psychological importance and convinced a number of pacifists on the left that some causes might be worth fighting for, thus helping to build the acceptability of war against Hitler.

In 1936 Hitler made perhaps his boldest gamble, against the advice of his generals, when he occupied the demilitarized Rhineland; there were protests but nothing more, even from the French, caught up at the time by domestic politics. Early in 1938 he seized Austria, after having systematically paralyzed the Austrian government through the activities of indigenous Nazis and by extraordinary personal abuse of Kurt von Schuschnigg, the Austrian chancellor. The independence of Austria had been of some concern to Italy, but the "Axis" concluded in 1936 between the German and Italian dictators proved strong enough and the task of watching over Austria tiresome enough to allow Mussolini to give Hitler free rein, and to put an end to any English and French hopes for Italy. There was little enough objection elsewhere: the Austrian regime had not been popular, and the Anschluss seemed yet another affirmation of nationality.

Hitler's next gamble was made by invoking the same principle, this time in support of the Sudeten Germans, who had been incorporated into Czechoslovakia at its creation. But beyond nationality, Hitler foresaw the elimination of Czechoslovakia, the most stable and liberal state in central and eastern Europe, by playing on the jealousies of her neighbors to the east and her discontented universities. Czechoslovakia's stability and liberalism had made her of particular interest to the Western powers, and her defense was guaranteed by the Russians, provided the French also would join. The principal response to this new threat, however, came from Neville Chamberlain, prime minister of England since 1937. A man of great administrative ability and of high though narrow rectitude, Chamberlain abhorred war and continued to believe that Hitler could be dealt with rationally and traditionally by agreement. In this case Czech concessions were to be the price of a general revision of the settlement of 1919. After his first visit to Hitler in September, 1938, Chamberlain persuaded the Czechs to give up the Sudeten frontier, territory that included besides the militant and discontented Germans the bulk of the country's defensive fortifications. When Chamberlain returned a week later with the Czech concessions, he was astonished to find that they were no longer acceptable, that Hitler had speeded up his timetable and had escalated his demands to include other Czech territories where there were Germans and the satisfaction of other minority claims as well. Chamberlain returned to London in a temper, and after the new terms were rejected by the Czechs, the British began moves toward mobilization. But Chamberlain made one more effort, at a four-power agreement between Italy, Germany, France, and Britain. Concluded in Munich on September 29, the agreement conceded the harshest of Hitler's terms, and the Czechs were given no choice but to accept or be abandoned. Chamberlain returned to London with what he most prized, an agreement that Britain and Germany would settle all their problems by consultation and never go to war again: it meant, he said on his return, "peace in our time."

Early in 1939 Germany eliminated what was left of Czechoslovakia; the Western powers were relieved of their military commitment by the apparent internal collapse of their ally. But, despite some diplomats who kept seeking terms for the final appeasement, most British subjects and statesmen, including even Chamberlain, had come to realize that Hitler was not to be trusted; Britain therefore scattered guarantees across eastern Europe. It was to one of those nations that Hitler next turned his attention: pressure on Poland not only aimed at redressing the German grievance about the eastern frontiers but gave expression to Hitler's bitter racial hatred against Slavs. Dramatically, Germany's design on her eastern neighbor turned into a new partition of Poland. Negotiations had been going on in a desultory and perhaps not wholly serious way between Russia and the Western powers; now aware of Russian military weakness, fearful of the German eastward movement and perhaps with aggressive designs of his own, Stalin entered on a nonaggression treaty with Hitler, signed on August 23, to the astonishment and confusion of Western ideologues who had believed fervently either that Hitler's Germany was a bastion of anti-communism or that Russia could have no truck with evil. But the two powers gained from the pact a temporary security for their own designs, and two days later Hitler ordered the attack on Poland, which began on September 1. After a last offer of negotiation, the British sent an ultimatum

to Germany on September 3; there was no response and by late afternoon
Britain and France were at war with Germany.

For Further Reading

Brogan, D. W., *France under the Republic (1870–1939)*.
Bullock, Alan, *Hitler: A Study in Tyranny*.
Holborn, Hajo, *The Political Collapse of Europe*.
Kirkpatrick, Ivone, *Mussolini: A Study in Power*.
Mowat, C. L., *Britain Between the Wars, 1918–1940*.
Seton-Watson, Christopher, *Italy from Liberalism to Fascism, 1870–1925*.
Thomson, David, *Democracy in France since 1870*.
Thorne, Christopher, *The Approach of War, 1938–1939*.

27   World War II

The First World War had ended on a note of high expectations, but disillusionment was not long in coming. The Peace of Versailles left all dissatisfied, although there is little warrant for attributing to it all the subsequent
ills of the world. The hopes centering on the League of Nations proved
illusory. The nineteenth-century liberal wave of which it was, in a sense,
the culmination soon began to recede. The United States endeavored to
pretend that it was not part of the world; victorious France, beset by fear
and weakness, and seeking to organize Europe for her safety, pursued an
incoherent policy, allowing the Nazi revival in Germany; Britain made
appalling misjudgments and became the chief advocate of appeasement.
European leadership, in the second half of the thirties, passed from the
hands of the victors to the vengeful Germans. Thus, after twenty years of
truce, came a renewal of hostilities, a recurrence of the key issue that the
earlier conflict had failed to resolve: Germany's bid for world power.

In keeping with their disregard for the niceties of legal procedure,
German forces invaded Poland on September 1, 1939. The Western
powers, Britain and France, honoring their obligation to Poland, after a
brief hesitation, formally declared war on Germany two days later. As in
1914, Germany enjoyed the advantage of better preparation while the
Western allies possessed greater potential. Speed was Germany's need, time
the allies' asset. As in the First World War, the German military perfor-

A.D.   1939   Nazi-Soviet Pact; Germany invades Poland; Britain and France declare war on Germany; partition of Poland between Germany and Russia

1939–1940   The "phony war"; first Russo-Finnish War

1940   Denmark and Norway overrun by Germany; Germany launches attack in the west; Churchill succeeds Chamberlain as prime minister; Battle and collapse of France; Dunkirk evacuation; French armistice; Vichy regime; De Gaulle launches Free French movement; Italy enters the war; Battle of Britain; destroyer-bases deal between U.S. and Britain; FDR reelected for third term

1941   Central and eastern European rearrangements; Lend-Lease legislation; Yugoslavia and Greece overrun; Hitler attacks Russia; Atlantic Charter; Japanese attack on Pearl Harbor

1941–1942   Germans reach Caucasus; Japanese spread over Southeast Asia, Indonesia, and the Pacific

1942   Battle of the Coral Sea; Battle of Stalingrad; El Alamein; all France occupied; North African landings

1943   Russia withdraws recognition from Polish government in exile; French Committee of National Liberation in Algiers; invasion of Sicily; Italian armistice; collapse of Fascist regime, meeting of Allied foreign ministers in Moscow; Teheran Conference of the Big Three; Cairo declaration re China

1944   Normandy landings; FCNL becomes provisional French government; Rome entered; Warsaw rising; liberation of Paris; Battle of the Bulge

1945   Yalta Conference of the Big Three; death of FDR; Harry S. Truman President; Germany surrenders; Hitler commits suicide; Potsdam Conference; first atomic bomb dropped, on Hiroshima; Japan surrenders

mance was impressive, but prompt victory eluded her and in the end she succumbed to the weight of incomparably greater resources.

Germany easily crushed Poland in three weeks, the mechanized Blitzkrieg demonstrating German military capabilities. In accordance with the secret terms of the Nazi-Soviet Pact, Russian forces moved in from the east, and the fourth partition of Poland took place, with a thoroughly dependent state, the *gouvernement général,* being set up in the section occupied but not annexed by Germany.

Then ensued a curious six-month pause, the "phony war." In keeping with the Maginot Line mentality, the French, instead of launching an offensive, waited passively behind that supposedly impregnable barrier. And the Germans did not attack. The war of words continued, during which attempts of neutral powers—the Low Countries, the Vatican— failed to move the belligerents. There had been little enthusiasm for war in Germany at first, but understandable elation at the easy victory in Poland; Hitler's intuition was proved right again and his prestige stood high. Conversely, the allies, especially the French, were still suffering from the prewar confusion of their irresolute policies and divided opinions.

The Soviet Union, coolly pressing its advantage, extended its influence through nonaggression pacts and the acquisition of naval bases in the three small Baltic countries. Then, in November, Russia attacked the recalcitrant Finns; this furnished the grounds for the expulsion of the Soviet Union from the League of Nations in December. Russia's performance was inglorious, but in March, 1940, Finland was forced to yield.

Since no accommodation could be found on the basis of the *fait accompli* Germany moved to further initiatives. In April, 1940, Denmark was overrun in the course of one day, and a skillfully managed operation swiftly gave the Germans control of Norway. There was little the Norwegians could do, though they fought hard, and the attempted allied assistance had to be abandoned by June.

The real war could now begin. Adopting a modified version of the 1914 plan designed to bypass French border fortifications, the Germans attacked both Holland and Belgium in May, to the accompaniment of the bombing of neutral, undefended Rotterdam, a demonstration of Nazi frightfulness. The German tactics were a demonstration of the validity of the prescient analysis of the future war which had been offered by a young French officer, Charles De Gaulle, a prophet without honor in his country. The major part of Holland was quickly overrun, but the breach of the Belgian fortifications, and most of all the breakthrough at Sedan, was a more serious matter. The massive use of tanks and air power brought the Germans to the Channel coast, trapping a portion of the French army and the relatively small, but well-armed and efficient British Expeditionary Force that had moved into Belgium.

These troops, along with the Belgian army, were caught in a narrowing ring of steel and fire, and driven to the sea. The Belgians withdrew from the struggle; then came the evacuation of allied forces from the Dunkirk beaches. A large proportion of the men reached England, but the British land force had been destroyed as an instrument of war.

Having regrouped their forces, the Germans and the French faced each other along the Somme at the beginning of June. The fate of battle was not long in doubt; the campaign of France turned into a complete rout. The Germans entered Paris on June 13. France was reduced to a state of chaotic confusion, much of the population seeking the elusive safety of disorderly flight southward. The German booty in prisoners of war and matériel was enormous. France had collapsed.

The French army had been the chief allied instrument of war; it now lay irretrievably broken. A major decision faced the French government: what hopes were there, behind the shield of the British navy, that adequate power might be rebuilt? Might not Britain seek accommodation with Hitler, possibly even at France's expense? French counsels were divided, but following the resignation of Premier Paul Reynaud, who favored continued resistance, and the advent of Marshal Henri Pétain in his place, the defeatist view prevailed. The aged hero of Verdun considered the war lost; he would not abandon the country but would use his prestige to shield his people and secure terms from the Germans. Hostilities ceased with the conclusion of an armistice on June 22, a ceremony that reenacted in locale and details the 1918 armistice, the ignominy of which it was symbolically meant to erase.

Italy had remained neutral at the outset of the war despite her pact with Germany, offering her unpreparedness as a pretext. Many efforts were made—by the allies, the United States, and the pope—to keep her neutral, but the unfolding of events in France convinced Mussolini that he must be present at the kill, if for no other reason than to be in a better position to assert his future claims. On June 10 he declared war on both Britain and France. Italy played an insignificant military role, and her poor performance in Greece, which she had attacked the preceding October, was calculated to confirm the view of those who held Italian military competence in low esteem.

Not all Frenchmen surrendered. Charles De Gaulle, now a two-star general and holding a minor ministerial post in Reynaud's cabinet, escaped to England at the last moment. On June 18, proclaiming that a battle had been lost but not the war, he called upon all Frenchmen to join him in continued resistance. This was the birth of the Free French movement. He found little response at first, for the French people, thoroughly demoralized, thought the war lost. At this point they put their trust in Pétain.

The terms of the French armistice were harsh, yet they could have been

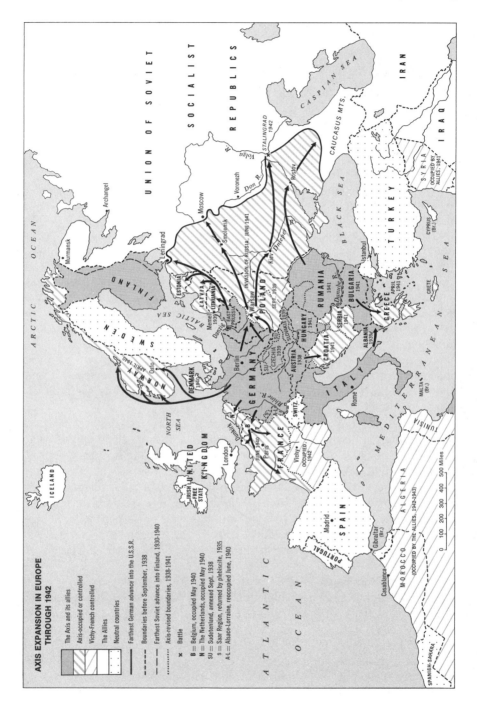

AXIS EXPANSION IN EUROPE
THROUGH 1942

The Axis and its allies
Axis-occupied or controlled
Vichy-French controlled
The Allies
Neutral countries

Farthest German advance into the U.S.S.R.
Boundaries before September, 1938
Farthest Soviet advance into Finland, 1930-1940
Axis-revised boundaries, 1938-1941

x = Battle

B = Belgium, occupied May 1940
N = The Netherlands, occupied May 1940
SU = Sudetenland, annexed Sept. 1938
S = Saar Region, returned by plebiscite, 1935
A-L = Alsace-Lorraine, reoccupied June, 1940

harsher. Hitler restrained himself because, defeated though she undoubtedly was, France still held important assets: her fleet and her overseas empire. To press her unduly might have thrown these assets into British hands. Conversely, Britain was deeply concerned lest these fall to the Germans; she too would not press France too hard. For a time the fleet and the empire were merely neutralized.

Though she would not make formal peace with the Germans, France was in effect out of the war. Her influence on its course could only be minimal. What little remained of the French army overwhelmingly gave its allegiance to the Vichy regime. Only some fragments of the empire in equatorial Africa and some scattered island possessions rallied to the Free French movement. Although that movement received some form of recognition from the British, on whom it was totally dependent, Vichy was undoubtedly the legal government of France. De Gaulle's initial gesture, quixotic as it may have seemed at the time, was important nevertheless, for in it lay the seed of the future reconstruction of France.

But in June, 1940, there was no question that Britain stood alone against the Nazis. The emergency brought out the staunchest qualities of the British people. The vacillating policy of the Chamberlain administration had come to an end at the time of the Norwegian invasion; in May, 1940, Winston Churchill, long an isolated and unheeded voice, succeeded Chamberlain as prime minister. Churchill infused his unquenchable energy and resolution into the prosecution of the war; for the moment he could offer little more than words, but these, magnificently eloquent, were an effective tool; the channel moat, for the last time perhaps, still made it possible for England to prepare her defenses.

In the summer of 1940 there was an epic battle in the British skies as the German Luftwaffe sought to crush the people's will to resist. It was a close call, but the combination of faulty German strategy and British technical skill turned the tide in September. This "Battle of Britain" had the same effect as the Battle of the Marne in 1914; Germany was not defeated, but compelled to engage in a struggle of indefinite duration and doubtful outcome.

The British accomplishment could not, however, prevent the organization of Europe by the Nazis and their allies. Spain's dictator, Franco, skillfully resisted Hitler's blandishments and adhered to his neutral status, but in effect collaborated with Germany. Vichy France's collaboration was not very satisfactory from the German point of view, but French resources could be and were commandeered. In September, 1940, Italy launched an offensive from Libya into Egypt, but it was checked and turned back, bringing German forces under the brilliant General Erwin Rommel into the North African theater.

Greece and her Balkan neighbors were the hinge where the southern and eastern theaters joined. In view of unchallenged German power on the continent outside of Russia, these small states of central and southeastern Europe endeavored to accommodate themselves to German demands as best they could. Hungary and Bulgaria, both of whom had territorial grievances stemming from the First World War, won benefits by cooperating with Hitler; conversely, Rumania suffered, losing some territory to Hungary and to the Soviet Union.

In Bulgaria German and Russian influences were in competition. Refusing a Russian guarantee, Bulgaria adhered to the Rome-Berlin-Tokyo combination in March, 1941, and allowed German forces into the country. Nazi negotiations with Yugoslavia seemed to be leading to a similar result until an unexpected coup ousted the regent. The Yugoslavs then opted for resistance to the Axis demands. Another demonstration of German efficiency and frightfulness (the bombing of Belgrade) was followed by an all-out invasion. Having disposed of Yugoslavia, the Germans went on to overrun Greece, incidentally rescuing the incompetent Italian operation in that country. The governments of both Yugoslavia and Greece went into exile, a fact pregnant with consequence, for at the end of the war they would appear as allies of the victors, in contrast with Hungary, Bulgaria, and Rumania.*

From mainland Greece the Germans went on to capture Crete, giving another impressive demonstration of the possibilities of air power. The British, who had diverted some forces from North Africa to the assistance of Greece, proved incapable of preventing this German success, and their depleted North African forces were also evicted from Libya. Pushing into the Middle East, the Germans gave assistance to an anti-British coup in Iraq, partly with the connivance of the Vichy regime. British troops rescued the situation, and one of the incidental consequences of the abortive coup was the virtual ouster of French influence from France's Middle Eastern mandates.

The continent, apart from Russia and some neutrals, was now under effective German control. Russia had lived up to the terms of the Nazi-Soviet Pact and even used her influence among continental Communists on Germany's behalf, but distrust persisted between the two partners. Hitler decided to dispose of the potential threat to his rear; on June 22, 1941, his forces crossed the Soviet border.

Surprisingly, and despite various warnings, the Russians' preparations were inadequate, and initially the Nazi war machine repeated its earlier successes. By the close of 1941 Moscow and Leningrad were under siege

---

* Rumania eventually threw in her lot with the Axis.

and the Germans had reached the Crimea. But Russia is a huge country, and her two classic assets, Generals Winter and Space, again saved the day. Despite frightful losses, the Russians managed to hold out. The stupid application of Nazi racial policy to Slavs turned what might have been a war of liberation from Communist tyranny into a struggle for national existence for the Russian people. They fought desperately and stopped the Nazi advance.

The third member of the Rome-Berlin-Tokyo triangle, Japan, had followed European events closely, taking advantage of the war to promote the organization of what was euphemistically called the "Greater East Asia Co-Prosperity Sphere." Pursuing her undeclared war with China, Japan also moved into Indochina after the French collapse. Britain and Holland were not in a position to resist a further Japanese advance southward, and Russia was neutralized by the signing of a nonaggression pact in April, 1941.

One country alone was in a position to offer possible resistance, the United States, which had clearly registered its hostility to Japanese aggression. But the United States was still laboring under the illusions born of the First World War; its first concern was to avoid involvement in the second. Indeed, the outbreak of war in 1939 had confirmed America's tendency toward isolation, though American sympathies were undoubtedly with the allied cause. The collapse of France was a shock, but the presidential election of 1940 was reminiscent of that of 1916, which Wilson had won behind the slogan, "He kept us out of war." President Roosevelt, while pursuing a somewhat ambiguous policy of assisting the allies within the bonds of the American neutrality legislation, was reelected for an unprecedented third term while promising not to involve American boys in a "foreign" war.

Britain was hard pressed at sea. German submarines were taking a heavy toll of her shipping, while her naval establishment had been relatively neglected. Roosevelt's destroyers-for-bases deal in September, 1940, transferred to Britain fifty overage American destroyers in exchange for 99-year leases on British bases in the western Atlantic that would be useful in the defense of the American continent, hence presumably enhancing its isolation. The extension of the zone of forbidden hostilities to 300 miles from the American shores and the Atlantic Charter in August, 1941, pointed in the same direction. Meanwhile the imaginative Lend-Lease Act had become law: the President was given wide discretion in assisting any country, even the Soviet Union, whose defense was deemed vital to the United States. American neutrality was stretching thin; it consisted of "all assistance short of war."

Yet the domestic debate went on in the United States, and it was

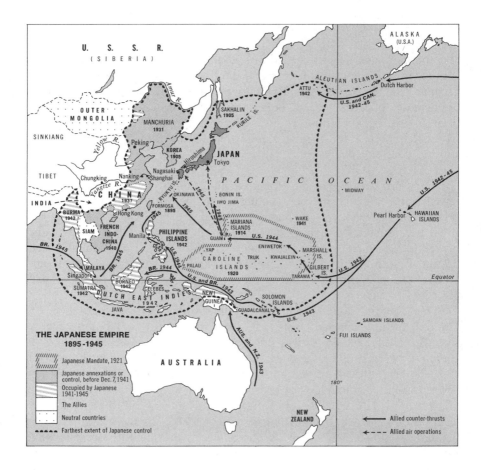

THE JAPANESE EMPIRE
1895-1945

- Japanese Mandate, 1921
- Japanese annexations or control, before Dec. 7, 1941
- Occupied by Japanese 1941-1945
- The Allies
- Neutral countries
- Farthest extent of Japanese control
- ← Allied counter-thrusts
- ←--- Allied air operations

resolved only by Japan. Taking a leaf from an earlier performance—the sneak attack on Russian Port Arthur in February, 1904—on December 7, 1941, Japanese aircraft struck the naval base of Pearl Harbor with telling results. The American reaction was an immediate declaration of war on Japan. This was followed by declarations of war by Germany and Italy against the United States, catapulting the country into the midst of the global conflict.

Americans never had doubts about the final result, and the war never came to America in the way that it did to much of the rest of the world. Behind the shelter of two oceans the American economy set about mobilizing its resources. Ultimately, these resources were the decisive factor in the outcome of the war, but in December, 1941, they were still largely potential. It took time to translate them into effective instruments of war.

As a consequence, the year 1942 marked the nadir of allied fortunes. The Germans reached the Caucasus while the Japanese overran much of the western Pacific and reached the gates of India. Axis forces in Africa were not far from Alexandria, and the prospects of a truly global strategy seemed open: a pincer movement from the Nile and the Caucasus that would engulf the Near East, and then turn toward India and effect a junction with the Japanese.

Since the British and the Russians were in desperate straits, the correct American decision was to give priority to the European and Mediterranean theaters, confining itself to a holding operation in the Pacific. Within a year of Pearl Harbor, sufficient resources had been accumulated to enable the allies to assume the offensive. Three almost simultaneous events turned the tide. The successful Russian stand at Stalingrad destroyed a whole German army and compelled a German retreat that would not stop until Berlin was reached. An Anglo-American force landed in Morocco and Algeria.* And a British offensive from Egypt was launched at El Alamein. Both African operations were successful; pushed from the west and the east, Rommel's Afrika Korps was finally smashed in Tunisia in May, 1943.

The writing on the wall was now clear, but German leadership lacked the element of rationality which had enabled Ludendorff to call a halt in 1918 when he became convinced that victory was no longer possible. Furthermore, the allies had adopted a policy of unconditional surrender: the war must go on until *Festung Europa* was completely reduced.

To achieve this result took another two years. In July, 1943, the allies overran Sicily; the collapse of Mussolini's Fascist regime followed. Seeking to escape further punishment, Italy sued for an armistice. However, announcement of the armistice led to the German occupation of most of the country, and the allies were compelled to inch their way at heavy cost over the length of the peninsula during the next two years. They reached Rome on June 4, 1944. Two days later the allied landings on the Normandy beaches began the reconquest of France. By the end of the year the fronts, both east and west, were nearing Germany. Nevertheless Hitler preferred Götterdämmerung to surrender. The Battle of the Bulge in the Ardennes Forest of Belgium in December stayed the allied advance only momentarily. Germany was overrun, Hitler committed suicide in his Berlin bunker, and on May 7, 1945, at Reims in France, the European phase of the war ended.

At the same time, the Japanese had been retreating in the Pacific. The air-sea battles of the Coral Sea and Midway in the middle of 1942 were the turning point. During the next two years the Japanese were gradually evicted from their island conquests, and by 1945 they were retreating in

* The North African landings resulted in a complete German occupation of France, though the French fleet was scuttled in Toulon harbor to keep it from the Germans.

Southeast Asia as well. The allies invaded the Philippines in October, 1944, the naval battle of Leyte Gulf marking the final crushing of the Japanese navy and air force.

The allies pushed relentlessly toward the Japanese home islands. The end came abruptly as a consequence of a revolutionary technical development: the atomic bomb. The first of these lethal weapons, exploded over Hiroshima on August 6, resulted in some 100,000 casualties. The second, dropped three days later on Nagasaki, induced the Japanese to surrender. The end came on September 2, 1945.

The war had resulted in the destruction of the power of all three members of the Rome-Berlin-Tokyo triangle; their future lay in allied hands, as did that of much of the rest of the world. The damage wrought during the long conflict was far greater than that of the First World War. Reconstruction at the most elemental level—the prevention of starvation, the repatriation of prisoners—was the most pressing concern, but important as it was it was overshadowed by the long-term problem of political and economic reconstruction. The impact of the Nazis' dreadful racial fantasies further exacerbated the situation. Some 6 million Jews and countless other innocents had been exterminated. The horrors of the concentration camps and gas chambers left memories that it would take a long time to erase. These profoundly affected the climate of the postwar world.

In 1919 many had looked upon the war as an interruption of the normality of peace, and thought it possible to return to the good old days of before 1914. No one in 1945 clamored for a return to the conditions of 1939. The Second World War was in many respects a continuation of the first, and it liquidated much of that war's incomplete business, but it left in its train another legacy of problems. Nevertheless, whatever the new world would be like, it was expected to be new.

The Nazi conquest had destroyed the structure of Europe. In certain cases, with Belgium and Holland, Denmark and Norway for example, whether their governments had gone into exile or stayed at home, there was little difficulty in restoration. The French situation, however, was different. The Vichy government of Marshal Pétain, hedging between collaboration and caution, had sought to create new institutions for France. But after recovery from the initial shock of defeat, under the stress of Nazi exactions, and especially after November, 1942, and as the tide of war turned, opposition to Vichy and to the Nazis began to increase. General De Gaulle's initial appeal had met with little response, and the allies showed considerable hesitancy in cooperating with his Free French. But after the North African landings nearly the whole of the French empire supported De Gaulle. A provisional government was organized in Algiers with De

Gaulle eventually in control. By 1944 the allies had little choice but to grant him recognition, although, especially in American quarters, it was grudgingly given. France thus managed to achieve representation among the victors in both the German and the Japanese armistices.

In France the Resistance had grown strong during the occupation. The Communists had played a large and honorable part in this movement—Russia after all was an ally. They commanded about one-quarter of the popular vote in French elections. Might the time be ripe for revolution? Whatever the answer, the war had laid the ground for appreciable changes in the social, no less than in the political, structure of France.

The Italian case presents some similarities with the French. There had been little enthusiasm for the war among the Italian people, one reason for the country's poor military performance. No sooner had the allies landed in Sicily than Fascism collapsed. The king dismissed Mussolini, who was imprisoned, and appointed Marshal Badoglio in his place in July, 1943. But Italy could not escape from the war so early. While she sought to enlist herself in the allied camp most of the country remained in German hands. Moreover, the Germans rescued Mussolini and set him up in the north as head of a puppet regime. It was a sad and sordid episode; Italy was beset by near civil war in addition to being a battle ground in the main struggle. The Italian Resistance, much of it, as in France, Communist, was both anti-German and anti-Fascist. As in France, the Communists commanded between a quarter and a third of the popular vote.

Both France and Italy, however, had been liberated by nations that eyed the rise of Communist influence in Europe with suspicion. In eastern Europe, where the liberating armies had been Russian, the situation was quite different. The Russians adopted a relatively simple stance, insisting that the liberated countries have governments friendly to them. This would have been reasonable, had not "friendly" and "subservient" been synonymous in their lexicon. The ironic truth was that authentic Communist sentiments were much stronger in France and Italy than in eastern Europe.

This led to all manner of complications, not least in the relations between the Russians and the Western powers. Differences between the Americans and the British pale into insignificance by comparison. Fighting a common enemy was a powerful binder of the alliance, but ideological differences between the Soviet Union and the West had only momentarily been put aside by the necessities of the war. Reciprocal distrust remained deep; Russian memories of Franco-British performance at Munich and Western memories of the Nazi-Soviet Pact could not be easily eradicated.

Once the danger of defeat was over and the prospects of victory began to brighten, increased emphasis on the political aspects of the war and on the implications of military decision was inevitable. In this respect Churchill and Stalin had a better understanding of the facts of power than President Roosevelt. That is why, for example, the British favored invading the Balkans; realizing that possession is nine points of the law, they hoped to occupy that area before Russia. But they were unable to convince the Americans, and the Red army controlled the region when the fighting stopped.

The effort to maintain the unity of the alliance found expression in several wartime meetings of the Big Three, Roosevelt, Churchill, and Stalin. The central and east European region was the sharpest focus of difference. As for Poland, there was little prospect that the Russians would relinquish the fruits of the Nazi-Soviet Pact; yet they agreed that there must be a separate Poland after the war. This raised the question of boundaries and the nature of the new Polish government. The Polish government in exile had been recognized during the war as the legitimate spokesman of the Polish people, but the Russians withdrew that recognition in April, 1943, granting it instead to a Polish Committee of National Liberation, essentially a Communist puppet. When the Poles rose against the Nazis in Warsaw in June, 1944, the failure of Russian assistance resulted in their being crushed, and as the Russians finally advanced through Poland the prospects of any authentically independent Polish regime became very dim.

Yugoslavia was another case in point. Exploiting internal tensions, most of all between Serbs and Croats, the Axis had broken up the country into its component elements. There arose in Yugoslavia two rival resistance movements: the Chetniks, adherents of the government in exile; and a Communist group led by Josip Broz (Tito). Thus, in addition to troubles with native collaborators, mainly Croatians, Yugoslavia faced virtual civil war. As time passed, the effectiveness of the Communists increased until they gained recognition from all the allies. When the country was liberated, it also asserted territorial claims against Italy. In 1945 there was a sharp confrontation in Istria and Julian Venetia between the western forces and the native Yugoslavian, largely backed by the Russians, until an uneasy truce was achieved and a temporary line of demarcation agreed upon between the two.

Czechoslovakia was by common consent restored in her pre-Munich borders, but although President Eduard Beneš, leader of the government in exile, persistently strove to maintain good relations with all the allies and accepted Russia's "amputation" of the extreme Ruthenian segment of his country, the effectiveness of Russian control over the whole of Czechoslovakia was not weakened. Hungary and Rumania had both waged war against Russia, and Finland had reentered the war on the German side. These nations were treated as defeated enemies. Bulgaria had been at war only with the Western allies. In order to exert her influence in her affairs, Russia now declared war on her. Greece, on the other hand, another point of conflict among the victors and, torn by virtual civil war, was liberated and occupied by Western forces. All these difficulties, of course, dwindled into insignificance compared to the problem of what to do with Germany.

These political issues, inseparable from the course of military operations, were discussed by the Big Three at Teheran in November, 1943,* and at Yalta in February, 1945. The latter meeting, held when the end of the war was in sight, was of crucial importance. While Japan and a future world organization were on the agenda, Germany was the chief subject under consideration, and its dismemberment was accepted in principle. The British insisted that France be given an equal voice in the discussion of German affairs, but France was not represented at Yalta—this had unfortunate consequences. No agreement could be reached on the troublesome Polish question; the promise to assist in the establishment of a democratic government there was in effect an evasion.

President Roosevelt was a very sick man at Yalta. Two months after his return, on April 12, 1945, he died. In the same month, following careful preparations, there met in San Francisco the conference from which the United Nations was born. In order to avoid a repetition of the awkwardness of 1919—the disowning of its child by the United States—the future world organization was deliberately divorced from the treaties of peace. The charter which emerged after two months of sometimes difficult discussions was little different in its essentials from the Covenant of the League: in deference to the facts of power, yet also glossing over some enormous differences, five permanent members of the Security Council —the United States, the Soviet Union, the United Kingdom, France, and China—were endowed with the power of veto.

On July 17, following the termination of hostilities in Europe, the Big Three met again in Potsdam, outside Berlin. Recriminations over Russian high-handedness in the east—the brutal assertion of power in Bucharest for example—countered by Russian ones on the score of Greece, led to no change in anyone's behavior or position. Germany was to remain under occupation, divided into several zones, deprived of a central government, disarmed, demilitarized, and de-Nazified. Berlin, within the Russian zone, was to be under quadripartite administration. By putting territory east of the Oder-Neisse line under Polish administration, the powers placed a heavy mortgage on the future. The division of East Prussia between Poland and Russia had the same effect. It was also decided that peace treaties would be drafted first with the other enemy powers, and a Council of Foreign Ministers was entrusted with the task. Undoing Hitler's notorious An-

---

* Immediately after this meeting came the meeting in Cairo between Roosevelt, Churchill and Chang Kai-shek; the conferees agreed that Japan must be reduced to her pre-1894 position, and Formosa was wrested from her.

schluss, the allies decided to deal with Austria as a separate entity. Like Germany she was divided into zones of occupation with Vienna under joint occupation and administration.

Much of Germany was rubble; its people were stunned, the general chaos compounded by the influx of Germans expelled from other parts of Europe. (Thus the German people were united, though hardly in the manner Hitler had intended.) But the pressing problems of economic reconstruction did not affect Germany alone. In many countries production had fallen to a fraction of the prewar level; indeed, the very structure of European society had been shaken, a fact which helped the Russians to capitalize on the situation. Great Britain, though bled white by the war, remained stable. There was no Communist threat in England, but the election that took place in July, 1945, resulted in victory of the reformist-socialist Labour party. Churchill, the architect of victory, was compelled to yield his place at Potsdam to Clement Attlee. Thus, as the postwar era began, the future of Europe remained unsettled; no one could say whether a true peace had been achieved or only, as in 1919, a truce.

Perhaps even more foreboding and uncertain was the situation created by the dropping of the atom bombs on Japan. No more striking manifestation of war as an instrument of change could be cited than this event. New weapons have been a familiar experience in the story of mankind, but what happened at Hiroshima sent a shudder of apprehension throughout the world. Primitive as it was, the first atom bomb raised the possibility of total destruction. How politics would deal with this problem was a question; the new development pointed with unusual sharpness to the urgency of an issue that has been in the making since the launching of modern science and technology. Could modern society, beset by the problem of its proliferating numbers, depending on highly complex economic relationships, and possessed of such lethal weapons, preserve freedom and individualism, even the human race itself? In this question lay perhaps the supreme irony of the struggle against the totalitarian regimes. Unlocking of the power of the atom raised the possibility of an age of unprecedented ease for mankind, but it plainly required the revision of certain modes of thought, and the adjusting of power relationships. This was the great issue that confronted the world at the end of World War II.

For Further Reading

Falls, C., *The Second World War: A Short History.*
Liddell Hart, B. H., *The Other Side of the Hill.*
Ryan, C., *The Longest Day.*
Trevor-Roper, H. R., *The Last Days of Hitler.*

The Brooding Present

28 Europe Since World War II

In 1940, after the collapse of France, Marshal Jan Smuts of South Africa delivered himself of the judgment that "France is gone in our day and perhaps for many a day." In 1945 it might seem that "Europe" could be substituted for "France" in that verdict, allowing for the exception of two peripheral entities, Britain and Russia. The Continental countries lay prostrate and powerless.

The first need was to restore social services and political order; the second was to draft formal treaties of peace. The Council of Foreign Ministers of the great powers set about this second task, and by 1947 treaties were made with Italy, Hungary, Bulgaria, Rumania, and Finland, though not with Germany and Austria. With two exceptions, the new map of Europe was not very different from that of 1937: the Soviet Union recovered much of Russia's loss from the First World War, and Poland was bodily shifted westward. The rest were minor changes. Broadly speaking, the application of self-determination remained the guiding principle, as it had been after the First World War.

The nature of domestic regimes was a different matter. In France Vichy disappeared and a new constitution established the Fourth Republic, largely a replica of the Third. In 1946 Italy became a republic. In both countries the structure of politics reflected a return to parliamentary democracy under a multiparty system, though the Communists greatly increased their strength. Catholic parties also grew in influence: in Italy the Catholics were strong enough to obtain a majority for some years. In France General De Gaulle "withdrew" in 1946 because he considered the new constitutional arrangements unsatisfactory; thereafter the country reverted to the pattern of ministerial instability so characteristic of the prewar period.

Both in France and in Italy the Communists were maneuvered out of

A.D.   1945   Surrender of Germany; San Francisco Conference;
                    The United Nations; Potsdam Conference; Labour
                    in office in Britain; surrender of Japan
             1946   Fourth French Republic; Italy becomes a republic;
                    Churchill's "iron curtain" speech in Fulton, Mis-
                    souri; De Gaulle "withdraws"
             1947   Communists out of government in France and in
                    Italy; Truman Doctrine; beginning of the Cold War;
                    India and Pakistan emerge to independence; UN
                    establishes State of Israel
             1948   Communist coup in Prague; Marshall Plan and
                    OEEC; Yugoslav-Soviet break
        1948–1949   The Berlin blockade
             1949   Signature of NATO Treaty; emergence of the West
                    German Federal Republic; the German Demo-
                    cratic Republic
             1950   The Korean War; Indonesian independence
             1952   Elizabeth II queen of the United Kingdom
             1953   Death of Stalin; Eisenhower President of the U.S.;
                    East Berlin rising; ECSC launched
             1954   Geneva conference and agreement re French Indo-
                    china; EDC proposal defeated in French parlia-
                    ment
             1955   Bandung meeting; Treaty of Peace with Austria;
                    Warsaw Pact; emergence of Nikita Khrushchev in
                    control

----

participation in the government in 1947. Yet in both, as in Britain and elsewhere, the nationalized sector of the economy was markedly expanded. Divided Germany offered initially a contrast between ruthless Russian exploitation in the east and in the west assistance given with a view to restoring the economy. The result was large-scale migration westward: western Germany had soon absorbed some 11 million refugees from Rus-sian-controlled areas.

In countries under Russian occupation matters were relatively simple. It did not take very long before dependable Communist regimes were established everywhere; Czechoslovakia, the last holdout, was brought into

1956   Twentieth Party Congress of U.S.S.R.; independence of Tunisia and Morocco; Hungarian rising crushed by Soviet intervention; Israeli attack on Egypt; Anglo-French intervention at Suez

1957   *Sputnik*

1958   Treaty of Rome launches the Common Market (EEC); De Gaulle called back to power; the Fifth French Republic; the Eisenhower Doctrine re the Middle East

1960   Abortive summit meeting in Paris; independence of the Belgian Congo; independence of French Black Africa; beginning of Sino-Soviet conflict

1962   Independence of Algeria; Cuban missile crisis

1963   France vetoes British application to Common Market

1964   Ouster of Khrushchev

1967   The Six-Day War between Israel and the Arab countries

1968   Student agitation and strikes in France; Warsaw pact countries occupy Czechoslovakia

1969   De Gaulle quits office; Pompidou president, American moon landing

1970–1971   Issue of Britain's adherence to the Common Market; Sino-American relations; problems of the American and world economies

---

line by a coup in February, 1948. There was one exception, and that a portentous one: in the summer of 1948, Marshal Tito, though still proclaiming himself a Communist, rejected Russian dictation. This first successful assertion of heresy within the Communist fold initiated a highly important line of future development.

Impotent Europe could not escape the impact of the Cold War, the larger contest between the two superpowers which had emerged from the hot war. The division became very sharp in 1947, with the proclamation of the Truman Doctrine—the American decision to take up the burden of assistance to Greece and Turkey that Britain felt unable to carry any longer—providing a convenient landmark of the change. Henceforth the United States would use its power to help those seeking to "contain" Communist expansion. The highly imaginative Marshall Plan for the economic rehabilitation of Europe which came into effect in 1948, apart from its very real humanitarian motivation, was a most successful instance of enlightened self-interest on the part of the United States; it did much to check Communism in the West.

It was a natural next step to reorganize military power in western Europe. The creation of the North Atlantic Treaty Organization (NATO) in 1949, an alliance of fifteen nations, subsequently extended to include both Greece and Turkey, accomplished this goal by announcing that they would consider an attack against any one of them an attack against all the NATO powers. But NATO raised some difficult questions to which the outbreak of the Korean War in 1950 gave added point. After the defeat of Japan, Korea had been divided into Communist and American zones. Following the successful Communist takeover of mainland China, an attack by the North Koreans against the south resulted in the intervention of the United Nations. But the United States carried by far the main burden of the war; in the Far East it was performing the same task of containing Communism as in the West. Thus it was all the more eager to organize Europe's military potential.

This brought the German question to the fore. The three sectors under western control were united into the Federal Republic of West Germany under the guidance of Konrad Adenauer, leader of the Christian Democratic party. A drastic currency reform in 1950 led to an outstanding economic recovery; one soon began to hear about *Wirtschaftswunder,* the German "economic miracle." But American interest in the rebuilding of military power in Europe led to the question of German rearmament, an alarming prospect to all who remembered the ruthlessness and brutality of Germany during the war. The so-called European Defense Community was long debated, and finally rejected by the French in 1954. However, subsequent negotiations led to Germany's rearmament and her participation in NATO.

The Communist world, allowing for the Yugoslav heresy, still presented a monolithic structure under the guidance of the Muscovite mother church. The death of Stalin in January, 1953, produced a contest for the succession finally resolved with the emergence of Nikita Khrushchev to a position of leadership. This raised new possibilities; Khrushchev's surprising attack on Stalin at the Twentieth Party Congress in 1956 induced hopes of change. Open opposition to Russian domination developed in some of the satellite countries. Poland managed to steer a middle course and thus staved off Russian intervention, but violence broke out in Hungary, where

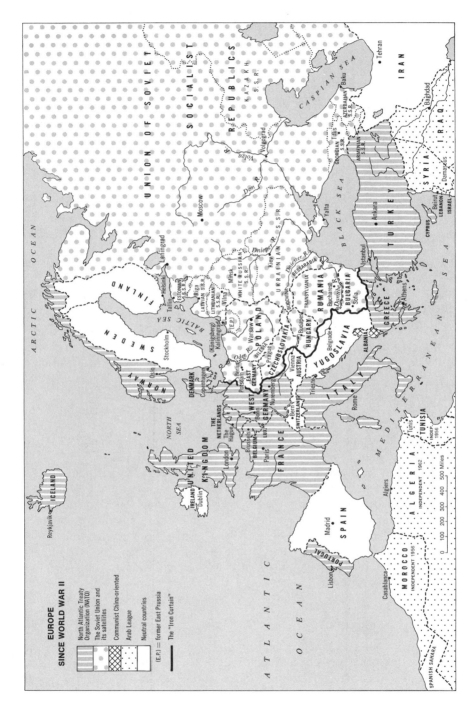

EUROPE
SINCE WORLD WAR II

North Atlantic Treaty
Organization (NATO)

The Soviet Union and
its satellites

Communist China-oriented

Arab League

Neutral countries

(E.P.) = former East Prussia

The "Iron Curtain"

a rebellion in Budapest was ruthlessly crushed by the Russian army in October, 1956. Neither the West nor the United Nations would help the frustrated Hungarians. Yet despite this assertion of Russian control it was clear that there were growing strains within the Communist structure.

But there were not merely strains; there were notable successes as well, especially in a field in which the United States had long claimed primacy—technology. In October, 1957, Russia launched *Sputnik,* the first earth satellite, a severe jolt to American pride, and a world-wide sensation. Despite this illustration of Soviet power, and even despite the failure of an attempted summit meeting in Paris in 1955, there seemed to be indications of a changing climate within the Soviet Union. Changes in leadership were no longer followed by executions. While the government continued its efforts to keep up with American armaments, which put a severe strain on the Russian economy, there were signs that the desire of the Russian people for a greater share of the goods of this earth might lead to a less bellicose Soviet stance in international affairs.

At the end of the war European nations still controlled much of the planet; the French empire, for example, had been a very useful asset to the allies. But the war intensified the desire for independence among colonial peoples, while the setbacks inflicted for a time by the Japanese also served to debase the prestige of white-skinned Westerners. Thus the war initiated a movement which in the course of two decades resulted in the virtual liquidation of all the European empires save the Russian.

By 1950 the Dutch, after some unsuccessful attempts at compromise, were evicted from their East Indian possessions, which emerged as an independent Republic of Indonesia. The British tried to adhere to an evolutionary policy for their huge empire. They relinquished India in 1947, but what the British had held together fell apart once independence was won: rivalries and bloody disputes resulted in the division of the vast subcontinent between India proper, largely Hindu, and Pakistan, predominantly Muslim. The British adopted a similar course of action elsewhere, notably in Africa. Most of the former British possessions retained membership in the Commonwealth, but British hopes of keeping the Commonwealth a unit of international importance proved an illusion.

The French attempt to reorganize their empire into a French Union was equally unsuccessful. France was evicted from the Levant and soon found herself mired in a desperate war in Indochina. In 1954, finally, under the leadership of Premier Mendès-France, the French disengaged themselves from Indochina, leaving the region as a problem, and later a dilemma, for other powers, particularly the United States. French protectorates over Tunisia and Morocco were abrogated in 1956, but Algeria

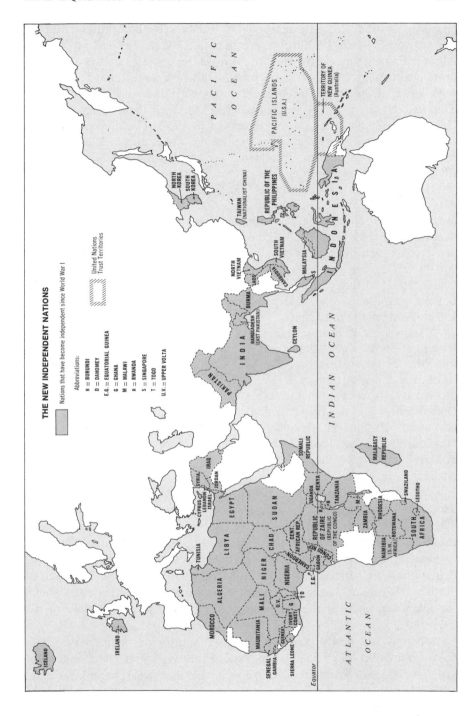

THE NEW INDEPENDENT NATIONS

Nations that have become independent since World War I

United Nations
Trust Territories

Abbreviations:

B = BURUNDI
D = DAHOMEY
E.G. = EQUATORIAL GUINEA
G = GHANA
M = MALAWI
R = RWANDA
S = SINGAPORE
T = TOGO
U.V. = UPPER VOLTA

had been incorporated into metropolitan France. This constitutional device did not work: while the European settlers, the colons, insisted on keeping Algeria French, the native majority sought to cut loose. A savage and prolonged conflict followed, a war fought with ruthlessness and brutality on both sides, while it produced increasing political dissension in France. This reached the point of threatened civil war, with the consequence that General De Gaulle came out of retirement in 1958. The outcome was the end of the Fourth Republic, instead of which was established the Fifth, of which De Gaulle became president, endowed with extensive powers, somewhat on the American model.

His leadership was paradoxical. De Gaulle had been expected to keep Algeria French; moving circumspectly, and arousing his erstwhile supporters to murderous fury, he gradually began to speak of Algerian independence. By 1962 he had accustomed the French electorate to the prospect of such independence, and in July, after a plebiscite, Algeria left the French empire. At the same time, decolonizing with a vengeance, De Gaulle freed virtually the whole of the rest of the French empire. His policies permitted the new independent states to retain important economic and cultural bonds with France.

The process of decolonization was attended by an unexpected episode. Late in 1956, France, Britain, and Israel launched an attack on Egypt after that country had nationalized the Suez Canal and proclaimed its intention to destroy the new state of Israel. The Egyptians fared poorly, especially against Israeli troops, but the threat of outside intervention, in which the United States and the Soviet Union momentarily joined, put a stop to the adventure. Britain and France suffered heavily in prestige from their bungled efforts, but Israel had given an impressive demonstration of its military capabilities, and notice of its firm intention to survive Arab hostility.

The United States played a complex and not always happy role in decolonization. Sympathetic a priori to the clamor for independence everywhere, it was insufficiently aware of the problems that the freeing of colonies must inevitably produce. In 1960, Belgium suddenly granted freedom to the Congo. Chaos was the result, and tentative American participation in the turmoil proved an embarrassment. Ironically, for much of the world, America, once the friend of aspiring nationalities everywhere, has taken the place of the former imperialist powers as the villain of the piece.

Most of the newly emerged states, a number of them very small, achieved membership in the United Nations. The unforeseen proliferation of members did not facilitate the operation of the world organization, in which Communist members cheerfully endorsed all anti-imperialist claims, seemingly oblivious to the persistent imperialism of the Russians.

The demise of empire might be taken as evidence of the decline of the former European great powers. Demoted from that rank indeed they were, but an unmitigated picture of decline would be highly misleading.

During the fifties, the German economic miracle had its counterpart elsewhere, especially in France and in Italy. After a long period of stagnation, France's population began to grow, with the important consequence of changing the age composition of the country. Everywhere the state interfered in the economy in behalf of recovery; extensive nationalization and planning became commonplace.

Another important and novel development also occurred in Europe: the havoc of two wars and the common loss of world power began to convince numbers of Europeans of the futility of internecine quarrels. The idea of European unity has a long background which nationalistic passions have never succeeded in destroying. Out of the 1950 proposal of French foreign minister Robert Schuman—the name of Jean Monnet deserves equal mention—the Coal and Steel Community was born (1953). These two basic industries were to be integrated, or "scrambled," in six countries, France, West Germany, Italy, Belgium, the Netherlands, and Luxembourg. The scheme, designed with a view to economic advantage as well as to decrease the possibility of war, prospered, and on January 1, 1958, the Treaty of Rome brought into existence the European Economic Community, usually referred to as the Common Market. The same six countries launched upon the ambitious undertaking of creating a free trade area among themselves and of integrating their entire economies. The Common Market was a resounding success—industrial tariffs, supposed to disappear by 1970, were reduced ahead of schedule—and the whole region boomed.

In the eyes of many of its advocates the Common Market was but a prelude to political integration, which offered, among other things, a possible solution of the German problem. The Europe of the Six is but a part of Europe, roughly coterminous with Charlemagne's empire, but it holds a vital core of some 235 million people. The Franco-German relationship, so different from what it was forty years ago, is of crucial importance, for Europe cannot "unite" without including both France and Germany in the merger.

There remains the question of Britain. That country, fallen upon hard times, faces troubles reminiscent in some respects of those of France after the First World War, when the cost of victory came too high. Unlike the rest of western Europe Britain did not enjoy the advantage of defeat. Attempts to continue to play a major world role, reliance on the Commonwealth or on the special link with the United States, have led only to disillusionment. Britain initially took an unfavorable view of the efforts toward European integration, of which she might have been the leader. EFTA (European Free Trade Association) has been no adequate answer to the Common Market, and Britain has been evolving toward the view that her future lies in Europe. Here is perhaps the most important issue for the Europe of the future: will the legacy of superseded quarrels result in continued division, or can Europe, returning to the legacy of both pagan and Christian Rome, become a major unit, comparable to the United States, the Soviet Union, and China, in the world tomorrow?

The changing face of the Vietnam war, the persistence of Sino-Russian differences, the divergences which have broken the unity of the Communist world, the possibility of change in the relationship between the United States and China, and many other issues, are problems which are not primarily European. Their importance bespeaks the passing of the European Age, yet a Europe united even in part would remain one of the major factors in the affairs of the world.

For Further Reading

Aron, R., *A Century of Total War.*
Brzezinski, Z. K., *The Soviet Bloc: Unity and Conflict.*
Djilas, M., *The New Class: An Analysis of the Communist System.*
Fontaine, A., *A History of the Cold War.*
Lichtheim, G., *The New Europe Today—and Tomorrow.*
Seton-Watson, H., *Neither War Nor Peace: The Struggle for Power in the Postwar World.*

29   The Cold War

The term "The Cold War" came into popular use in 1947: it was the title of a pamphlet by Walter Lippmann critical of certain views expressed by George F. Kennan (writing as Mr. X) in a widely read and discussed article, "The Sources of Soviet Conduct." Yet, as Mr. Kennan later observed in his memoirs, he had already set down these views in government memoranda two years before, in early 1945. Indeed, one may date the beginning of the Cold War, in its more restricted sense, from about that time—in the last year of the Second World War, with the emergence of

A.D. 1939 German-Soviet nonaggression treaty
      1941 Germany invades Soviet Union; Pearl Harbor
      1943 Discovery of Katyn massacre; U.S.S.R. rupture with
            Polish government in exile; Teheran Conference
      1944 Normandy landing; pro-Soviet Polish National Committee
            created; Warsaw uprising; Churchill-Stalin agreement
            in Moscow; civil conflict in Greece
      1945 Yalta Conference; pro-Soviet Groza government formed
            in Rumania; Potsdam Conference; first atomic bomb
            dropped, on Hiroshima; Moscow Conference
      1946 Churchill's "iron curtain" speech in Fulton, Missouri
      1947 Announcement of "Truman Doctrine" for aid to Greece
            and Turkey; Marshall Plan launched; creation of Comin-
            form
      1948 Communist coup in Prague; Tito's Yugoslavia expelled
            from Cominform; beginning of Berlin blockade
      1949 North Atlantic Treaty signed; Chinese People's Republic
            proclaimed
      1950 North Korean invasion of South Korea; Atlantic Council
            agrees on measures of West German rearmament
      1953 Death of Stalin
      1956 Khrushchev denunciation of Stalin; Gomulka becomes
            First Secretary of Polish Communist party; abortive
            Hungarian uprising
      1957 Khrushchev defeats "anti-Party group"; launching of
            first Soviet *Sputnik*
      1959 Fidel Castro victory in Cuba
      1960 Revelation of Sino-Soviet rift
      1961 Abortive Bay of Pigs invasion in Cuba; erection of Berlin
            wall
      1962 Cuban missile crisis

issues (and the search for methods of dealing with them) that were to disrupt the wartime alliance of the United States, the Soviet Union, and Great Britain against the Axis powers.

The Cold War can, of course, be given broader meanings that encompass the breakup of the Big Three Alliance and the onset of the postwar Soviet-American antagonism. One could say that a state of cold war has marked the relations of the Soviet Union with the other leading powers ever since the cessation of open conflict between the new Bolshevik regime and the "imperialists" in the early 1920's. The hostility between "Communism" and "capitalism," or between "totalitarianism" and "democracy," sometimes enlarged to signify a cultural, almost ethnic, conflict between "East" and "West"—all very unsatisfactory but misleadingly handy terms— has been a major feature of the international scene for half a century. Cold war can be defined, too, as a form of conflict taking place below the level of hot war in a thermonuclear age, that is, as a means of pursuing antagonistic aims at a time when the full use of material power appears unbearably costly and destructive for all concerned. Although there were numerous limited hot wars and skirmishes in the decades after 1945, the threatening mushroom cloud in the background influenced profoundly the international climate in those years. Both of these definitions of "cold war" are extremely general, however, and concern virtually the entire range of recent international affairs. The present chapter limits itself to the narrower conflict.

In retrospect it is apparent that the Big Three Alliance, called into being by World War II, was never a closely knit coalition of mutual trust. In addition to the twenty years of enmity that lay behind it, both the Western powers and the Soviet Union harbored suspicions that the other might conclude a separate peace with the Axis if it seemed advantageous to do so. Stalin's role in partitioning eastern Europe with Germany during the period of the Nazi-Soviet Pact (1939–1941) and the Anglo-American delays in launching a second front in Europe in 1942 and 1943 contributed importantly to these mutual suspicions. A revealing indication of this mood on the Russian side is Stalin's remark in 1944, reported by the Yugoslav Communist Milovan Djilas: "Perhaps you think that just because we are the allies of the English that we have forgotten who they are and who Churchill is. They find nothing sweeter than to trick their allies. . . . And Churchill? Churchill is the kind who, if you don't watch him, will slip a kopeck out of your pocket."

This persistent mutual suspicion was accompanied by the bickering over relative contributions and sacrifices that seems to be a part of all "grand alliances." The Cold War as such, however, was precipitated and took form in eastern Europe, initially in disputes concerning the postwar status of Poland and Rumania. The discord first surfaced in Poland, but the Cold War actually started in Rumania. It is worth looking into these two disputes briefly, since they illustrate many of the problems and ambiguities associated with the Cold War as it later expanded. Even in the afterlight of a quarter-century it is difficult to determine the extent to which the crisis concerning these two countries was a consequence of Soviet intentions, present from the outset, to dominate these two states and remodel them in its own image, the unhappy but possibly avoidable crossing of wires in the mutual reading of intentions, or simply that Poland and Rumania happened to be the loci of an essentially unavoidable rupture of a wartime alliance that had lost its function with the anticipated defeat of the common menace, Nazi Germany.

From the summer of 1941 on, the Polish question was confused by the interplay of two related but distinct issues: (1) whether Poland was to regain the eastern territories lost under the unsavory circumstances of the Nazi-Soviet Pact, and (2) whether the Poles would be free to determine their own domestic political and social order. Most Poles naturally connected the two, seeing the restoration of the eastern territories as a legitimate restitution and as a sign of good faith that the tradition of partition and dismemberment was at an end. Great Britain and the United States were less than enthusiastic about the restoration of the 1939 frontier, which contained large numbers of non-Poles, and they proved to be unwilling to make this the occasion for a break with the Soviet Union. On the contrary, they were inclined to argue that chances for decent Soviet-Polish relations and the preservation of Polish independence depended upon Poland's willingness to acquiesce in the permanent loss of the lands beyond the so-called Curzon Line. As for the Soviet Union, it was clear from the beginning that it intended to reclaim all territories gained and incorporated in the years 1939–1941. Whether, if these demands had been acceded to gracefully at the beginning (in all likelihood a political impossibility for any representative Polish regime), the Russians would have been content to let the Poles create a regime of their own choosing remains an open question. We have no real knowledge of Soviet plans and intentions in those years.

Given these incompatible interests and intentions a clash of some sort was probably inevitable despite the continuing common need to fight Hitler. The Polish government in exile in London and the Soviet regime came to an open breach in 1943 as a consequence of the German discovery of mass graves of Polish officers in the Katyn forest—a massacre almost certainly perpetrated by the Russians, though for reasons that remain obscure. Shortly thereafter Stalin threw his weight behind a Polish Communist group as the nucleus for the future government of Poland. The abortive Warsaw uprising of August, 1944, which Stalin icily refused to assist, or permit to be assisted, produced a real, though not publicized, crisis of confidence in the Big Three Alliance. Still, at the Yalta Conference in February, 1945, the Allies did arrive at formulas regarding the frontiers of Poland and the composition of its government, which, while stacked in the Soviet Union's favor, seemed to give promise of an agreed-upon solution. Indeed, a fully Communist-controlled government did not emerge until 1947, by which time the situation throughout eastern Europe had deteriorated beyond hope of Soviet-Western agreement. The Polish question, then, had seriously darkened allied relations but did not lead to an explicit breach.

In the case of Rumania, in contrast, overt disagreement among the allies developed in a relatively short span of time; the forcible installation of the Communist-dominated Groza government in March, 1945, a government which the United States and Great Britain refused to recognize, may be said to mark the beginning of the Cold War, before the final defeat of Germany or the first explosion of an atomic bomb. Although a territorial issue—Bessarabia and northern Bukovina—also divided Rumania and the Soviet Union, it was not central. Rather, the ouster under Soviet insistence of a post-armistice coalition government and the installation of a regime effectively controlled by the Communists directly and flatly affected the domestic structure and independence of Rumania. This was no native revolution; the Rumanian Communists came to power through the will and the presence of the Soviet Union. Occurring a few weeks after the Yalta Conference, it was clearly not in accord with the Declaration on Liberated Areas, which provided for broadly representative interim governments as well as for the holding of early free elections. It did correspond, however, to the terms of the Churchill-Stalin agreement of October, 1944 (Roosevelt did not participate in this agreement but knew of it), which had in effect assigned spheres of influence in southeastern Europe (ostensibly only for a period of military occupation following the expulsion of the Germans), with Greece falling to Great Britain, but Rumania to the Soviet Union. It is evident that Stalin regarded this agreement, rather than the more general provisions of the Yalta agreement, as operative. Throughout 1945 the United States and Great Britain rejected the Groza government as being in contravention to the Yalta agreement; the Soviet Union strongly supported it. There was a fleeting possibility, arrived at in the Moscow Conference of December, 1945, of a mutually acceptable formula involving token representation of non-Communists in the government and the holding of free elections. This quickly broke down: the Soviet Union would not accept elections that would assuredly return an anti-Soviet majority in a country on its frontiers. Although the Western powers did in fact recognize the Groza government and did sign a peace treaty with it, and although King Michael was not forced to abdicate until 1947, the Rumanian impasse was never really resolved, and it hung over all the post-Yalta conferences of the Great Powers until the conferences themselves eventually broke down.

The Polish and Rumanian crises point up two prominent problems and quandaries in the Cold War. First, was the major Soviet concern territorial and defensive, did it want only to strengthen its western approaches and have regimes on its periphery that were "friendly" enough to accept the necessary measures, or was it intent upon imposing its own form of social and political organization on all states within its effective reach (perhaps as the only way it could conceive to assure a "friendly" regime)? Second, was the way to deal with the power vacuum resulting from the destruction of Hitler's empire the classic one of agreed-upon spheres of influence (certainly Stalin's preference, at least for the short run) or was it the Wilsonian principle of self-determination, through the holding of free elections? Unfortunately, the United States and Great Britain did not see eye to eye on this matter, with the result that in the critical year 1945 the policies of the Western allies were not always in consonance. The confusions resulting from this difficulty in reading intentions and from conflicting strategies for resolving the problem of power and influence in eastern Europe contributed greatly to the escalation and extension of the Cold War.

In the three years after the end of the Second World War the Cold War expanded and deepened—in Bulgaria, Yugoslavia, Albania, Hungary, and, most dangerously, in a divided and occupied Germany, with its capital, Berlin, deep inside the Soviet zone of occupation. The February, 1948, Communist coup in Prague ended the independence of the last non-Communist regime in east central Europe (with the interesting but precarious exception of Finland at the north, and Greece, in the throes of a civil war, at the south). The Cold War spilled into the Middle East, with the revival of the perennial Straits question and the sharp dispute over the continued Soviet occupation of northwestern Iran. In February, 1946, Stalin reintroduced the theme, muted during the war, of the inevitability of conflicts under "imperialism." Winston Churchill, in his speech at Fulton, Missouri, the next month, referred to the "iron curtain" that was dividing Europe.

Increasingly the Cold War colored other international problems, not only the peace treaties with the defeated Axis powers, Germany and Japan, but also the civil war that was to rage in China until the victory of the Chinese Communists in 1949. The announcement in March, 1947, of the Truman Doctrine—American aid and support for Greece and Turkey on the fringes of the Soviet imperium—has been taken by some as inaugurating the Cold War. Quite clearly the conflict was well in progress by that time, but the Truman Doctrine did indicate that the United States was moving beyond diplomacy and verbal protest to throw its own power and resources into the conflict. While the creation of the Communist Information Bureau (Cominform) in October, 1947, was a somewhat pale and limited resurrection of the old Comintern, it showed that for the Soviet side, too, the world was now divided into hostile Communist and "imperialist" camps.

The year 1948 witnessed both a climax and a testing point in the Cold War, but also a foreshadowing of things to come. The Communist coup in Czechoslovakia, destroying a democratic regime that had sought desperately to maintain good relations with the Soviet Union and to serve as a bridge between the two worlds, seemed to mark the end of any hope for accommodation. Four months later the Soviet Union imposed a blockade on Berlin. The blockade, and the airlift which was successfully mounted to counter it, gave some definition to the nature and precarious limits of a Cold War at the advent of the age of atomic and thermonuclear weaponry. The crisis was passed without a violent confrontation, but the margin of tolerance between a Western abandonment of its position in Berlin and an open test of strength between predominant Soviet land power (still mauled from the war, but massive and on the scene) and predominant American air power (with a growing atomic arsenal) was extremely narrow.

In the same month, June, 1948, occurred the first of a set of events that in the subsequent two decades was significantly to alter one of the major premises of the Cold War. The Tito regime in Yugoslavia was expelled from the bloc of Communist states. This rift within the newly created Soviet cosmos, while not immediately destructive of its unity—indeed, Draconic steps to impose conformity were the immediate consequence— did display the uncertain foundations of a system that attempted to be at once monolithic and multinational.

Perhaps the single most salient feature in the evolution of the Cold War from its origins in the concluding phase of the Second World War to its establishment as an international fact of life and a label for the times by 1948 is that while the mounting conflict between the Soviet Union and the Western powers was reciprocal it was not symmetrical. This is of some importance for understanding the dynamics of the Cold War and the debates and historical controversies that accompanied it. Soviet-Western relations were reciprocal in that the actions of one side profoundly affected those of the other. In this respect the Cold War is intelligible only as a sequential, escalating contest. In many of its twists and turns it provides classical examples of the mutually produced exacerbations that mark great power politics. At the same time, the relationship was not a symmetrical one despite much talk about the rivalry of superpowers and the creation of mirror images. Several obvious points of "asymmetry" in the antagonism may be offered. Thus, Soviet insistence upon having "friendly regimes" on its western frontiers meant in effect the imposition of Communist regimes; Western insistence upon free elections meant in effect regimes unfriendly to the Soviet Union. Hence, the controversy was not one that could be resolved by the outcome of elections, but involved the acceptability of self-determination itself. Second, once the options of mutual agreement or accommodation seemed closed the choices open to American policy were framed in the debate "containment versus liberation"—holding the line against further Soviet expansion or undertaking to "roll back" the extension of Soviet control in Europe. While these formulations were ambiguous and did not adequately define the range of choices open to the United States, they were, nonetheless, the alternatives for popular and passionate debate in this country in the 1950's. It is reasonable to suppose that debates of some type were also going on in the Soviet Union during these years, when the unpleasant consequences of the collapse of the alliance were making themselves felt. Yet quite obviously the terms of the debate were not, and could not have been, the same in the Soviet Union. Third, the strategic implications of control over eastern Europe were quite different for the Soviet Union and for the United States and Great Britain. A Continental power occupying much of the great Eurasian heartland, Russia clearly looked upon its western approaches (whether its intentions were defensive, offensive, or a mixture of both) in a quite different light from that of the United States or Great Britain, both offshore powers as far as Europe was concerned and both acutely concerned over an irreversible tilting of a traditional European balance of power, the fulcrum of which was somewhere in central Europe. Fourth, and related to this, in the immediate postwar years there was a vast lack of symmetry between the land-based Soviet Union with its armies-in-being and close to the scene and the more remote if fearfully destructive aerial-atomic potential of the United States. Finally, at the level of ideology there was a profound lack of symmetry between the perceptions, goals, and expectations of the Communist leaders and those of the Western leaders. Even granting, as seems quite likely, that in his later years Stalin was hardly a revolutionary and indeed had a real mistrust of any spontaneous revolutionary impulse that would not be firmly under his control, still, his view of the international scene and of the relations between states was not that of a Churchill, a Roosevelt, a Truman, or an Attlee.

Exclusive emphasis upon the reciprocal features of the Cold War can too easily lead to a kind of Olympian neutralism about the conflict and its sources, just as too exclusive emphasis upon one or another feature of asymmetry can lead to a "good guys—bad guys" view of this dangerous and disheartening period of history. Much of the rather fruitless debate about the origins and causes of the Cold War stems from such selective oversimplification.

In the years after 1948 the term Cold War came to describe a whole complex of international tensions seen as deriving from the bipolar antagonism of the two superpowers, the Soviet Union and the United States. Certain things happened to the meaning of the Cold War in consequence. The North Korean invasion of South Korea in June, 1950, was read as a part of this pattern of conflict, but with the war now becoming hot. The Asian conflict in turn increased fears of a military attack in Europe and led to a certain shift in emphasis from efforts to bolster European economic recovery, as through the Marshall Plan, to defending Europe militarily by strengthening NATO and moving toward West German rearmament. The vast anticolonial movement in Asia and Africa, an impulse that had its own roots and was bound to make its appearance in one form or another in the aftermath of the Second World War, was also warped, by both sides, into the Cold War polarization—with eventually unfortunate consequences for all concerned.

By the time of Stalin's death in March, 1953, the atmosphere of the Cold War had also penetrated into the domestic climate of both sides. From 1948 on, the Communist party line in Russia and in the satellites became tougher and tougher, partly to achieve an impregnable front against the imperialist enemy, partly to guard against the Titoist heresy, though partly, no doubt, for reasons of purely domestic infighting. In the United States the Cold War, combined with the separate but apparently related challenges in the Far East, produced the phenomenon that has been loosely labeled McCarthyism, although a temper of frustration and suspicion had been mounting for some time before the Senator cometed across the scene.

Stalin's death did not end the Cold War, but it did lead to a series of changes within the Soviet Union and the Soviet bloc that significantly modified the setting. The struggle for succession within the Kremlin, the gingerly efforts to move away from some of the excesses and rigidities of Stalinism, the growing restiveness in the east European satellites, the appearance of "thaws" and "new courses"—all pointed to some shift in the foundations of that vast imperium Stalin had created and the creation of which had been the central occasion for the Cold War. A climax was reached in 1956, with Khrushchev's denunciation of Stalin at the Twentieth Congress of the Soviet Communist party, with the successful Polish move to a more independent status, and with the violent spasm of the Hungarian Revolution.

The events of 1956, however, while demonstrating that important changes had taken place, also demonstrated the persistence of certain decisive features of the Cold War. For if 1956 served to demolish the Stalin myth as well as the pretension that Soviet Communism was a freely accepted and popular way of life, it also showed that when the chips were down, as in Hungary, the Soviet Union had the power and the will to maintain its position in eastern Europe. The failure—and, it should be said, the inability, except at fearful cost—of the United States to exercise its will in the Hungarian crisis rather effectively ended the theme of "liberation" or "rollback" which had been one of the planks in the domestic debate about the Cold War since the onset of the conflict. From this time on, there was relatively little talk—there had never been much action—about freeing the nations of eastern Europe.

Following on the heels of the crisis in eastern Europe, and in part a consequence of it, was the tremendously important schism between the two major Communist powers, the Soviet Union and China, which festered and then erupted between 1957 and 1960. The impact on the Communist world of this rift and of the appearance of two rival centers of Communist ideology and influence lies beyond the scope of this chapter, but it was bound to affect the nature of the Cold War. More than the Titoist heresy, more than other departures, defections, or attempted defections, the Sino-Soviet break was instrumental in destroying the image of the Communist bloc as having a single will and purpose.

Nikita Khrushchev's emergence from the post-Stalin interregnum as the new leader in 1957 did not effectively counter this drift toward divisiveness within the Communist bloc. Indeed, his rather erratic policies and style of behavior contributed to sharpening the Sino-Soviet conflict. The seven years of Khrushchev's leadership, from 1957 to 1964, did, however, lead to some modifications in the content of the Cold War. Soviet-American relations alternated between efforts at some type of détente and, after *Sputnik,* an intensified race in the missile and space programs. The "third world" became increasingly the object of international attention and competition. A critical intersection of these two trends occurred with the Cuban missile crisis in October, 1962. Like earlier major Soviet-American confrontations in the Cold War—notably the Berlin blockade in 1948 and the Hungarian Revolution in 1956—the resolution of the crisis seemed to carry a dual message: the United States was forced to face the unwelcome fact of a hostile, virtually Communist regime close at hand in the Western Hemisphere; the Soviet Union failed dramatically in its effort to exploit this fact by playing thermonuclear brinkmanship.

In the 1960's there was throughout the world a growing sense that times were changing, if not necessarily for the better. The term Cold War,

which had become a blanket description to cover most postwar antagonisms, came to seem less and less appropriate, and the phrase itself fell out
of usage, except in historical studies, which now attempted to put the Cold
War "in perspective" or to describe its rise and fall. No statesman now
liked to have the epithet Cold Warrior hurled at him. Somehow the equally
ambiguous term "peaceful coexistence" had crept in.

Several reasons, apart from the mere passage of time and boredom with
a turn of speech, may account for this fading of the image of the Cold War.
For one thing, the characterization of the world as bipolarized seemed an
increasingly inapplicable and inaccurate way of describing the international
scene in the 1960's. Despite the tremendous resources and military destruc-
tiveness at their disposal, the Soviet Union and the United States did not
dominate the globe as they appeared to in the two preceding decades.
China was contending with Russia for at least the moral and ideological
leadership of the Communist world. In the West, France, under De Gaulle,
had moved off on a course of its own determination. The Vietnamese
conflict had come to absorb a high percentage of American attention and
energies. The lines of cleavage in Africa and the Middle East were following their own logic and no longer fell into the force field of two superpowers.

In central and eastern Europe, the place of origin of the Cold War,
further change was taking place. True, the problem of a divided Germany
remained, and as the periodic alarms and crises involving Berlin demonstrated (notably the building of the Berlin wall in 1961), it was still a most
refractory and dangerous one, capable of bringing the Cold War back into
very sharp focus and even of leading to a disaster of incalculable proportions.

Among the Communist states of eastern Europe, one after another
came to mark out its own course. Albania had broken with Khrushchev by
1960 and held to neo-Stalinist orthodoxy in fear of Yugoslavia. Later
Rumania and then Czechoslovakia, previously exceptionally docile regimes,
asserted their freedom of action, the one primarily in the area of foreign
economic and defense policy, the other in domestic liberalization.

The apprehensive and at times forceful response of the Soviet Union
reflected the alarm with which its leadership witnessed these changes,
especially as they corresponded in part to moods within its own population.
But on the whole these changes and crises caused far less reaction in the
United States than had the events of the 1940's and 1950's. Clearly something had happened to the Cold War even in eastern Europe.

In sum, it appeared that while the Soviet Union and the United States
would continue to have a relationship not inappropriately described as
Cold War—recent history and habits by now ingrained would probably

assure that for some time—by the end of the 1960's this particular relationship was only one among a number in the world at large. Cold War no longer seemed fitting as a general description of a new age which was at once hotter and less controllable and yet displayed increasing revulsion to the idea of war as such, hot or cold. After a quarter of a century under the sign of the Cold War the world was groping its way toward different configurations and different styles.

For Further Reading

Fontaine, Andre, *History of the Cold War.*
Halle, Louis J., *The Cold War as History.*
Hammond, Paul Y., *The Cold War Years: American Foreign Policy Since 1945.*
McNeill, William H., *America, Britain and Russia: Their Cooperation and Conflict, 1941–1946.*

30   Latin America in Ferment

From the mid-nineteenth century to the Spanish-American War in 1898 the world at large was little aware of Latin America. The brief rule in Mexico of the French Emperor Maximilian caused a flurry of interest, but his death in 1867 before the firing squad of Benito Juárez was soon followed by the seemingly perpetual dictatorship of Porfirio Díaz (1876–1911). Giant Brazil was held together for almost half a century by the paternalistic Emperor Pedro II until the Republic dismissed him in 1889. The one nation that steadily progressed economically and politically was Argentina, whose beef and wheat were consumed by the more industrialized nations. Throughout most of Latin America the economies of the nineteen nations that had won their independence became increasingly dependent on a few products exported to Europe and the United States. Most emigrants from Europe seeking homes in the New World considered the United States more attractive, and the foreign travelers who had earlier found the newly liberated nations exotic places to visit and report on had few successors. Cultural, economic, or political developments in Latin America rarely held the attention of any foreign nation for long.

The nations south of the Rio Grande began to come of age internationally after 1900, but the pace was slow until Fidel Castro won Cuba in

A.D.   1898   Spanish-American War
            1910   Revolution begins in Mexico
            1912   Universal compulsory male suffrage law passed in
                    Argentina
            1916   First popularly elected president in Argentina, Hipó-
                    lito Irigoyen
            1918   Student movement begins in Córdoba, Argentina
            1930   Getúlio Vargas begins 15-year rule in Brazil; the
                    depression comes to Latin America
       1934–1940   Lázaro Cárdenas stabilizes Mexico, implements the
                    revolution, expropriates foreign oil properties
                    (1938)
       1943–1955   Perón dominates Argentina
            1952   Bolivian Revolution
            1959   Fidel Castro triumphs in Cuba
            1961   Bay of Pigs invasion of Cuba fails; Trujillo assassi-
                    nated, ending 31-year dictatorship in the Domini-
                    can Republic
            1962   Missile crisis between Russia and the United States
            1965   First Pan-American Assembly on Population meets
                    in Colombia; President Lyndon Johnson sends
                    Marines to the Dominican Republic
            1970   Salvador Allende elected president of Chile

1959. The Mexican Revolution beginning in 1910 wrought great changes in Mexico, but nowhere else, and until World War II Latin America was little seen and not much heard on the international scene. The Good Neighbor Policy of Franklin D. Roosevelt turned some attention and aid southward, but his successors in the White House showed little interest because they were engaged in the enormous United States effort during World War II and the Cold War era which followed. Events like the Bolivian Revolution of 1952 or the stirring of the masses in the other tradition-bound republics roused little interest in the United States. However, Castro's triumph set in motion events that dramatized the explosive nature of Latin America's problems and their significance to the world at large, and the Cuban missile crisis between Soviet Russia and the United States in October, 1962, was the shock that put Cuba and Latin America on the map as never before.

Western Europeans and others realized that a dispute between the nuclear giants over a Caribbean island could put all civilization in mortal peril. Governments and universities hastened to examine the political, cultural, and economic conditions of this relatively unknown continent. Research institutes devoted to Latin American affairs sprang up throughout the United States; millions of dollars were made available by Washington and private foundations. Similar institutes were established in Great Britain, France, East and West Germany, and Japan. Soviet writings on Latin America grew from 3 titles in 1918 to 4,200 during 1960–1964. One result of this activity was that in a decade more serious studies of Latin America appeared than in the entire previous century.

The facts revealed in these studies are somber and puzzling. The economic position of a few countries has improved, but the leaders and people of this vast region are more disturbed and dissatisfied than ever before. They have entered the world scene, but are distinctly unhappy with their position, and a spirit of disenchantment is pervasive.

Clearly Latin America is in ferment, but no one pattern of distress may be found in this vast area, and the enormous variety of peoples, economies, and prospects makes generalization difficult. Mexico survived the fires of the revolution of 1910–1920, although the country's population declined by a million people. Large landowners, newspapers, banks, professors, and much of the government bureaucracy disappeared in the holocaust. Confusion followed for twenty years, but beginning with General Lázaro Cárdenas' presidency (1934–1940) there was progress. The Revolution slowed down; some claim that it has stopped altogether because one political party (Partido Revolucionario Institucional) dominates the country and thus far has won all elections. But the country has passed beyond its profound social revolution to achieve a special kind of stability which gives it a unique position in Latin America.

In sharp contrast to Mexico, proud of its Indian past and determined to achieve an independent position in the world even against its powerful neighbor to the north, is Argentina, which has been in the political doldrums since the fall of Juan Domingo Perón, who, with his charismatic wife Eva, revolutionized this wealthy country between 1943 and 1955. Perón continued some traditional policies—opposition to the United States and determination to be the leader in Latin America—and adopted a program of economic nationalism long advocated by important groups. But however much Perón resembled the typical Argentine caudillo, he brought one new and powerful element, the workers, into the mainstream of national life. His political power rested solidly on the army and the workers. Perón gave industrialization a forward thrust and assured an improvement of the workers' living conditions, but at the expense of the agricultural and pastoral sector of the economy. On balance when the armed forces rose in 1955 and the dictator fled, many Argentines, particularly the middle and upper classes, felt profound relief, for the corruption and pillaging of the Perón regime had brought Argentina close to economic and moral disaster.

The smoke of the fires Perón lighted still hangs over Argentina, and Peronism is still a dominant issue in Argentine political life. The uncertainty left in his wake affected all groups: labor unions, landowners, army, church, industry, and political parties. Both elected presidents, Arturo Frondizi (1956–1962) and Arturo Illía (1963–1966), were removed by the army before their terms ended. The wounds Perón inflicted on the body politic have not yet healed, nor has the economic balance between agriculture and industry been worked out. The Peronistas remain as an important political force, but in typical Argentine fashion they too are divided; the country has not yet created a true community. Perón gave the workers for the first time in Argentine history significant material benefits and a new sense of personal dignity, but Peronistas are not yet fully accepted by other powerful political elements. The army, therefore, has stepped in and shows little disposition to relinquish its control.

Portuguese-speaking Brazil is the country in Latin America with the most of everything—the most inflation, the most voters, the most workers, the most consumers, the most illiterates, and the greatest economic potential. Its population of about 100 million increases by more than 2 million every year, an increase larger than the total population of many other Latin American countries. Brazilians have been proud that in a hemisphere of sharply divisive racial strains they alone have evolved a culture marked by the fusion of European, Indian, and Negro stocks, and that, situated among countries where violence has often occurred, they have rarely used force to settle their disputes.

The immense size and diversity of Brazil are the overriding facts of its existence. This large tropical world, 3,294,000 square miles in area, would hold the entire continental United States with room for an extra Texas; it has the largest river in the world, the Amazon; two of its waterfalls, Iguassú and Paulo Afonso, are higher than Niagara; the island of Marajó at the mouth of the Amazon is as big as New England. Brazil produces much of the world's coffee (despite Africa's increasing competition), grows more bananas than any other country, possesses in Itabira an iron deposit estimated at more than a billion tons, and is so rich in plants that some 50,000—one-fourth of all known species—are found within its borders.

Yet Brazil has developed slowly and erratically. The abolition of Negro slavery in 1888 and the fall of the Empire in 1889 led to a series of uncertain Republican years; Brazil entered the modern world only in 1930, when Getúlio Vargas began his largely benevolent rule. A master politician who well understood the needs and aspirations of his people, he shrewdly played off the army, big business, and labor against one another and used regional rivalries to hold power until his suicide in 1954. During unprecedented social and economic ferment, which he encouraged by his support for economic nationalism and by laws protecting workers, Vargas was sufficiently flexible and skillful to hold Brazil together like a twentieth-century Emperor Pedro II.

No president after Vargas has demonstrated his ability in political maneuver; each has faced mounting economic and social problems. Juscelino Kubitschek (1956–1960) built the new capital Brasília but impoverished the country thereby. Jânio Quadros, elected president in 1960 by the largest popular vote in Brazilian history, proved an unpredictable leader. When he unexpectedly resigned in August, 1961, he plunged Brazil into a prolonged political crisis.

Since 1945 the army has been the decisive force in Brazilian politics. Traditionally disposed to uphold the established government and to guarantee constitutional and civilian rule, it has intervened whenever it considers Brazil threatened from any direction. It removed Vice-President João Goulart, who had succeeded Quadros, because it did not trust him, and replaced his left-leaning regime in 1964 with a military-dominated, middle-class supported government under Marshal Humberto Castelo Branco, who in November, 1965, by decree abolished existing political parties and substituted one "official" party and one "loyal opposition." The election of Marshal Artur da Costa e Silva by Congress in October, 1966, introduced another uncertain element in the country's confused situation.

LATIN AMERICA IN 1970

European possessions

★ National capitals

0   500   1,000 Miles

When the marshal assumed the presidency in March, 1967, he promised to "humanize" the revolution. Instead he and the other stern army figures who succeeded him in power have apparently decided that Brazil's many problems can only be solved in a harsh military spirit. The relatively peaceful period of Brazilian history apparently has now ended.

At the turn of the century, in his classic *Revolt in the Backlands,* Euclydes da Cunha described the poor, ignorant fanatics of the northeast led by António Conselheiro. The shock inspired by this book was forgotten once the army had destroyed these rebels. But the poor and dispossessed in Brazil cannot be ignored today. No matter who holds political power in Brazil, or indeed in most Latin American countries, one persistent, inescapable problem remains: extremely rapid population growth. Before the year 2000, some 600 million Latin Americans will probably share the hemisphere with 300 million North Americans. This problem is connected with all the great questions at issue today.

Will Latin America, assisted by the United States, be able, in John F. Kennedy's words, "to satisfy the basic needs of the American peoples for home, work and land, health and schools" without major convulsions of governments and societies? Will the policy of "armed conflict" which Castro proclaimed in August, 1967, at the first meeting of the Latin American Solidarity Organization, achieve its radical aim to rouse the masses to overthrow the present power structures by force? Will reforming groups in Latin America, such as the Christian Democratic parties in several countries and Chile's socialist government led by Marxist Salvador Allende, elected in 1970 to a six-year term as president, be able to find a way to achieve economic and social justice by evolution rather than revolution? Many thoughtful and intelligent groups in Latin America do not accept guidance from either Washington or Havana, and are determined to change their societies by their own methods for their own national purposes.

At this point in history, Latin America is struggling to enter the society of developed nations and to play a larger role in the world. The struggle sometimes becomes bitter, the range of problems is comprehensive: "What is under debate," says Luiz Auguiar Costa Pinto, "is the whole heritage of the archaic society—the economic, political, and intellectual heritage—as well as the archaic society itself—its structures, its values, its prospects." One controversial but inescapable element in the discussion is the widespread opposition expressed inside and outside Latin America to United States intervention—cultural, economic, political, and military. While this debate goes on, the forces representing entrenched tradition, liberalizing evolution, and open revolt confront one another with increasing hostility. No one can predict the outcome with certainty, but fundamental and unexpected changes are possible. For in Latin America there has long existed, as Robin Humphreys has emphasized, both a revolt against tradition and a tradition of revolt.

For Further Reading

Adams, Richard, et al. (eds.), *Social Change in Latin America Today.*
Graham, Richard (ed.), *A Century of Brazilian History Since 1865.*
Hanke, Lewis, *Contemporary Latin America.*
Lambert, Jacques, *Latin America: Social Structures and Political Institutions.*

31   The Middle East Since 1940

During the Second World War, major campaigns were fought along the borders of the Middle East—in the Caucasus, Greece, Crete, the Western Desert of Egypt, and in Ethiopia—but the region itself escaped unscathed. However, a cataclysm of such magnitude could not but have deep repercussions, and in fact the war shattered the social and political order which had been established through European influence. In addition to the revolutionary ideas let loose in the region, there was the presence of several hundred thousand allied troops, whose upkeep added hundreds of millions of dollars to the foreign exchange reserves of the various countries, but also created shortages and raised prices sharply, exacerbating social tensions. The allied powers—especially the British—understandably subordinating local considerations to overall strategy, made the Middle Eastern governments take unpopular measures and, where necessary, as in Iraq and Iran in 1941, and in Egypt in 1942, coerced or overthrew such governments. And, more generally, the war interrupted or reversed the process of imperial disengagement in the region. The result was to intensify the already great political ferment and to increase nationalist resentment of the occupying powers.

The end of the war was, therefore, the signal for repeated attempts to end foreign control. These were generally successful, since the local forces could usually enlist the support of the United States, and sometimes that of Britain and the Soviet Union as well. Thus France, which had formally granted independence to Lebanon and Syria in 1943, was forced by Britain and the United States to withdraw its troops from those countries by 1946. In Iran withdrawal of American, British, and under strong American pressure, Soviet forces early in 1946 was followed by the collapse of a Soviet-sponsored separatist government in Azerbaijan. Anglo-Egyptian negotiations were fruitless until 1954 when, thanks to United States efforts, an agreement was reached. Two years later, British troops were withdrawn from the Suez Canal zone, paving the way for the granting of independence to the Anglo-Egyptian Sudan. In Iraq, repeated attempts to amend the 1930 treaty with Great Britain were unsuccessful, but British forces were withdrawn following the conclusion of the Baghdad Pact in 1955. As regards the smaller countries, Jordan received independence in 1946, Cyprus in 1960 (after prolonged guerrilla fighting), Kuwait in 1961, and Southern Yemen in 1968.

A.D.   1941   Anglo-Soviet troops occupy Iran; Riza Shah deposed and replaced by son

           1945   Formation of Arab League

   1945–1947   Azerbaijan crisis

           1946   French troops evacuate Lebanon and Syria; Britain recognizes independence of Transjordan (Jordan)

           1947   Truman Doctrine promising support to Greece and Turkey; United Nations partition of Palestine, evacuation of British troops

           1948   Proclamation of State of Israel

   1948–1949   Arab-Israeli war

           1949   First of series of military revolts in Syria

           1951   Nationalization of oil industry in Iran

           1952   Military revolution in Egypt overthrows monarchy and establishes republic

           1954   Anglo-Egyptian Treaty providing for evacuation of British troops

           1955   Baghdad Pact

           1956   Granting of independence to Sudan; nationalization of Suez Canal; Anglo-French-Israeli invasion of Egypt

           1958   Military revolt in Iraq ends monarchy

           1962   Civil war in Yemen, overthrow of monarchy

           1967   Arab-Israeli war

           1968   Independence of Southern Yemen

In Palestine reconciliation of Arab and Zionist aspirations proved impossible. A United Nations resolution in 1947, partitioning the country, was followed by the withdrawal of British troops and fighting first between Zionists and Palestine Arabs and then, after the proclamation of the State of Israel in 1948, between it and the neighboring Arab countries. Hostilities erupted repeatedly, as in the "Six-Day War" of 1967, an overwhelming Israeli triumph that resulted in the occupation of important parts of Egypt, Jordan, and Syria. Diplomatic and commercial relations remain broken; no solution has been found for repatriating the 750,000 Arab refugees who fled Palestine after the creation of Israel, and the danger that Arab-Israeli conflict may trigger a third world war remains grave.

The unity imposed on the greater part of the Middle East by the Ottoman Empire broke down after the First World War, and that provided by Britain's predominance disappeared after the Second. Since then various attempts, both internal and external, to unite the Middle Eastern countries have met with little success, and the region has been the scene of conflicts between the Great Powers. American and British efforts to bring Middle Eastern countries into a defense pact or alliance have also generally failed. A Middle East Defense Pact proposal of 1951 foundered on Egyptian opposition. The Baghdad Pact, concluded in 1955, linked Iran, Pakistan, and Turkey with Britain, but the only Arab country to join was Iraq, which withdrew in 1959.

The main internal attempt at integration was that of the Arab League, founded in 1945, to promote political and economic cooperation among its members. This too has had little success because of the clash of rival dynastic and national ambitions and divergent interests. The various Fertile Crescent schemes, aiming at uniting Syria, Lebanon, Palestine, Jordan, and Iraq under the Hashimi royal house—one of whose branches ruled Iraq and another Jordan—were thwarted by Egypt and Saudi Arabia, while Egyptian leadership has been opposed by Iraq, Jordan, and Saudi Arabia. Two unions formed in 1958, the United Arab Republic between Egypt and Syria and the Arab Union between Iraq and Jordan, soon broke down. In addition to these conflicts between the Arab states, and between them and Israel, there have been tensions between Turkey and Syria, Iran and Iraq, Iran and the United Arab Republic (Egypt), and Iraq and Kuwait.

Local quarrels have both invited, and been aggravated by, Great Power intervention. A series of crises centered on Syria in 1955–1957 led to an American-Soviet confrontation. Egypt's nationalization of the Suez Canal in 1956, and the subsequent attack on that country by Britain, France, and Israel, led to United Nations action and to American and Soviet pressures, compelling withdrawal of the invading forces. The civil war in Lebanon in 1958, and the support given to the rebels by the United Arab Republic

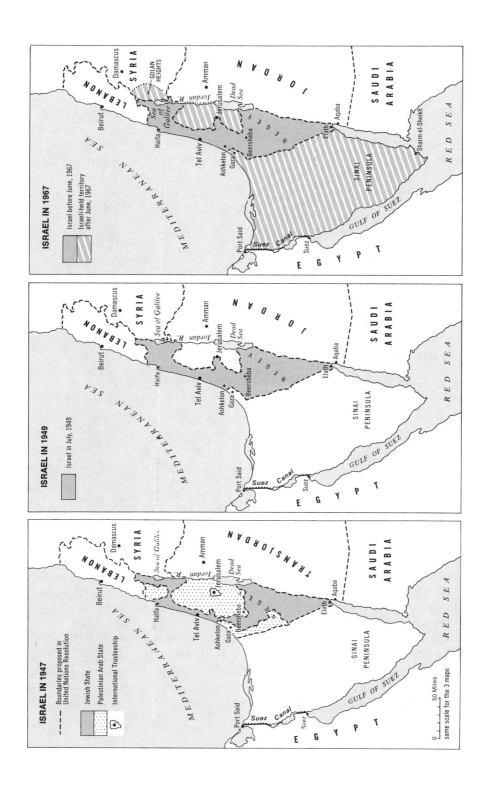

ISRAEL IN 1947

- - - Boundaries proposed in United Nations Resolution

Jewish State

Palestinian Arab State

International Trusteeship

DAMASCUS •
SYRIA
LEBANON
Beirut •
Sea of Galilee
Jordan R.
Amman •
Jerusalem
Dead Sea
TRANSJORDAN
SAUDI ARABIA
Haifa •
Tel Aviv •
Ashkelon •
Gaza •
Beersheba •
N E G E V
Elath •
Aqaba •
MEDITERRANEAN SEA
SINAI PENINSULA
GULF OF SUEZ
RED SEA
Port Said •
Suez Canal
Suez •
E G Y P T

0   50 Miles
same scale for the 3 maps

ISRAEL IN 1949

Israel in July, 1949

Damascus •
SYRIA
LEBANON
Beirut •
Sea of Galilee
Jordan R.
Amman •
Jerusalem
Dead Sea
JORDAN
SAUDI ARABIA
Haifa •
Tel Aviv •
Ashkelon •
Gaza •
Beersheba •
N E G E V
Elath •
Aqaba •
MEDITERRANEAN SEA
SINAI PENINSULA
GULF OF SUEZ
RED SEA
Port Said •
Suez Canal
Suez •
E G Y P T

ISRAEL IN 1967

Israel before June, 1967

Israeli-held territory after June, 1967

Damascus •
SYRIA
GOLAN HEIGHTS
LEBANON
Sea of Galilee
Jordan R.
Amman •
Jerusalem
Dead Sea
JORDAN
SAUDI ARABIA
Haifa •
Tel Aviv •
Ashkelon •
Gaza •
Beersheba •
N E G E V
Elath •
Aqaba •
Sharm-el-Sheikh •
MEDITERRANEAN SEA
SINAI PENINSULA
GULF OF SUEZ
RED SEA
Port Said •
Suez Canal
Suez •
E G Y P T

(Syria and Egypt), provoked a landing of U.S. Marines—and Soviet counterprotests. In the civil war which broke out in Yemen in 1962 Egypt backed the republican forces, and Saudi Arabia and Jordan supported the royalists. Egypt in turn received Soviet arms and aid, and similar support reached the royalists from the British-ruled territories of South Arabia; in addition the United States, anxious to preserve the stability of Saudi Arabia and the other oil-producing countries, used pressure to prevent the fighting from extending beyond the borders of Yemen. And following the 1967 war, the Arabs have received Soviet backing and the Israelis American.

In sum, although international relations in the Middle East are being determined by the countries of the region to a far greater degree than before, the influence of the Great Powers is still considerable and, in some circumstances, decisive. This power is exercised not so much through direct force as through diplomatic pressure and the supply of financial aid and arms to the Middle Eastern governments.

In most of the regimes established after the First World War under British and French influence, power was exercised mainly by the landlords and upper middle class. These regimes broke down after the Second World War. At present three main types of government prevail: military dictatorships with a strong nationalist and socialist orientation; traditional monarchies engaged in modernizing their countries; and liberal parliamentary democracies. Syria's military revolt of 1949 was the first of many, in the course of which the ruling officer groups, drawn mainly from the lower middle class, came to apply increasingly radical policies. In Egypt the 1952 coup overthrew King Farouk—whose scandalous behavior had discredited the monarchy—and the country was ruled by officers led by Gamal Abdel Nasser—a burly officer of lower-middle-class origin whose experience of the disastrous campaign against Israel in 1948–1949 had led him to start the secret Free Officers Movement. This regime has reoriented foreign policy, drastically reduced Western influence through the use of Soviet countervailing power—in the process securing vast amounts of aid from both sides—and sought to establish Egyptian leadership in the Arab world. In the name of Arab Socialism, it has also deeply transformed the country's internal structure, extending economic and educational opportunities to the masses, breaking the economic and political power of the former ruling classes, and curtailing the appreciable measure of intellectual and political liberty previously prevailing. In Iraq the army coup which overthrew the monarch in 1958 failed to produce any leaders of stature, and the country has been torn by armed conflicts between military and political factions and by civil war between Arabs and Kurds. Similarly, in Yemen the officers who led the revolt of 1962 failed to get control over the whole country, and the war between them and royalist tribes continues.

The surviving monarchies in Iran, Jordan, Kuwait, and Saudi Arabia have so far succeeded, thanks to the loyalty of their armies, in the twofold task of staving off internal onslaughts, often supported by more radical neighbors, and rapidly modernizing the economic and social structure of their countries. This has necessitated some far-reaching changes, such as the Iranian land reform of 1963, which greatly reduced the power of the landlords, and the political and administrative reorganization in Saudi Arabia. Their task has been facilitated by oil revenues in Iran, Kuwait, and Saudi Arabia and American and British aid in Jordan.

In Turkey the one-party rule established by Mustafa Kemal Atatürk continued under his successor and faithful lieutenant İsmet İnönü, who in spite of his advanced age had retained much intellectual vigor, realized that Turkey was ripe for a multiparty system, and commanded the widespread respect required to make the transition possible. The 1945 elections were contested by the Democrat party, which in 1950 took office. The following decade saw much economic and social progress, but this was accompanied by rising prices, imbalances, repressions, and growing tensions which exploded in the army coup of 1960. In contrast with other Middle Eastern countries, however, the more radical army officers failed to gain control of the movement, and power was gradually handed back to civilians.

Lebanon's constitutional system has also endured, surviving a bloodless revolution in 1952 and a short but devastating civil war in 1958. Here the main tensions have been between Christians and Muslims, aggravated by struggles between rival ideologies and power groups in the other Arab states. Similarly, Israel's broad-based democracy has not been threatened by fairly frequent changes in party alignments. Thanks to the high educational and social level of its people and to considerable, some would say lavish, foreign aid, the country has overcome the difficulties posed by isolation from its Arab neighbors and the task of absorbing well over a million immigrants, most of them Oriental Jews with cultural values different from those of the predominant Western-born or native Israelis.

After 1945 Middle Eastern oil resources—which at present amount to 60 per cent of world reserves—were rapidly developed and the producing countries bordering the Persian Gulf now account for more than 25 per cent of world output and more than 50 per cent of exports. Oil revenues, which are running at over $3 billion a year, play a dominant part in their budgets and serve to finance a large part of the region's expenditure on defense and development.

Industrialization is also proceeding at an accelerating pace, and in several countries manufacturing and mining now account for a fifth or more of the gross national product. Transport and communications have developed rapidly; railways and ports have been built, roads have been vastly extended and improved, and a network of airlines covers the region. However, as in other underdeveloped regions, agricultural output has generally lagged behind the rapid population growth (3 per cent per annum in several countries), and the Middle East, formerly a net exporter, has become increasingly dependent on imports of grain, mainly from the United States. The Middle East has also had heavy deficits in its balance of payments which have been met by very large amounts of aid from the United States, the Soviet Union, Western Germany, Britain, and other countries. Thanks to oil and foreign aid, the rate of economic growth in most Middle Eastern countries has been distinctly above that of other underdeveloped regions, and the level of living is higher than ever before.

The progress achieved has, in the main, taken place within the framework of private enterprise. But in all countries the government has played a leading part, contributing heavily to investment, extending social services, and seeking to secure greater social justice through taxation and, in several countries, land reform. In Egypt since 1961, and later in Syria and Iraq, the bulk of industry, finance, and transport has been nationalized and a socialist system is well under way. And in the whole region socialist ideas, drawn from west European, Russian, and Chinese sources, are capturing the allegiance of the intelligentsia, along with nationalism. Generally, the two beliefs amalgamate to form the same kind of socialist nationalism which is widespread in other underdeveloped regions.

The size of the intelligentsia is growing rapidly, because of the expansion of education and the increase of the urban population. For the first time in history more than half the boys and nearly half the girls in the Middle East are attending school and hundreds of thousands of students of both sexes are receiving higher education. Particularly noteworthy has been the expansion of technical and scientific education and research. Middle Eastern scientists are making an appreciable contribution to the progress of their countries, and a few are doing work which has wider significance. Similarly, the literature being produced in the region has reached a high level, and works written in Arabic, Hebrew, Persian, and Turkish have been translated into various Western languages. Among the most distinguished are the novelists Samuel Agnon, the Nobel Prize winner, and Haim Hazzaz in Israel, the novelists and short story writers Nagib Mahfuz and Yusif Idris in Egypt, Mahmut Makal and Kemal Yashar in Turkey, and Sadiq Chubak and Jalal Ali Ahmad in Iran.

Except in Israel and Lebanon, illiteracy is widespread but may be expected to fall sharply in the next decade or two. In the meantime other media are reaching the masses: transistor radios have opened the remotest villages to the outside world, and movies and television are now available in the smaller towns. Rural electrification and the spread of social services are transforming still further the outlook of the peasants who still constitute the bulk of the population. Thus the Middle East, so long left behind by history, torn by tensions, perplexed by conflicting ideologies, facing grave economic and social difficulties, but with renewed vitality and hope, is making its way into the modern world.

For Further Reading

Berger, Morroe, *The Arab World Today.*
Fein, Leonard, *Israel.*
Hurewitz, J. C., *Middle East Politics: The Military Dimension.*
―――― (ed.), *Soviet American Rivalry in the Middle East.*
Karpat, Kemal (ed.), *Political and Social Thought in the Contemporary Middle East.*
Shwadran, Benjamin, *The Middle East, Oil and the Great Powers.*

32   Africa Since 1945

In 1945, independence for African states in the reasonably near future seemed an absurdity to the colonial powers. Nor were there many African political leaders who thought it plausible to demand it. The French government had made its view very clear at the Brazzaville Conference of 1944, stating: "The establishment one day of self-governments in the colonies, even a day far off, is to be eliminated from any consideration." The British Report of the Commission on Higher Education in West Africa in June, 1945, was less negative but equally complacent: "Somewhere, in West Africa within a century—and what is that in the life of a people—a new African State will be born."

In East and Central Africa, it is not clear that anyone expected that there would ever be an *African* state. Rather, a significant segment of those in positions of authority looked forward to the gradual devolution of power primarily to the white settler community, a modified version of the Union of South Africa, albeit one more devoted, it was hoped, to the Crown.

Indeed, with one or two possible exceptions, it is doubtful that there existed in 1945 a genuine African nationalist movement anywhere on the continent. Such political organizations as did exist demanded changes that would end various discriminations of the colonial governments, but usually within the context of pledges of loyalty to the imperial system. There was,

A.D.   1944   Brazzaville Conference of French Union
        1945   Fifth Pan-African Congress, Manchester
        1948   Nationalist Party comes to power in Union of South Africa
        1952   Overthrow of King Farouk in Egypt; Mau Mau emergency proclaimed in Kenya
        1954   Algerian war of independence begins
        1955   Bandung Conference
        1956   Independence of Sudan, Tunisia, Morocco
        1957   Independence of Ghana
        1958   Referendum in French Africa; conference of Independent African States, Accra; All-African People's Conference, Accra; independence of Guinea
        1960   Year of Africa (independence of 17 states); Congo crisis breaks out; Katanga secession
        1961   Creation of Casablanca and Monrovia groups; Angola rebellion begins (first in Portuguese Africa)
        1962   Algeria gains independence; end of Katanga secession
        1963   Creation of Organization of African Unity
        1965   Unilateral Declaration of Independence by Southern Rhodesia
        1966   Coups in Nigeria (death of Balewa) and Ghana (fall of Nkrumah)
        1967   Secession of Biafra
        1970   End of Biafra secession

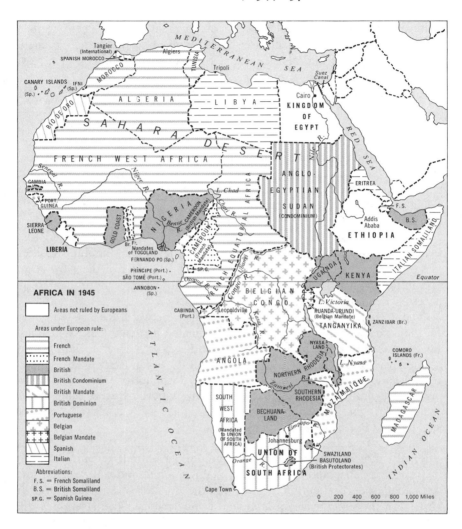

to be sure, an avant-garde: those who met in Manchester in October, 1945, at the Fifth Pan-African Congress and bluntly demanded independence. This group included not only such great figures of the pan-African movement as W. E. B. DuBois and George Padmore but many who would later become leading nationalists: Kwame Nkrumah (Ghana), Jomo Kenyatta (Kenya), Hastings Kamuzu Banda (Malawi), and Obafemi Awolowo (Nigeria).

Yet despite the attitude of the colonial powers and the timidity of African political organizations, the years after 1945 saw the continuous, rapid, and accelerating decolonization of much of Africa. There were at least four major factors that most of those involved on the African scene in 1945 had not taken into consideration, two external to the continent, two internal to it.

One was the impact of Asian developments on African affairs. The independence of India and Pakistan in 1947 placed Great Britain squarely on the path of creating a multiracial Commonwealth, and the influence of Gandhi and the Indian Congress party was to be felt throughout British Africa. The abortive decolonization of Indochina in 1946 made the French Union face squarely the issue of independence as an option, and had an immediate effect on political sentiment in North Africa and Madagascar which in turn affected French black Africa. The proclamation of the Chinese People's Republic in 1949 had a clear bearing, partially insofar as it affected the world balance of power, but more directly as it led to a period of Chinese-Indian friendship culminating in the Bandung Conference of 1955. The consequent emergence of the concept of the Afro-Asian bloc, in the United Nations and elsewhere, was of critical importance to the success of decolonization in Africa.

The second factor was the world struggle between the United States and the Soviet Union. As the struggle terminated its acute Cold War phase and became an armed truce (or "competitive coexistence"), dating from the Geneva Conference of 1954, the U.S.S.R. began actively to support African nationalist movements. The eventual response of the United States was to give limited and tacit but important support to these same movements and to put pressure on its NATO allies (Great Britain, France, Belgium, and Portugal) to decolonize rapidly.

These two external factors greatly facilitated the work of African nationalist movements, but internal conditions in Africa account basically for their emergence and the response of the colonial authorities. The third factor that escaped attention in 1945 was the ripeness of most territories in Africa for the emergence of nationalist movements. The strains of the colonial period had begun to reach a critical point. Urban-educated elites were beginning to butt hard against the limitations to their advancement inherent in the colonial situation. On all the fronts they pushed—in the civil service and other bureaucracies, in local political structures, in commercial enterprises—they found barriers or obstacles to their hopes and ambitions.

The rural peasants were no happier with their situation. Peasant turbulence and rebellion had been a constant of the colonial scene. The declining authority of most traditional chiefs (because of the ambiguous role they were called upon to play by colonial authorities) combined with the increasing usurpation of land for cash-crop production (by those of traditionally high status and, in some areas, by white settlers) was leading to acute discontent. The link between the discontent of the educated elite and the peasants was provided by "lower-middle-class" elements (junior clerical personnel, artisans, schoolteachers, health personnel, skilled workers) whose numbers grew significantly during World War II. The economic recession of the early postwar years, combined with a decline in real wages, made this stratum willing to join a mass nationalist movement that would canalize the various discontents into a demand for political independence.

The fourth factor to account for the misperceptions of 1945 was the failure to anticipate the nature of the response of the colonial administrations. Both colonizers and colonized thought administrations would respond to nationalism by repression. This was indeed the initial response everywhere. Repression, however, has its costs, and in most of Africa after 1945 the costs turned out to be too high. In areas where there were few white settlers and not much mineral wealth, pure repression seemed very expensive indeed for the metropolitan power. Almost immediately, Britain and France decided to mix repression with political and economic concession. As the pressure continued, the investment in education and health burgeoned, and the cost of resisting nationalism mounted steadily. There came a point at which the costs of maintaining the territory became greater than those of letting it go. This was reinforced by the following consideration: if in the late nineteenth century one of the motives of establishing colonial rule was the establishment by European powers of preemptive monopolies (a game which, if one plays, all must play), so it was in the later period that if one goes (decolonizes), others are pressured to go (and also are more willing to go). The various European powers began to discover the economics of neocolonialism and slowly became aware that, under certain conditions, it made economic sense to pull out. These conditions involved an accord with the urban educated elite of a transfer of power to them in return for a continued involvement in the ex-colonial international economic network. When they realized this fact (a realization which occurred at different moments for different powers), they shifted their policy.

Great Britain took the lead. Independence of the Indian subcontinent and the gradual withdrawal from the Middle East was matched by early moves to decolonize the Anglo-Egyptian Sudan and British West Africa. Successive constitutional reforms culminated in independence for the Sudan in 1956, and for the Gold Coast in 1957. The constitutional path was slower in Nigeria because of the split in the nationalist movement, reinforced by the establishment of a federal system in 1951. However, regional self-government was achieved in 1956 and independence in 1960.

In British East and Central Africa, constitutional reform was complicated by the presence of white settlers. Particularly in Kenya and Southern Rhodesia the settlers intended that whatever devolution of powers might occur should go to them as a group rather than to the black majority. Indeed, to ensure that this was so, white settlers sought to achieve federations of the strong settler territory with its immediate neighbors, among other reasons lest power be turned over to black Africans in the neighbors and thus affect by example the settler territories. In East Africa, the federation was to bring together settler-dominated Kenya with Uganda and Tanganyika. In Central Africa, it was to bring together settler-dominated Southern Rhodesia with Northern Rhodesia and Nyasaland. The federation idea ran aground in East Africa because of spirited resistance in Uganda (leading to the exile of the Kabaka of Buganda, an important traditional ruler, from 1953 to 1955) and the outbreak of Mau Mau insurrection in Kenya in 1952. However, Central Africa was more fertile ground, and in 1953 the British established the Federation of the Rhodesias and Nyasaland. As a result, African nationalists in Nyasaland and Northern Rhodesia had to seek withdrawal from and dissolution of the Federation as a prerequisite to their own independence (such dissolution being accomplished only in 1963).

The French government at first was deeply resistant to the idea of independence or self-government in any form. Algeria had known violent repression in 1945. Madagascar was the scene of a bloody rebellion in 1947. The Ivory Coast had its famous "incidents" in 1949. Tunisia had *fellaghas* (guerrillas) beginning in 1953. The Sultan of Morocco was deported because of his nationalist sympathies in 1953. It was only in 1954, the year of the Geneva Accords on Indochina, that the French government, then led by Pierre Mendès-France, granted internal autonomy to Tunisia. This led to independence for both Tunisia and Morocco in 1956. Part of the reason for the rapidity, however, was the desire to resist decolonization in Algeria, where the war for independence had begun in late 1954. The combination of the Algerian war and the imminent independence of the Gold Coast (Ghana) helped to push the French to a willingness to grant limited self-government to French black Africa and Madagascar under the Loi-Cadre of 1956 which became full autonomy under the De Gaulle referendum of 1958 (except Guinea, which opted for independence) and then to independence for 14 separate states in 1960.

The accelerating pace affected other colonial powers as well. Italy, as a defeated Axis power in World War II, had little choice. The United Nations had already decided in 1949 that Libya would become independent in 1951 and Somalia in 1960. Belgium was directly affected by the French developments. It was only in 1956 that the political future of the Congo became a matter for public discussion and only in January, 1959, following the granting of autonomy to neighboring French Congo, that the first serious political troubles occurred in the Congo. The haunting example of Algeria led the Belgians to concede rapidly and grant independence on June 30, 1960.

Thus when Harold Macmillan, then prime minister of the United Kingdom, told the Houses of Parliament of the Union of South Africa on February 3, 1960, that a "wind of change" was sweeping Africa, his hearers were shocked at the unwelcome statement but not unaware of what he was talking about. At the United Nations, 1960 was called the Year of Africa because 14 former French colonies, the Belgian Congo, Somalia, and Nigeria all achieved independence (and admission to the UN) that year. Independence had taken the form of a downward sweep of the continent: Libya in 1951; Tunisia, Morocco, and the Sudan in 1956; Ghana in 1957; Guinea in 1958; virtually the whole of the northern half of the continent by 1960 (with the notable exception of Algeria).

Furthermore, in the course of this downward sweep, pan-Africanism had gained much ground. In April of 1958 the first Conference of Independent African States was convened at Accra, in Ghana. The eight then-independent states committed themselves to joint international activity, in the United Nations and elsewhere, on behalf of African liberation movements. And what is striking is that this grouping bridged black and Arab Africa for the first time in a significant way. This conference was followed in December, 1958, by a nongovernmental All-African People's Conference, also in Accra, which brought together political leaders and trade unions from all over the continent, from both independent and colonized states, even including the Union of South Africa.

Thus, 1960 was a highpoint of achievement and optimism for African nationalism. Yet it is also a turning point away from optimism, for it saw the outbreak of the Congo troubles, the first internal crisis of major proportions in an independent African state and one which had direct consequences for the liberation of southern Africa, for African unity, and for the role of outside powers on the African continent.

Within the first month of the Congo's independence, its army rebelled, Katanga province seceded, the Belgians invaded, and the Congo appealed for UN assistance, which it got in the form of contingents of troops from a large number of countries, including many African states. By September the governing alliance in the Congo had split, two rival groups claiming to be the legitimate government. By November, each group controlled substantial territory of the Congo (and Katanga still was governed by the secessionist regime). It was not until mid-1961 that the two claimants to central power were fused, and only in December, 1962, was the Katangese secession definitively put down. In the meantime, and in many ways because of the Congo crisis, the African world changed.

The whites of southern Africa took heart and decided to halt the downward sweep of African liberation. Its thrust was still strong enough to bring about the independence of six more countries in East and Central Africa from 1961 to 1964, but the movement rapidly decelerated. An alliance came to be forced in the so-called white redoubt of southern Africa between South Africa (since 1961 a republic and not a member of the Commonwealth), the white regime in Southern Rhodesia, and Portugal (concerned for Angola and Mozambique).

The Congolese crisis affected the United States, drawing the nation into African affairs with a new intensity. Until 1960 the United States played the role of the benign, mildly anticolonial outsider. After 1960 it was to become the most influential outside power on the African continent and one whose benignity many Africans would contest.

The independent states of Africa, faced with the two-way split in the central governments of the Congo, were forced to take sides. They grouped themselves into two blocs, each supporting one faction in the Congo but proceeding from there to positions on other issues, such as Algeria and the Cold War. The "radical" bloc was known as the Casablanca group, the more "moderate" as the Monrovia group. This split among African independent states broke the African unity which had been created between 1958 and 1960. Once the Congolese split was temporarily healed in 1961 and Algeria received its independence in 1962 it was possible for the Casablanca and Monrovia groups to merge into the Organization of African Unity (OAU) at Addis Ababa in May, 1963, but the basis of compromise was fragile.

The Congo merely crystallized this split among Africans; it did not create it. The independence of a large number of African states meant that the nationalist movements, now in power, had to make decisions, opt for solutions, make both internal political choices and international alliances. In the majority of cases, the leadership of the nationalist movement represented an urban educated elite who saw the end of colonial rule as a removal of the barriers they had felt to their own advancement in terms of political power and economic rewards. They were quite content to reap the rewards of their struggle, rewards which were likely to be far more ample in the immediate future if good economic relations were maintained with ex-colonial powers and the developed world in general.

For some nationalists this attitude was a betrayal of previous ideals and promises: it would replace colonialism with neocolonialism. This postindependence split was made more acute by the fact that those with the more radical vision retained power in some independent states. Thus the split was not only within independent states but between states. Furthermore, similar groups in neighboring countries were in contact one with the other. The links of radical groups, in power in one country and out of power in another, led quickly to charges by some of the Monrovia states of "subversion." In the polarization initiated by the Congo issue, these charges became a major bone of contention between certain African independent states.

A second source of contention was support for independence movements in nonindependent African states. The Casablanca states gave high priority to political and military aid to liberation movements, and resented the more limited and often only verbal support such movements found in many of the Monrovia states.

The compromise of the OAU was essentially that the Casablanca powers renounced their "subversive" support of opposition movements in Monrovia states in return for a more active commitment by Monrovia powers to African liberation movements in southern Africa. A special African Liberation Committee (ALC) was established under the OAU to coordinate financial and military assistance to liberation movements. This compromise, however, soon became obsolete. The independent states began to run into more serious internal difficulties than "subversion," and it took more than the ALC to liberate southern Africa.

The internal political difficulties of contemporary independent African states derived from two aspects of their situation which became increasingly evident as the first euphoria of achieving sovereignty wore off. One was the fragility of the state machinery. Armed with brief histories as nation-states and consequently thin national solidarities, and faced with severe economic problems, many citizens—*especially* the educated ones—fell back on ethnic (so-called tribal) solidarities to assure their protection and advancement as individuals. This led to nepotism, ethnic riots, and secessionist movements. It has made these states susceptible to outside political pressure. No African nation was exempt from this phenomenon.

Second, there was the uncertainty of state revenues. Demands for state expenditures for education, job creation, infrastructure, and welfare grew steadily while revenue did not keep pace, partly because of a relative decline in world commodity prices and partly because a reduction of East-West tension resulted in cuts in foreign aid, loans, and subsidized purchase prices. As a result the state budgets suffered an increasing gap which led to internal squeezes.

Neither conservative nor radical regimes were able to cope with these dilemmas adequately. The result was a series of coups, yet the new regimes coped with the problems no better than their predecessors. The successor regimes tended, however, not to be radical ones.

Thus, the period beginning in 1963 has seen coups, attempted coups, mutinies, and plots in almost every African nation—French-speaking or English-speaking, North, West, Central, and East. In the process, there

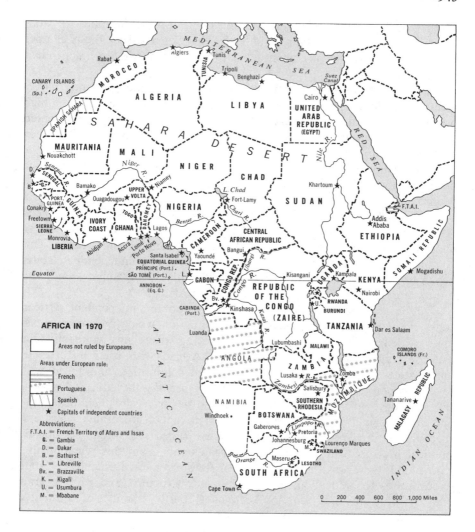

AFRICA IN 1970

Areas not ruled by Europeans

Areas under European rule:

French

Portuguese

Spanish

★ Capitals of independent countries

Abbreviations:
F.T.A.I. = French Territory of Afars and Issas
G. = Gambia
D. = Dakar
B. = Bathurst
L. = Libreville
Bv. = Brazzaville
K. = Kigali
U. = Usumbura
M. = Mbabane

occurred the second Congo crisis from late 1963 through early 1965 which threatened the existence of the OAU; the downfall of "radical" regimes in Ghana and Mali; and the series of tragedies that have plagued Nigeria, Africa's most populous state (two military coups, riots, the secession of Biafra, civil war). As crisis piled on crisis, it became very difficult for the African states to devote much attention to liberating southern Africa.

Meanwhile, the plans of the OAU's African Liberation Committee were repeatedly frustrated. They had hoped that Portugal would give up its colonies with the application of a little force. They had hoped that Great Britain would bring Southern Rhodesia to independence under majority rule. They had hoped that the World Court would rule that South Africa had violated its mandate in Southwest Africa. They had hoped that, eventually, the collapse of these "buffer" units would permit a successful revolution in South Africa. Instead, Portugal resisted strongly the armed revolts in Angola, Portuguese Guinea, and Mozambique. The white settlers of Rhodesia made a "unilateral declaration of independence" in 1965 and the British failed to use force to stop them. (A UN economic boycott has proved ineffectual.) The World Court threw out the Southwest Africa case on a technicality in 1966. South Africa not only severely repressed its underground movements; it even began to acquire black client states in independent Africa. Liberation movements in southern Africa had to retrench for the long haul.

Thus, Africa saw a moment of very swift change, particularly around 1960. Many states came to independence. This rapid change of the political map was made possible by a particular conjuncture of a favorable international climate (East-West competition) and accumulated African frustration, which had ripened into revolutionary zeal.

Independence released and appeased those frustrations. It has, to be sure, created new, even worse ones, but these have not yet ripened. And the international climate has become less permissive for Africa since 1960. The continent has entered into a phase of internal difficulties which are largely cordoned off and ignored by the rest of the world. This phase will probably last until the internal strains become more intolerable and the world system becomes less able to contain African eruptions.

For Further Reading

Davidson, Basil, *Which Way Africa?*
Green, Reginald, and Ann Seidman, *Unity or Poverty? The Economics of Pan-Africanism.*
Wallerstein, Immanuel, *Africa: The Politics of Unity.*

33   The New Asia

Since World War II, Asia* has undergone profound changes. The war itself resulted in a drastic restructuring of power relations in the region. It also released forces which have subsequently changed the face of Asia and fundamentally altered its role in world affairs.

* For the purposes of this discussion, "Asia" is understood to mean the countries stretching from Korea to Pakistan.

A.D. 1945 Dropping of first atomic bombs; Soviet entry in the Pacific war; Japanese surrender and the end of World War II in Asia

1946 Unsuccessful U.S. attempt to mediate Nationalist-Communist conflict in China and renewal of Chinese civil war; independence of the Philippines

1947 Independence of India and Pakistan

1948 Independence of Burma; outbreak of Communist-led rebellions in Burma and several other Southeast Asian areas; assassination of Gandhi in India

1949 Communist victory over Chiang Kai-shek's regime in China and establishment of the People's Republic of China under Mao Tse-tung; independence of Indonesia under Sukarno

1950 Sino-Soviet alliance; outbreak of Korean War

1951 Japanese peace treaty and U.S.–Japan security treaty; start of Korean peace negotiations at Panmunjom; India's first Five-Year Plan

1953 Truce in Korea; China's first Five-Year Plan; election of Magsaysay as president of the Philippines

1954 Geneva Conference and French withdrawal from Indochina; establishment of SEATO (Southeast Asia Treaty Organization)

1955 Bandung Conference of Asian-African leaders; start of U.S.–China Geneva-Warsaw talks

1957 Malayan independence; Sukarno's introduction of "guided democracy" in Indonesia; revolt in Sumatra and outer islands of Indonesia

---

In the years since 1945, Asia has been swept by political and social revolutions. The colonial and traditional regimes that existed before the war have been replaced by a wide variety of new states. And powerful new forces—nationalism, Communism, the drive for self-determination, and demands for social change—have shaped the development of the region.

Processes of modernization and economic growth have also accelerated. Most of the new leaders in Asia are dedicated to social change, rather than to the preservation of tradition-rooted values. The drag of tradition

1958   "Great Leap Forward" in China; "offshore islands" crisis
       on China coast
1959   Tibetan revolt; Chinese-Indian border incidents
1960   Open debate in Sino-Soviet relations; renewed conflict in
       Vietnam; revision of the U.S.-Japan security treaty
1962   China-India border conflict; Geneva Conference on Laos;
       Ne Win coup d'état in Burma
1964   China's first nuclear test; death of Nehru; Indonesian
       "confrontation" with Malaysia
1965   Attempted Communist coup in Indonesia, resulting in
       military control under Suharto; major U.S. intervention
       in Vietnam; India-Pakistan conflict over Kashmir
1966   "Great Proletarian Cultural Revolution" and purge of Liu
       Shao-chi in China; opening of Asian Development Bank;
       founding of ASPAC (Asian and Pacific Council)
1967   Founding of ASEAN (Association of Southeast Asian Na-
       tions)
1968   Cessation of U.S. bombing of North Vietnam and start of
       Paris negotiations on Vietnam
1969   Sino-Soviet border conflict; Nixon's "Guam Doctrine";
       U.S. agreement with Sato government on the return of
       Okinawa to Japan; death of Ho Chi Minh in North Viet-
       nam; growth of Japanese gross national product makes
       Japan third-largest economy in the world
1970   Overthrow of Sihanouk and U.S. military intervention in
       Cambodia
1971   Announcement of planned Nixon trip to Peking

---

has been strong, however, and the gap between aspirations and accomplishments has in many places created frustration, instability, and conflict.

Despite the instability of the region, and the enormous internal problems facing Asian countries, most of the new nations have been incorporated into the Western-created international system. (Communist China,
however, has been only partially absorbed into the system. The United
States and a sizable number of other non-Communist nations have not yet
recognized the Peking regime, and the regime has only recently gained

United Nations membership. It has, though, established diplomatic relations with approximately fifty Communist and non-Communist states.) In a variety of ways, the new nations are increasingly active participants in world politics.

In the power balance in Asia itself, two countries, one Asian and one Western, emerged into dominant roles in the postwar period. The hostile confrontation between these two—Communist China and the United States —has, for most of the period, been the most important single influence shaping the configuration of power relations in the region. Mainland China, genuinely unified for the first time in a half-century, and ruled by a Communist regime, has attempted to assert its regional primacy and has called for world-wide Communist revolution. The United States, victorious in World War II, and directly involved in Asia as never before, has attempted to maintain the power balance in Asia, "contain" China, and combat the spread of Communism. In the latter 1960's, however, the power balance became increasingly complex. Japan began to reemerge as a potent economic power, and the Soviet Union, partly as a result of its disputes with China, increased its diplomatic activity in the region. As a result, a multipolar four-power balance seemed to be emerging.

The extent of revolutionary changes in Asia can be grasped only if one compares the situation of today with that which prevailed prior to World War II. Before the war, most of Asia was dominated by external powers, first by Western nations, and then by Japan, which rose to challenge the West and attempted to conquer much of Asia in the process.

European colonial nations, most notably Britain, France, and the Netherlands, controlled almost all of South and Southeast Asia. (Only Thailand was able to preserve its independence by playing the French and British against each other.) While embryonic nationalist movements had begun to grow in the region, they were still weak and ineffective. The United States had projected its power into part of the area, as a result of the Spanish-American War, and it ruled the Philippine Islands; however, it had promised to grant independence to the Philippines—although this promise was yet to be fulfilled.

Russia, which had expanded steadily eastward throughout the nineteenth century, had encroached on all of China's borderlands and established firm control in eastern Siberia and the Maritime Provinces. Its expansionist drive in northeast Asia had been blocked by Japan, but after the Bolshevik revolution its Communist government still exerted pressures at many points on China's periphery. It also attempted to stimulate Communist revolutions in many Asian countries; except in China, however, Communist movements had achieved little success prior to World War II.

China had been able to maintain a precarious independence, despite internal decay and external pressure, but it was already undergoing a process of revolutionary change. The impact of the West in the nineteenth century had helped to undermine the 2,000-year-old Chinese imperial system, and following the collapse of the Manchu dynasty in 1911, the country was weak and divided. Both the Western powers and Japan competed for influence in China and severely compromised its sovereignty. However, the nationalist movement led by the Kuomintang, which came to power in the late 1920's, had begun to unify and modernize the country, even though it faced a serious internal challenge from the Communists and from 1937 on was engaged in a fight for survival against Japanese aggression.

Japan was the only Asian nation which, in response to the nineteenth-century impact of the West, had been able not only to preserve its independence but also to carry out a program of rapid modernization. As it built up its industrial and military strength, it first joined the Western powers in their imperialist encroachments on the Asian mainland (in the process defeating China and Russia, in wars fought, respectively, in 1894–1895 and 1904–1905), then embarked on a major war against China in 1937, and finally, in 1941, decided to challenge both the United States in the Pacific and the European powers in Southeast Asia.

Both Japan's initial successes against the Western powers in the war, and then its ultimate defeat, fundamentally altered the character of Asia as it had existed before 1941. It is no exaggeration, in fact, to say that out of the war there emerged a new Asia.

For a brief period Japan expelled the Western powers from Asia and controlled a large part of the region from Korea to Burma, but by 1945 Japan itself was devastated and prostrate. Occupied by American troops, it was forced to give up its imperial pretensions, disarm, and draw into its home islands.

China, although a victorious power, emerged from the war gravely weakened and internally divided. Even though the Nationalist government was initially able, with American support, to reassert control over China's major cities, it faced a major challenge from the Chinese Communists, who during the war had built a powerful peasant-based revolutionary army and controlled most of the countryside in north China. Despite American efforts to mediate the Kuomintang-Communist conflict, China was plunged into open civil war in 1946.

The United States, whose military forces had been primarily responsible for Japan's defeat in the Pacific, found itself in the immediate postwar situation as the only real power in most of the region. As the occupier of Japan and South Korea, and the unsuccessful mediator of civil conflict in

China, it was drawn deeply into Asian political affairs. Except where American power was exerted, the region was in many respects a power vacuum.

The Soviet Union, which had entered the Pacific war in its closing days, was able, however, to reinject itself into the power equation in Asia, at least to a degree. It temporarily occupied China's Manchurian provinces and North Korea, and while promising to support the Chinese Nationalist government, it proceeded to give indirect support to the Communists in their struggle against the Nationalists.

In Southeast Asia, although the United States fulfilled its pledge to grant independence to the Philippines, the European powers at first attempted to reestablish prewar patterns of colonial rule. They soon discovered, however, that they were incapable of doing so. The strong anticolonial, nationalist movements which had sprung up throughout the region during the war were led by men who demanded immediate independence.

Similar nationalist movements had developed in South Asia, and by 1947 Britain, acquiescing in the face of the new forces, began granting independence, to India, Pakistan, Burma, and Ceylon. In Southeast Asia, however, the Dutch and French were less willing to recognize the revolutionary changes that had taken place, and it was not until they had fought bitter, unsuccessful, colonial conflicts that they agreed to withdraw from Indonesia, in 1949, and Indochina, in 1954. (The Geneva Conference which ended the French-Vietnamese struggle left Indochina divided; Laos and Cambodia were separated from Vietnam, and Vietnam was divided at the 17th parallel between Communist and non-Communist regimes.)

The struggles between the Dutch and Indonesians, and between French and Vietnamese, were by no means, however, the only conflicts which kept much of Asia in turmoil in the immediate postwar years. Many conflicts occurred between competing Asian leaders and groups. While nationalism was clearly the predominant new social-political force in the emerging nations, Communism was a strong competitor, and in the late 1940's Communist parties attempted to seize power through violent struggles in many Asian countries.

In China, after full-scale civil war erupted in 1946, the Communists—who already controlled large areas of the country and constituted, in effect, a state within a state—soon achieved major military successes in Manchuria and north China. Weakened by disintegrative processes that had sapped its vitality during World War II, the Nationalist regime deteriorated rapidly. By 1948, the balance of military power in the struggle shifted in the Communists' favor, and by the fall of 1949 they had achieved control over most of the country. The Nationalists under Chiang Kai-shek retreated to Taiwan (Formosa), where they continued to maintain a competitive regime which still exists today—a de facto separate regime which claims to be the government of China but has no prospect of regaining control of the China mainland.

In October, 1949, the Communists set up a new regime in Peking, the People's Republic of China headed by Mao Tse-tung. It immediately established relations with the other Communist states (except Yugoslavia) and in February, 1950, signed a thirty-year Treaty of Friendship, Alliance, and Mutual Assistance with the Soviet Union. As Mao put it, China "leaned to one side." The basic realignment of China's entire international position which this involved had a great and immediate impact not only on Asia but on the entire world balance.

During this same period, Communist parties in many other parts of Asia challenged the new non-Communist nationalist leaders and made their own bids for power. In fact, during 1948, with Soviet encouragement, Communist rebellions broke out or were intensified throughout much of South and Southeast Asia—in Indonesia, Malaya, Burma, the Philippines, and India, as well as in Indochina. The Chinese Communist regime, after it was established, gave strong moral support to these insurrections.

For a period of time, the Communists threatened to topple many of the new non-Communist regimes. But eventually it became clear that most Communist parties did not have sufficient support to succeed. Only in Indochina, in fact, were the Communists able to capture a significant part of the nationalist movement. Elsewhere, the insurrectionary struggles ultimately failed, and by 1950–1951 many Asian Communist parties started shifting toward less violent tactics.

Communal strife, based on religious and other cultural differences, also created turmoil in many parts of Asia. Establishment of independent states did not automatically create consensus within the new nations, solve the problems of nation building, or eliminate deep-rooted conflicts within and among them. The most serious of the communal conflicts was the one that broke out between Hindus and Muslims in India and Pakistan at the time of independence in 1947. It left a residue of bitterness which has caused tensions in that area ever since.

In the context of both the instability which characterized the new Asia in the early postwar years and the Cold War between the Communist and non-Communist nations that had already started in Europe, the establishment in 1949 of a strong, dynamic, and militant Communist regime in China, allied with the Soviet Union and openly proclaiming its belief in world-wide revolution, had a disruptive impact. The new sense of threat in Asia felt by many non-Communist nations was then magnified when, in mid-1950, Communist North Korea, with Soviet backing, launched an attack on South Korea.

The Korean War was a major turning point in the postwar history of

Asia. During 1949 and early 1950, the United States appeared to be disengaging its power from any involvement in the affairs of the Asian mainland. It had dissociated itself from the defense of the Chinese Nationalist regime on Taiwan and was "letting the dust settle," apparently in preparation for ultimate recognition of the new Chinese Communist regime.

The Korean War fundamentally changed the situation. Not only did the United States and other United Nations forces go to the defense of South Korea; Washington also announced its intention to "neutralize" the Taiwan Strait, thereby preventing Communist takeover of Taiwan and reengaging American forces in the Chinese conflict. Then, after Chinese Communist troops crossed the Yalu River in late 1950, the major fighting in Korea was between Chinese and American forces.

The Korean War stimulated the United States to rearm and to start building a network of military alliances in Asia, designed to "contain" China and check any further expansion of Communist control or influence. Between 1951 and 1954 military pacts were signed between the United States and Japan (a peace treaty, without Chinese participation, was also concluded with Japan in 1951), the Philippines, South Korea, and Nationalist China, and in 1954 the multilateral Southeast Asia Treaty Organization (SEATO) was formed, including Thailand, the Philippines, Pakistan, the United Kingdom, Australia, New Zealand, and France, as well as the United States.

The war also left a heritage of mutual suspicion and enmity in both the United States and Communist China. The United States evolved a policy of "pressure and diplomatic isolation" directed against Peking, and the main elements of this policy—nonrecognition of the Chinese Communist regime, opposition to its seating in the United Nations, an embargo on all American trade with mainland China, and opposition to other contacts with it—were all to persist long after a truce had brought the fighting in Korea to a halt in 1953.

Only a minority of the new Asian nations were predisposed, however, to join the United States in anti-Communist military alliances or in its efforts to isolate Communist China. Influenced in part by residual anti-colonial feelings which created suspicion of American motives, in part by sympathy for China as an Asian and "socialist" state, and in part by preoccupation with their own internal problems, a majority of Asian states, especially in South and Southeast Asia, chose to adopt a posture of neutralism or nonalignment.

International crises in Asia did not end when the Korean truce was signed in 1953. Almost immediately, attention shifted to Indochina, where the war between the French and the Communist-led Viet Minh (under Ho

Chi Minh) intensified. Both the United States and the Chinese Communists increased their support of the combatants. However, when the fighting reached a high pitch in 1954, the major participants agreed to negotiate. The Geneva Conference held that year resulted in a temporary settlement which, like the one in Korea, halted the fighting but failed to produce a viable political agreement or unification of the country.

In late 1954 and early 1955, Communist China precipitated still another crisis by launching an intense bombardment of the Nationalist-held offshore islands lying near the China coast. When the United States responded by increasing its defensive support of the Nationalists, the crisis gradually abated.

The atmosphere in Asia changed substantially in 1955 when the historic Bandung Conference that met in Indonesia heralded a period of reduced tension, greater moderation in Chinese Communist policies, and increased attempts at collaboration among the Asian and other non-Western countries. The principal leaders of 29 Asian and African nations attended this meeting, where Peking's Premier Chou En-lai, together with Nehru of India, played a leading role. The conference was a dramatic symbol of the rising importance of the new nations in world affairs, but it did not lead to real unity among them. In fact, when a decade later an attempt was made to convene a second such meeting, the effort failed.

The almost uninterrupted series of international crises which kept Asia in a state of high tension during the early 1950's tended to determine the world's image of the region, but many of the most significant developments of the period were actually taking place within the Asian states themselves, rather than in their external relations. Major political, economic, and social transformations were under way, as great efforts were made, in both the non-Communist and the Communist nations, to modernize and spur economic growth.

In their initial years in power, the Communist leaders in China were able, with impressive speed, to unify most of the country and build a totalitarian apparatus of power. They also carried out domestic programs of social revolution and rehabilitated the economy they had inherited. Then, in 1953 they launched China's first Five-Year Plan, modeled on Stalin's plans in the Soviet Union. Under the slogans of "socialization" and "industrialization" they collectivized agriculture, as well as socializing industry and commerce, and initiated a fairly rapid process of growth. On balance this was a period of significant economic achievement in China, during which the economy grew at an average rate of 6 to 8 per cent a year (in GNP), and industrial output more than doubled.

Serious problems remained unsolved, however, as agricultural output lagged and population soared, and in 1958 the Chinese Communists turned to radical new policies—establishment of communes in the countryside and total mobilization of labor for a "great leap forward" in both agriculture and industry. The failure of these policies created a serious economic crisis during 1959–1961, set China's development program back by several years, and tarnished the Chinese Communist "model" of development, which prior to the "great leap forward" had had a significant impact on many Asian leaders. In contrast with the 1950's, China made little progress economically in the 1960's.

Throughout the 1950's, Communist China was also convulsed by numerous "mass campaigns" designed to reindoctrinate the population and restructure society. These slackened during the post-"leap" crisis, but after 1962 new campaigns were launched, leading to a massive "great proletarian cultural revolution" in 1966. Party chairman Mao Tse-tung, with the backing of some of China's military leaders, including Lin Piao, Peking's minister of defense, mobilized the youth of the country into Red Guards units, to combat "erosion" of the revolution, and to attack the party and government bureaucracies. As it developed, the campaign shattered the unity of the regime's leadership and developed into a major power struggle. Mao purged a large proportion of the regime's top party and government leaders, and the army had to step in to run the country. After the Ninth Party Congress was held in early 1969, efforts were made to reunify the badly disrupted society and rebuild the party, but progress was slow.

Despite Communist China's growing military establishment and international influence, from the late 1950's on, Communist China experienced major setbacks in its foreign as well as domestic policies. At the end of 1957 it abandoned the moderation of the "Bandung period" and put renewed emphasis on revolutionary militancy, precipitating the second offshore islands crisis in 1958, as well as border conflicts with India in 1959 and 1962, and exerting pressure again on many Asian countries on its periphery.

Sino-Soviet relations seriously deteriorated during the late 1950's. This was a result not only of ideological problems and basic differences regarding world strategy (including policy toward the United States) but also of serious clashes of national interests. Moscow, in Chinese eyes, failed to give adequate backing to Peking in both the second offshore islands crisis and the border conflicts with India, and it reneged, the Chinese claimed, on promises to support Peking in its program to develop nuclear weapons. Bitter Sino-Soviet debates broke out in 1960, and by 1963—after the Soviet Union had signed a limited nuclear test ban treaty with the United States—the Chinese and Russians, instead of collaborating, were engaged in intense competition throughout the world Communist movement and the underdeveloped world. The deterioration of Sino-Soviet relations had a great impact on the entire world balance, just as the signing of the Sino-Soviet alliance also had a little more than a decade earlier. By 1969 tension between the two countries was such that border incidents brought them close to war.

In the early 1960's, Peking's interest turned increasingly toward the underdeveloped nations, in Africa and Latin America as well as Asia, but during 1965–1966 China experienced serious setbacks in these regions too, and found itself increasingly isolated internationally. Its loss of prestige from these developments was only partially offset by its success in exploding its first nuclear device in 1964. During the "cultural revolution," in the latter 1960's, China retreated into fairly extreme isolation. In 1969, however, it began to look outward again and renew its diplomatic activity abroad. Then, in early 1971, Peking adopted a dramatically new and more flexible policy toward the United States and invited President Nixon to visit Peking.

Japan, during most of these years, was largely insulated from the violence and conflict that afflicted so much of the rest of Asia, but it too underwent internal transformations which, though peaceful, were in many respects no less significant. During the American occupation, many reforms were introduced, with the aim of democratizing as well as demilitarizing Japanese society. Equally important, as the Cold War developed, and the United States began treating the Japanese as allies rather than defeated enemies, Japan was able to repair the wartime damage to its economy, and then it rapidly rebuilt Japan into a modern, industrialized nation of the first rank.

In the mid-1950's, despite some American pressure on Japan to rearm, strong pacifist tendencies and constitutional barriers to rearmament led successive Japanese governments to rely primarily on American power for their national security. Left-wing groups strongly opposed Japan's security treaty with the United States, and some Japanese groups favored moves toward neutralism, but the conservative governments in power argued for continued reliance on American forces for protection; this enabled Japan to limit its defense expenditures to a minimum and greatly facilitated the growth of its civilian economy. In the latter 1960's, however, Japanese defense forces did grow somewhat, and debate on security policies increased. Nevertheless, the Liberal Democratic government in power signed the treaty barring nuclear proliferation, and opposition in Japan to major rearmament remained strong.

The economic growth rate in Japan in the latter 1950's and 1960's, which was one of the highest in the world, was nothing short of phenomenal. The Japanese themselves referred to it as an "economic miracle." As a consequence, living standards rose significantly, and Japan enjoyed a high degree of domestic political tranquillity. Despite the existence of a strong socialist opposition to the government and considerable disaffection among intellectuals, Communism remained a relatively weak force.

Abroad, the expansion of Japan's foreign trade and aid paralleled the growth of its domestic economy, and Japan became a major force in the world economy. In the 1950's and early 1960's, the Japanese were slow to try to reassert any major political role in international affairs. Closely tied to the United States, both by the Japanese-American security treaty and by trade, Tokyo generally followed Washington's lead on foreign policy issues. Like the United States, for example, it pursued a nonrecognition policy toward Peking, although it did promote trade and nonofficial contacts with Communist China. It was cautious about trying to assert any role of political leadership in Asia. In the latter 1960's, however, Japanese leaders were groping toward a more independent foreign policy, and it seemed likely that even without major remilitarization they would gradually assume, because of their great economic power and growing political influence, a role of greater leadership in non-Communist Asia. The return of Okinawa by the United States to Japan in 1969 symbolized Japan's search for a more independent posture.

In contrast with China, India after independence created a Western-type constitutional regime and adopted moderate democratic, socialist methods to pursue its goals of modernization and economic growth. Like China, and unlike Japan, however, it had to struggle with enormous domestic problems created by extreme poverty, agricultural backwardness, and a population lacking many of the skills essential for modern development. Under the leadership of Jawaharlal Nehru and the Congress party, it made some impressive gains, but accomplishments clearly lagged behind aspirations.

The heritage of British legal and administrative skills was a great asset to independent India, but this fact alone did not provide easy answers or automatic solutions to the country's enormous difficulties, political as well as economic. Huge refugee problems and Hindu-Muslim communal strife plagued the government right after independence, and the tasks of creating a unified nation, coping with linguistic regionalism and other divisive forces, and finding a viable balance between political centralization and decentralization posed continuing challenges.

In 1951, nevertheless, the Indian government was able to launch the first in a series of five-year development plans. Compared with the Chinese development program, India's plans placed greater stress on voluntarism and democratic methods, improvement of consumer welfare, and a balance between agriculture and industry as well as between state and private enterprise. While the pace of development in India was slower than that in

China in the 1950's, it avoided the kind of social upheaval that Chinese policies produced and did not encounter major setbacks comparable to those which resulted in China from the failure of the Communists' most radical policies, such as the "great leap forward." Even though progress in India took place at a relatively moderate rate, it nevertheless was impressive in many respects. It did not, however, produce immediate solutions to such basic problems as the nation's insufficiency of food and the necessity to rely on large-scale foreign economic assistance.

In foreign affairs, India's most immediate and pressing problem following independence was its dispute with Pakistan over control of Kashmir, which periodically erupted into open conflict, in both the 1950's and the 1960's. (When Pakistan, which had received large-scale American military assistance in the 1950's, concluded that the United States would not help it assert its claims to Kashmir, it turned in the 1960's increasingly toward Communist China for support.) Civil conflict erupted in East Pakistan in 1971 and the resulting flow of refugees to India created severe new strains in Indian-Pakistan relations, posing the danger of war.

On the broader world stage, India pursued a policy of nonalignment, dissociated itself from the Cold War, and attempted to promote "peaceful coexistence." It was particularly insistent, until 1959, on the need to establish friendly relations with Communist China. Under Nehru, who emerged as perhaps the most influential world-wide spokesman for the neutralist nations, India was able to play a far larger role in international affairs than its actual economic and military strength warranted.

India's hopes for friendship with Communist China, and for Sino-Indian collaboration in promoting world-wide "peaceful coexistence," were rudely shattered, however, when serious clashes took place on the Sino-Indian border in 1959 and 1962, and Peking adopted an openly hostile attitude toward the New Delhi government. The Chinese Communists simultaneously took steps to try to improve relations with all of India's neighbors—Pakistan, Afghanistan, Nepal, Burma, and Ceylon—in an effort to isolate India politically and reduce its international influence. These developments, and the death of Nehru, caused a significant decline in India's international prestige. Within India, hostility toward China grew, and apprehension about a potential threat from the north took its place, alongside the problem of relations with Pakistan, as a major continuing preoccupation of Indian policymakers. In response to the new situation, the Indian government, while still proclaiming its faith in nonalignment, fostered closer relations with both the Soviet Union and the United States, and looked to both for greater economic and military support. In 1971 relations between India and the U.S. deteriorated but India and the Soviet Union signed a 20-year friendship pact.

The most volatile and unstable region in Asia during most of the postwar period was neither Northeast Asia nor South Asia, but Southeast Asia. During the first two decades after the war, insurrections, coups d'état, and wars were endemic in the region and affected almost every Southeast Asian state.

Vietnam (formerly part of Indochina) was the prime focus of major military conflict which involved the great powers as well as local contestants for power. The uneasy truce between the Communist north and non-Communist south that resulted from the Geneva Conference of 1954 lasted for only a brief period. In the late 1950's and early 1960's the Communist-led Vietcong and National Liberation Front renewed the struggle in the south, with substantial and growing support from North Vietnam in the form of men and supplies. Before long the conflict posed a real threat to the continued existence of the non-Communist regime in the south, and in response to this situation the United States greatly increased its level of intervention, especially from 1965 on, pouring large numbers of American troops into South Vietnam and initiating bombing raids on the north to reduce its flow of aid. Both Communist China and the Soviet Union countered with increased material assistance to North Vietnam, although they were unable to cooperate effectively in doing so and both refrained from open intervention with their own forces. Over time the intensity of the conflict mounted. Many attempts were made to find a basis for a negotiated settlement, and after the United States halted its bombing of North Vietnam in October, 1968, negotiations were initiated in Paris, but as of mid-1971 no substantial progress had been made. Mounting casualties in Vietnam and growing antiwar sentiment at home led President Lyndon Johnson to decide in 1968 not to run for reelection. After Richard Nixon assumed the presidency, he began a gradual withdrawal of U.S. troops under a policy of "Vietnamization." He also put forward his "Guam Doctrine," or "Nixon Doctrine," calling for reduced American military responsibilities in Asia. Partly as a result, the Vietnam War became a less intense political issue in 1969. When, after a coup in Cambodia overthrew Prince Norodom Sihanouk, Nixon ordered United States troops into Cambodia, antiwar sentiment broke out again with even greater intensity, and Cambodia became more deeply involved in the war. However, as the withdrawal of American forces proceeded in 1970–71, fighting declined to a low level. But the prospects for a political settlement remained uncertain as of mid-1971.

In Laos, a similar conflict between Communist and non-Communist forces destroyed the tranquillity of this small, isolated nation; it too involved the major powers. In the early 1950's the Communist-led Pathet Lao, with North Vietnamese support, seized control of two northern provinces in Laos and initiated an insurrectionary struggle against the existing non-Communist government. A temporary settlement that would have incorporated the Pathet Lao into the government was agreed upon in 1957, but by 1959 the conflict was renewed, with the Russians and Chinese giving assistance to one side and the Americans providing support on the other. To deal with the crisis a new Geneva Conference was convened in 1962; its participants signed agreements calling for guarantees of Laos' independence and neutrality, and the major Laotian factions agreed to the formation of a coalition government. Despite these agreements, the struggle for power soon broke out again, and the Pathet Lao seized sizable portions of the country. The government was able to prevent a Communist takeover, however, and the struggle continued, although at a relatively low level of violence by comparison with the war in Vietnam. By 1971, however, the future of Laos seemed dependent mainly on the outcome of the Vietnam War, and the direction of future American policy.

Elsewhere in Southeast Asia, the Communist insurrections which had taken place in the late 1940's and early 1950's in Burma, Malaya, and the Philippines were effectively brought under control by the mid-1950's, but almost every small country in the area faced recurring threats to its stability. However, faced by the twin dangers of potential subversion at home and increased influence exerted by a powerful and militant Communist China to the north, they responded in a variety of ways.

Thailand decided to abandon its traditional neutrality and aligned openly with the United States. It joined SEATO—the only mainland Southeast Asian nation to do so—and when the United States intervened in Vietnam on a large scale, Thailand cooperated by providing air bases to the American forces. By 1970, however, when it appeared that an eventual reduction of the United States military role in Asia was likely, the Thais began to show increased interest in broadening relations with the other major powers. At home, ruled by a conservative monarchy and military dictatorship, Thailand escaped much of the social upheaval characteristic of the region, although it was troubled by localized Communist-led guerrilla activity—in the north and northeast of the country, and in the south on the Malayan border. In the latter 1960's Peking gave strong moral support to these guerrillas, but Chinese material support remained limited.

Cambodia, also led by a conservative government under Prince Sihanouk, resisted internal change and was successful in maintaining a fairly high level of domestic stability. But, fearful of pressures from its immediate neighbors—South Vietnam and Thailand—it sought security by proclaiming its neutralism and at the same time establishing closer ties with Communist China. For many years Sihanouk succeeded in surviving politically, preserving Cambodia's independence, and insulating most of Cambodia from the conflicts in neighboring Vietnam and Laos, but to do so he allowed the North Vietnamese to create military sanctuaries in Cambodia. In 1970 he was overthrown by a coup. United States and South Vietnamese forces then intervened in Cambodia to attack North Vietnamese positions, while Sihanouk, with Chinese political support, set up an exile government. By mid-1971 Cambodia had become increasingly involved in the Vietnam War.

The government of Burma was harassed throughout the 1950's by many internal challenges, from a variety of separatist as well as Communist groups, and from Chinese pressures on its border as well. Frustrated by the ineffectiveness of civilian-led democratic institutions, General Ne Win staged a coup d'état in 1962 and established a military government. Thereafter, Burma not only reaffirmed its long-standing neutralism but retreated into extreme isolation, attempting to minimize its contacts with both the Communist and the non-Communist powers. Domestically, it attempted to implement its own brand of "socialism" under a strict military dictatorship.

Malaya, for most of the decade prior to achieving independence in 1957, was preoccupied with the task of defeating a major Communist insurrection. Thereafter, under Tunku Abdul Rahman, it achieved considerable success in creating a functioning democratic political system and fostering economic growth. It still faced major problems at home, however, most notably the problem of improving relations between the Malays and Chinese, the two major ethnic groups in its population, and in the late 1960's renewed Malay-Chinese conflict resulted in a major crisis which led to a temporary suspension of the constitution. (In almost every Southeast Asian country, unassimilated overseas Chinese minorities have exercised economic power out of proportion to their numbers. Southeast Asian governments have imposed many controls on them, and over time pressures for acculturation or assimilation have increased.) In its foreign policy, Malaya—after independence—while avoiding formal membership in any Western-led alliance, continued to rely on British and Commonwealth forces for its protection, particularly against threats from Indonesia, which militantly opposed a plan to create a greater Malaysia incorporating Singapore and part of Borneo. Even after the British decided to withdraw their forces, Kuala Lumpur was able to convince Australia and New Zealand to continue military support. Continuing tensions and problems complicated relations between Malaysia and Singapore, but in the latter 1960's relations between Malaysia and Indonesia greatly improved.

The Philippines, under President Ramon Magsaysay, successfully suppressed the Communist-led Hukbalahap rebellion in the early 1950's, and, like Thailand, it joined SEATO and clearly aligned itself with the United

States. However, despite the fact that its democratic institutions, modeled on those of the United States, introduced democratic processes of government, the government was slow to attack the nation's basic social problems or to mobilize its resources effectively for economic development. In the latter 1960's, in fact, deteriorating conditions were accompanied by renewed insurrectionary activity, which raised basic questions about the future stability of the country.

Indonesia, the largest and potentially the richest nation in Southeast Asia, encountered some of the greatest difficulties in creating a viable state after independence. Under Sukarno, the republic started its existence with high hopes, but ineffective government soon resulted not in progress but in political and economic deterioration. In 1957 Sukarno ended parliamentary democracy and introduced what he called "guided democracy." A major revolt then broke out against the government, in Sumatra and the eastern islands, and it was suppressed only with great difficulty. Thereafter, Sukarno moved increasingly toward personal rule, based on a delicate balance of forces between non-Communist army officers and local Communist leaders (who led a party that was not only the largest organized political group in Indonesia but the largest Communist party in Asia, outside of China).

In his foreign policy, although Sukarno proclaimed a neutralist position, in the late 1950's he became increasingly strident in his denunciations of the United States and other Western "imperialist" powers and greatly strengthened his ties with both Communist China and the Soviet Union. In Southeast Asia he aggressively opposed the plan to create Malaysia, and through his policy of "confrontation" exerted strong pressure against it.

External adventures did not halt the process of deterioration within Indonesia, however. In the fall of 1965 there was an attempted coup d'état in which the Communists tried to seize power. Indonesia's anti-Communist military leaders took over instead, and bloody reprisals throughout the country decimated the Communist party. The new leaders under General Suharto then proceeded to end the "confrontation" policy directed against Malaysia, and slowly eased Sukarno out of power. They also reduced their ties with the Communist countries and restored friendlier relations with the United States. At home they took steps to halt the process of economic decline, and with multilateral foreign economic assistance they were able to make some progress.

In short, two decades after World War II, Asia was still unstable and was still undergoing great changes. Most of Asia now consisted of independent countries, rather than colonial domains, but the new nations varied greatly in their interests, problems, and course of development, and the problems of nation building were enormous.

Not only was Asia divided between Communist and non-Communist countries; among both the Communists and the non-Communists there were tremendous differences. The tendencies toward bipolarity which characterized the 1950's were followed by increasing multipolarity in the 1960's.

New elite groups and political leaders had emerged in every Asian state, and they were all dedicated to political, economic, and social change. However, they looked in many different directions for "models" and inspiration, and each nation was trying to reshape its policy, economy, and society in its own way, drawing on many ideas from both the non-Communist and the Communist nations as well as from their own Asian traditions.

Apart from the leaders in Communist China and its small Asian Communist neighbors, a majority of the new leaders in Asia professed belief in some form of parliamentary democracy comparable to that in the West. But it proved no easy task in many of the tradition-rooted agrarian societies of Asia to transplant Western political forms into settings where some of the most basic prerequisites for effective, stable democracy were lacking. As a result, even though democratic institutions and processes appeared to be taking root in some Asian countries—such as Japan, the Philippines, and Malaya—in others—such as Burma, Indonesia, Thailand, and Korea—when democratic institutions faltered, military coups occurred. Throughout Asia, however—even in the countries ruled by Communist parties or military dictatorships—there was a notable increase in mass political participation.

Throughout Asia, also, modern science and technology were spreading fairly rapidly (in part as a result of vastly expanded mass education), and all the new states, whatever their political system, were attempting to promote processes of economic growth. Industrialization was increasing in many areas, and new seeds and agricultural methods held forth the promise of a "green revolution" that might greatly increase food output. Here again, however, there was great variety in the approaches to development adopted in different countries (even though some form of planning by government authorities became almost universal), and in the degree of success achieved. Not only in Japan, but in a number of other countries as well—including Nationalist China, South Korea, and Malaya—impressive growth rates and rising living standards were actually realized, but in some others—for example, Burma—there was little real success. The two most populous Asian nations—Communist China and India—using very different methods, both initiated significant planned programs of development, but both faced enormous continuing problems in implementing them.

"Asian solidarity"—a powerful slogan in the 1950's—proved to be a will-o'-the-wisp, at least in the short run, as conflicting interests of many sorts continued to divide the states in the region. Some forms of limited regional collaboration among the non-Communist nations of Asia did slowly evolve, however, and in the mid-1960's it appeared as if this trend might become increasingly important.

The most serious unresolved active conflicts in the region were those in the three Indochinese states, Vietnam, Laos, and, as of 1970, Cambodia as well. The future peace and stability of the region depended in considerable part on whether, and how, these conflicts could be resolved.

Relationships between the major powers involved in Asia were undergoing considerable change at the start of the 1970's. Whereas in the 1950's and part of the 1960's the balance was essentially a bipolar one, involving hostile confrontation between Communist China and the United States, as a result of the Sino-Soviet split the balance became increasingly a triangular one in the 1960's, and then, with American talk of partial disengagement and the rapid reemergence of Japan's influence, it seemed destined to become a four-power balance in the 1970's.

By the latter 1960's, war between China and the Soviet Union appeared to be, in some respects, a greater danger than any major U.S.-Chinese conflict. Gradually, there were some signs of reduced tension between the United States and China. Both President Johnson and President Nixon called for greater contacts with the Peking regime. In 1969 the United States reduced its restrictions on China travel and trade. Finally in 1971 Peking and Washington startled the world with the announcement that President Nixon would meet with Chinese leaders in Peking before May 1972. The results of this meeting will have a profound effect on the entire pattern of big power relations in Asia.

In Asia as a whole, the processes of modernization and social change seemed destined to continue, and Asian nations could be expected steadily to emerge into roles of increased international importance. What the trend of events in the period immediately ahead would be seemed to depend on the answers which history would give to a variety of key questions. When and how would the conflicts in the Indochina area end? Would any rapprochement between the United States and China be possible? Could war between China and the Soviet Union be avoided? What role would the Japanese play in the region? Would a four-power balance be stable? Would peaceful cooperation among Asian nations grow? None of these questions can presently be answered with certainty.

For Further Reading

Butwell, Richard, *Southeast Asia Today and Tomorrow—Problems of Political Development.*

Clubb, O. Edmund, *Twentieth Century China.*
Fairbank, John K., *The United States and China.*
Gordon, Bernard K., *The Dimensions of Conflict in Southeast Asia.*
Ho, Ping-ti, and Tsou, Tang (eds.), *China in Crisis.*
Jan, George P. (ed.), *International Politics of Asia: Readings.*
Kahin, George McT. (ed.), *Governments and Politics of Southeast Asia.*
Langer, Paul F., *Japan, Yesterday and Today.*
Mason, Philip (ed.), *India and Ceylon: Unity and Diversity.*
Morris-Jones, Wyndraeth H., *Government and Politics of India.*
Reischauer, Edwin O., *The United States and Japan.*
Schurmann, Franz, and Schell, Orville (eds.), *The China Reader,* Vol. 3:
    Communist China.
Sen Gupta, Bhabani, *The Fulcrum of Asia.*
Tilman, Robert (ed.), *Man, State and Society in Contemporary Southeast Asia.*
Ward, Robert E. (ed.), *Political Development in Modern Japan.*

34   The United States Since World War II

Alone among the great powers, the United States emerged from World War
II practically unscathed; except for the bombing of Pearl Harbor and
damage to installations on islands in the Pacific, no American territory was
ever attacked, and while nearly 300,000 American soldiers and sailors died
in battle, these losses, too, were insignificant when compared to the 7.5
million Russians, the 2.2 million Chinese, the 3.5 million Germans, the 1.2
million Japanese, who were killed, or to the lesser but proportionately
heavy casualties suffered by Britain, France, and the other belligerents.
Nevertheless, few nations were more changed by the war than the United
States.

To begin with, the war destroyed American isolationism. The nation
had never really been isolated from affairs in the rest of the world, but as
late as the 1930's large elements in the population turned their backs
psychologically on most of the rest of humanity. Isolation had been produced by a strange combination of insularity and idealism. Separated from
Asia and Europe by great oceans and intent upon the development of a
continent, Americans had little reason to devote their energies to foreign
affairs, or so it seemed. Their sense of their own uniqueness and virtue,
products of their democratic system and the rich natural resources of their
land, made them look on other peoples as either (in the case of Europeans) evil and corrupt or (in the case of most others) benighted. Al-

A.D.   1946 Employment Act creates Council of Economic Advisors

1947 Truman Doctrine and the Marshall Plan

1949 North Atlantic Treaty Organization approved

1950 Outbreak of the Korean War

1950–1960 Sale of television sets averages over 7 million a year; by 1960, 88 per cent of all households have television

1954 Supreme Court declares racially segregated schools unconstitutional

1956 Martin Luther King, Jr., organizes Montgomery, Alabama, bus boycott

1958 First commercial jet airplanes in service

1962 Cuban missile crisis

1963 Assassination of President John F. Kennedy

1964 Student riots at the University of California, Berkeley

1965 President Lyndon B. Johnson "escalates" the Vietnamese War; Education Act provides first comprehensive federal aid to education; race riot in Watts district, Los Angeles, California

1968 Assassination of Martin Luther King, Jr.

1969 Astronauts land on the moon

though many persons had always regretted this isolationism, recognizing that events in the rest of the world vitally affected American interests and believing that the nation had an obligation to spread and share its political and economic advantages, it took the war to convince the great majority that this was the proper way to look at the question. By 1945 technology had caused the protecting oceans, so to speak, to evaporate, the excesses of the totalitarians had reaffirmed Americans' faith in their own values, and the desperate condition of so much of the rest of humanity had touched them deeply and made them willing, even eager, to share some of their wealth with those less fortunate.

But the postwar internationalism contained also a strong illiberal element—it was in part a new imperialism, a reflection of American power. The military and industrial might generated in order to defeat the Axis powers, capped by the enormous force of the atom bomb, still an American monopoly, made the United States seem like a colossus among pygmies when the war ended. Although Russia quickly demonstrated that it, too, possessed tremendous strength, this merely stimulated American competitiveness, and combined with genuine dislike of Communist repression of individual self-expression and fear of Soviet expansionism to produce the Cold War. That conflict aside, however, American internationalism had its aggressive side. Huge sums were spent to rehabilitate Europe and help underdeveloped regions to improve themselves, but the nation collectively and American businessmen individually also poured billions into foreign nations for purely material purposes, often without regard for the welfare of the people who were affected by this investment. And when conflicts developed between the desire to help others and the supposed national and personal interests of Americans, these were usually resolved in a narrowly selfish way. Thus the United States, while committed to aiding poverty-stricken Latin American countries, repeatedly supported reactionary and undemocratic regimes in the hemisphere either because they were anti-Communist or because they were willing to make favorable economic arrangements with Americans, often at the expense of their own people.

The war also affected American foreign policy in another unfortunate manner: its "lessons," like most of the lessons of history, were applied too literally by the postwar generation to its own problems. First of all, the idea of appeasement was almost totally rejected. Failure to move soon enough to check the Nazis had undoubtedly cost the United States and Europe heavily, but the refusal to "appease" nondemocratic governments, especially Russia, was often carried to unreasonable and self-defeating extremes after 1945. The idea that the United States must intervene to thwart aggression *anywhere* if it was not itself to be overrun, put into effect most disastrously in Vietnam during the administration of Lyndon

Johnson, but more or less accepted by every postwar President, resulted in a severe straining of American resources and also in the undermining of the faith of many nations in America's good intentions. It was probably inevitable, given the wealth and power of the United States, that many small and poor nations would resent and envy America, but the policy of intervening diplomatically and even militarily in every corner of the globe at the first sign of trouble and often without the invitation of the local populace was bound to exacerbate these feelings. More important, the growth of nationalism in the underdeveloped countries and the fragmentation of the unity of the Communist powers made the fear that a Russian Hitler might soon seek world domination progressively more unrealistic, and in any case, events repeatedly demonstrated that the United States simply could not, through its own determination, control the course of history all over the world. The result was a great loss in American prestige abroad and an enormous waste of American resources that had serious domestic repercussions.

At home the chief effect of the war was to confirm the American commitment to the basic principles of the welfare state and a managed, as distinct from a laissez-faire, economy. Wartime demand had finally ended unemployment and restored full prosperity, and experience had demonstrated the soundness of the major New Deal reforms. The Employment Act of 1946, establishing a Council of Economic Advisors to plan policies aimed at promoting employment, production, and purchasing power, gave the force of law to an attitude toward the role of the government in managing the economy that only a generation earlier had seemed to millions the antithesis of free-enterprise capitalism. Even when the Republicans regained control of the White House under Dwight D. Eisenhower, the new point of view remained in force. Eisenhower neglected many problems related to social welfare, and his stress on budget balancing caused a series of minor depressions (euphemistically called "recessions"), but he did not even suggest the repeal of New Deal laws, and his talk about the virtues of individualism and free enterprise, if not mere talk, never went much beyond suggestion.

Nevertheless, and despite Eisenhower's enormous personal popularity, his less than forceful application of the new tools for managing the economy caused widespread public dissatisfaction, and when John F. Kennedy succeeded to the presidency in 1961 after having campaigned on the promise to "get the country moving again," the time was ripe for more positive action. Instead of seeking to stimulate the economy by increasing government spending, which would either drain off funds from the private sector or, if not paid for by increased taxation, trigger an inflationary spiral, Kennedy suggested a sharp reduction in taxes, which would free private capital for new investment and stimulate consumption, and thus demand. This policy of deliberately unbalancing the budget ran into considerable opposition, but in the brief period of national chagrin after Kennedy's assassination in November, 1963, President Johnson persuaded Congress to act. The result fully bore out the hopes of the plan's sponsors; the gross national product increased at a swift pace, unemployment declined sharply. Reversing the process to slow down the boom and check inflation, equally important in the view of economists, proved much more difficult to achieve for political reasons. Despite a rapid upward movement of prices, Congress hesitated to raise taxes, delaying until 1968 when a 10 per cent "surcharge" was added to the federal income tax. Inflation seemed at the end of the sixties a perennial problem. Nevertheless, the argument had become one of means, not of principle—that the economy could and must be managed by the government was no longer challenged.

General prosperity, freedom from fear of a major depression, rapid economic expansion, a sharp increase both in the standard of living of the people and in the kinds of goods and services available to them, made the immediate postwar era a time of complacency for most Americans. For the middle-class majority, conditions had never been so good, and they were improving at a spectacular rate. Antibiotics almost eliminated the dangers of contagious diseases. Television brought the world into everyone's living room while the jet airplane enabled millions to see the world at first hand with remarkable ease and at relatively low cost. Every form of leisure activity—from golf, skiing, and boating, to the spectator sports, to concert and theater going, reading, and a dozen others—experienced an unprecedented boom. A style of life that had once been the exclusive privilege of the upper levels of society was suddenly opened up not merely to white-collar workers but also to factory laborers and other wage earners. Educational opportunities proliferated, the population of American colleges rising in the 1950's and 1960's from well under 3 million students to well over 6 million. Home ownership soared, as millions of wage-earning city dwellers found themselves able to afford houses in the burgeoning suburbs. Electronic computers, performing in seconds calculations that human brains could not manage in years, speeded the flow of business, freed countless thousands from drudgery, and made possible enormous scientific advances in a variety of fields that promised still greater material rewards. Space itself was conquered, as Americans, responding to the challenge posed by *Sputnik,* the first Russian earth satellite, in 1957, swiftly developed a series of extraterrestrial vehicles, culminating in the first landing of men on the moon in July, 1969.

Yet despite, and to a degree because of, the new progress, grave social problems soon began to surface. One involved the downtrodden condition of American Negroes. For two centuries a dreadful race prejudice had survived in the United States for a variety of reasons. Its origin lay in slavery—the age-old monument to human selfishness and unreason. It was reinforced by the effects of slavery on the slaves; the belief that black "savages" were so inferior that they might rightfully be kept in bondage like horses and cattle was a self-fulfilling prophecy, for the system crushed many of the slaves psychologically and by preventing their education kept them ignorant and undeveloped and thus by practical standards actually inferior to their masters. Unsophisticated observers, seeing the behavior of the *average* bondsman—the exceptions were conveniently ignored—could easily conclude that as a race Negroes lacked potential for the higher human achievements, and that even from their own point of view they were better off as slaves than as free men. Most white men who advocated reform of the system did so on humanitarian or paternalistic grounds, and sought not true equality for blacks but merely the amelioration of their wretched condition.

The Civil War destroyed slavery but it did not produce equality. The experiment of Reconstruction was a flat failure, and by the early twentieth century the Negro tenth of the population was mired in what at best could be called second-class citizenship. World War I brought some economic improvement, World War II still more. The reaction to Hitler's nonsense about race and his slaughter of 6 million Jews because of their supposed racial inferiority could not help stirring the consciences of many white Americans. The performance of Negro troops in the war inspired a new respect for their courage and patriotism, and the shortage of labor produced by the wartime boom enabled many blacks both to improve themselves economically and to develop new self-respect. Less immediately obvious but in the long run probably more important, social research in the 1920's and 1930's had proved that Negroes were not physiologically or mentally inferior to whites, but that their low estate was the result of the very repression that white prejudice had imposed upon them.

By the early 1950's the true nature of this prejudice was clear to the majority of educated Americans. The Supreme Court decision in *Brown* v. *Board of Education* (1954) outlawing segregation in the public schools was based on this awareness that their environment, not their genes, made Negroes "inferior." The entire civil rights movement followed logically, but not, alas, smoothly, from the same premise. Two forces checked the movement. Once the injustice of repression was admitted by the oppressors, Negroes naturally began to *demand,* not merely to plead for, full equality. (They too, perhaps, had unconsciously believed themselves inferior to whites.) Their demands offended the really deep prejudices of many whites who, if allowed to preserve the comfortable paternalism of the past, would have willingly "improved" the Negroes' position. More significantly, the mass of lower-middle-class whites had never really grasped the relationship between the behavior of Negroes and their environment. They saw results as causes—black poverty, black crime, black "shiftlessness" still seemed to indicate congenital flaws in the Negro character. Such white men also felt strongly the pressure of the new black competition—for jobs, for places in already crowded schools, for housing, for all the other advantages of modern life. Thus, while it was obvious that equal treatment would benefit everyone, achieving equality was no easy matter. Black aggressiveness took the form of riots, demands for "compensation" for past injustices, even talk of a new black-inspired segregation and a separate black nation. A white "backlash," although mostly bluster, further rent the fabric of society. By the end of the sixties Negroes had improved themselves enormously, but this improvement was merely a measure of how depressed their condition had been. The nation was still paying a heavy price for having so long held its black citizens in bondage.

Poverty was in large measure a by-product of the race problem, but it was also paradoxically related to the character of prosperity. The marvelously efficient American system of production was based on a complex technology that required highly skilled labor to make it function. Automation eliminated many jobs, of course, but also created new ones; the difficulty lay in the fact that the demand for unskilled labor declined while that for skilled labor rose. The need for well-educated workers expanded, too, so that many posts existed that were beyond the capacity of a large percentage of the population. While high-paying jobs for engineers and technicians went begging, thousands of willing workers could not find decent employment. The poverty problem was also related to urbanization and the emergence of an impersonal civilization that destroyed men's sense of individual accomplishment and weakened both their will to work hard and their sense of being necessary parts of a social organism. In turn this led to a breakdown of community loyalty, the casting off of moral restraints, and a retreat into passivity and self-indulgence. The welfare state, conceived of as a humane way to deal with misfortune, a kind of social insurance, was thus to a degree corrupted and corrupting.

Young people were particularly hard hit by the complexities of modern life. The poor and the dull tended to give up or strike out resentfully at a world they did not make and could not change. The affluent and intelligent, in increasing numbers, tended to "drop out." Reared in comfortable circumstances by indulgent parents, they did not seem capable of enduring frustrations of any sort. Trained by well-meaning but complacent teachers to be idealists, they looked at the irrationalities and injustices around them and (failing to recognize that these were inevitable aspects of the human condition that men of good will must seek to ameliorate but must learn to live with) concluded that they were living in a uniquely rotten society. Many became revolutionaries of the spirit; others were overwhelmed by their contempt and turned to drugs and other deviant forms of behavior.

The senseless and apparently unending war in Vietnam was only one of the causes of youth's discontent. The two great wars of their century seemed to prove that patriotism was a force for viciousness and destruction alone, while the revolution in communications and the general decline of provincialism made nationalism appear an anachronistic form of political organization. The nuclear bomb, they correctly understood, made war not merely horrible but absurd. Yet while millions suffered from actual deprivation and millions more from exasperating, spirit-crushing social inconveniences, the nation was spending billions on its gigantic military machine.

Materialism, racism, the "rat race" of modern life, further offended the young idealists and strengthened their natural tendency to rebel against the values of their fathers. The very complexities of the social problems of the age which made their elders gravitate toward moderation, compromise, and "consensus" made young people insist on one or another absolute. But perhaps most of all, they suffered from the general sense of individual powerlessness that was psychologically frustrating to all men in a world of gigantic, impersonal institutions. Old and young, rich and poor, found it ever more difficult to make an identifiable impact on society. Egos demanded expression. Labor, thought, and feeling commonly produced everything but this sense of purpose—unless directed toward some destructive goal. The greatest statesmen could not achieve true world peace, but a single demented zealot could start a war. Martin Luther King and a host of dedicated followers could not eliminate racial prejudice, but a sordid drifter, shooting King down from ambush, could cause a dozen cities to burn. In an important way, the violence and disorder that plagued the nation was produced not so much by social injustice as by the desperate need of confused individuals to express themselves.

Of course, none of these terrible and terrifying conditions has yet destroyed American society; all are under attack from a hundred directions. What the outcome will be is for the future, not for the historian, to determine.

For Further Reading

Carmichael, S., and Hamilton, C. V., *Black Power*.
Congressional Quarterly Service, *Congress and the Nation: 1945–68*.
Galbraith, J. K., *The New Industrial State*.

Goldman, E. F., *The Crucial Decade—and After.*
Halle, L. J., *The Cold War as History.*
Harrington, Michael, *The Other America.*
Malcolm X, *Autobiography.*
Riesman, David, et al., *The Lonely Crowd.*

35   The State of Culture Today

In present-day discussions of the contemporary scene the main topic is: Are we seeing the breakdown of our civilization?

Sooner or later, the sophisticated person who reads or hears such discussions reminds himself that to the living "the times" always seem bad; in most eras many voices cry out against the visible decadence; in every generation—and especially to the aging—the world has always been going to the dogs. By showing that life continues and new energies arise, the study of history cannot help inspiring skepticism about the recurrent belief in decline.

But sophistication—and skepticism—should perhaps go a step further and ask why that same phenomenon recurs; in other words, the historical-minded should look into the meaning and cause of the undying conviction of decadence. One cause, one meaning, is surely that in every era some things are in fact dying out and the elderly are good witness to this demise. Manners, styles of art and politics, assumptions about the aim of life or the nature of man and of the universe change as inevitably as fashions in dress; and just as no one could deny that men's stiff collars two inches high have vanished into the attic of history, so no one should deny that less tangible entities—say, the idea of "a man of honor"—have vanished too. The very words look quaint and evoke no answering emotion. What is involved here is of course the vivid faith and the cultural form, not the underlying reality that there are always honest and dishonest men. If, then, such faiths and forms are considered good by a generation that grew up to value them, that generation will experience at their passing a legitimate feeling of loss.

The very notion of change, of which the twentieth century makes such a weapon in the advocacy of every scheme, implies the notion of loss; for in society as in individual life many desirable things are incompatible—to say nothing of the fact that the heedlessness or violence with which change takes place brings about the incidental destruction of other useful attitudes and institutions. In 1971, for example, one can ask whether all over the world the idea of a university has not been damaged, without hope of

A.D.   1870   Education Acts passed in most countries of western Europe: free compulsory education; beginnings of industrial literacy

          1871   End of Franco-Prussian War; beginning of armed diplomacy leading to 1914

          1889   Paris World's Fair: the Eiffel Tower and the triumph of machinery; London dockers' strike

    1890–1905   The new Romanticism: Symbolism; Art for Art's Sake; Decadence; Post-Impressionism

    1890–1910   Invention or discovery of: the automobile; serum therapy; Diesel engine; Kodak roll film; motion pictures; heavier-than-air flying machine; fingerprinting; striptease; tuberculin; appendectomy; plastic surgery; color photography; wireless; artificial diamonds; spinal anesthesia; psychoanalysis; Mendelian genetics; histidine; radioactivity; vacuum tube; artificial insemination; organ transplant; quantum theory; relativity; Salvarsan for syphilis; anaphylaxis; artificial materials from resins and cellulose

    1894–1906   The Dreyfus Affair: the intellectuals a new political force

    1895–1917   The emergence of Marxism and Syndicalism; *Reflections on Violence* (1908); the suffragettes; the coming "century of the child"

          1900   "The Yellow Peril"; Western envoys besieged in Peking and relieved by a European army under a German general

    1900–1911   The century turns; Art Nouveau and the new democratic life—penny press, peace crusades, Balkan Wars, international crises

    1905–1915   The Cubist Decade—innovation in all the arts, notably architecture

    1914–1918   The Four Years' War, ultimately the First World War, shatters European power

    1919–1939   "Between Wars"—unrest and indifference under the sway of diminished intelligence; culture imitative, regressive, and derisive of itself; second youth movement and yearning for peace

1929–1939   World-wide economic depression

1939–1945   The Second World War; military application of scientific power, culminating in atomic explosion at Hiroshima

1945 ff.   The Age of Anxiety; the Cold War in a divided world; local wars linked with decolonization and universal shrinkage of power; the race to reach the moon: ostentation and propaganda

1964   The cellular revolution: internal and external disorder, the third youth movement, and the second women's liberation; decay and stasis of institutions; art against society; anti-art against the culture and the self; the absurd and the obscene in the effort at destruction or recovery; the drug experience and the experience of dissolution

----

recovery for a very long time. This conclusion, if correct, has nothing to do with the merits of the cause that produced the onslaught: the historian notes results in the way an insurance assessor notes a broken shopfront.

Before one can go on to assess with the same detachment the extent to which the hitherto dominant Western civilization is damaged or dying, one must be reminded of still another historical datum, which is that entire civilizations do perish. The tremendous endings of Greece or Rome are not a myth. Life somehow continues after the fall, to be sure, but it is that very "somehow" which tells us that something above mere existence has disappeared. That something is what we call civilization. It is an expression of collective life cast in determinate ways, an expression which includes power, "growth," a joyous or grim self-confidence, and other obvious signs of a going concern. But it consists also of tacit individual faith in certain ideals and ways of life, seconded by a general faith in the rightness of the whole. It follows that widespread disbelief in those intangibles and the habits they produce in day-to-day existence brings on the dissolution of the whole.

The only question then is: How deep goes the disbelief? For history shows both big and little decadences. Decadence means "falling off," and it is possible for a civilization to experience a lesser fall from trust in its own ways without wrecking the entire fabric. The passage from what we call the High Middle Ages to the Renaissance and Reformation is one such falling away and new beginning. The era of the French Revolution is another. At both these moments—roughly the end of the fourteenth century and the end of the eighteenth century—Europe saw old institutions crumble, long-accepted thoughts dissolve, feelings fade away, and new ones take their place.

Those times were "epochs," which strictly speaking means *turnings*. The old system comes to what looks like a halt, during which all the familiar things seem empty or wrong. Despair, indifference, the obsession with cruelty and death, the Samson-complex of wanting to bring down the whole stupid edifice on one's head and the heads of its retarded upholders —these passions seize the souls of the young generations and turn them into violent agents of change, or else into what we now call dropouts from society. From both the activists and the negators come the new ideas and ideals which permit the march of civilization to continue. But it can also happen that not enough new ideas, no energizing hopes, emerge, and civilization falls apart in growing disorder, mounting frustration, and brainless destruction.

The judgment as to which took place at a given moment in the past is naturally easier to make than the judgment as to which is happening now. But it is again possible to draw guidance from history and take an inventory of significant activities and institutions so as to gauge the degree to which fruitful novelty is keeping pace with obvious destruction. The state in which we find government, religion, morality, social intercourse, language, the arts, and that ultimate basis of civilized life, public hope, permits us to form at least a tentative conclusion about the magnitude of the present *epoch*.

Government is first in the list and first in importance. Many would disagree, but that is in itself a symptom of the contemporary condition. For sixty years or more, advanced opinion in the West has regarded politics and politicians as beneath contempt and the State as an imposition and an imposture. The law and its enforcers are increasingly held in opprobrium as mere tools of "the power group," variously defined but deemed to have won its position largely by fraud and force.

Meanwhile crime stalks the capitals of the world, and its suppression is neither feasible nor in keeping with enlightened thought. The value of the State can stand no higher than the utility of its laws, which in turn must command public support and approval. Though the Western system of justice is perhaps the most solicitous ever devised to protect the rights of the accused, its administration has bogged down, and the march of mind has substituted the idea of illness and treatment for that of evil intent and penalty. Doctrines on the subject are, however, confused, with resulting disparities in pleading, sentencing, and paroling which can only wind up as manifest injustice.

Overcrowded and antiquated prisons provoke justifiable riots, and while some prisoners linger awaiting trial, others escape or revolt or come to the end of their sentence after a much abridged term. Nine years is the usual length of the "life" sentence that replaces the "cruelty" of capital punishment. But recidivism is high, robbery with violence is common and enjoys a large immunity, and the criminally insane when released repeat their senseless horrors—the fit counterpart of what is practiced upon them during their periods of confinement. As in so many realms of social existence, Western man has all the right ideas except that which would turn them into actualities. The net result is contempt for law, for the State that enforces it, and for the governors that still believe in both.

If we ask whether this marks a decadence, we need only observe that the present outlook contrasts sharply with that of a century ago, when the citizen took pride and satisfaction in being an amateur lawyer and parliamentarian. The constitution, the electoral campaign, the jury, and the vote ruled the imaginations of men. The courts and other public authorities earned the respect of the vast majority; they were regarded as the creations of the sovereign people, and such respect and origins helped them to function. Today these same ideas and words evoke only derision. Law-abiding, law-and-order, are terms of contempt meaning hypocrisy or cynicism. The police are considered a kind of malignant growth on the body politic, and among some that body itself is felt to be a usurpation of evil forces over simple human nature. These changes mark the end of the liberal ideal, which saw in universal suffrage for self-government and in the rule of law the keys to a good society. So far is this ideal sunk that the rightness of any minority has become an axiom, and more and more people feel themselves to be not sovereign, but shamefully oppressed—a desperate minority.

In the place of the former attitude toward the State stands what might be called for short the Marxist analysis. It does not of course stem from Marxist propaganda alone; but its spirit is that which informs the literature of Marx and his disciples; it is the spirit of exposure and revelation, the animus of the war against appearances, in search of a reality made up of conspiracies and their victims. It does not so much examine as classify and denounce.

It is a democratic spirit insofar as the passion for equality naturally stimulates envy and suspicion; but it is also a racist spirit in that it attributes virtues and violated rights to one group, wickedness and wrongful supremacy to another. In this sense, visibly, women are a race oppressed by the race of men; the old and the "square" are races unjustly dominant over the race of the "under thirty"—and so on. *La guerre des races* is fought in every public place and public print.

Its aim is still tinged with traditional liberalism to the extent that it takes thought of the "forgotten man" (and woman); while in its indignation it also shows the puritanical spirit of inquisition which belongs to the vigilant free press and which works on the premise that every person and event has its inside (and dirty) story. But with or without cause, the net effect cannot but be lowering, whether the target be a man or an institution, a regime or a "race." This is true even when nothing discreditable is revealed: the act of digging-to-uncover tells its own accusatory tale and reduces public faith in what is.

From the point of view, not of what is thus tarnished, but of the art of governing taken in the abstract, it is clear that the incessant eroding of faith and trust must in the end nullify all public authority and with it the general will. When the general will does not habitually prevail over particular wills, nothing is left but the arbitrary acts of improvised centers of power.

The evidence for this conclusion is seen today in the myriad demonstrations occurring all over the world, sometimes against dire oppression, more often against perfectly legal but unpopular measures, and sometimes again from habit, with no defined object in mind, save expressing hostility to whatever is established. The word Establishment, torn from its precise meaning, now denotes any institution, even benevolent (such as the fire department), which is tainted with having existed prior to the mood of protest.

Another name for that mood is Civil Disobedience, also a term divorced from its true meaning, which was: defiance of a bad law to show that it was bad, by accepting the consequences of breaking it. Now Civil Disobedience is the breaking of any law so as to show that existing society commits injustices at large, and on this ground the lawbreaking asks to be excused. The riots, protests, sit-ins, and strikes have this in common that they substitute the pressure of group blackmail for the force of law and put both the law and the officers of government on the defensive as usurpers.

In countries that have traditions and charters of popular sovereignty, these outbreaks are protected by the guaranteed rights of assembly and petition, though the physical destruction, obscene libel, and disruption of ordinary life which now mark "protest" go far beyond the right of assembly and petition as originally defined, and could not be envisaged as a right by any sane instrument of government. The interpretation of a violent act as "a statement" is correct only in the context of revolution. The falling away here is from the idea of systematic government itself.

In countries where liberalism never won a firm seat—generally those of eastern Europe, Asia, and Latin America—these extreme ways of political action may seem to be indigenous and familiar: coups d'état, street riots, and assassinations apparently continue their long history. They have provided in the past a rough substitute for general elections and a fitful tempering of despotism. But nowadays these uses of force have taken on a new aspect. Formerly, an uprising was an act of civil war; force was met with force, men died, and no one was astonished. Now uprisings large and small, kidnappings and killings of hostages, and highjackings of planes are expected to be acknowledged as legitimate means of communication between the people and their governors. Vandalism and riot having become channels of free opinion, authority must be patient, must withhold force and enter into negotiations, often on the simple terms of "Accept all our demands, or we shall do worse."

What Western civilization is witnessing, in short, is the last phase of the great emancipation promoted in the eighteenth century, and that last phase resembles the first, when all enlightened men agreed that authority and the State were always and a priori in the wrong. Whenever this feeling holds, any retaliation is necessarily "against the people" and thus a crime. What was then theory is now practice backed by the same theory: écrasez l'infâme now serves against any agency of restraint. Intellectual opinion leans automatically toward the objector, supports local animus against any central authority, and protests against all sanctions. In other words, power has ceased to be legitimate except when the people take it into their hands. If, as is only fair, we entertain the possibility that this conclusion is justified by enormous, incurable evils on the part of those who rule, then the decadence is from both sides, and the structure of civilization no longer has either faith or power to sustain itself with.

Under the populism now become universal—since even the totalitarian regimes profess to embody it: the "People's Republic," the People's Party, or whatnot—a perpetual referendum or plebiscite would be required to bring into being a new kind of sovereignty. But "total consultation" is hardly workable for the day-to-day conduct of government, if indeed continuous participation in public affairs is compatible with the other demands of civilized existence. At the present time, in nations not ruled by a dictatorship, the verdict on many issues is more and more often rendered by groups which are or which imitate professional revolutionary cells. To the degree that students all over the world have taken a hand in politics, that is the pattern they have successfully adopted for quick results.

The original model of rule by collective resistance and organized menace has of course been legalized and at work in the West almost since the start of the period under review: the trade unions, wielding the strike, the closed shop, and various other devices for coercing their own members have taught the public the power not only of disruption but even of mere interruption. To sum up, rule by direct-action groups is gradually replacing rule by individuals supposedly free, who delegate their unit of power to a legitimate authority.

In this political transformation, the only difficulty is to fashion a group coherent enough to coerce by these means. The trade unions took eighty years to win their privilege. But with the rising interdependence of industrial needs and services, smaller and smaller groups can disrupt the common life and bring about partial or total surrender. Success televised inspires imitation, just as local grievances, real or fancied, inspire revolt. A decision by a zoning board or a school superintendent, or again, the appointment of an unpopular person, even to a private institution, suffices to set off the indignation needed to create ad hoc parties of protest. "Regular channels" being both slow and suspect, "confrontation" ensues. Thanks to the floating feelings of aggression generated by other factors within industrial society—feelings kept fresh by report and example—the natural tendency is toward "action," a slogan which ensures that today in many parts of the world forces are ready at a word to storm city hall, break up a public hearing, ravage a university, or detonate an embassy.

The international scene has of course displayed this kind of behavior for a long while. Profit-by-outrage is an old game. The twentieth century has only added its peculiar tone of vulgar arrogance and boastfulness, aimed at impressing the home front. But the kidnapping and ransoming of envoys, the storming of embassies and the hatred of foreigners on grounds of "policy" take us back to the primitive times, the Venetian days, of diplomacy. All in all, the growing resemblance between the traditional anarchy of the great powers and the anarchy within each nation marks the decline of the very idea of nation.

And yet, when a principle happens to be invoked as the reason or occasion for modern outbreaks against the state, the principle generally belongs to the established liberal-socialist collection: it is "Down with imperialism"—or racism, or capitalism. Outbursts of hostility directed at another country usually spring from one or more of these same principles. No new ones, no practical or utopian schemes of society or plans of life, have yet emerged. This has significance for the observer assessing Western civilization's chances of survival. What strikes such an observer is that besides being unoriginal, these old-new ideals and doctrines are also undisputed. The evil which the doctrine attacks may still exist, but it exists without support from any principle widely held. Just as all regimes are "for the people," so all responsible groups and classes are "for equality and justice" and "against poverty and discrimination." Imperialism (colonialism) has no proponents left; racism as an overt policy is restricted to the southern tip of Africa; and capitalism has been so modified that it is at many points indistinguishable from communism, itself also hybridized. Nobody supports the view that the poor are necessary to society or that "inferiors" exist or have a role to play in some hierarchical order. Egalitarianism is affirmed as universally as pauperism is condemned.

Indeed, the only political ism surviving in full strength from the past is nationalism. This was partly to be expected from the liberation of so many colonies simultaneously, beginning in the 1920's. But this nationalism differs from the old in two remarkable ways: it is not patriotic and it does not want to absorb and assimilate. On the contrary, it wants to shrink and to limit its control to its own small group of like-minded we-ourselves-alone. It is in that sense racist, particularist, sectarian, minority-inspired. In truth, it flourishes as an expression of the antinomian passion which is the deepest drive of the age. In Asia and Africa the fission of kingdoms and regions into smaller states, and of these states again into smaller ones, shows an impatient mistrust of all central authority, regardless of its source or form. In Europe, nearly every "old" nation has one or more "subnations" demanding independence—Scotland and Wales from England; Brittany from France; Catalonia from Spain. The rage for absolute freedom is virulent. Ireland is in civil war. Little Belgium is rent by strife between two linguistic groups, and her great university has had to be split into two. Germany is a gerrymander. To the east and south, Balkanization has been overlaid but not extinguished by Soviet domination. Cyprus is a battlefield. In the Far East unity, never great, is less and less. No sooner is Pakistan free of that imperial monster India than East Pakistan cries out for liberation from the imperial monster West Pakistan.

In the United States the struggle to enforce the Constitution upon the South is still going on as if the federal union were trying to interfere in a foreign country, while a black nationalism demands (and in small ways obtains) total segregation. In Canada, French nationalism has likewise turned from sullen resistance to armed violence. And everywhere, regardless of doctrine or regime, the same ferment works inside common institutions under the name of decentralization. When sex adds its explosive force, the movement is called Women's Liberation.

In short, the one political and social ideal, the one motive power of the time is Separatism, no matter what other rags of older philosophy it masquerades under. If this is not yet Breakdown, it is undeniably Breakup.

Further evidence comes to us from the churches in the form of ecumenism (counterpart of populism), and of "the Underground" (counterpart of revolution). That the Catholic Church, long the model of hierarchical organization, should revise its doctrines with the aid of a large representative assembly is nothing new. What is new is that the rather impolitic decrees subsequent to the Second Vatican Council should be flouted by groups of priests who maintain that they are "not attacking" the authority they defy. The same contention is made by individuals in every church. Ministers take a stand against their governing synods on this or that article of faith, on ritual or private conduct, and call the public to witness whether their autonomy is not in truth justified by the act of challenge itself.

As in the rest of society, the one new idea is that authority exists to ratify the decisions of its declared enemies. Time has not yet shown whether such an arrangement can continue beyond phase one, that is, its first application by the first dissidents. At the moment, the assumption is warranted. Responsible and "wise" authorities hesitate to find heresy, to unfrock or disqualify, not so much afraid as ashamed of wielding any power at all, imbued as they are with the principle of whatever is is wrong.

A frequent characteristic of dissolving times is—almost by definition —their tendency to blur distinctions of purpose and of function. Men and institutions find themselves desiring to fuse aims, activities, and moods formerly held separate. This urge is in keeping with the main drive, which is to *undo,* to remove barriers and recover a primal unity of being with other men. It is the will to mix, merge, and forget. The business conglomerate is a conspicuous example. It owes its being not alone to diversification for commercial safety, but to a sort of reckless and derisive pleasure in flouting industrial specialization: the new corporation produces bathroom fixtures with the right hand and art books with the left. The supermarket and shopping center similarly bring the consecrated chapel for the weary next to the concourse of groceries which has made them so. Students have sought and won the right to eat in libraries and make love in dormitories. The church succeeds in attracting new young worshipers by combining the service with their favorite combo; while a rebellious priest thinks he has made an important religious point by marrying a couple in a subway station.

It is not so far-fetched as it may seem at first to find in the Cold War itself a conglomerate of acts and attitudes which matches this general liking for the mixed and indeterminate. The Cold War is a potpourri of diplomacy, verbal aggression, secret violence, assassination, and open fighting on shifting fronts. Peace is seldom signed, armistices are not kept, partitioned countries stay dismembered, and everybody talks peace and disarmament simultaneously with world revolution and armed intervention for abused nationhood. If either side—or indeed any human group—did believe in the rightness of its system, the spectacle would surely be different. We may think ourselves fortunate that the crusading spirit is dead, or that the fear of atomic war does govern the imagination of peoples; nevertheless, a genuine conviction against the Cold War, a strong skepticism about all ideology, would also achieve a different outcome—a different diplomacy, less childish provocations, and more sober efforts at peacemaking. An observer's tenable conclusion on looking at the Cold War is not that other times and nations have secured peace and good will by simply wanting it, but that those tougher, clearer, less sentimental periods did not bear the mark of the hybrid in all things as we inescapably do. What makes it inescapable is our preference for it.

The arts, of course, have been our instructors. They are always tempted by mélange and ambiguity, and now many practitioners prove by example that machinery and sculpture and painting are one, as life is one. The theater in the round means to refute the error that theater means show, and kindred dramatic groups try to rub out the distinction between player and audience by circulating, sometimes in the nude ("the way we are all born"), among the spectators. Hundreds of other examples of the alloyed arts will suggest themselves.

And perhaps one can go further and infer that the forces at work to eliminate differences between the sexes also aim at an ultimate unity. The former division of labor in the family—home and job—has largely disappeared. The young dress and grow hair alike, or nearly. The appeal of pornography and promiscuity, the publicity desired for the sexual act, and the charm exerted by the commune as domestic unit—all imply the partly conscious intent to get rid of the individual, with his rigid contours, in favor of a more homogeneous human material. To this end the taking of drugs contributes its share of abolition by removing the no doubt arbitrary limits of the real. Partakers maintain that drugs afford an expansion of consciousness, hence a liberation from the narrow and sterile life of reason. It might be more accurate to say that by drowning consciousness in sensation, drugs bring the user back to the starting point of his development, when he had to organize experience and draw the lines he now wishes to erase. The modern artist has done little else for eighty years than use sensation and purposeful confusion to restore (not expand) aboriginal consciousness.

The link between this important emotion and the quasi-religious feeling among the young is easy to trace. The dropout, the communard, the flower people are preaching or practicing a kind of primitive Christianity, though so far without a messiah. Like the early Christians they say no to the Empire and spurn its tolerant advances. They prefer a life without possessions, fixed abode, or clear relationships. The Essenes, too, we are told, picked up a clean garment at the next port of call, leaving behind the one just worn. Likewise—it is well known—primitive churches are always accused of sexual looseness. The charge is probably true. But its meaning of course differs for the practitioner and his critic. The religious neophyte bases his life on the law of love, in which there are no dividing lines. Stranger, acquaintance, friend, lover, relative are all one. Chance and impulse replace system and convention. Only by being simple and poor, natural and good, can the world be saved from Caesar and his legions (read: General Motors and the Pentagon).

Such a life is at first deliberately marginal. It is only because others tolerate and feed the dropouts and first Christians that they survive; but the force of their example is not to be measured by their numbers or their visible influence. For their appeal is to an emotion buried in every member of the high civilization, buried indeed in every human being: the impulse to knock down the building blocks so painfully erected; the longing to start afresh; the Crusoe fantasy and Walden instinct. Strictly speaking, these feelings are delusive. Crusoe had a shipful of civilized products or he would have perished, just as Thoreau brought with him an ax, a bag of nails, some beans, and other forms of capital. But feelings are stronger than facts when it is a question of bringing a civilization to its close; for the particular feelings that demand renewal at any cost have behind them the tremendous force of unreasoning hate against what must seem to a passionate man an endless series of cages. "I feel something within me," said the Chieftain from the North, "that compels me to burn Rome."

The attitude in our churchmen and churchgoers which responds kindly to such feelings argues a lack of faith not simply in the government of the church but in the government of God. Reports of high church attendance alternate with reports of widespread religious indifference. These statistics are probably equally correct. They do not impinge on the plain fact that religious fervor is rare and commands no intellectual support. Nietzsche's observation of eighty years ago that "God is dead" was taken up again recently as a liberating idea. But all it records is the upshot of the long secularization of life since the seventeenth century. What it states is that the citizens of the modern industrial world do not habitually reckon with Providence or appeal to a deity. They reckon with and appeal to machinery, medicine, money, the enemy on the other side of various curtains, and the forces of the unconscious. These are not gods. Even when feared or trusted too far, these forceful entities of the modern world are neither worshiped nor selflessly served. Science has been called a religion, and the analogy has meaning as regards its revelations of nature, but no one sings "O Science, our help in ages past"—the relation of grateful intimacy, of mutual love, is wanting.

Men in Western civilization have thus been thrown back wholly on themselves, and they find themselves wanting. They see more and more clearly that they are not in control of their individual lives or collective destiny, and that their simplest practical goals elude their reach. Because of increasing populations, because of the dread momentum of things— machines and their products—it appears harder and harder for anyone to accomplish any purpose, even one that commands general agreement. To get pollution out of the air or provide housing or realize the theoretical possibilities of communication and transportation become mighty "problems" whose solutions recede further and further away. It is doubtless from this growing feeling of impotence in the midst of technique that the heirs of 2,500 years of Western culture develop the anger of frustration leading to vandal revolt. Technique and reason, being shown powerless, are called unnatural.

Liberal thinkers down to very recent days had been confident that education would be the civilizing force sustaining orderly government in a good society. The experiment of democratic education was tried with enthusiasm and at great cost, relative to what any earlier civilization had done. And the effort still continues, though with growing dismay. For it now appears that education too has its limits. Literacy cannot be spread indefinitely but turns back on itself; teachers cannot be mass-produced at will like cars; and worst blow of all, the beneficiaries of free schooling resist or scorn the benefit. Accordingly, the latest "solution" offered the once-hopeful world is: "de-schooling society." It sounds like a new-found freedom.

When closely examined, the problem turns out to be not an educational one, not the removal of ignorance, but the need for the school to effect a magical reconciliation of the pupil with society, perhaps with life itself. Seeing the poor, the rich, and the middling all contributing their quota of vandals and dropouts of school age, seeing "the young" as a new class or race in open warfare with the world, the liberal imagination of educators and social philosophers concludes that here is one more witness to the bankruptcy of "bourgeois values." Like representative government, like capitalism, like traditional religion, the culture that the West has been painstakingly fashioning since Renaissance and Reformation has ceased to serve.

This verdict which condemns the bourgeoisie or middle class as responsible for the individual and collective evils of the age is not being uttered today for the first time. Nor was it first pronounced by the Marxians or their predecessors and successors in socialism. As we shall see in a moment, it is not a purely economic indictment in any case. When the anti-bourgeois commonplaces, which are now nearly two hundred years old, are repeated today in newspapers or in liberal households, they imply something more—and other—than the need to rescue the poor from the "tyranny of the powerful." They imply, to begin with, confusion of thought and self-disgust. After all, our conception of the general welfare springs from liberal thought itself, and liberal thought is a bourgeois creation. In the same way, "the rights of the people" are not in opposition to the "materialism" which is imputed to the bourgeois as a sin, for surely the rights of the people and the welfare of the people include their material prosperity.

And topping these paradoxes is the supreme one that the present spiritual distress and revolutionary surge come at a time of general affluence and high productivity; a time, moreover, when thanks to industry Western civilization has reversed the age-old proportions of rich and poor. It is certainly our shame that 15 to 20 per cent of our most advanced populations are in want, yet it is not by accident that the ratio is no longer what it ever used to be—20 per cent in comfort and 80 per cent in want. But nothing is harder to bear than the contrast between what is and what might be. Machine civilization's power to create wealth has given mankind a glimpse of universal plenty, and when we find ourselves far from abundance on a global scale, our impatience turns into fury.

And if we look deeper still than these matters of common anguish and revolutionary propaganda, we come upon signs that even a much nearer approach to planetary prosperity would not in fact relieve our pain. Just as when John Stuart Mill, then a young liberal reformer, fell into a deep depression and asked himself whether the instant realization of all his hopes would make him happy, and he answered no, so today the realization of the Western world's practical concerns would not reconcile and make happy its chief denouncers. It might make the poor and disfranchised happier, but one may wonder for how long, since those already free from want, tyranny, ignorance, and superstition declare themselves the most oppressed and miserable of men and willingly risk all they have in order to smash the system.

This abolitionist outlook, as was said a moment ago, is not new and not radical in the political sense. It is moral and aesthetic, and it was first given form by the artists who came to maturity during or shortly after the French Revolution. It was then that art took over the role that religion had formerly played in holding up to the impure world the divine promise and reproach of a pure one. With the Romanticists, the city of God became the vision of art. It was then also that the bourgeois citizen became an object of hatred and contempt, because he believed in the world—in trade, in politics, in regular hours, a steady life, a safe marriage, sound investments, and a paunchy old age. His moral complacency and artistic philistinism made him appear the enemy of all generous emotion, the antithesis of everything spiritual and selfless in man.

The great popular and national disillusionment after the failure of

revolution in 1848 intensified this antagonism. With the onset of industrialization, the uglification of cities, the degradation of the poor, the demagogy
and sensationalism of the penny press, the cheapening of taste through the
early crude mass production, the raucousness of advertising, the emotional
disturbances connected with the change from manual to mechanical work
that makes man a cipher—with all these and a dozen other consequences
of man's entry into the industrial age, the moral and aesthetic conscience of
the West, manifesting itself through its artists, began to repudiate society as
a whole. This manifold denunciation is what Flaubert and Ruskin, Baudelaire and William Morris, are all about—and not only they, but hundreds
of others in every language of Europe. Their despair is universal and the
depicted evil remarkably uniform. In American literature its recording goes
from Melville to Mark Twain and Henry Adams and then to Dreiser and
Scott Fitzgerald.

After 1870 in Europe, two movements prepare the present embattled or
alienated stance of the arts. One movement takes the path of withdrawal,
self-enclosure in the "genuine" world of spirit and sensation. Its present-
day continuation may be seen in all the groups, hippie or other, which take
every means to secede from society and the common self, including the
chemical means called drugs. The results, thanks to the despised technology that manufactures heroin and LSD, are extreme, but the tradition is, as
it were, respectable. Bohemia was the first form of Hippieland, and it is
more than a hundred years since Baudelaire justified the "artificial paradise" of drug taking as a necessary antidote to urban life.

The other movement was from the start activist and used art to shock
the bourgeois into a realization of his own turpitude. The line from the
Naturalists and satirists of the eighties (Zola, Jarry) through the Futurists,
Surrealists, Dadaists, and Expressionists to the Existentialists and others of
our contemporaries is perfectly clear. Indeed, the explosive substance and
devices change remarkably little. The poets since Laforgue are virtually
one (minor) poet. The dose of shock is merely increased to keep up with
the inevitable inflation of all effects. When Genêt becomes an artistic hero
and civic model on the strength of being a gifted thief and homosexual, or
when novelists and playwrights depict torture, madness, rape, and copro-
philia in parables meant to shine upon the paying public the light of self-
reformation, then surely the entire bourgeois class aimed at has been fully
convinced of its abominableness. For all the while the less violent writers
and dramatists have preached from the same book. Joyce and Gide and
Proust and D. H. Lawrence and E. M. Forster "show up" the bourgeois
and "his" society, dig down into the murk of motive, and prove that not a
word can be said for things as they are.

The arts of storytelling being almost wholly devoted to this propaganda, it was left to music and the plastic arts to satisfy the inarticulate emotions of a hard-driven society. And it is certainly true that since the first decade of this century the appeal of line, color, and sound has outstripped that of words. But even if many of the compositions in concrete or pigment or tone have furnished the aesthetic pleasure that strengthens the soul, many more have had the effect—intended or not—of once again "facing" the beholder with the despair and disharmonies of his own life. The cult of originality, the growing need of artists to singularize themselves within the growing mass of the talented, has encouraged the strong and arrogant to administer ever more brutal shock treatments to the public. This has meant more than merely abandoning representation or simple one-step abstraction from objects. First "the work" has been reduced to mere sensation; then the beholder has been excluded by saying that painting is only an act of the painter's, preferably a random act, as in dripping or throwing paint on canvas; finally the artist has eliminated himself, either by repudiating the making of objects or by preferring to collect and assemble and exhibit oddments from the junkheap of civilization.

In music a parallel development has occurred, though more difficult to make clear because of apparent exceptions. Still, the insistence of some experimenters that silence is more important than sound, or the great efforts made to impress concertgoers with the "elemental" by tapping on the frame of a piano with mallets—all these reductions and innovations betoken a desire common to many artists to achieve at least two ends in one: to exert some form of violence on the public and to disinfect art from any suggestion of past humanity. Dehumanization both condemns present man as vile and concentrates his gaze on the raw materials—noise, color, line, words as words, all to be taken with forced innocence.

There is, besides, the necessity of the modern artist to avoid comparison with the crushing legacy of earlier art, the masterpieces produced since the Renaissance that have exhausted all possible forms and genres and left to present performers only the choice of sterile imitation or total abstention.

All this taken together supplies the meaning of the label "anti-art," which has significantly united different kinds of avant-garde. "Anti-" is the effective bond. It corresponds precisely to the political, religious, and emotional need to be rid of whatever lingers on from yesterday. And it stimulates that emotion as well. The hunger is for a completely purged existence, an environment like a blank slate. Considering the radical hatred, the unforgiving thoroughness behind all these separate moves toward the perfect emancipation, the student of contemporary culture hazards a guess that the relaxing of manners and morals is rather a consequence than a cause of the social disarray.

The blank slate anticipated from razing everything to the ground is wanted for the purpose of writing upon it the mark and merit of a new man. The new man must therefore prepare himself to be new. He has to be young. With the aid of prophetic elders, he widens and deepens the gap separating him from his progenitors. He has in this way persuaded the civilized world that "the young" exist as an absolute. The abandonment of civility, soap, the mother tongue, and other features of inherited manners makes vivid the distance. The feeling that honesty need no longer control dealings with "those others" is logical as well—it is at any rate common to revolutionists and other killers. Still more radical is the transformation of sex into something indeterminate, depersonalized, and therefore weakened in emotional associations—perhaps weakened also in sensual pleasure through the absence of the usual barriers.

Communal living in conditions of Asiatic indifference goes with this reduction of consciousness of the self and within the self to the mood. The individual is thus made ready for the political struggle. From the immediacy of frustration, which makes the industrial state and its "bourgeois values" hateful, to the immediacy of the will, which aims at settling something by violence if need be, is a straight path that can be traveled in either direction. Whether the act succeeds or helplessness prevails, another stroke has helped bring down the city of the world which the vision of art has made so intolerable.

Nor is the world intolerable because it lacks "reasonable" or humane intentions. Such elements are not unknown among us, but ignored; and they are ignored because the difficulty of turning a good and approved plan into a reality has become monumental. There stands in the way all that democracy has decreed shall be respected—the right of individuals and groups to be consulted and conciliated. In that abstract form, no one can or would want to object to this right of resistance. But in actuality the resistance includes both sensible and ignorant criticism, both legitimate and dishonest interests, both wise and stupid apprehension; which is why in the once excellent New England town meeting it may now take eight years to settle the site of a new high school after the decision to build it has been taken. Such examples also tell us why everybody is starved of the pleasures of accomplishment, why everybody talks like a lunatic about Creativity, why there are myths about national goals and planning ahead.

The combination of these objective facts with the insistent propaganda against "the system" is what produces the state of mind in which total decadence—falling away, dissolution—is possible and, indeed, likely. The artists and intellectuals of the century have done their work so well that most bourgeois themselves, for all their advanced years and their innate philistinism, feel strong stirrings of sympathy with the young who want to devour them and with the minorities that want to replace them. Guilt is as strong a bourgeois tradition as complacency, and in every great revolution of mankind the victims (or a good segment of them) can be counted on to help. Today one finds throughout Western civilization men in high places who freely confide their self-hatred and openly envy their antagonists— and sometimes subsidize them in secret.

But the inchoate movement for renovation is not so simple as even this double twist would suggest. Among the young there are, as always, manipulators of others' ideals; they have set plans and sure techniques, but their goal is indistinct. Among the idealists (and sometimes within the rebel himself) there is a split in the method of making all things new. The cry of Participation heard in Europe and America points to this uncertainty. Participation means sharing the power, but this in turn means entering the Establishment, joining the bourgeois and working with them. Is this practicable, even if conceivable? The young and the dispossessed are no more sure of the answer than are the factory workers who also want Participation in management: independence and responsibility tug opposite ways. The only settled point is that the new man, the new Left, the new wave, the new cry in art, films, dress, lingo, or morals, toil together to hasten the work of time and oblivion.

If it were not for the striking convergence of these forces in our own day, there would be no point in discussing the nature of the so-called crisis in Western civilization, the character of the turning point which we are said to have reached or passed or sighted ahead. And the books of Spengler, Toynbee, Riencourt, Pickman, and others would not furnish (via their reviewers) catchwords and arguments for general conversation. The frame of mind of a high civilization is always self-conscious, but perhaps none before ours has attained such an extreme of self-consciousness. We owe this sensitivity to the length of our memory, that is, to our historical studies; to the speed of our communications, which give us no respite wherein to take the world as it is; to the peculiarity of our literature and our psychology, both introspective and ruthless in dissecting and imputing motives, suspicious of the slightest self-satisfaction; to the bleakness of our science, which shows us a purposeless universe of not even rational design; and finally to the fears which our great cleverness has raised up for us— fear of atomic destruction, fear of overpopulation, fear of our massed enemies; and in daily life, fear of all the diseases, mishaps, and dangers that our technology advertises in warning. It seems very apposite and not wholly accidental that one of the most popular genres of casual literature is the spy story: in it everyone sees himself as the lonely soul hiding among enemies, guilty actor and frightened fugitive, and at the same time freed from the usual restraints of honor; ready to kill for the cause, while frequently uncertain what the cause is and whether the enemy spy is not one's

closest fellow, all others being the Establishment—order, system, police—
the Kafkaesque bureaucracy.

These speculations, like the appeal of this pseudocharacter, the spy, fall
within the realm of sensibility. They constitute no positive evidence of our
historical condition, for the sensibility and its taste in popular literature can
change overnight without leaving a trace. Yet the circumstances and events
embraced in this ultimate chapter do permit us to say that Western civilization does not appear to contain in any class, in any nation, a healthy
reserve of animal faith. Rather, faith is on the list of shortages, like all
other natural resources. But much more than they, faith is needed for
action, innovation, risk-taking, heroism. The spy who wants to come in
from the cold obviously lacks this warming fire within. He carries on from
duty, and when he talks of "the cold" he is only projecting his inner lack of
natural heat.

It may be hazarded as a historical generality that the periods of
creation, and even the effectiveness of single movements, occur when the
vision of Possibility is vivid to many minds, when it is obvious that the
ground can be made level and ready to be built on. Then the presence of
obstacles and opposition is only another incentive to struggle. The uphill
fight is going to be rewarded by an incomparable view from the summit
won. This was the feeling widespread among the gifted at the height of the
eighteenth century, and again in the great flowering of Romanticism. It
sprang up once more after the *fin de siècle* lassitude, as our own century
began. The Cubist Decade was a great producer of models. Then came the
great catastrophe of the Four Years' War of 1914–1918, which not only
swept from the earth innumerable young geniuses, but showed the Western
world that it could not protect civilization from its own stupidity or evil
impulse.

The spirit of the West has never really recovered from that shattering.
Lately, scholarship has come to see that for half a century we have been
living on the ideas generated during the two decades before that war, 1895
to 1914. In science, art, technology, philosophy, social and political
thought, all the new principles were set forth with finality, from aviation,
wireless, and motion pictures to abstract art, city planning, aesthetic
simultaneity, quantum physics and genetics, relativity and psychoanalysis.
We have only elaborated those teachings, or tried, when we could, to evade
them by jumping back to earlier models, quite in vain. The question now is
whether the events we are witnessing are preparing another open and level
ground for a reawakened animal faith and the creation of undreamed-of
new things, or whether on the contrary our sullen doings have reached
repetition in futility.

While "awaiting confirmation or adversity," as the poet put it, we can
recapitulate and take stock each for ourselves. There is no doubt that

regarding the outer shell or container of civilization, which is the State, all our efforts tend against aggregation and toward disintegration. Yearning and action alike are moving us toward the small, self-contained unit which can be "free." Maybe it is a wise unconscious preparation for the time when atomic war has pulverized all large-scale existence and the survivors must be content with the isolated "villa" (= settlement) of late Roman times. In that case the deliberate pigsty mode of communal life which many of the young cultivate is a sign of remarkable prescience.

But it is also possible that the centrifugal force that drives us all to flee the octopus organization and the remote control of unseen hands, so that we may huddle with a few friends, bemoan our lot or demonstrate against it, will suffer a check. Anarchy, whether permissive or fostered by intemperate leaders, goes so far; then it generates repression. The present assumption that protest warrants every license may well end in a blood bath; or even without it, in a tyranny more relentless than any of recent date, and vindictive in proportion to the arrogance of those who provoked it into being. With such a repression would come necessarily a puritanism of the most searching kind. Artists, free thinkers, and free lovers who currently denounce the Western nations as police states would from their future labor camps long for the good old days.

In either event, the present failure of authority is a prime symptom. It tells us that on the all-important question of how to live together, the contemporary world has not a single new idea to offer, not one.

The next diagnostic point is the question of morals and religion. Morality, like religion, has the double aspect of satisfying an emotional need and serving a social purpose. Without morality—some inner restraint —society must assign two policemen to watch every citizen day and night. And without a religion which sustains conduct or at least organizes the facts of life and the cosmos, men seek in vain for the meaning of their existence. Not all can find in art or science a substitute justification, and even private ambition or calculated hedonism demands special gifts. Great populations without a goal outside themselves will turn to nationalistic war or race hatred to find the call to transcendence that the human spirit requires. On these points too, at the present time, the Western mind is mute. Popular revivalist religion captures only a few more souls than does subtle philosophic or aesthetic religiosity, leaving a void for the seven devils of partisan hatred to disport in. As for the embodiment of the fundamental decencies through manners and conduct, we have not as a civilization even begun to think about—let alone discuss—what would be desirable for an overcrowded industrial world. We have only drifted into the casual style, of which the extremes incite to a dangerous disgust with one's fellowman.

Art and science, just mentioned, look like better grounds for self-congratulation. Within our period both have gained enormously in prestige and support. Their practitioners are in fact the only admired leaders of the civilization. Ostensibly, then, art and science are flourishing, which argues a "healthy society." But are they healthy in themselves and in their relation to mankind? The metaphor of health is misleading in all such questions—a healthy malignancy kills the patient. The arts are not malignant, but as was shown above they are hostile, dehumanized, unnaturally self-conscious. They mean to awaken the complacent to their condition of sin and they succeed. But how long must the lesson last? And what does perpetually teaching it do to the propagandist himself? The imagination of disaster is a great gift, but after the disaster what? Cassandra's employment ends with her success. One congenial conclusion about the contemporary arts is that they are performing the great task of detaching us from all old models of feeling, seeing, and thinking, in preparation for the indescribable new.

Science, too, has little to say *comprehensively* to this civilization. It is none too well integrated within itself. One thinks not merely of the thirty to forty particles that have been found "basic" to matter-energy (not a simple plan, surely); one thinks also of the proliferating specialties, each with its private language and its stream of discoveries that do not somehow cohere and settle any large subject. It has become a matter of pride that science is never done: her name is Penelope. But if that is so, then science is not what its founders expected, a source of knowledge; rather, it is an absorbing activity, whose results can never give its patron civilization any conception of the world, much less of that other fugitive, man.

There is not even, for the educated, the prop of an all-embracing speculative philosophy. Ethics and metaphysics are no longer subjects for self-respecting philosophers to think about. For half a century or more, professional thinkers have preferred to analyze language, to attempt the quantification of the intuitive, or to uncover the rational bases of science. The next-door neighbors of philosophy—psychology and theology—leave the intelligent layman equally uncared for amid a plethora of myths and metaphors, of "personal statements" and "scientific" studies: there is no mediation or reconcilation between Ouspensky and Dr. Kinsey. As for the common man, he has been left more than ever at the mercy of his penchant for superstition. Technology as advertised supplies the miraculous, aided by science talking of inhabited planets, while astrology enlivens the newspapers and unidentified flying objects the heavens.

To be sure, science is now wedded to technology and faithful in its service. Many who are close to the work retain their enthusiasm for the future of civilization, precisely because technology can create abundance and replenish or eke out the supply of natural goods. But there are two obstacles on the road to material welfare. One is how to distribute it. Western nations have never found the way—the pitiful Common Market is the furthest they have attained in mellowing international trade. Internally they are stumped by political facts; in the United States at least, abundance rots in silos while our own poor and others starve. None of this proceeds from ill will, blindness, or indolence—except insofar as these vices afflict every inhabitant of the globe and preclude paradise.

The second and worse barrier to technological blessedness is that it has created conditions of life that more and more people find unendurable. There is no need to rehearse the cries of pain. They form the daily chorus of anguish—in common talk, in the newspapers, in plays and novels, in the grave studies of sociologists and psychiatrists. Against this sort of testimony no argument and no promise will avail. When the sweetness of life, such as it is at the best of times, vanishes altogether, the weak go under and the strong go elsewhere.

So as the last third of the century opens we find both the social and the political impulses at one in urging flight or destruction; from science and the arts, little or no solace; from religion hardly a clear pointer to duty or justification. The observer feels himself carried back among the prophets and thaumaturgists of St. Augustine's day, with no better guide than dumb instinct to find the way out. If these are not the signs of an emphatic ending, they look uncommonly like it.

Remains one question: if the description is correct, if it is an ending, a thoroughfare leading into the desert, of what magnitude is the predictable pause and turn? To answer this is to push the observer beyond his limits. He can safely say that we are seeing something of greater moment than the close of neoclassicism at the end of the eighteenth century. What is dying out now is the individualism and high art of the Renaissance, the fervor of the Reformation, the hopes of liberalism, the zest of the free and patriotic nation-state. But is it more than the close of a brilliant half-millennium? Is it akin to the fall of Rome, the death of paganism, and the turmoil of barbarian clusters under a primitive and precarious Christianity?

Or is it some third phenomenon—for where are now the vigorous, untroubled barbarians and the heroic bishops and missionaries bearing the Word? Meditation is the best answer, and from it at least one assurance will emerge, which is that as long as man exists, civilization, art, society, and science also exist in germ. Man's civilization is not identical with *our* civilization, and the building or rebuilding of states and cultures, now or at any time, is more becoming to our nature than longings and lamentations.

For Further Reading

Barzun, Jacques, *Science: The Glorious Entertainment.*
Brown, Norman O., *Life Against Death.*
Gilbert, Felix, *The End of the European Era.*

Gray, Francine, *Divine Disobedience.*
Linder, Staffan B., *The Harried Leisure Class.*
Lukacs, John, *The Passing of the Modern Age.*
Ortega y Gasset, *The Revolt of the Masses.*
Trilling, Lionel, *The Opposing Self.*
Wilson, Colin, *The Outsider.*

Index

72 73 74 75 76 9 8 7 6 5 4 3 2 1